A Distant Soil™

Colleen Doran

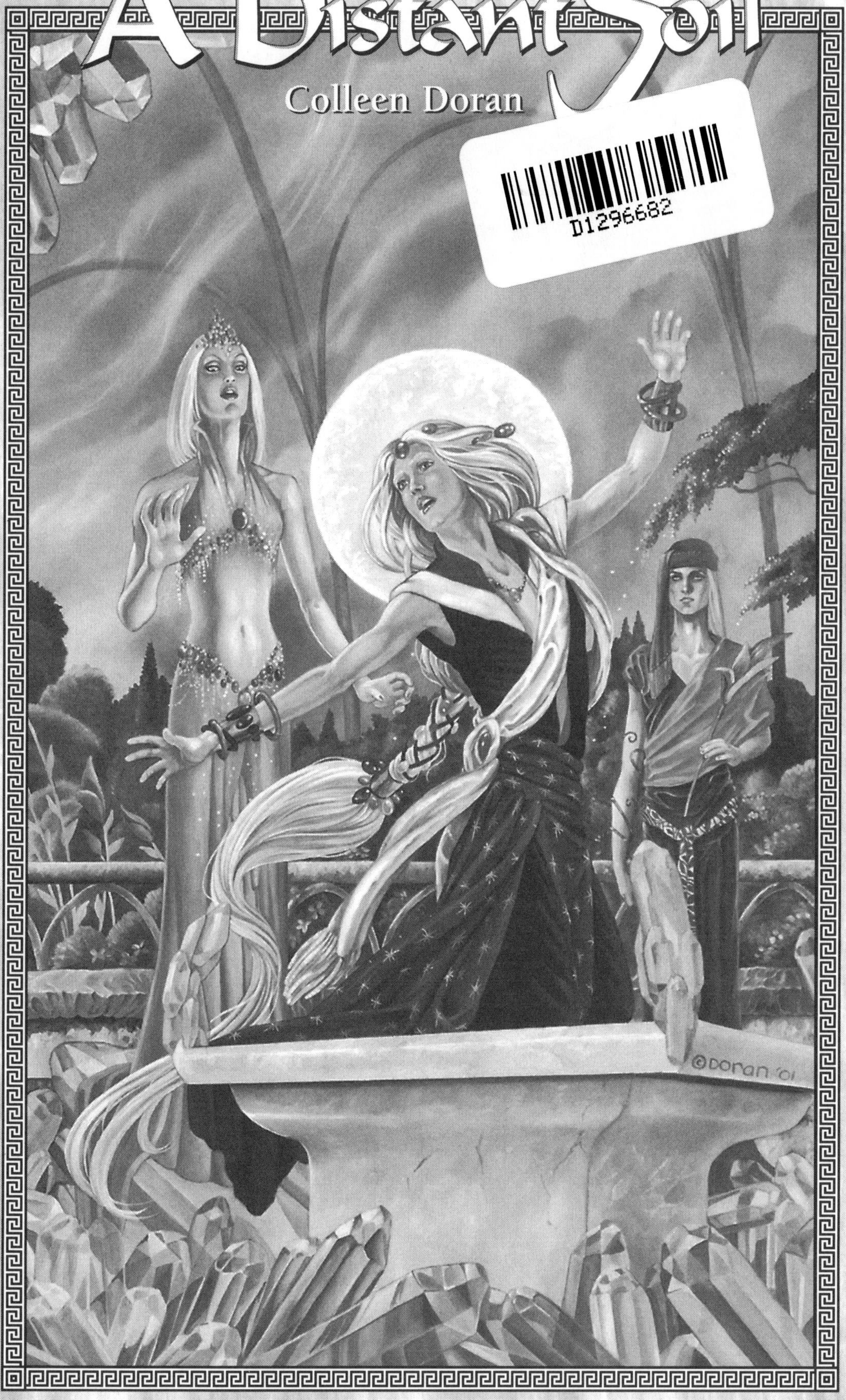
©Doran '01

Colleen Doran

A Distant Soil™
The Aria III

Previous volumes in this series:
Book 1 A Distant Soil: The Gathering,
Book 2 A Distant Soil II: The Ascendant.

Other books featuring the work of Colleen Doran:
Anne Rice's The Master of Rampling Gate
Walt Disney's Beauty and the Beast
Wonder Woman: The Once and Future Story
Sandman: Dream Country
Sandman: A Game of You
The Big Book of Scandal
The Big Book of Martyrs
The Big Book of Bad
The Big Book of the 70's
The Big Book of Wild Women
Two Fisted Science.

Portions of this volume originally published in single
magazine issues A DISTANT SOIL™ 26-31
by Image Comics® and Aria Press. Copyright© 1998-
2001. Colleen Doran. All right reserved.

First Printing
Image Comics
1071 N. Batavia St., Ste A
Orange. CA 92867

Printed in Canada
ISBN # 1-58240-201-9

IMAGE COMICS

PUBLISHER
Jim Valentino

DIRECTOR OF PRODUCTION
Brent Braun

DIRECTOR OF MARKETING
Anthony Bozzi

ART DIRECTOR
Doug Griffith

GRAPHIC DESIGNER
Kenny Felix

ACCOUNTING MANAGER
Traci Hale

ACCOUNTING ASSISTANT
Cindie Espinoza

INVENTORY CONTROLLER
Sean O'Brien

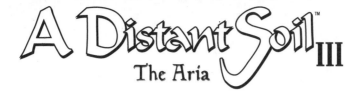

A Distant Soil™ III
The Aria

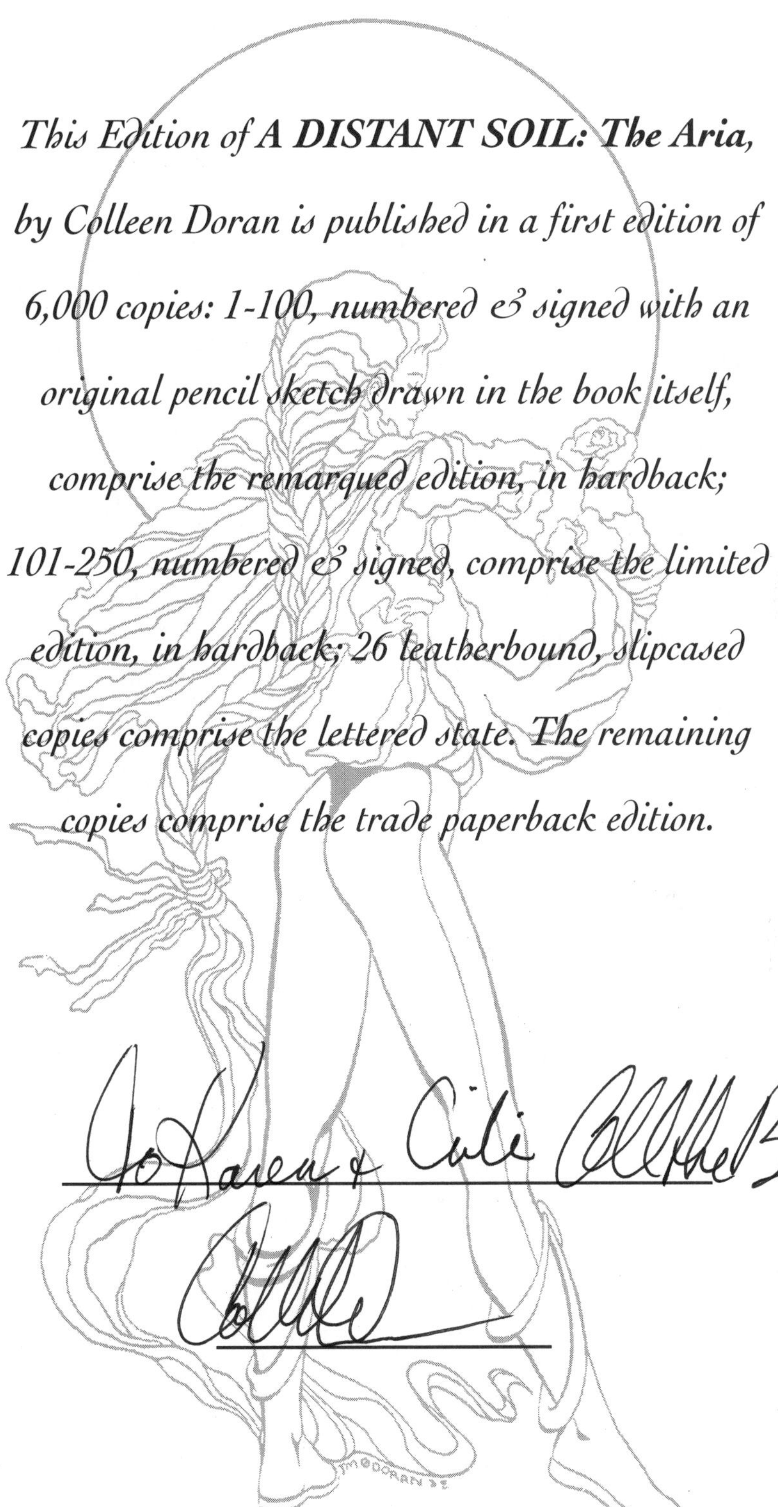

*This Edition of A **DISTANT SOIL: The Aria**,*
by Colleen Doran is published in a first edition of 6,000 copies: 1-100, numbered & signed with an original pencil sketch drawn in the book itself, comprise the remarqued edition, in hardback; 101-250, numbered & signed, comprise the limited edition, in hardback; 26 leatherbound, slipcased copies comprise the lettered state. The remaining copies comprise the trade paperback edition.

To Karen & Cile All the Best

This one's just for Mom.

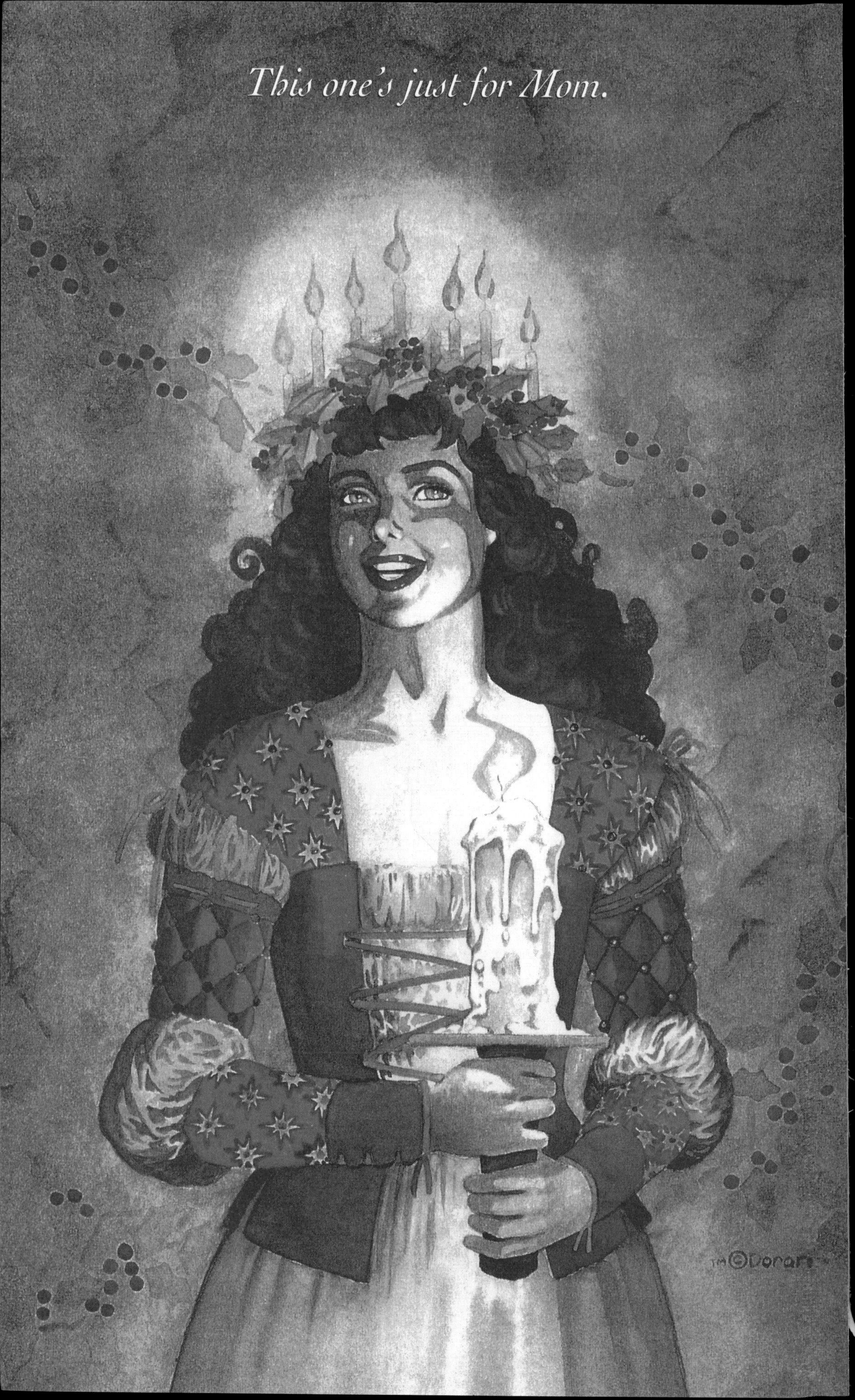

A Distant Soil™ III
The Aria

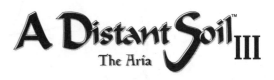

Colleen Doran
CREATOR

Anita Doran
ASSISTANT

Mary Gray
COPY EDITOR

Jason

Liana

Rieken

Rienrie

D'mer

Dunstan

Minetti

Kirov

Kovar

Beys

Basl

Jason and Liana are the children of Aeren, a fugitive from the planet Ovanan. Both children possess extraordinary psychic abilities, but Liana was born with the power of the Avatar, the religious leader and protector of Ovanan. The Avatar's power can only be controlled by one being at a time and as long as Liana lives, she is a threat to Ovanan, which has sent its massive warship Siovansin to Earth to assassinate her.

Rieken, the leader of the Ovanan resistance movement and his bodyguard D'mer, have also come to Earth in human guise to gather a brave team of human men and women to infiltrate the *Siovansin* and destroy Ovanan's evil Hierarchy.

Jason, captured by Ovanan agents, is drugged and appears to die from an overdose. Rienrie, a physician working for the Resistance, slips Jason into a coma and delivers him safely to Resistance

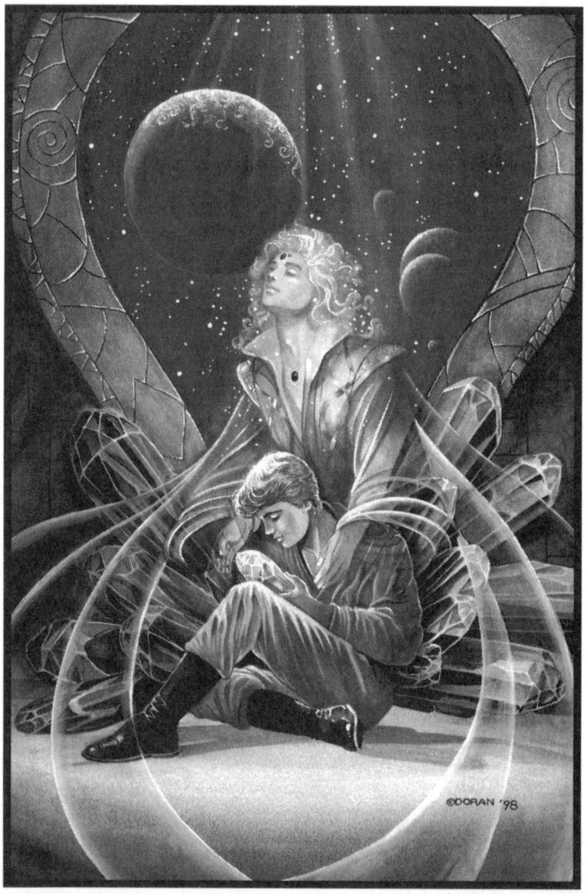
©DORAN '98

Liana

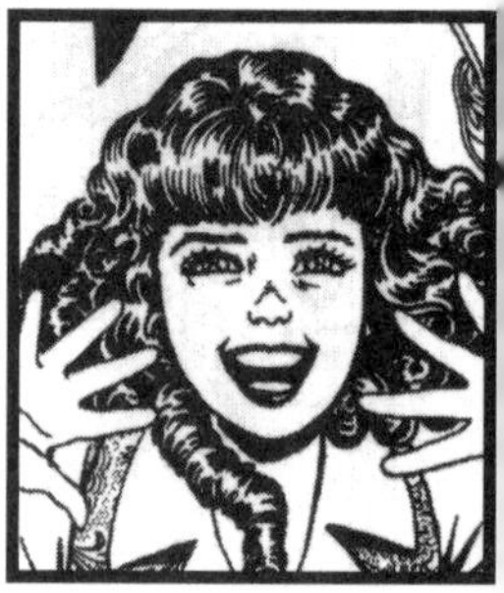

Jason

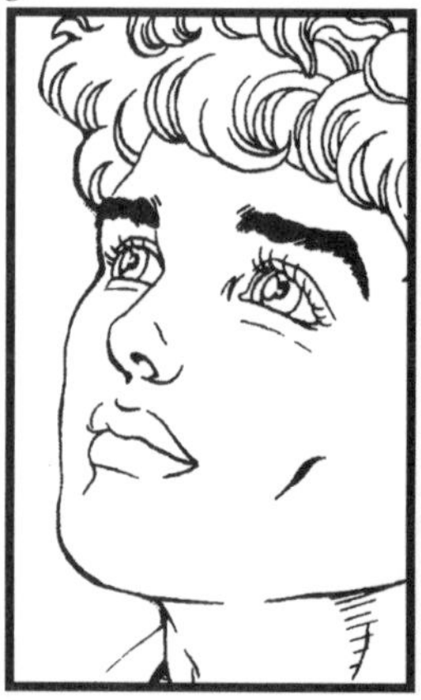

WHAT HAS GONE BEFORE

headquarters deep in the bowels of the *Siovansin*. Meanwhile, another battle occurs in the other-dimensional world, Avalon, a place where legends live and the only thing standing between Earth and the forces of the Dark are the Gates, protected by King Arthur and the Knights of the Round Table. Sir Galahad falls defending one of these Gates and stumbles through it, landing in our world where he joins Liana and her new companions Brent, Reynaldo and Chris. All agree to aid Liana and the Resistance.

Meanwhile, Rieken and D'mer have recruited Corrine and her magician sidekick Dunstan, Minetti a policeman, and Serezhe Kirov, a Russian dissident, as well as the beautiful Bast, an Ovanan shapechanger in exile. She discovers Rieken's terrible secret: he is, in fact, the Avatar Seren himself, in reality a pawn of the Ovanan Hierarchy.

Galahad

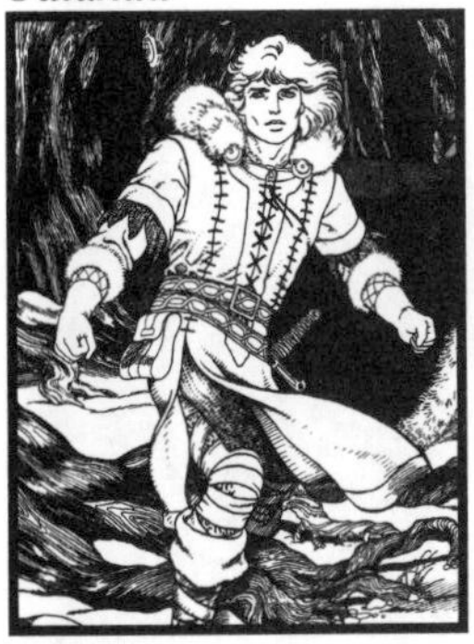

Rieken

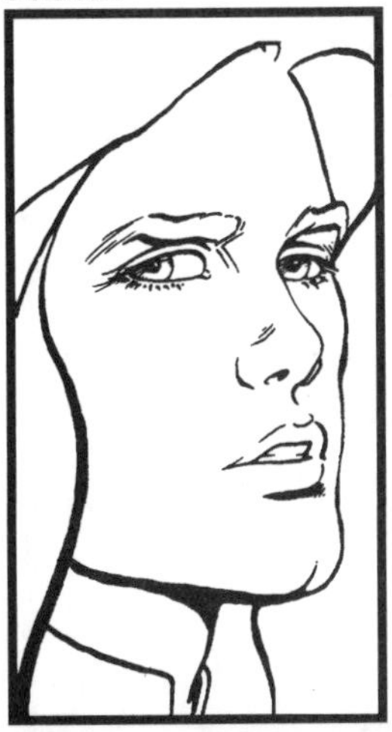

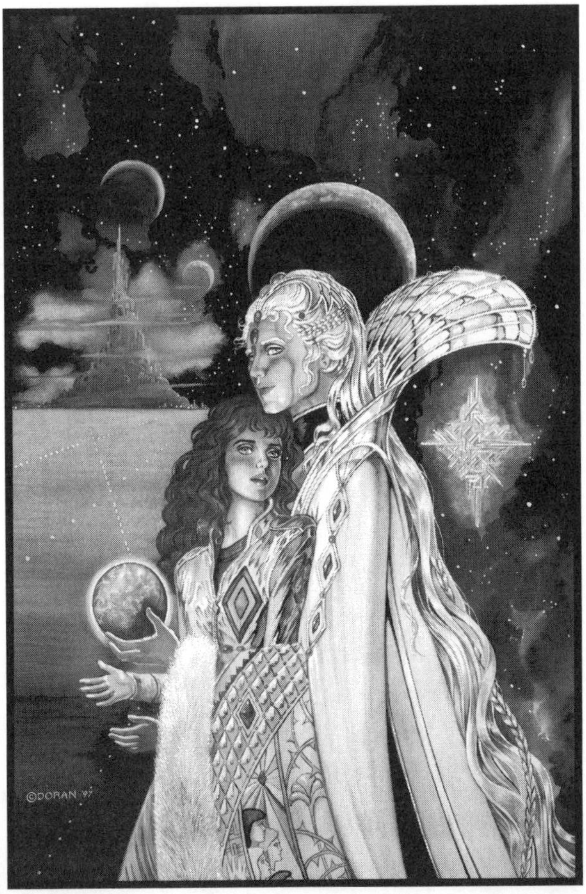
©DORAN '97

Dunstan
Minetti
Corrine
Niniri
Ninivir
Brent
Serezha
Chris
Merai
Sere
Vinyr

Dunstan
Minetti
Corrine
Niniri
Ninivir
Brent
Serezha
Chris
Merai
Sere
Vinyr

Rieken's champions are discovered and confronted by a Hierarchy warship. Rieken draws on the Avatar's power to destroy the warship so they can escape, but the Hierarchy senses the Avatar's touch on the power of the Collective and the sadistic Sere pays a call at the Avatar's apartments to interrogate him. She slaughters most of the Avatar's staff but is stopped by Major Kovar before she can invade Seren's private chambers. Niniri of the Hierarchy arrives, theorizing that the child-Avatar Liana destroyed the ship and orders Sere to leave the Avatar in peace.

Meanwhile, Rieken's champions accustom themselves to their new surroundings and D'mer attends Rieken, who is in trance, exhausted after destroying the warship.

In the *Siovansin*, Jason has recovered from his overdose. The beautiful Resistance leader Beys takes Jason on a tour of the ship and tries to convince him to join their cause. She wants him to help the Resistance kill the Avatar. Jason is suspicious of their motives and is disturbed by the strange customs of Ovanan. The Resistance

D'mer

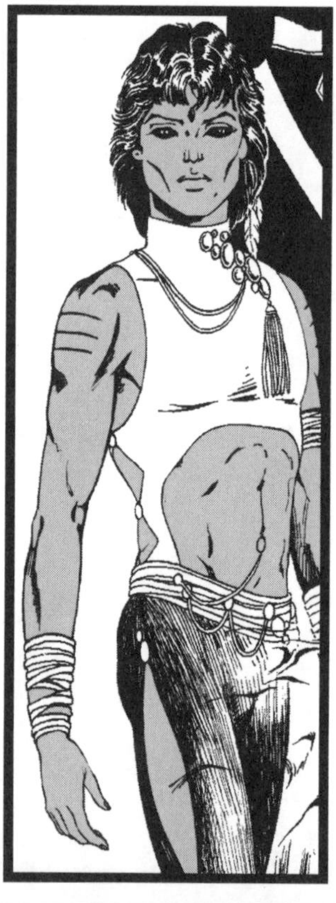

Bast

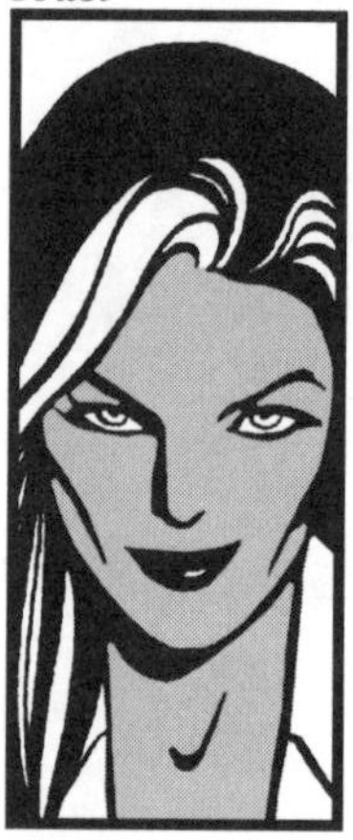

Minetti

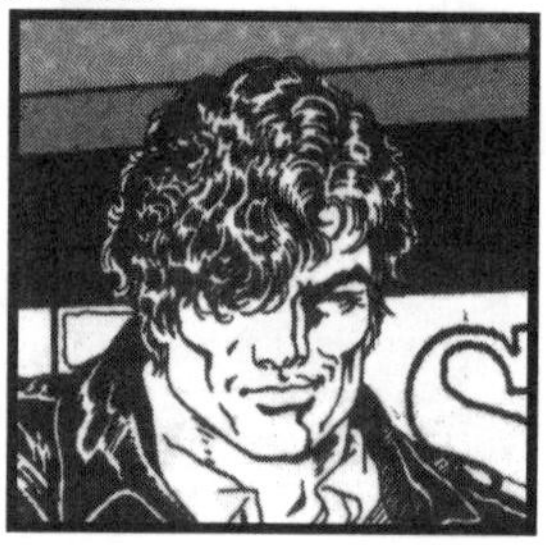

Corinne

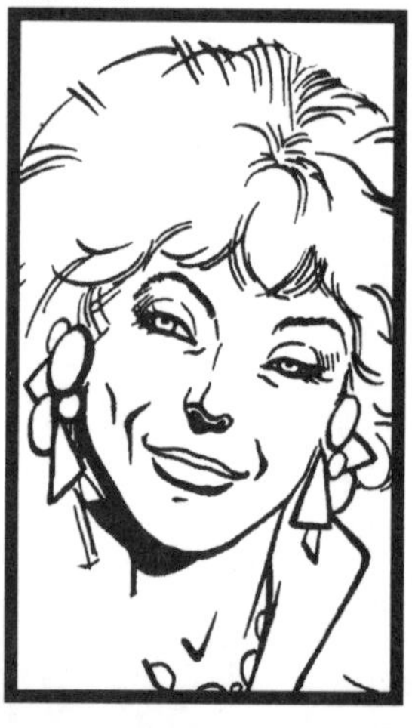

Dunstan

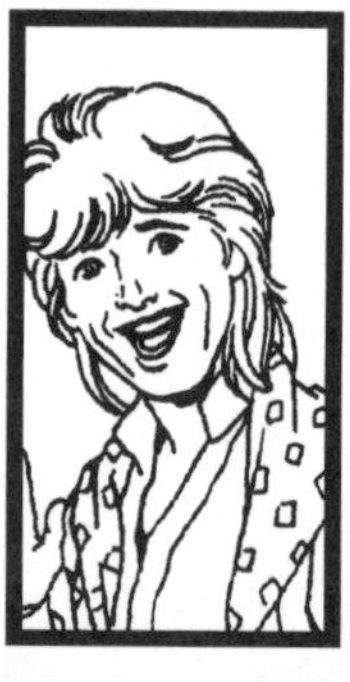

WHAT HAS GONE BEFORE

is equally suspicious of Jason and worries that he may be a Hierarchy spy. Jason agrees to undergo a Resistance initiation if the Resistance agrees to tell him everything they know of his father, who began the Resistance movement before he fled Ovanan.

While Jason is subjected to a painful Resistance initiation, Liana learns to control her power under the tutelage of Bast. Bast and Rieken begin a passionate affair (to the distress of D'mer who has secretly been Rieken's lover for some years), and Jason falls deeply in love with Beys who uses psionically charged crystals to bend the boy to her will.

The Hierarchy also faces a crisis when one of their own, the seer Merai, kills himself in the grip of one of his terrifying visions. Desperate for a replacement, they choose Prince Emeris, an extremely powerful psionic whose sartorial splendor is matched only by his capacity for cruelty. D'mer was once Emeris's slave and Emeris

Niniri

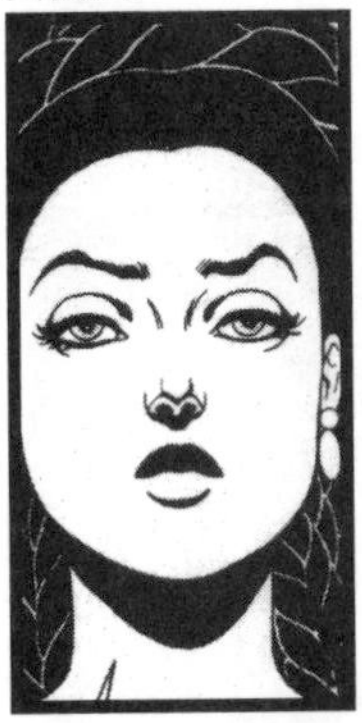

Beys

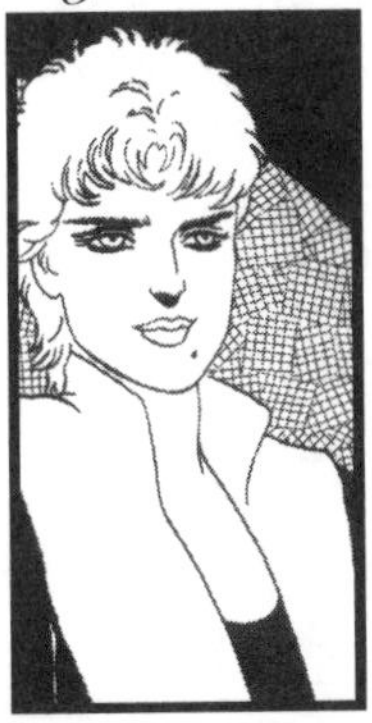

Major Kovar

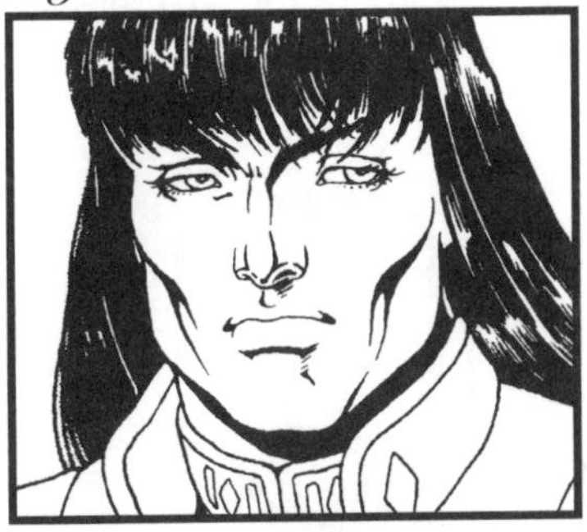

Siovansin

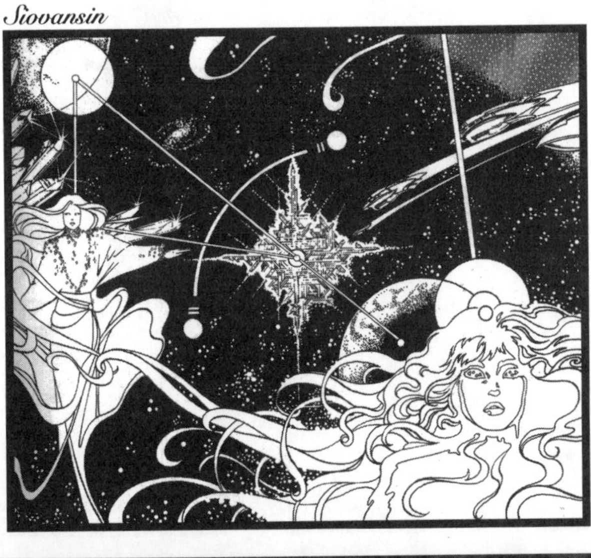

Sere

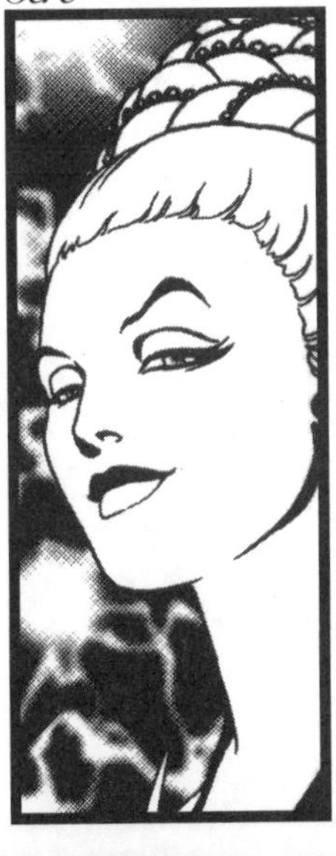

Jason

Liana

Rieken

Rienrie

D'mer

Dunstan

Minetti

Kirov

Kovar

Beys

Bast

has an old dispute with the Avatar. He plans to use his new power as one of the Hierarchy to get D'mer back.

Upon their return to the *Siovansin*, Rieken makes desperate plans to save D'mer from Emeris. Distressed by the Avatar's devotion to a slave, Rieken's servant Jorvana attempts to kill D'mer.

Jason has spent his time on the *Siovansin* training to carry out the Resistance's master plan: the assassination of the Avatar. On his journey to the Avatar's chambers, he is recognized by one of the guards who captured him on Earth. While he flees, several of the Resistance are killed, and one guard escapes to relay the news to the Hierarchy that Jason is still alive. The healer who saved him, Rienrie, commits suicide upon capture, but not before the Hierarchy learns the location of the Resistance safehouse.

Rieken and several of his champions travel to the depths of the *Siovansin* to meet with their Resistance allies, successfully passing the scrutiny of the mysterious Irishai who warn Rieken that the safehouse has been compromised and soldiers are capturing

Chris

Ninivir

Jorvana

Merai

Meris

Rienrie

WHAT HAS GONE BEFORE

everyone they find Below. Chris is shot and killed by a sniper, but the others escape.

Upon their return to the Avatar's apartments, Rieken learns of the plot to murder D'mer and allows D'mer his revenge: he gives Jorvana a fiery end.

Devastated by the betrayal of his trusted servant, and heartsick at the death of Chris, Rieken retires to his bedroom and orders Kovar to arrange funeral services for Christopher.

While the others attend the ceremony, Rieken sleeps in the company of his many pets. Jason, however, has managed to evade the heavy security of the Avatar's house and slips inside Rieken's room. Leaning over the sleeping figure of the man he has come to kill, Jason lifts his hand to strike...

Brent

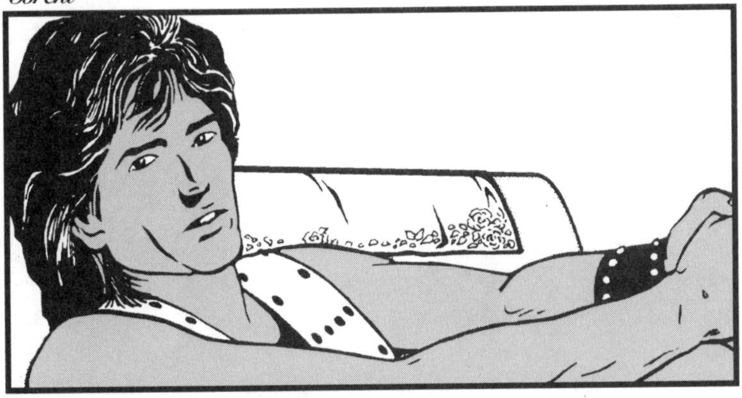

Serezha

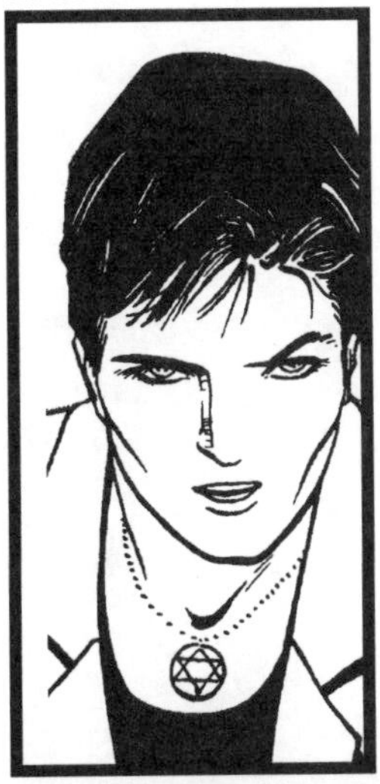

Reynaldo

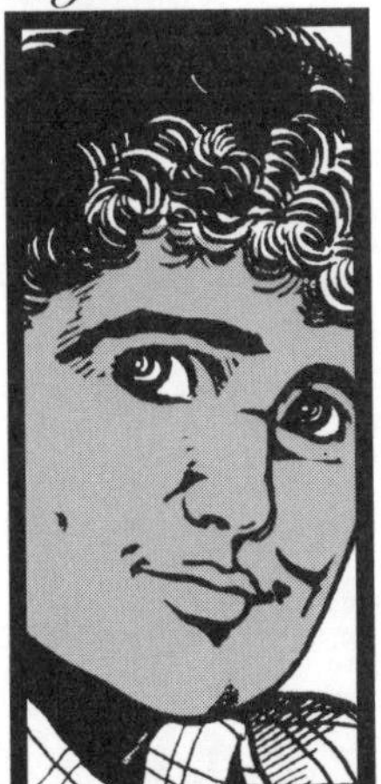

Vinyr

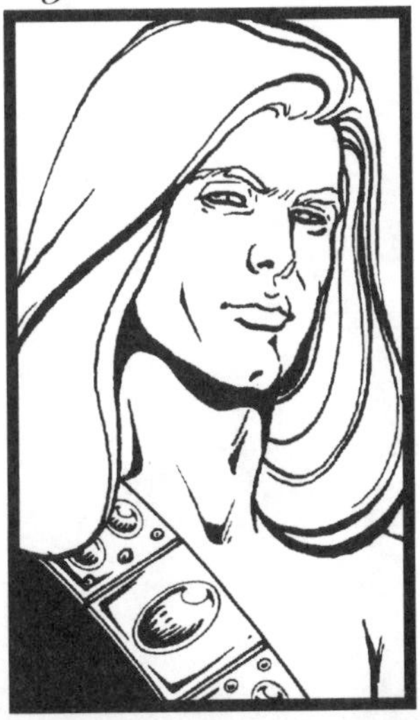

Dunstan
Minelli
Corrine
Niniri
Ninivir
Brent
Serezha
Chris
Merai
Sere
Vinyr

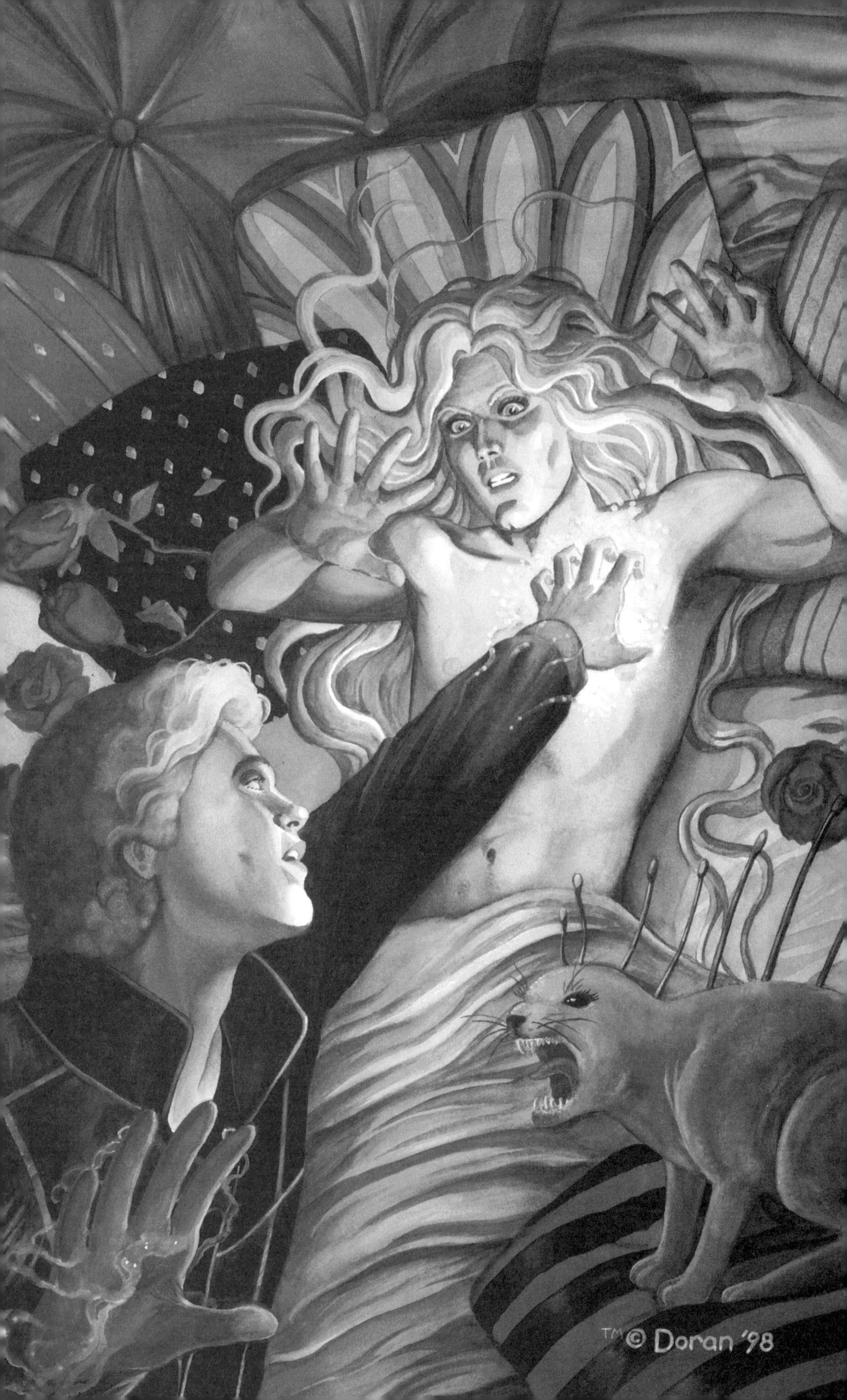
TM © Doran '98

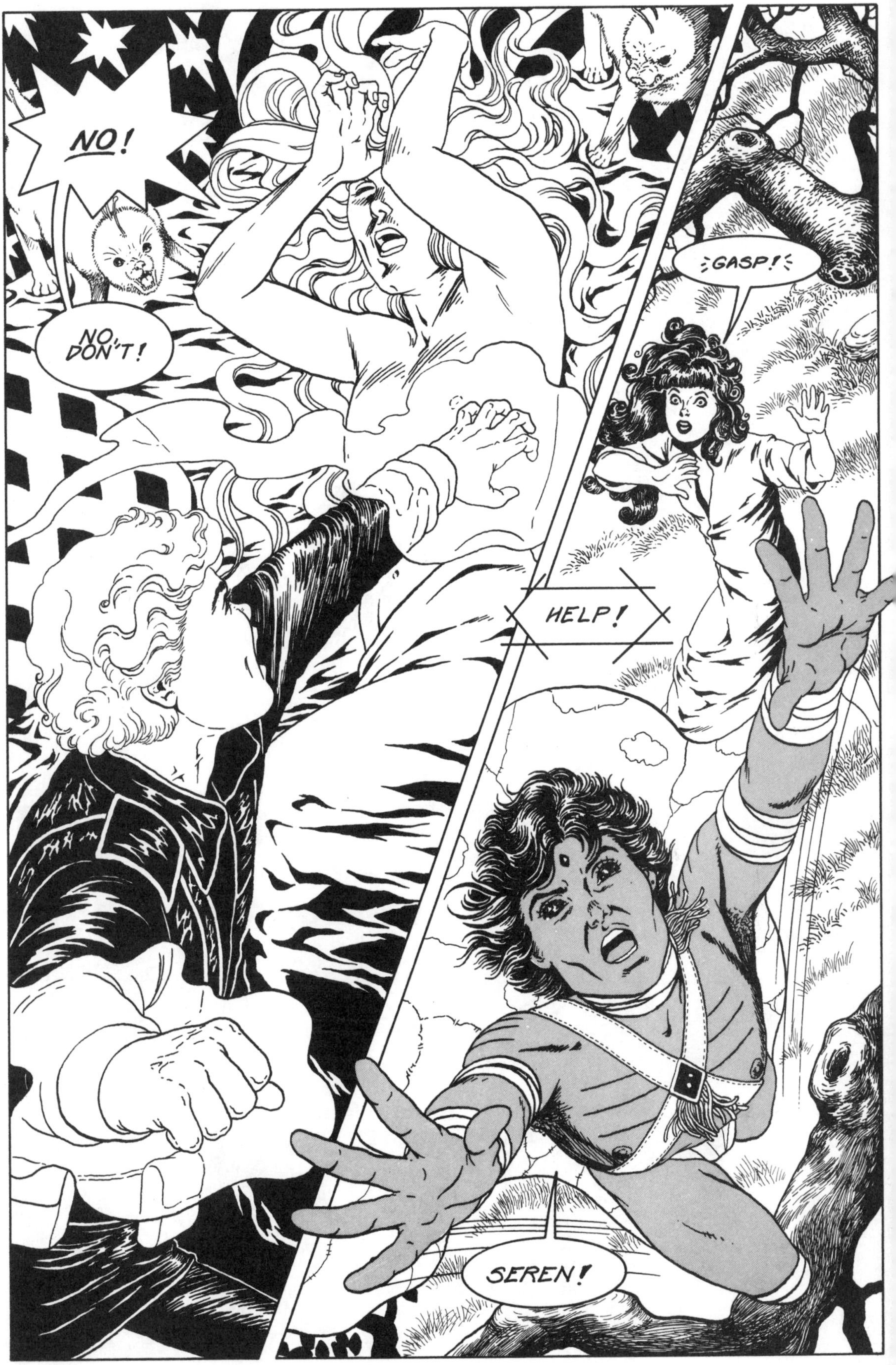
NO!
NO, DON'T!
GASP!
HELP!
SEREN!

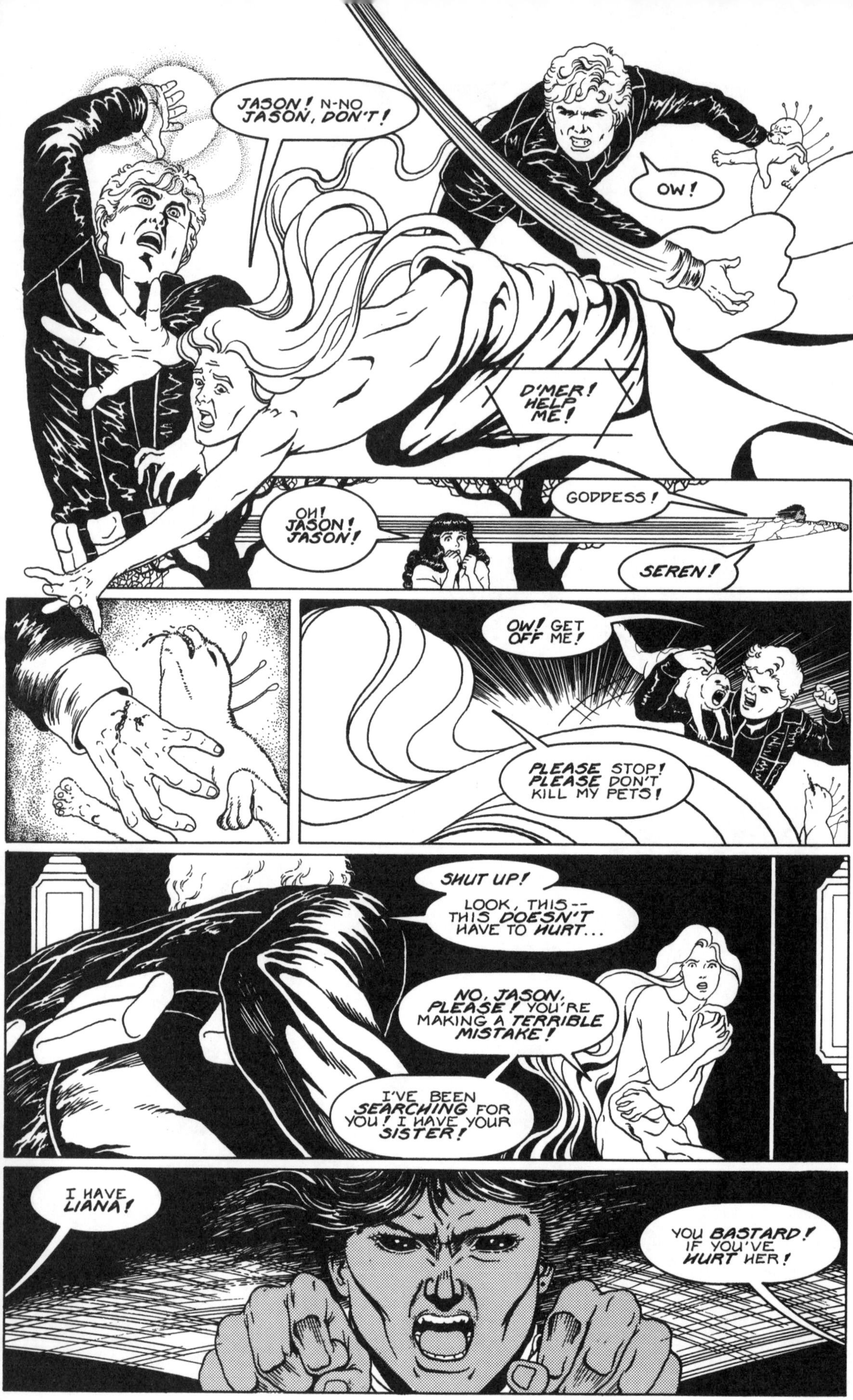
JASON! N-NO JASON, DON'T!
OW!
D'MER! HELP ME!
OH! JASON! JASON!
GODDESS!
SEREN!
OW! GET OFF ME!
PLEASE STOP! PLEASE DON'T KILL MY PETS!
SHUT UP!
LOOK, THIS-- THIS DOESN'T HAVE TO HURT...
NO, JASON, PLEASE! YOU'RE MAKING A TERRIBLE MISTAKE!
I'VE BEEN SEARCHING FOR YOU! I HAVE YOUR SISTER!
I HAVE LIANA!
YOU BASTARD! IF YOU'VE HURT HER!

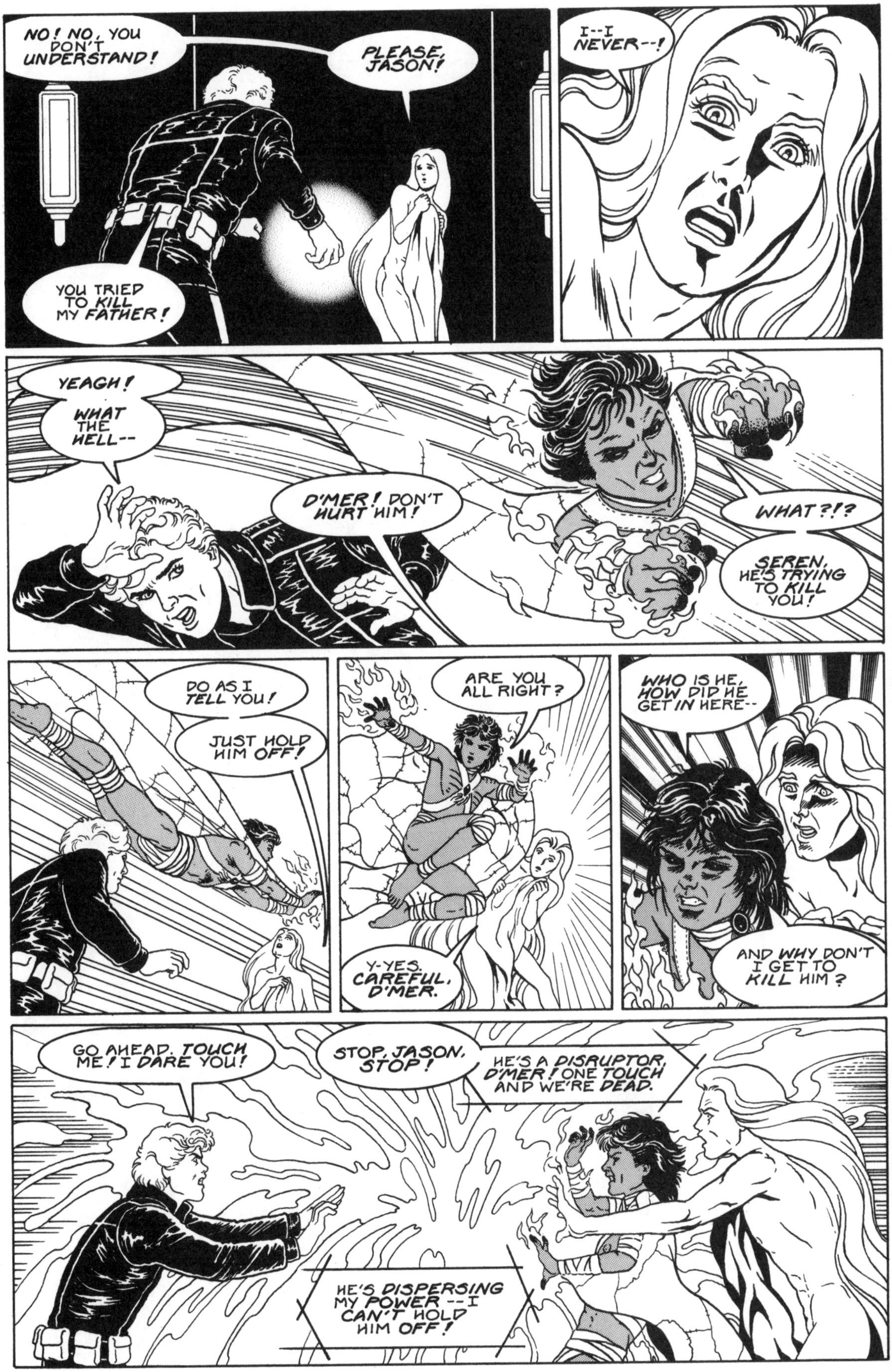
NO! NO, YOU DON'T UNDERSTAND!
PLEASE, JASON!
YOU TRIED TO KILL MY FATHER!
I--I NEVER--!
YEAGH!
WHAT THE HELL--
D'MER! DON'T HURT HIM!
WHAT?!?
SEREN, HE'S TRYING TO KILL YOU!
DO AS I TELL YOU!
JUST HOLD HIM OFF!
ARE YOU ALL RIGHT?
Y-YES. CAREFUL, D'MER.
WHO IS HE, HOW DID HE GET IN HERE--
AND WHY DON'T I GET TO KILL HIM?
GO AHEAD. TOUCH ME! I DARE YOU!
STOP, JASON, STOP!
HE'S A DISRUPTOR, D'MER! ONE TOUCH AND WE'RE DEAD.
HE'S DISPERSING MY POWER--I CAN'T HOLD HIM OFF!

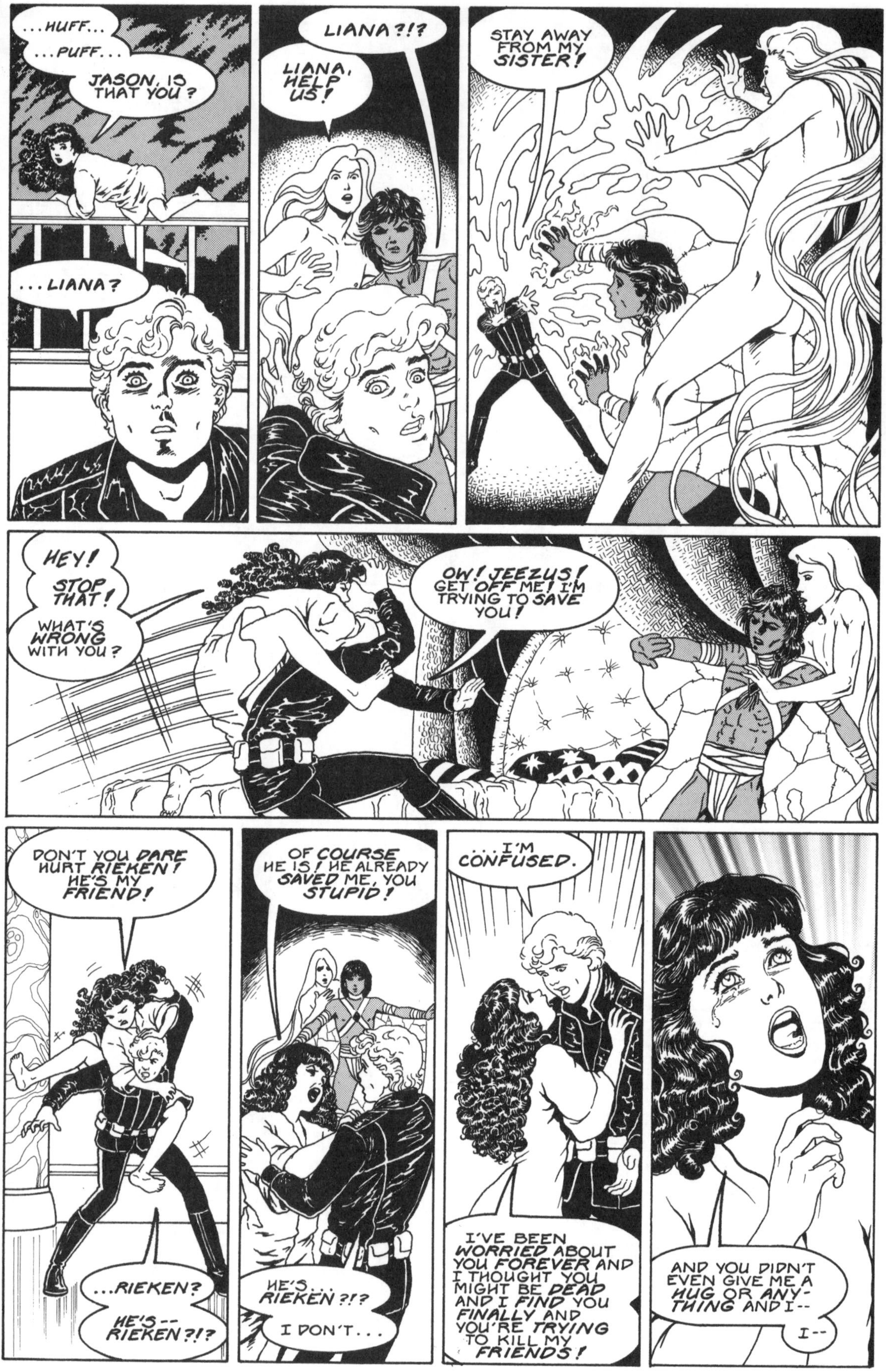
...HUFF...
...PUFF...
JASON, IS THAT YOU?
...LIANA?
LIANA?!?
LIANA, HELP US!
STAY AWAY FROM MY SISTER!
HEY! STOP THAT! WHAT'S WRONG WITH YOU?
OW! JEEZUS! GET OFF ME! I'M TRYING TO SAVE YOU!
DON'T YOU DARE HURT RIEKEN! HE'S MY FRIEND!
...RIEKEN?
HE'S-- RIEKEN?!?
OF COURSE HE IS! HE ALREADY SAVED ME, YOU STUPID!
HE'S... RIEKEN?!?
I DON'T...
...I'M CONFUSED.
I'VE BEEN WORRIED ABOUT YOU FOREVER AND I THOUGHT YOU MIGHT BE DEAD AND I FIND YOU FINALLY AND YOU'RE TRYING TO KILL MY FRIENDS!
AND YOU DIDN'T EVEN GIVE ME A HUG OR ANY-THING AND I--
I--

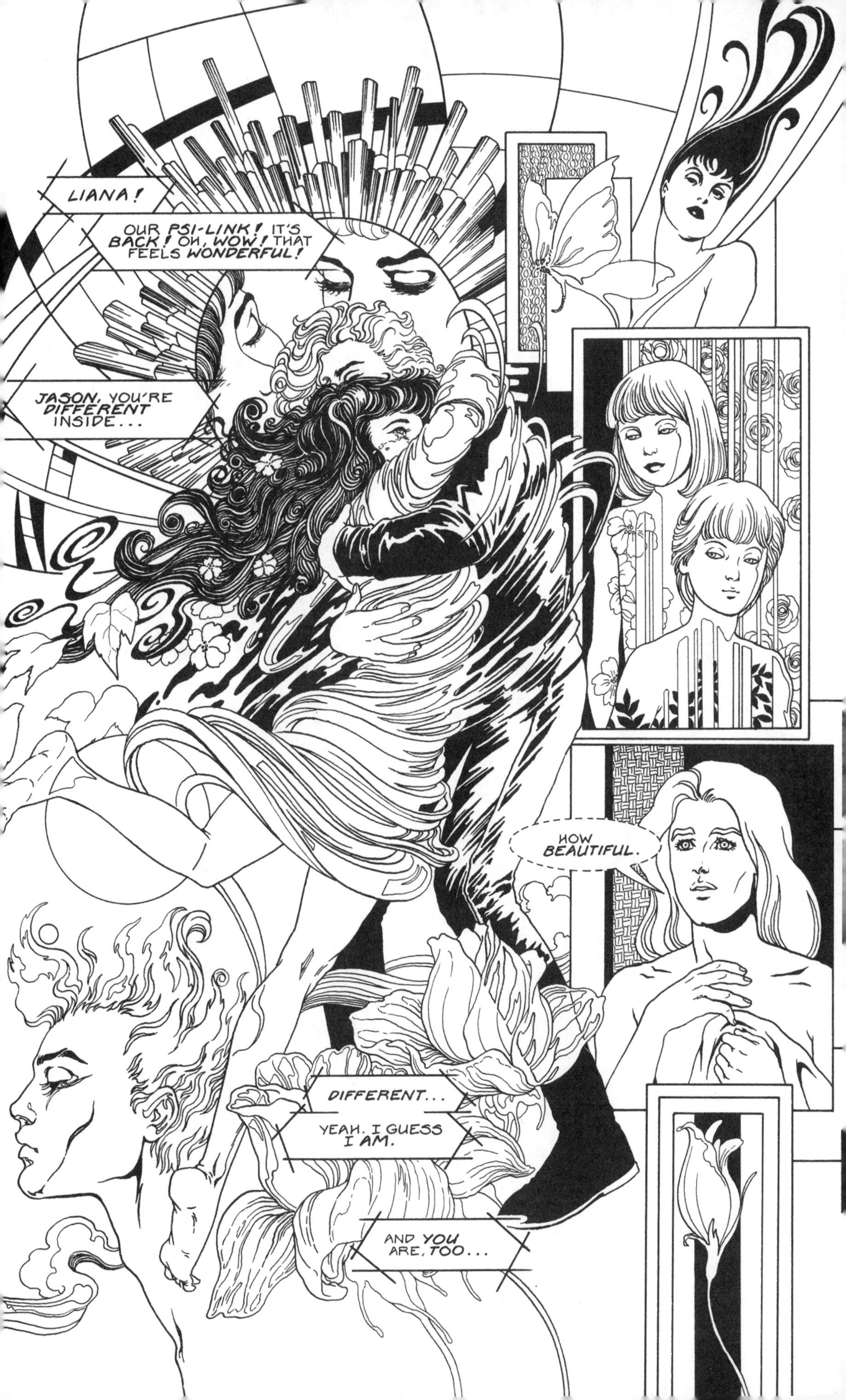
LIANA!
OUR PSI-LINK! IT'S BACK! OH, WOW! THAT FEELS WONDERFUL!
JASON, YOU'RE DIFFERENT INSIDE...
HOW BEAUTIFUL.
DIFFERENT...
YEAH. I GUESS I AM.
AND YOU ARE, TOO...

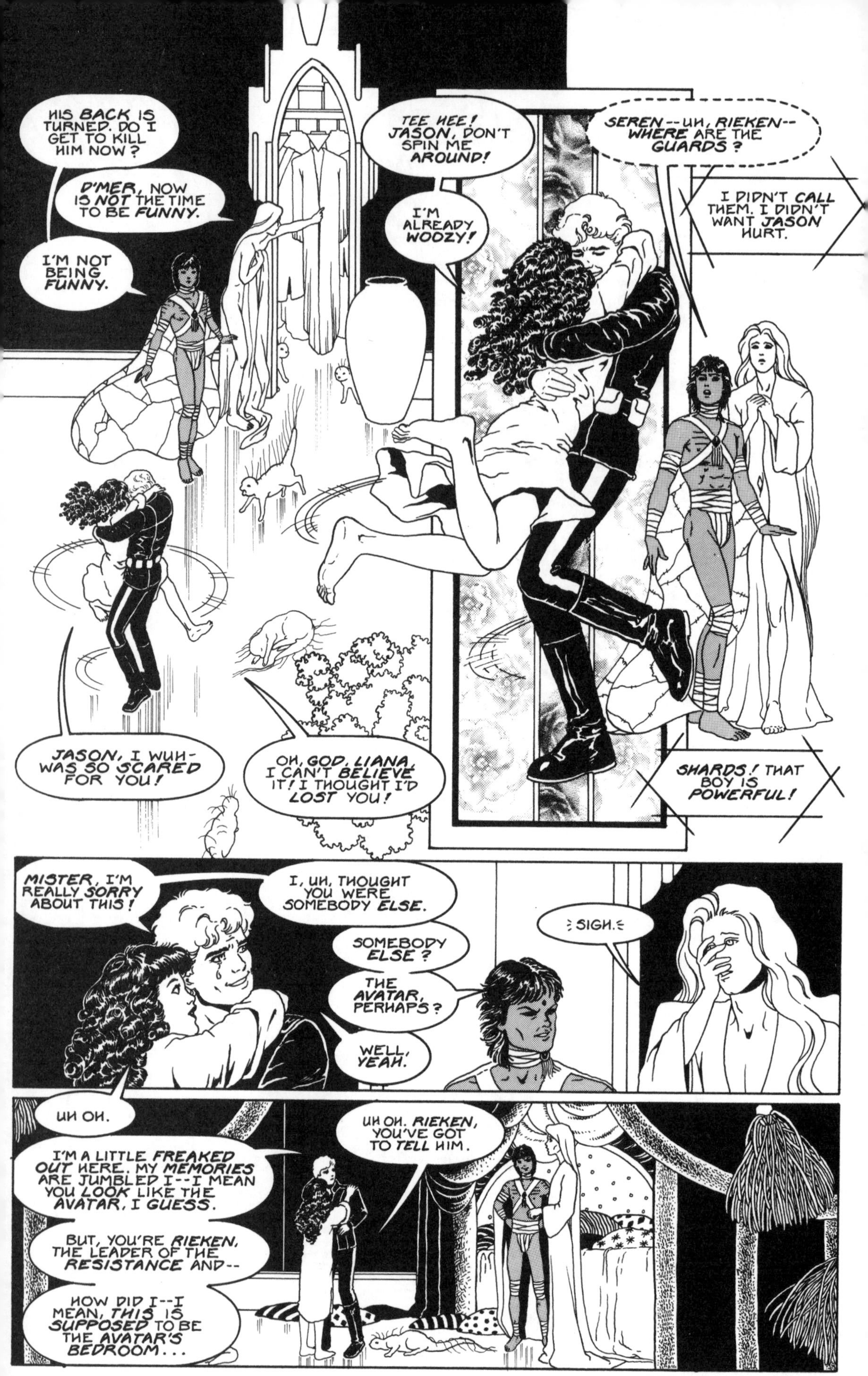
HIS BACK IS TURNED. DO I GET TO KILL HIM NOW?
D'MER, NOW IS NOT THE TIME TO BE FUNNY.
I'M NOT BEING FUNNY.
TEE HEE! JASON, DON'T SPIN ME AROUND!
I'M ALREADY WOOZY!
SEREN--UH, RIEKEN--WHERE ARE THE GUARDS?
I DIDN'T CALL THEM. I DIDN'T WANT JASON HURT.
JASON, I WUH-WAS SO SCARED FOR YOU!
OH, GOD, LIANA, I CAN'T BELIEVE IT! I THOUGHT I'D LOST YOU!
SHARDS! THAT BOY IS POWERFUL!
MISTER, I'M REALLY SORRY ABOUT THIS!
I, UH, THOUGHT YOU WERE SOMEBODY ELSE.
SOMEBODY ELSE?
THE AVATAR, PERHAPS?
WELL, YEAH.
SIGH.
UH OH.
I'M A LITTLE FREAKED OUT HERE. MY MEMORIES ARE JUMBLED I--I MEAN YOU LOOK LIKE THE AVATAR, I GUESS.
BUT, YOU'RE RIEKEN, THE LEADER OF THE RESISTANCE AND--
HOW DID I--I MEAN, THIS IS SUPPOSED TO BE THE AVATAR'S BEDROOM...
UH OH. RIEKEN, YOU'VE GOT TO TELL HIM.

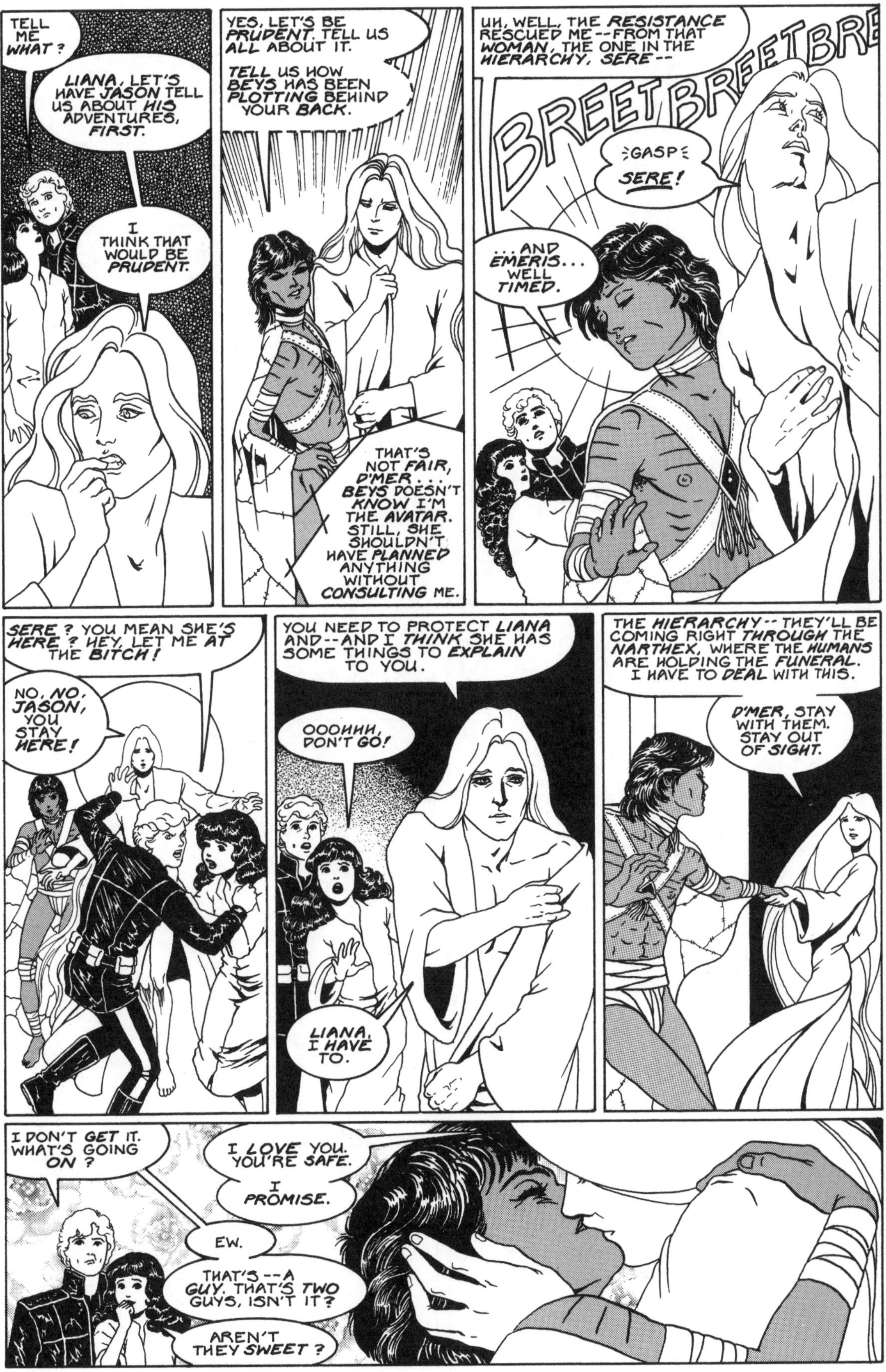
TELL ME WHAT?
LIANA, LET'S HAVE JASON TELL US ABOUT HIS ADVENTURES, FIRST.
I THINK THAT WOULD BE PRUDENT.
YES, LET'S BE PRUDENT. TELL US ALL ABOUT IT.
TELL US HOW BEYS HAS BEEN PLOTTING BEHIND YOUR BACK.
THAT'S NOT FAIR, D'MER... BEYS DOESN'T KNOW I'M THE AVATAR. STILL, SHE SHOULDN'T HAVE PLANNED ANYTHING WITHOUT CONSULTING ME.
UH, WELL, THE RESISTANCE RESCUED ME--FROM THAT WOMAN, THE ONE IN THE HIERARCHY, SERE--
BREETBREETBRE
GASP SERE!
...AND EMERIS... WELL TIMED.
SERE? YOU MEAN SHE'S HERE? HEY, LET ME AT THE BITCH!
NO, NO, JASON, YOU STAY HERE!
YOU NEED TO PROTECT LIANA AND--AND I THINK SHE HAS SOME THINGS TO EXPLAIN TO YOU.
OOOHHH, DON'T GO!
LIANA, I HAVE TO.
THE HIERARCHY--THEY'LL BE COMING RIGHT THROUGH THE NARTHEX, WHERE THE HUMANS ARE HOLDING THE FUNERAL. I HAVE TO DEAL WITH THIS.
D'MER, STAY WITH THEM. STAY OUT OF SIGHT.
I DON'T GET IT. WHAT'S GOING ON?
I LOVE YOU. YOU'RE SAFE.
I PROMISE.
EW.
THAT'S--A GUY. THAT'S TWO GUYS, ISN'T IT?
AREN'T THEY SWEET?

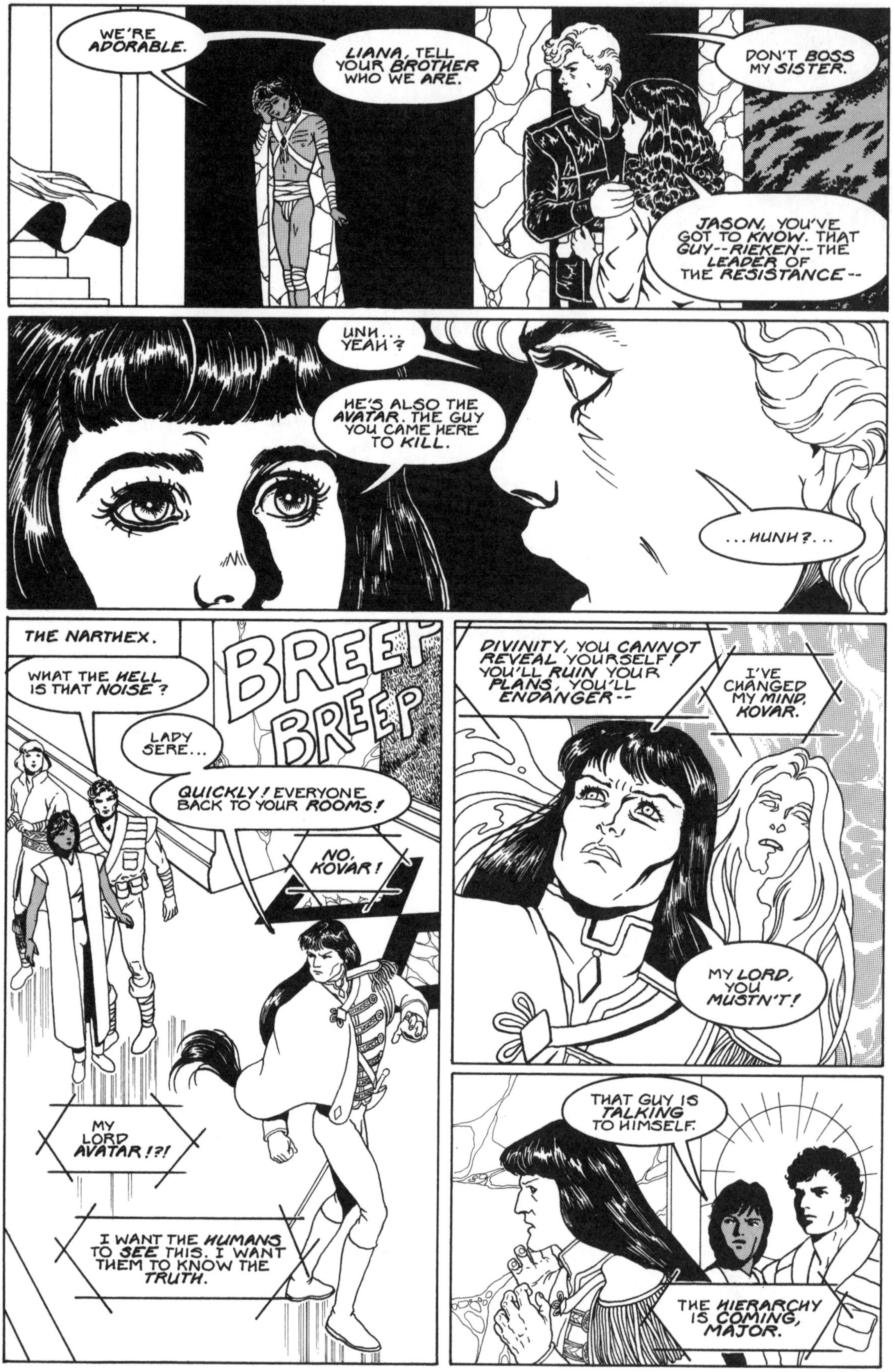
WE'RE ADORABLE.
LIANA, TELL YOUR BROTHER WHO WE ARE.
DON'T BOSS MY SISTER.
JASON, YOU'VE GOT TO KNOW. THAT GUY--RIEKEN--THE LEADER OF THE RESISTANCE--
UNH... YEAH?
HE'S ALSO THE AVATAR. THE GUY YOU CAME HERE TO KILL.
...HUNH?...
THE NARTHEX.
WHAT THE HELL IS THAT NOISE?
BREEP BREEP
LADY SERE...
QUICKLY! EVERYONE BACK TO YOUR ROOMS!
NO, KOVAR!
MY LORD AVATAR!?!
I WANT THE HUMANS TO SEE THIS. I WANT THEM TO KNOW THE TRUTH.
DIVINITY, YOU CANNOT REVEAL YOURSELF! YOU'LL RUIN YOUR PLANS, YOU'LL ENDANGER--
I'VE CHANGED MY MIND, KOVAR.
MY LORD, YOU MUSTN'T!
THAT GUY IS TALKING TO HIMSELF.
THE HIERARCHY IS COMING, MAJOR.

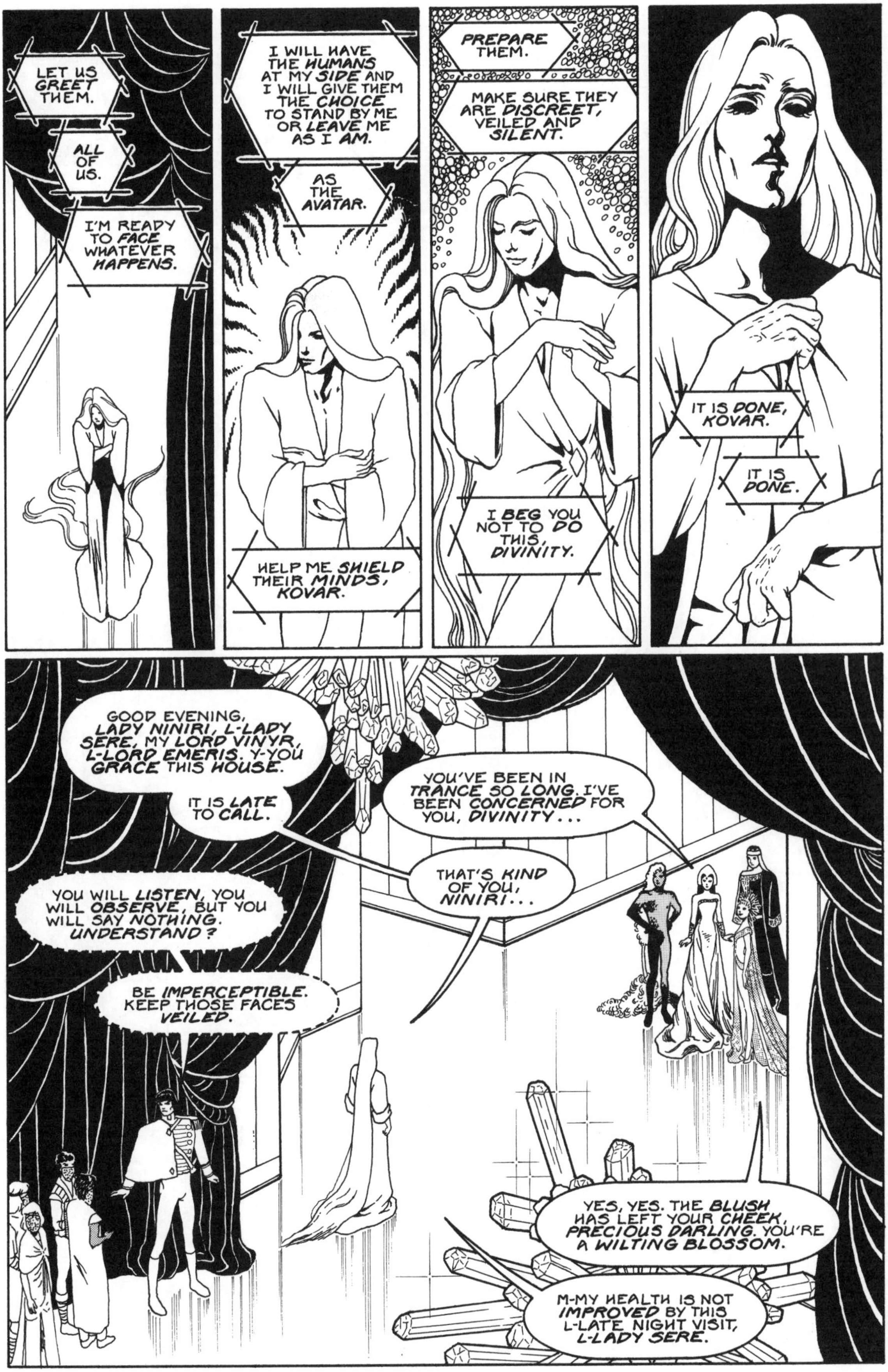
LET US GREET THEM.
ALL OF US.
I'M READY TO FACE WHATEVER HAPPENS.
I WILL HAVE THE HUMANS AT MY SIDE AND I WILL GIVE THEM THE CHOICE TO STAND BY ME OR LEAVE ME AS I AM.
AS THE AVATAR.
HELP ME SHIELD THEIR MINDS, KOVAR.
PREPARE THEM.
MAKE SURE THEY ARE DISCREET, VEILED AND SILENT.
I BEG YOU NOT TO DO THIS, DIVINITY.
IT IS DONE, KOVAR.
IT IS DONE.
GOOD EVENING, LADY NINIRI, L-LADY SERE, MY LORD VINYR, L-LORD EMERIS. Y-YOU GRACE THIS HOUSE.
IT IS LATE TO CALL.
YOU'VE BEEN IN TRANCE SO LONG. I'VE BEEN CONCERNED FOR YOU, DIVINITY...
THAT'S KIND OF YOU, NINIRI...
YOU WILL LISTEN, YOU WILL OBSERVE, BUT YOU WILL SAY NOTHING. UNDERSTAND?
BE IMPERCEPTIBLE. KEEP THOSE FACES VEILED.
YES, YES. THE BLUSH HAS LEFT YOUR CHEEK, PRECIOUS DARLING. YOU'RE A WILTING BLOSSOM.
M-MY HEALTH IS NOT IMPROVED BY THIS L-LATE NIGHT VISIT, L-LADY SERE.

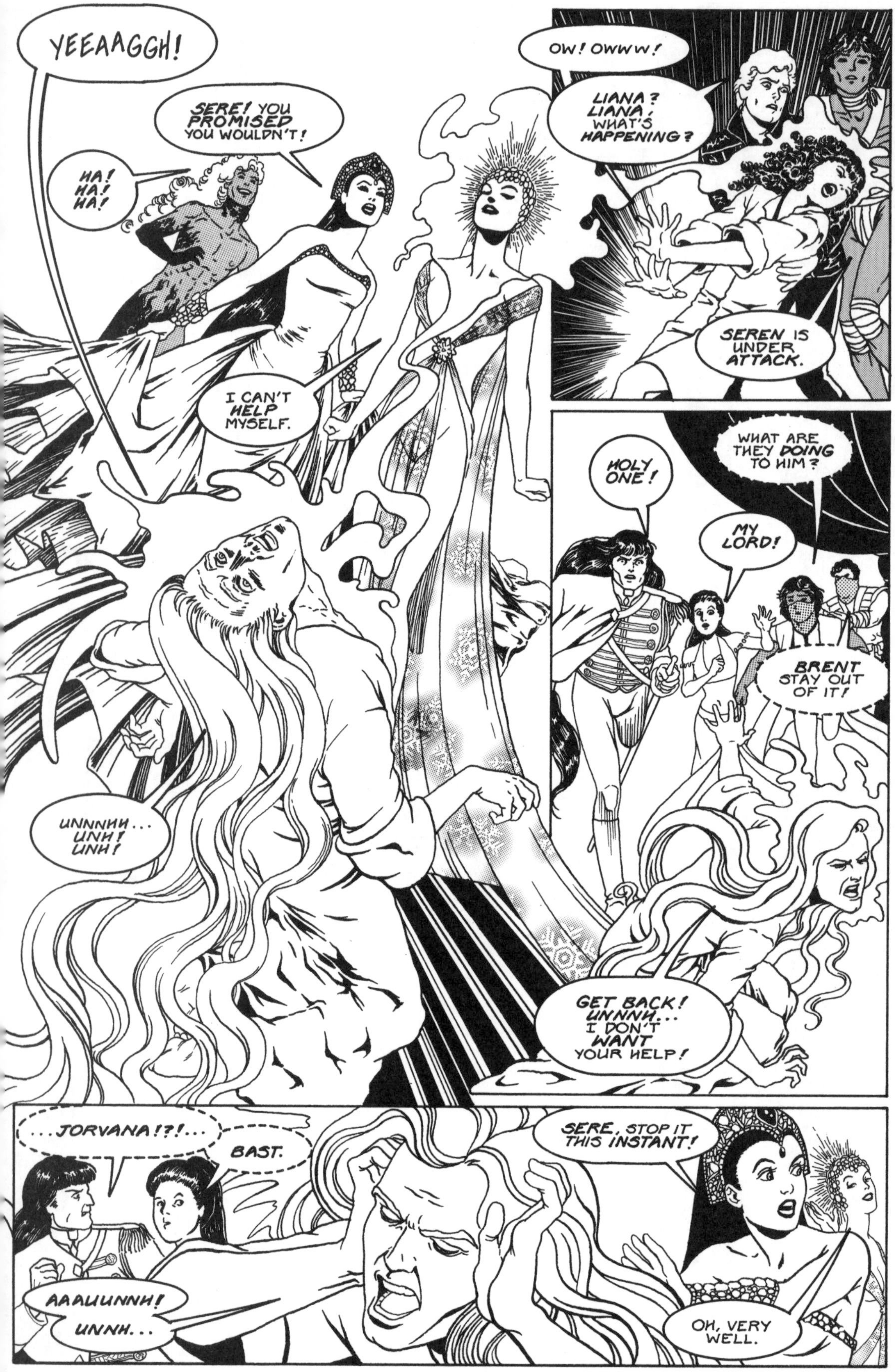
YEEAAGGH!
SERE! YOU PROMISED YOU WOULDN'T!
HA! HA! HA!
I CAN'T HELP MYSELF.
UNNNHH... UNH! UNH!
OW! OWWW!
LIANA? LIANA! WHAT'S HAPPENING?
SEREN IS UNDER ATTACK.
HOLY ONE!
WHAT ARE THEY DOING TO HIM?
MY LORD!
BRENT STAY OUT OF IT!
GET BACK! UNNNH... I DON'T WANT YOUR HELP!
...JORVANA!?!...
BAST.
SERE, STOP IT THIS INSTANT!
AAAUUNNH! UNNH...
OH, VERY WELL.

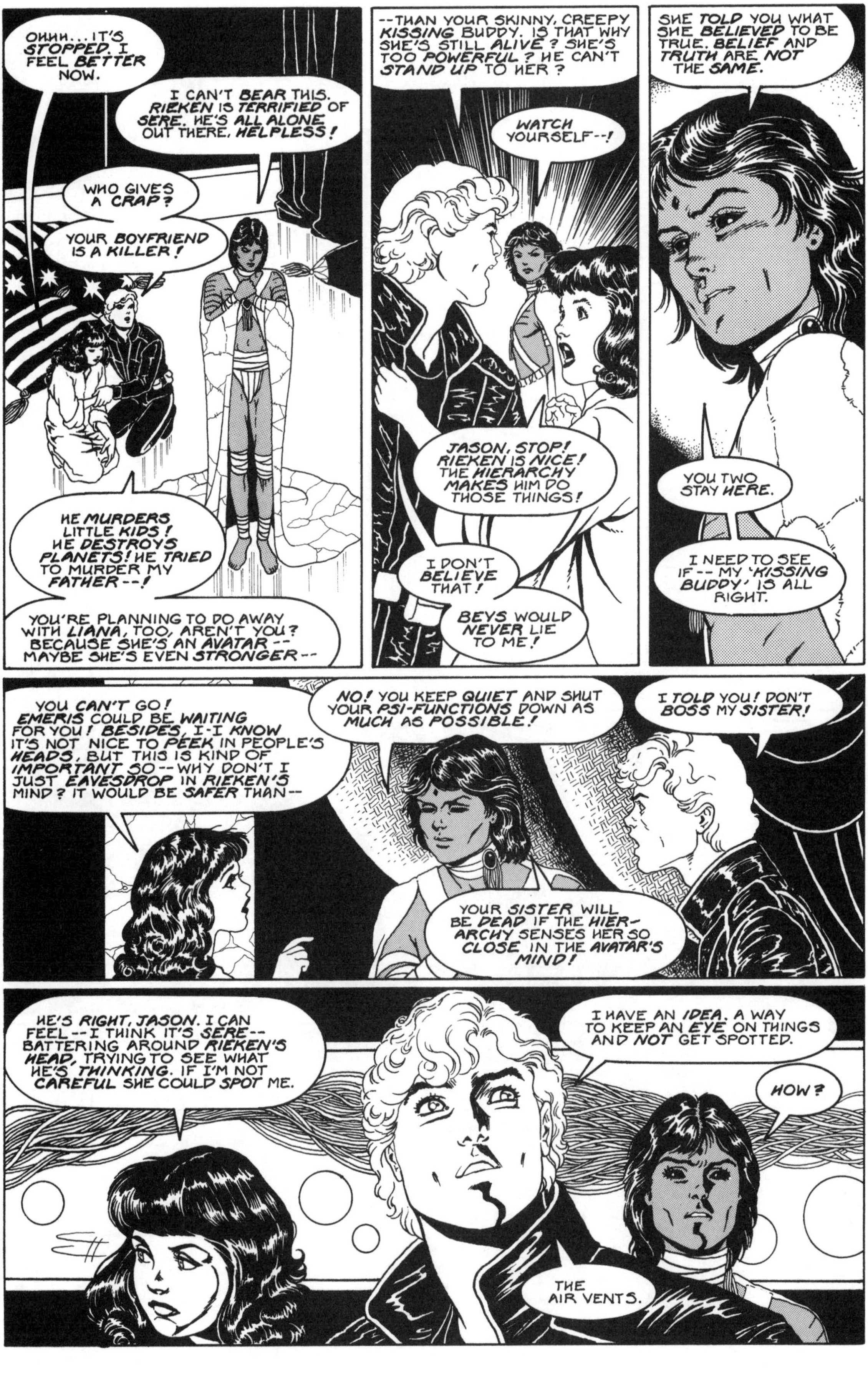
OHHH... IT'S STOPPED. I FEEL BETTER NOW.
I CAN'T BEAR THIS. RIEKEN IS TERRIFIED OF SERE. HE'S ALL ALONE OUT THERE. HELPLESS!
WHO GIVES A CRAP?
YOUR BOYFRIEND IS A KILLER!
HE MURDERS LITTLE KIDS! HE DESTROYS PLANETS! HE TRIED TO MURDER MY FATHER--!
YOU'RE PLANNING TO DO AWAY WITH LIANA, TOO, AREN'T YOU? BECAUSE SHE'S AN AVATAR-- MAYBE SHE'S EVEN STRONGER--
--THAN YOUR SKINNY, CREEPY KISSING BUDDY. IS THAT WHY SHE'S STILL ALIVE? SHE'S TOO POWERFUL? HE CAN'T STAND UP TO HER?
WATCH YOURSELF--!
JASON, STOP! RIEKEN IS NICE! THE HIERARCHY MAKES HIM DO THOSE THINGS!
I DON'T BELIEVE THAT!
BEYS WOULD NEVER LIE TO ME!
SHE TOLD YOU WHAT SHE BELIEVED TO BE TRUE. BELIEF AND TRUTH ARE NOT THE SAME.
YOU TWO STAY HERE.
I NEED TO SEE IF-- MY 'KISSING BUDDY' IS ALL RIGHT.
YOU CAN'T GO! EMERIS COULD BE WAITING FOR YOU! BESIDES, I-I KNOW IT'S NOT NICE TO PEEK IN PEOPLE'S HEADS, BUT THIS IS KIND OF IMPORTANT SO--WHY DON'T I JUST EAVESDROP IN RIEKEN'S MIND? IT WOULD BE SAFER THAN--
NO! YOU KEEP QUIET AND SHUT YOUR PSI-FUNCTIONS DOWN AS MUCH AS POSSIBLE!
YOUR SISTER WILL BE DEAD IF THE HIER-ARCHY SENSES HER SO CLOSE IN THE AVATAR'S MIND!
I TOLD YOU! DON'T BOSS MY SISTER!
HE'S RIGHT, JASON. I CAN FEEL--I THINK IT'S SERE-- BATTERING AROUND RIEKEN'S HEAD, TRYING TO SEE WHAT HE'S THINKING. IF I'M NOT CAREFUL SHE COULD SPOT ME.
I HAVE AN IDEA. A WAY TO KEEP AN EYE ON THINGS AND NOT GET SPOTTED.
HOW?
THE AIR VENTS.

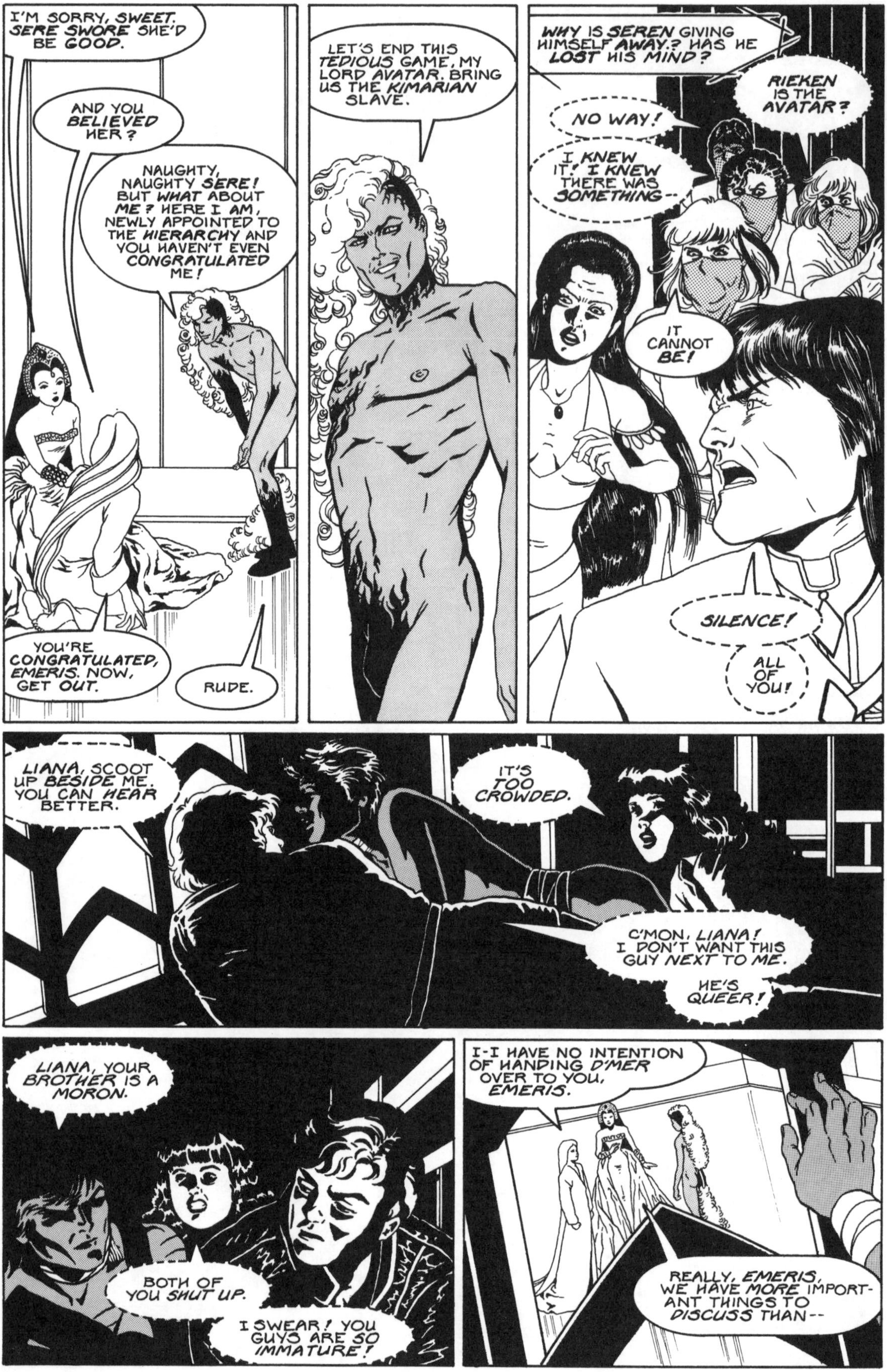
I'M SORRY, SWEET. SERE SWORE SHE'D BE GOOD.
AND YOU BELIEVED HER?
NAUGHTY, NAUGHTY SERE! BUT WHAT ABOUT ME? HERE I AM, NEWLY APPOINTED TO THE HIERARCHY AND YOU HAVEN'T EVEN CONGRATULATED ME!
YOU'RE CONGRATULATED, EMERIS. NOW, GET OUT.
RUDE.
LET'S END THIS TEDIOUS GAME, MY LORD AVATAR. BRING US THE KIMARIAN SLAVE.
WHY IS SEREN GIVING HIMSELF AWAY? HAS HE LOST HIS MIND?
RIEKEN IS THE AVATAR?
NO WAY!
I KNEW IT! I KNEW THERE WAS SOMETHING--
IT CANNOT BE!
SILENCE!
ALL OF YOU!
LIANA, SCOOT UP BESIDE ME. YOU CAN HEAR BETTER.
IT'S TOO CROWDED.
C'MON, LIANA! I DON'T WANT THIS GUY NEXT TO ME.
HE'S QUEER!
LIANA, YOUR BROTHER IS A MORON.
BOTH OF YOU SHUT UP.
I SWEAR! YOU GUYS ARE SO IMMATURE!
I-I HAVE NO INTENTION OF HANDING D'MER OVER TO YOU, EMERIS.
REALLY, EMERIS, WE HAVE MORE IMPORTANT THINGS TO DISCUSS THAN--

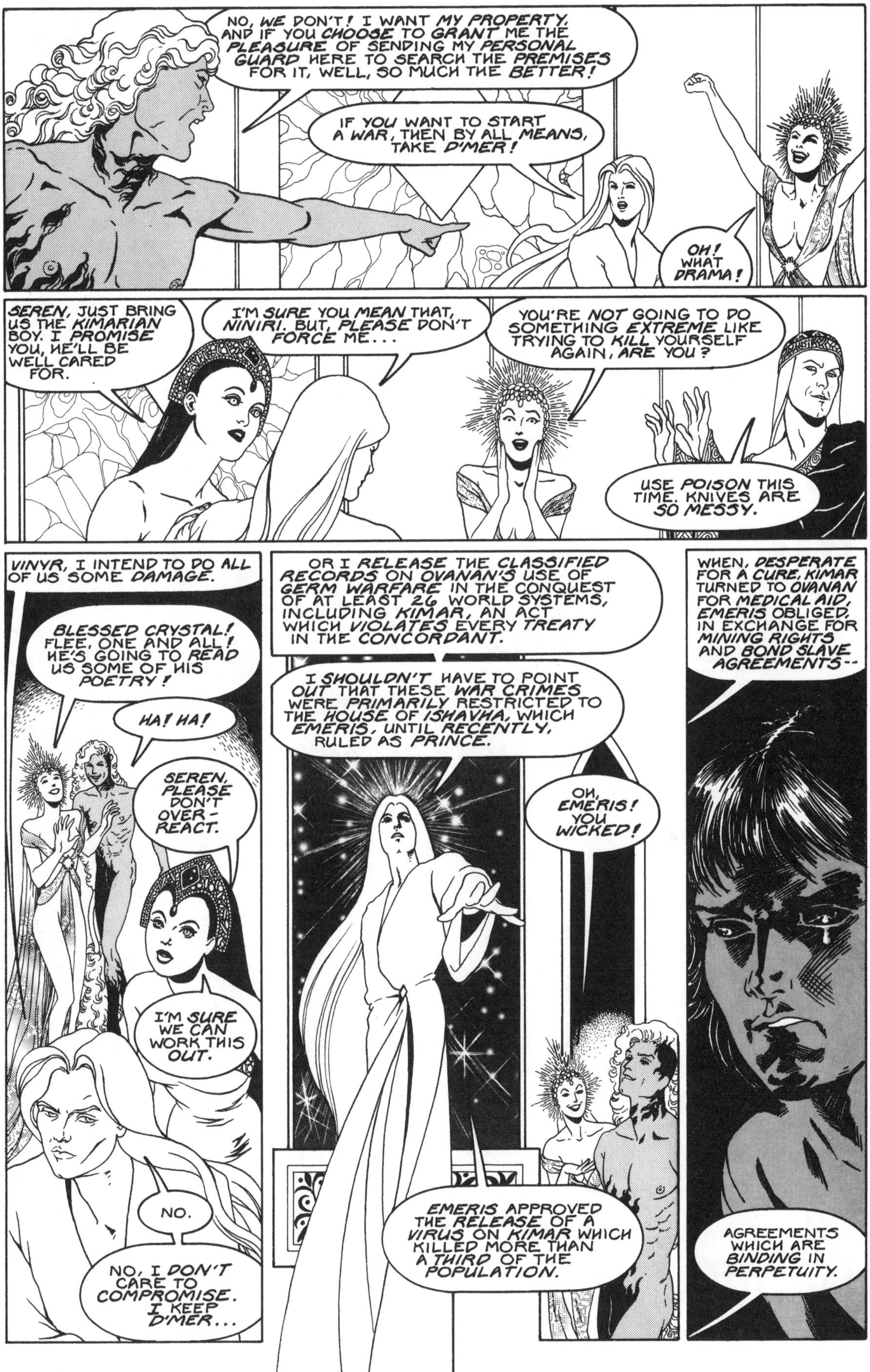
NO, WE DON'T! I WANT MY PROPERTY. AND IF YOU CHOOSE TO GRANT ME THE PLEASURE OF SENDING MY PERSONAL GUARD HERE TO SEARCH THE PREMISES FOR IT, WELL, SO MUCH THE BETTER!
IF YOU WANT TO START A WAR, THEN BY ALL MEANS, TAKE D'MER!
OH! WHAT DRAMA!
SEREN, JUST BRING US THE KIMARIAN BOY. I PROMISE YOU, HE'LL BE WELL CARED FOR.
I'M SURE YOU MEAN THAT, NINIRI. BUT, PLEASE DON'T FORCE ME...
YOU'RE NOT GOING TO DO SOMETHING EXTREME LIKE TRYING TO KILL YOURSELF AGAIN, ARE YOU?
USE POISON THIS TIME. KNIVES ARE SO MESSY.
VINYR, I INTEND TO DO ALL OF US SOME DAMAGE.
BLESSED CRYSTAL! FLEE, ONE AND ALL! HE'S GOING TO READ US SOME OF HIS POETRY!
HA! HA!
SEREN. PLEASE DON'T OVER-REACT.
I'M SURE WE CAN WORK THIS OUT.
NO.
NO, I DON'T CARE TO COMPROMISE. I KEEP D'MER...
OR I RELEASE THE CLASSIFIED RECORDS ON OVANAN'S USE OF GERM WARFARE IN THE CONQUEST OF AT LEAST 26 WORLD SYSTEMS, INCLUDING KIMAR, AN ACT WHICH VIOLATES EVERY TREATY IN THE CONCORDANT.
I SHOULDN'T HAVE TO POINT OUT THAT THESE WAR CRIMES WERE PRIMARILY RESTRICTED TO THE HOUSE OF ISHAVHA, WHICH EMERIS, UNTIL RECENTLY, RULED AS PRINCE.
OH, EMERIS! YOU WICKED!
EMERIS APPROVED THE RELEASE OF A VIRUS ON KIMAR WHICH KILLED MORE THAN A THIRD OF THE POPULATION.
WHEN, DESPERATE FOR A CURE, KIMAR TURNED TO OVANAN FOR MEDICAL AID, EMERIS OBLIGED, IN EXCHANGE FOR MINING RIGHTS AND BOND SLAVE AGREEMENTS--
AGREEMENTS WHICH ARE BINDING IN PERPETUITY.

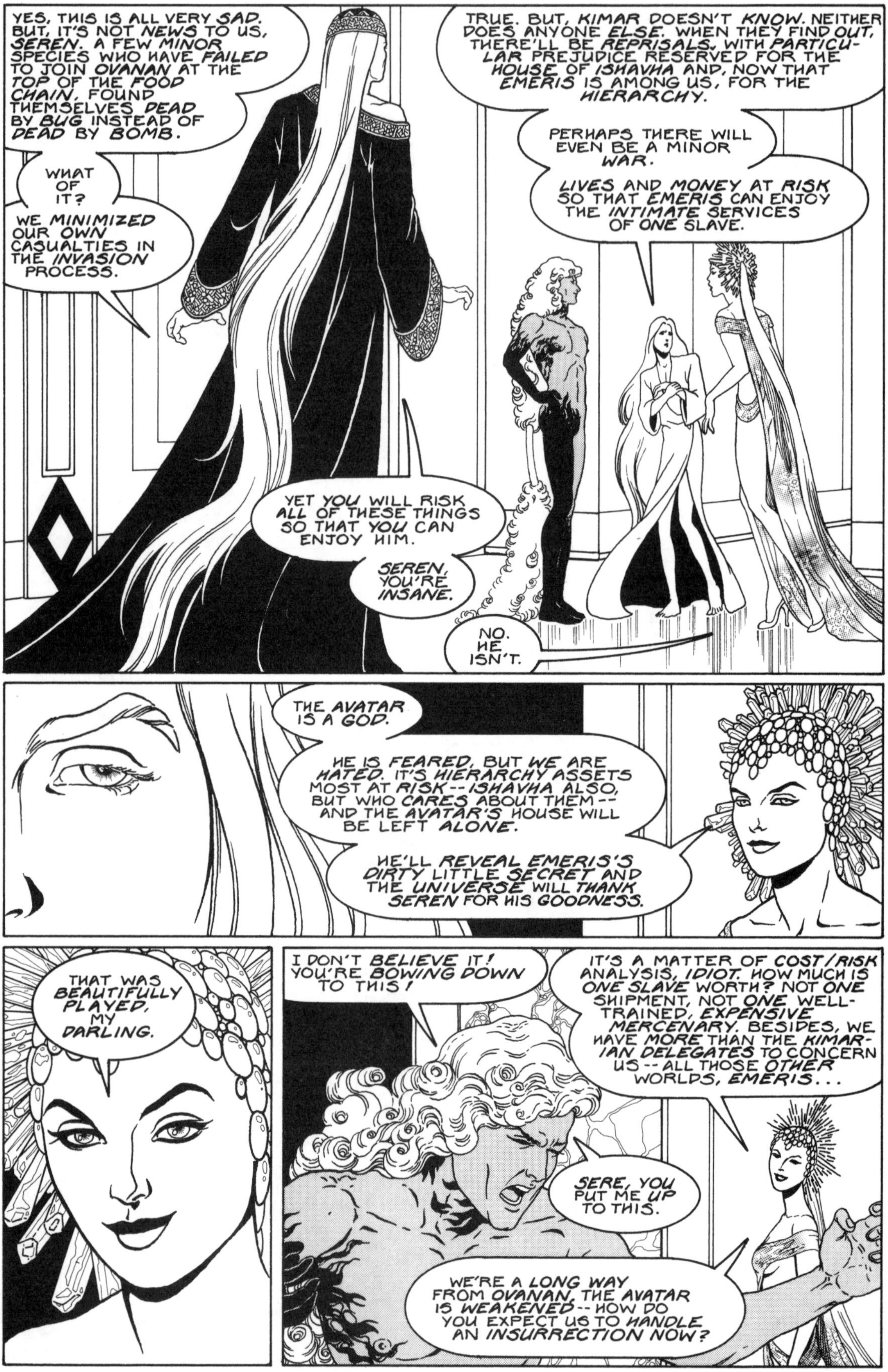
YES, THIS IS ALL VERY SAD. BUT, IT'S NOT NEWS TO US, SEREN. A FEW MINOR SPECIES WHO HAVE FAILED TO JOIN OVANAN AT THE TOP OF THE FOOD CHAIN, FOUND THEMSELVES DEAD BY BUG INSTEAD OF DEAD BY BOMB.
WHAT OF IT?
WE MINIMIZED OUR OWN CASUALTIES IN THE INVASION PROCESS.
TRUE. BUT, KIMAR DOESN'T KNOW. NEITHER DOES ANYONE ELSE. WHEN THEY FIND OUT, THERE'LL BE REPRISALS, WITH PARTICULAR PREJUDICE RESERVED FOR THE HOUSE OF ISHAVHA AND, NOW THAT EMERIS IS AMONG US, FOR THE HIERARCHY.
PERHAPS THERE WILL EVEN BE A MINOR WAR.
LIVES AND MONEY AT RISK SO THAT EMERIS CAN ENJOY THE INTIMATE SERVICES OF ONE SLAVE.
YET YOU WILL RISK ALL OF THESE THINGS SO THAT YOU CAN ENJOY HIM.
SEREN, YOU'RE INSANE.
NO. HE ISN'T.
THE AVATAR IS A GOD.
HE IS FEARED, BUT WE ARE HATED. IT'S HIERARCHY ASSETS MOST AT RISK -- ISHAVHA ALSO, BUT WHO CARES ABOUT THEM -- AND THE AVATAR'S HOUSE WILL BE LEFT ALONE.
HE'LL REVEAL EMERIS'S DIRTY LITTLE SECRET AND THE UNIVERSE WILL THANK SEREN FOR HIS GOODNESS.
THAT WAS BEAUTIFULLY PLAYED, MY DARLING.
I DON'T BELIEVE IT! YOU'RE BOWING DOWN TO THIS!
IT'S A MATTER OF COST/RISK ANALYSIS, IDIOT. HOW MUCH IS ONE SLAVE WORTH? NOT ONE SHIPMENT, NOT ONE WELL-TRAINED, EXPENSIVE MERCENARY. BESIDES, WE HAVE MORE THAN THE KIMARIAN DELEGATES TO CONCERN US -- ALL THOSE OTHER WORLDS, EMERIS...
SERE, YOU PUT ME UP TO THIS.
WE'RE A LONG WAY FROM OVANAN, THE AVATAR IS WEAKENED -- HOW DO YOU EXPECT US TO HANDLE AN INSURRECTION NOW?

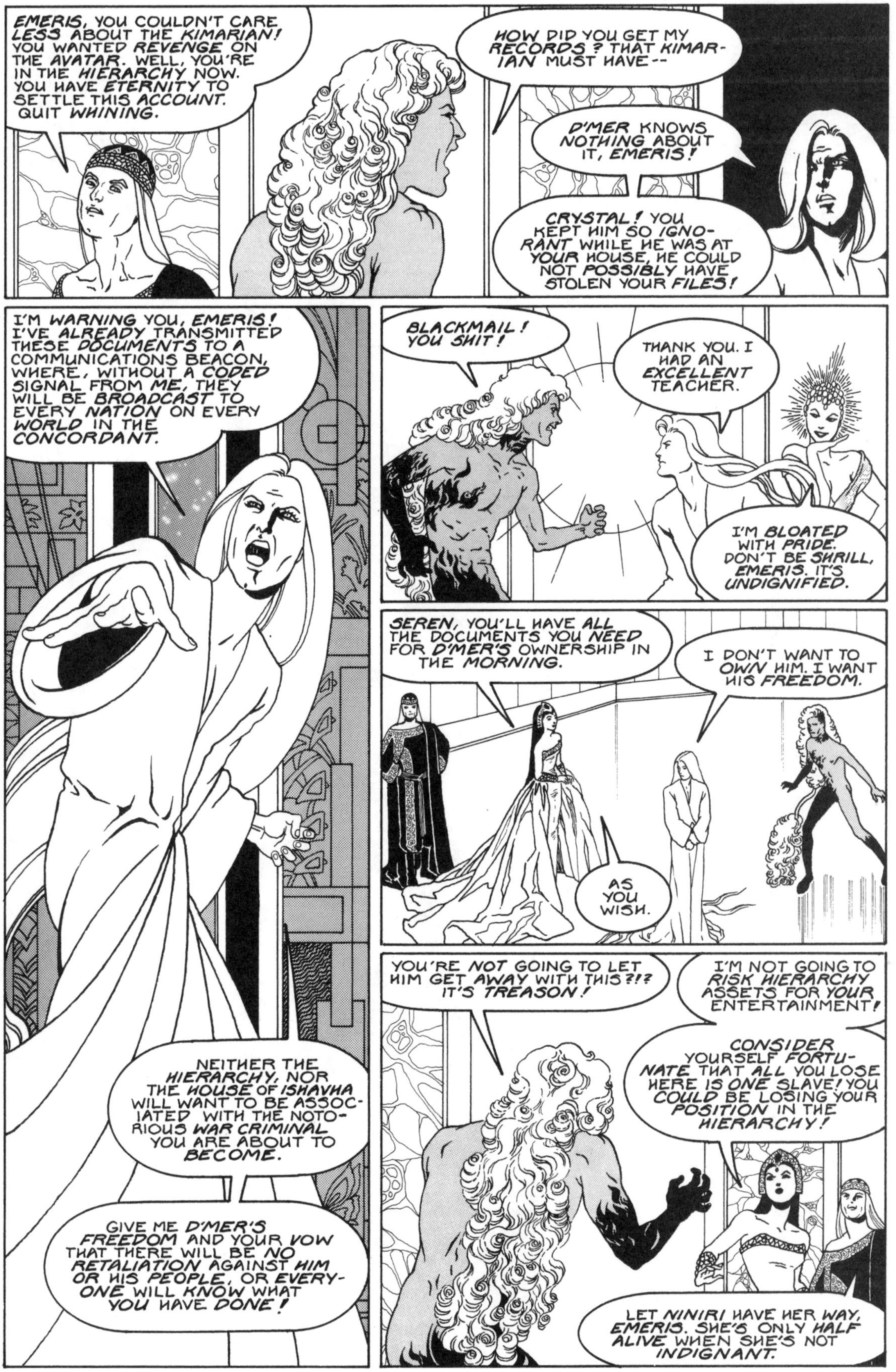
EMERIS, YOU COULDN'T CARE LESS ABOUT THE KIMARIAN! YOU WANTED REVENGE ON THE AVATAR. WELL, YOU'RE IN THE HIERARCHY NOW. YOU HAVE ETERNITY TO SETTLE THIS ACCOUNT. QUIT WHINING.
HOW DID YOU GET MY RECORDS? THAT KIMARIAN MUST HAVE--
D'MER KNOWS NOTHING ABOUT IT, EMERIS!
CRYSTAL! YOU KEPT HIM SO IGNORANT WHILE HE WAS AT YOUR HOUSE, HE COULD NOT POSSIBLY HAVE STOLEN YOUR FILES!
I'M WARNING YOU, EMERIS! I'VE ALREADY TRANSMITTED THESE DOCUMENTS TO A COMMUNICATIONS BEACON, WHERE, WITHOUT A CODED SIGNAL FROM ME, THEY WILL BE BROADCAST TO EVERY NATION ON EVERY WORLD IN THE CONCORDANT.
NEITHER THE HIERARCHY, NOR THE HOUSE OF ISHAVHA WILL WANT TO BE ASSOCIATED WITH THE NOTORIOUS WAR CRIMINAL YOU ARE ABOUT TO BECOME.
GIVE ME D'MER'S FREEDOM AND YOUR VOW THAT THERE WILL BE NO RETALIATION AGAINST HIM OR HIS PEOPLE, OR EVERYONE WILL KNOW WHAT YOU HAVE DONE!
BLACKMAIL! YOU SHIT!
THANK YOU. I HAD AN EXCELLENT TEACHER.
I'M BLOATED WITH PRIDE. DON'T BE SHRILL, EMERIS. IT'S UNDIGNIFIED.
SEREN, YOU'LL HAVE ALL THE DOCUMENTS YOU NEED FOR D'MER'S OWNERSHIP IN THE MORNING.
I DON'T WANT TO OWN HIM. I WANT HIS FREEDOM.
AS YOU WISH.
YOU'RE NOT GOING TO LET HIM GET AWAY WITH THIS?!? IT'S TREASON!
I'M NOT GOING TO RISK HIERARCHY ASSETS FOR YOUR ENTERTAINMENT!
CONSIDER YOURSELF FORTUNATE THAT ALL YOU LOSE HERE IS ONE SLAVE! YOU COULD BE LOSING YOUR POSITION IN THE HIERARCHY!
LET NINIRI HAVE HER WAY, EMERIS. SHE'S ONLY HALF ALIVE WHEN SHE'S NOT INDIGNANT.

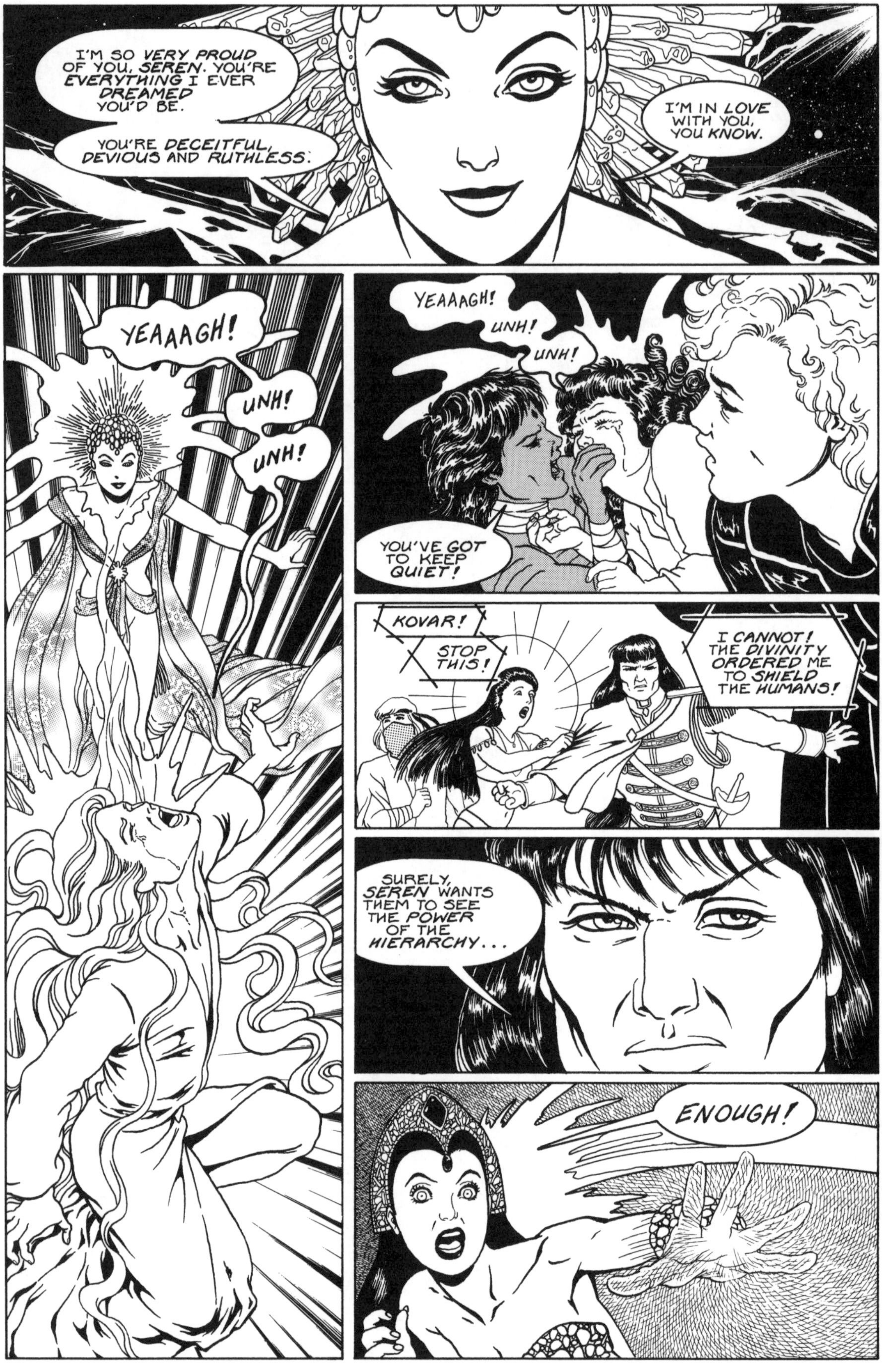
I'M SO VERY PROUD OF YOU, SEREN. YOU'RE EVERYTHING I EVER DREAMED YOU'D BE.
YOU'RE DECEITFUL, DEVIOUS AND RUTHLESS.
I'M IN LOVE WITH YOU, YOU KNOW.
YEAAAGH!
UNH!
UNH!
YEAAAGH!
UNH!
UNH!
YOU'VE GOT TO KEEP QUIET!
KOVAR!
STOP THIS!
I CANNOT! THE DIVINITY ORDERED ME TO SHIELD THE HUMANS!
SURELY, SEREN WANTS THEM TO SEE THE POWER OF THE HIERARCHY...
ENOUGH!

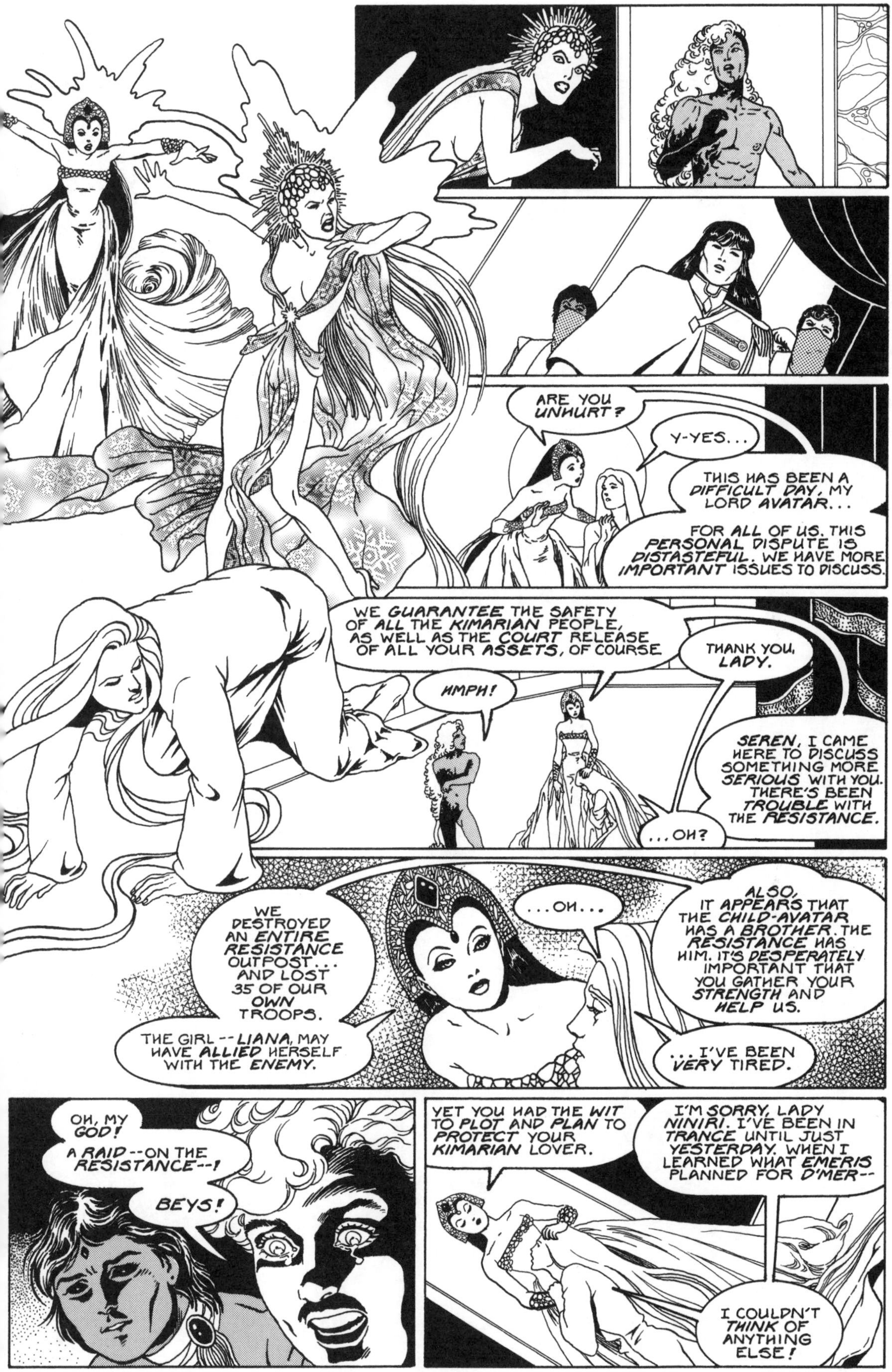
ARE YOU UNHURT?
Y-YES...
THIS HAS BEEN A DIFFICULT DAY, MY LORD AVATAR...
FOR ALL OF US. THIS PERSONAL DISPUTE IS DISTASTEFUL. WE HAVE MORE IMPORTANT ISSUES TO DISCUSS.
WE GUARANTEE THE SAFETY OF ALL THE KIMARIAN PEOPLE, AS WELL AS THE COURT RELEASE OF ALL YOUR ASSETS, OF COURSE
THANK YOU, LADY.
HMPH!
SEREN, I CAME HERE TO DISCUSS SOMETHING MORE SERIOUS WITH YOU. THERE'S BEEN TROUBLE WITH THE RESISTANCE.
...OH?
WE DESTROYED AN ENTIRE RESISTANCE OUTPOST... AND LOST 35 OF OUR OWN TROOPS.
THE GIRL --LIANA, MAY HAVE ALLIED HERSELF WITH THE ENEMY.
...OH...
ALSO, IT APPEARS THAT THE CHILD-AVATAR HAS A BROTHER. THE RESISTANCE HAS HIM. IT'S DESPERATELY IMPORTANT THAT YOU GATHER YOUR STRENGTH AND HELP US.
...I'VE BEEN VERY TIRED.
OH, MY GOD!
A RAID--ON THE RESISTANCE--!
BEYS!
YET YOU HAD THE WIT TO PLOT AND PLAN TO PROTECT YOUR KIMARIAN LOVER.
I'M SORRY, LADY NINIRI. I'VE BEEN IN TRANCE UNTIL JUST YESTERDAY. WHEN I LEARNED WHAT EMERIS PLANNED FOR D'MER--
I COULDN'T THINK OF ANYTHING ELSE!

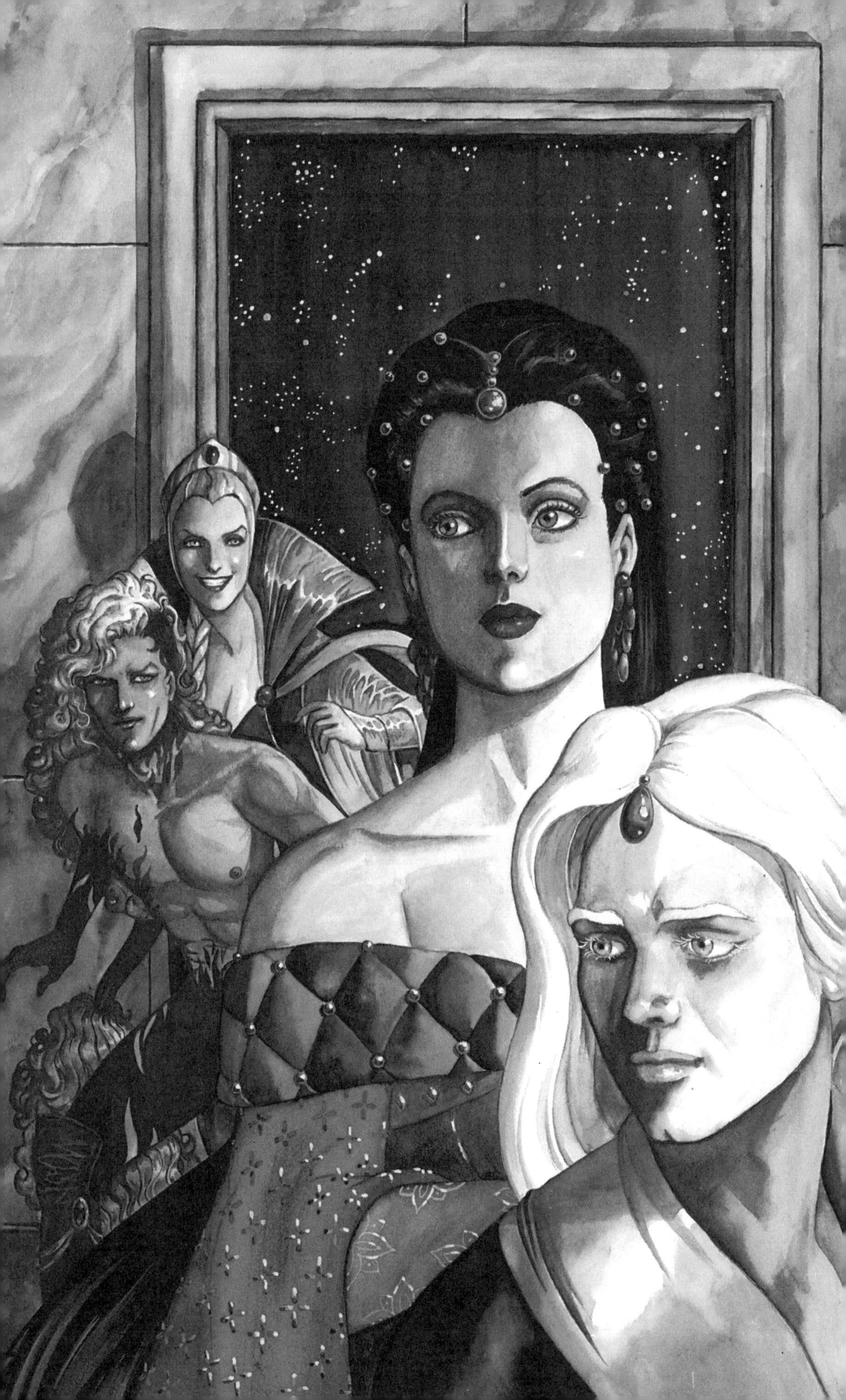

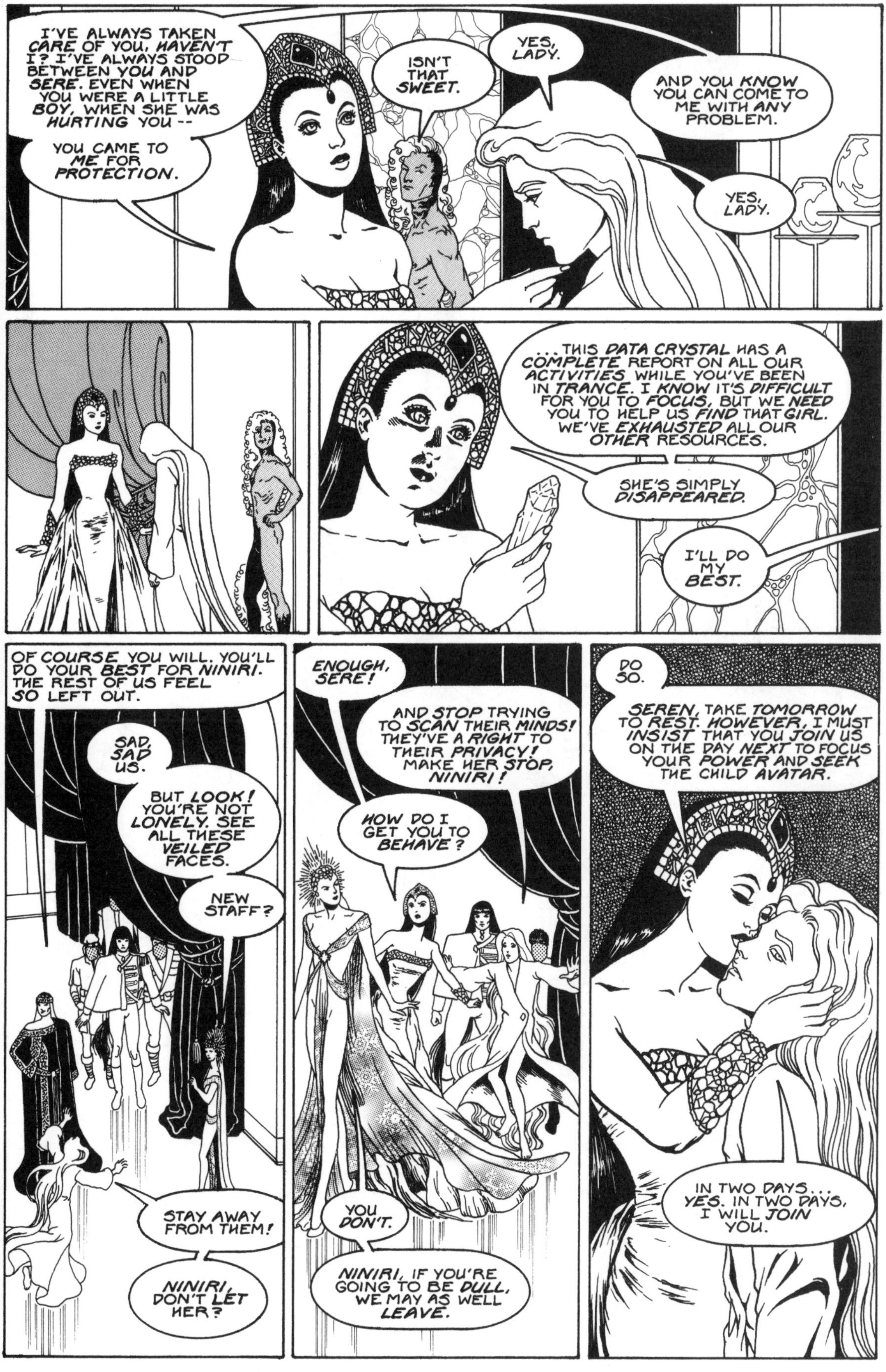
I'VE ALWAYS TAKEN CARE OF YOU, HAVEN'T I? I'VE ALWAYS STOOD BETWEEN YOU AND SERE. EVEN WHEN YOU WERE A LITTLE BOY, WHEN SHE WAS HURTING YOU --
YOU CAME TO ME FOR PROTECTION.
ISN'T THAT SWEET.
YES, LADY.
AND YOU KNOW YOU CAN COME TO ME WITH ANY PROBLEM.
YES, LADY.
...THIS DATA CRYSTAL HAS A COMPLETE REPORT ON ALL OUR ACTIVITIES WHILE YOU'VE BEEN IN TRANCE. I KNOW IT'S DIFFICULT FOR YOU TO FOCUS, BUT WE NEED YOU TO HELP US FIND THAT GIRL. WE'VE EXHAUSTED ALL OUR OTHER RESOURCES.
SHE'S SIMPLY DISAPPEARED.
I'LL DO MY BEST.
OF COURSE YOU WILL. YOU'LL DO YOUR BEST FOR NINIRI. THE REST OF US FEEL SO LEFT OUT.
SAD, SAD US.
BUT LOOK! YOU'RE NOT LONELY. SEE ALL THESE VEILED FACES.
NEW STAFF?
STAY AWAY FROM THEM!
NINIRI, DON'T LET HER?
ENOUGH, SERE!
AND STOP TRYING TO SCAN THEIR MINDS! THEY'VE A RIGHT TO THEIR PRIVACY! MAKE HER STOP, NINIRI!
HOW DO I GET YOU TO BEHAVE?
YOU DON'T.
NINIRI, IF YOU'RE GOING TO BE DULL, WE MAY AS WELL LEAVE.
DO SO.
SEREN, TAKE TOMORROW TO REST. HOWEVER, I MUST INSIST THAT YOU JOIN US ON THE DAY NEXT TO FOCUS YOUR POWER AND SEEK THE CHILD AVATAR.
IN TWO DAYS... YES. IN TWO DAYS, I WILL JOIN YOU.

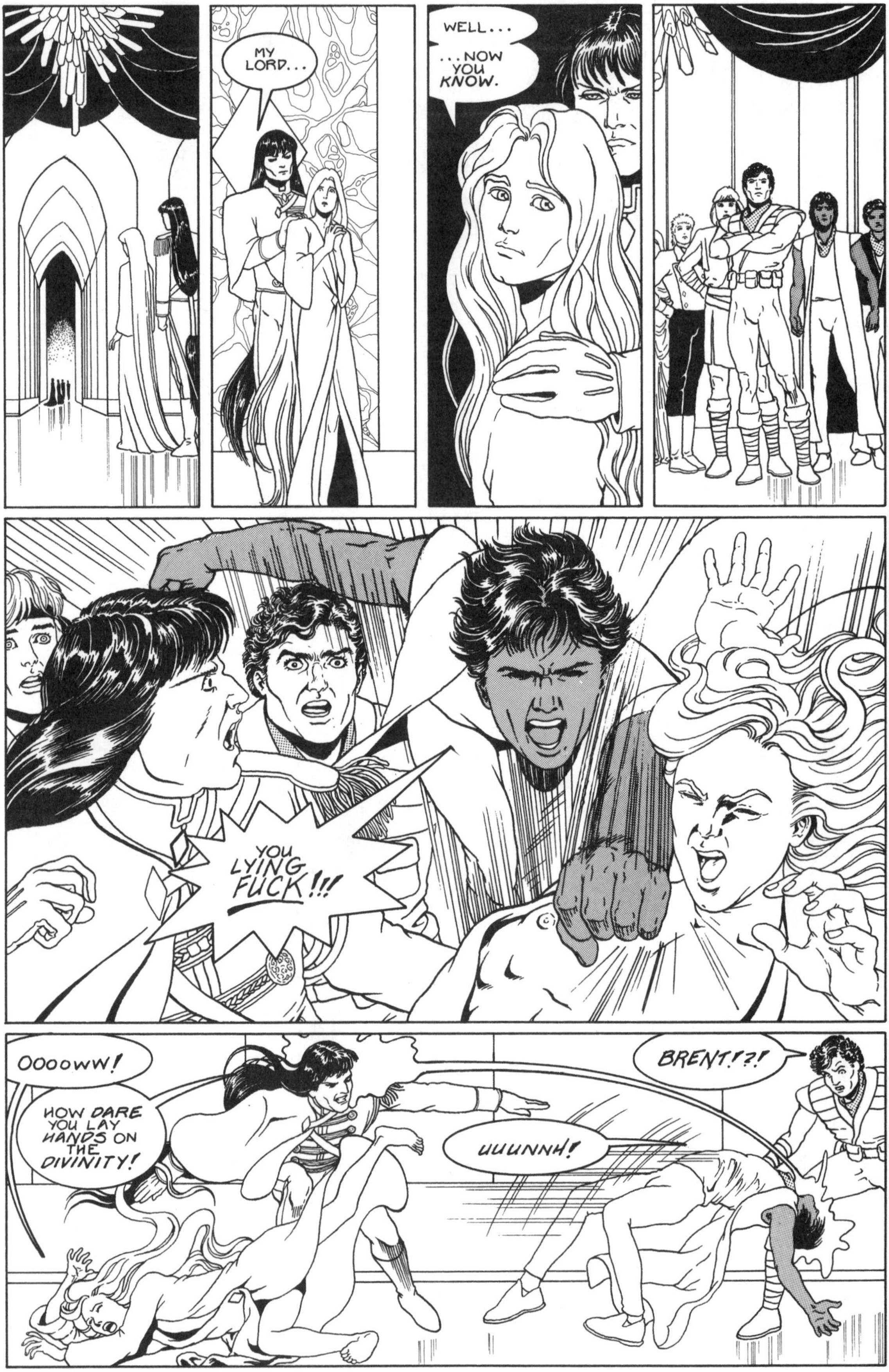
MY LORD...
WELL...
...NOW YOU KNOW.
YOU LYING FUCK!!!
OOOOWW!
HOW DARE YOU LAY HANDS ON THE DIVINITY!
UUUNNH!
BRENT!?!

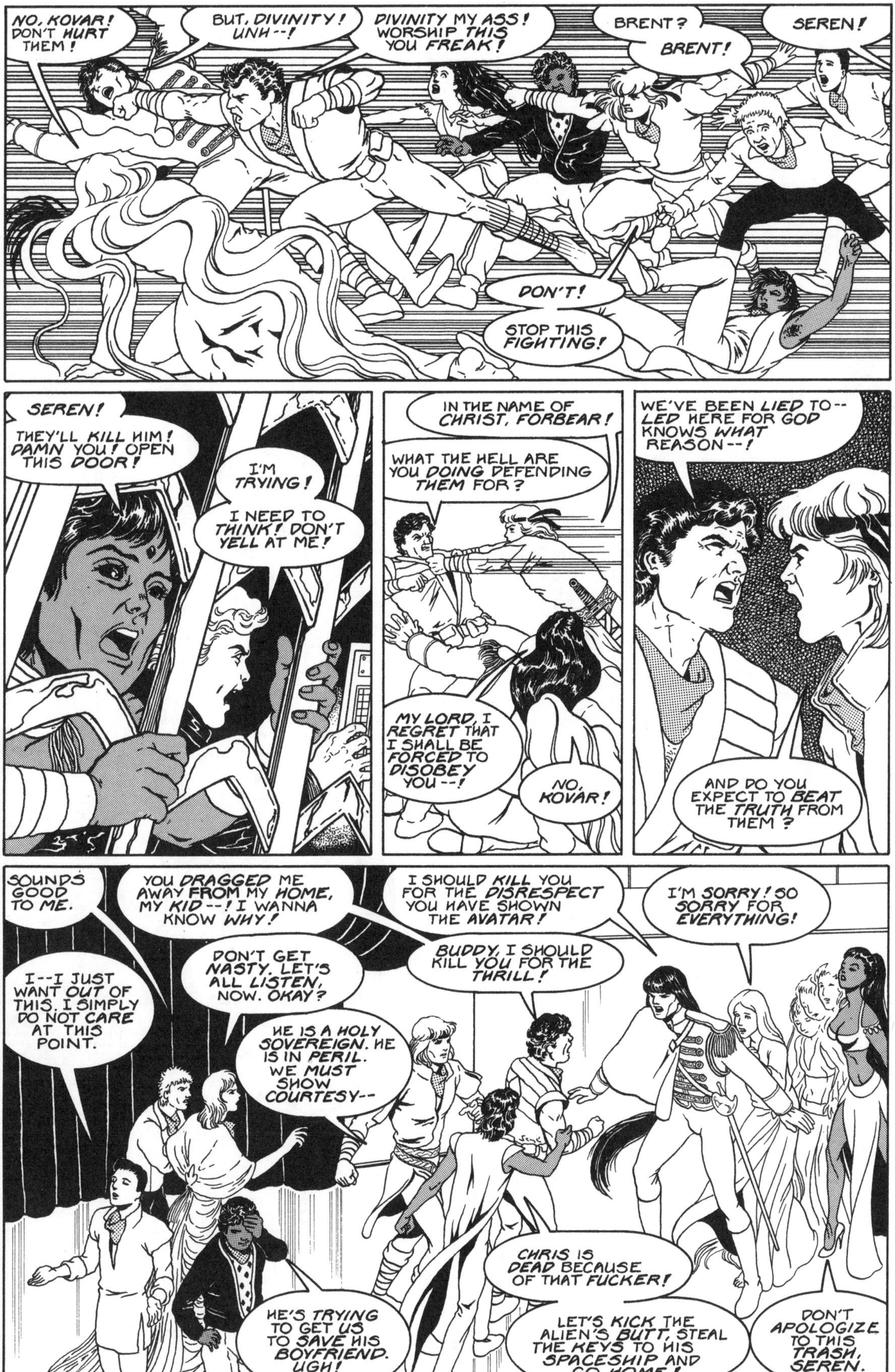

NO, KOVAR! DON'T HURT THEM!
BUT, DIVINITY! UNH--!
DIVINITY MY ASS! WORSHIP THIS YOU FREAK!
BRENT? BRENT!
SEREN!
DON'T!
STOP THIS FIGHTING!
SEREN!
THEY'LL KILL HIM! DAMN YOU! OPEN THIS DOOR!
I'M TRYING!
I NEED TO THINK! DON'T YELL AT ME!
IN THE NAME OF CHRIST, FORBEAR!
WHAT THE HELL ARE YOU DOING DEFENDING THEM FOR?
MY LORD, I REGRET THAT I SHALL BE FORCED TO DISOBEY YOU--!
NO, KOVAR!
WE'VE BEEN LIED TO-- LED HERE FOR GOD KNOWS WHAT REASON--!
AND DO YOU EXPECT TO BEAT THE TRUTH FROM THEM?
SOUNDS GOOD TO ME.
YOU DRAGGED ME AWAY FROM MY HOME, MY KID--! I WANNA KNOW WHY!
I SHOULD KILL YOU FOR THE DISRESPECT YOU HAVE SHOWN THE AVATAR!
I'M SORRY! SO SORRY FOR EVERYTHING!
I--I JUST WANT OUT OF THIS. I SIMPLY DO NOT CARE AT THIS POINT.
DON'T GET NASTY. LET'S ALL LISTEN, NOW. OKAY?
BUDDY, I SHOULD KILL YOU FOR THE THRILL!
HE IS A HOLY SOVEREIGN. HE IS IN PERIL. WE MUST SHOW COURTESY--
CHRIS IS DEAD BECAUSE OF THAT FUCKER!
HE'S TRYING TO GET US TO SAVE HIS BOYFRIEND. UGH!
LET'S KICK THE ALIEN'S BUTT, STEAL THE KEYS TO HIS SPACESHIP AND GO HOME!
DON'T APOLOGIZE TO THIS TRASH, SEREN.

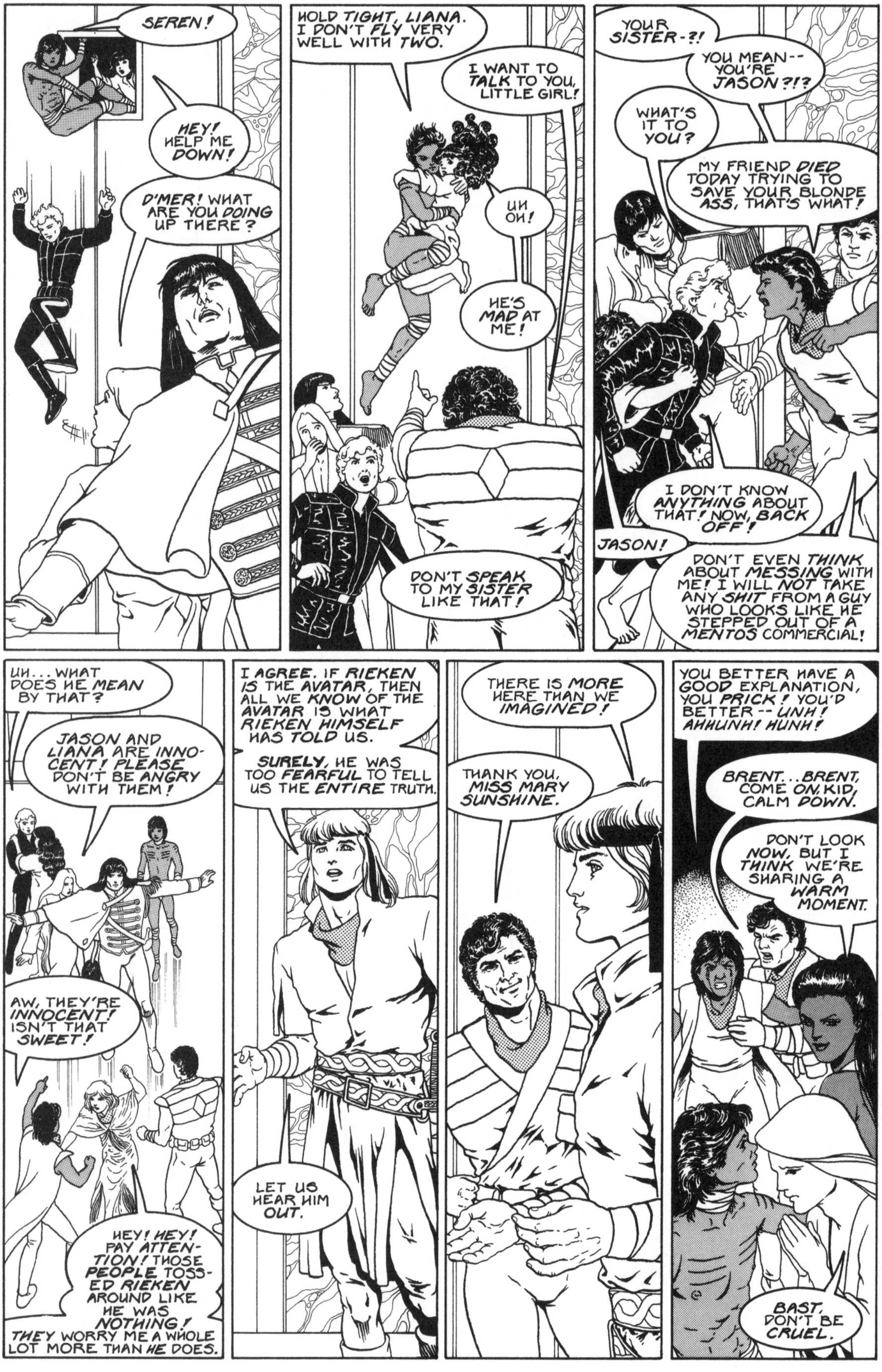
SEREN!
HEY! HELP ME DOWN!
D'MER! WHAT ARE YOU DOING UP THERE?
HOLD TIGHT, LIANA. I DON'T FLY VERY WELL WITH TWO.
I WANT TO TALK TO YOU, LITTLE GIRL!
UH OH!
HE'S MAD AT ME!
DON'T SPEAK TO MY SISTER LIKE THAT!
YOUR SISTER-?!
YOU MEAN-- YOU'RE JASON?!?
WHAT'S IT TO YOU?
MY FRIEND DIED TODAY TRYING TO SAVE YOUR BLONDE ASS, THAT'S WHAT!
I DON'T KNOW ANYTHING ABOUT THAT! NOW, BACK OFF!
JASON!
DON'T EVEN THINK ABOUT MESSING WITH ME! I WILL NOT TAKE ANY SHIT FROM A GUY WHO LOOKS LIKE HE STEPPED OUT OF A MENTOS COMMERCIAL!
UH... WHAT DOES HE MEAN BY THAT?
JASON AND LIANA ARE INNOCENT! PLEASE DON'T BE ANGRY WITH THEM!
AW, THEY'RE INNOCENT! ISN'T THAT SWEET!
HEY! HEY! PAY ATTENTION! THOSE PEOPLE TOSSED RIEKEN AROUND LIKE HE WAS NOTHING! THEY WORRY ME A WHOLE LOT MORE THAN HE DOES.
I AGREE. IF RIEKEN IS THE AVATAR, THEN ALL WE KNOW OF THE AVATAR IS WHAT RIEKEN HIMSELF HAS TOLD US.
SURELY, HE WAS TOO FEARFUL TO TELL US THE ENTIRE TRUTH.
LET US HEAR HIM OUT.
THERE IS MORE HERE THAN WE IMAGINED!
THANK YOU, MISS MARY SUNSHINE.
YOU BETTER HAVE A GOOD EXPLANATION, YOU PRICK! YOU'D BETTER -- UNH! AHHUNH! HUNH!
BRENT... BRENT, COME ON, KID, CALM DOWN.
DON'T LOOK NOW, BUT I THINK WE'RE SHARING A WARM MOMENT.
BAST, DON'T BE CRUEL.

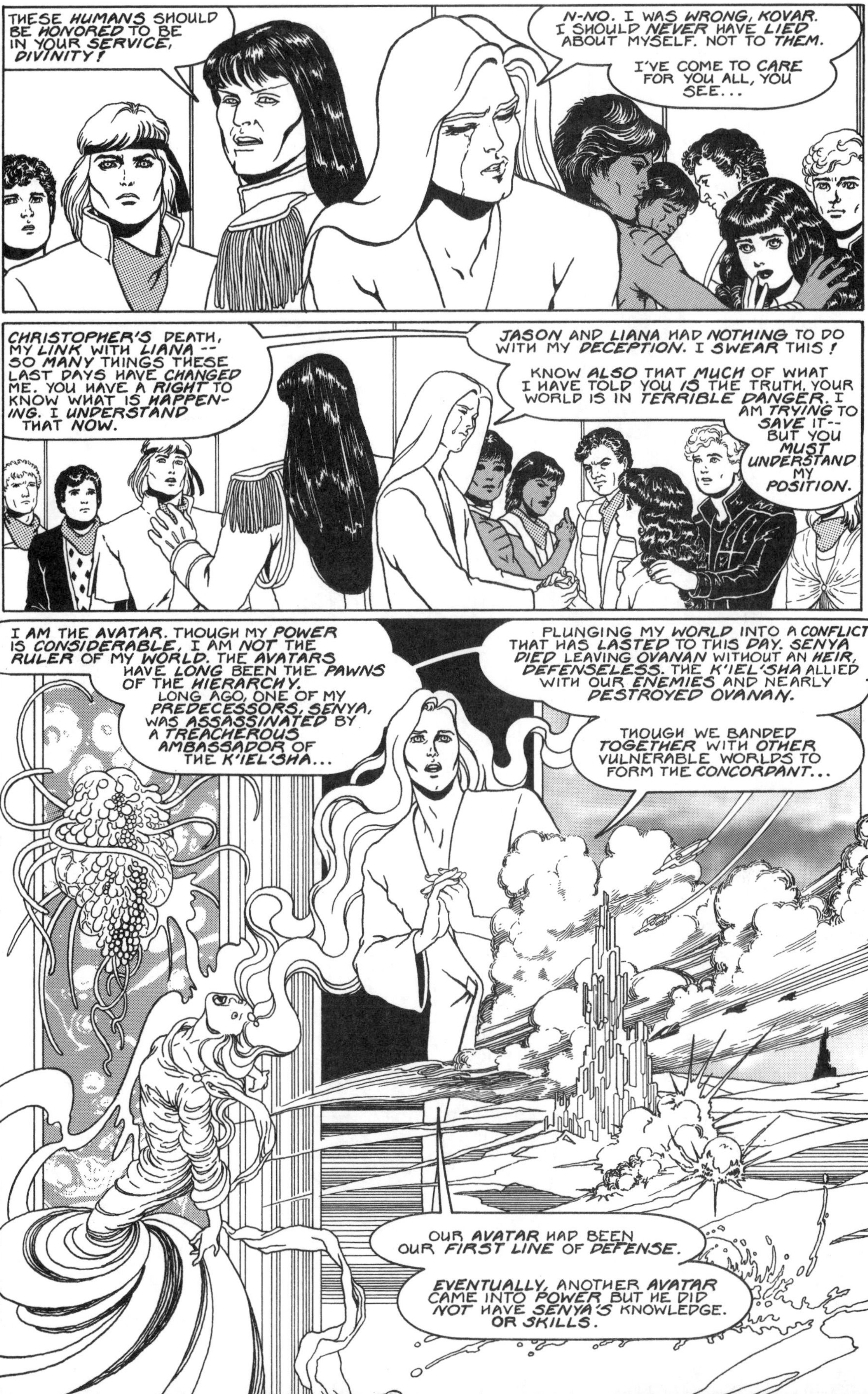
THESE HUMANS SHOULD BE HONORED TO BE IN YOUR SERVICE, DIVINITY!
N-NO. I WAS WRONG, KOVAR. I SHOULD NEVER HAVE LIED ABOUT MYSELF. NOT TO THEM.
I'VE COME TO CARE FOR YOU ALL, YOU SEE...
CHRISTOPHER'S DEATH, MY LINK WITH LIANA -- SO MANY THINGS THESE LAST DAYS HAVE CHANGED ME. YOU HAVE A RIGHT TO KNOW WHAT IS HAPPENING. I UNDERSTAND THAT NOW.
JASON AND LIANA HAD NOTHING TO DO WITH MY DECEPTION. I SWEAR THIS!
KNOW ALSO THAT MUCH OF WHAT I HAVE TOLD YOU IS THE TRUTH. YOUR WORLD IS IN TERRIBLE DANGER. I AM TRYING TO SAVE IT-- BUT YOU MUST UNDERSTAND MY POSITION.
I AM THE AVATAR. THOUGH MY POWER IS CONSIDERABLE, I AM NOT THE RULER OF MY WORLD. THE AVATARS HAVE LONG BEEN THE PAWNS OF THE HIERARCHY.
LONG AGO, ONE OF MY PREDECESSORS, SENYA, WAS ASSASSINATED BY A TREACHEROUS AMBASSADOR OF THE K'IEL'SHA...
PLUNGING MY WORLD INTO A CONFLICT THAT HAS LASTED TO THIS DAY. SENYA DIED LEAVING OVANAN WITHOUT AN HEIR, DEFENSELESS. THE K'IEL'SHA ALLIED WITH OUR ENEMIES AND NEARLY DESTROYED OVANAN.
THOUGH WE BANDED TOGETHER WITH OTHER VULNERABLE WORLDS TO FORM THE CONCORDANT...
OUR AVATAR HAD BEEN OUR FIRST LINE OF DEFENSE.
EVENTUALLY, ANOTHER AVATAR CAME INTO POWER BUT HE DID NOT HAVE SENYA'S KNOWLEDGE. OR SKILLS.

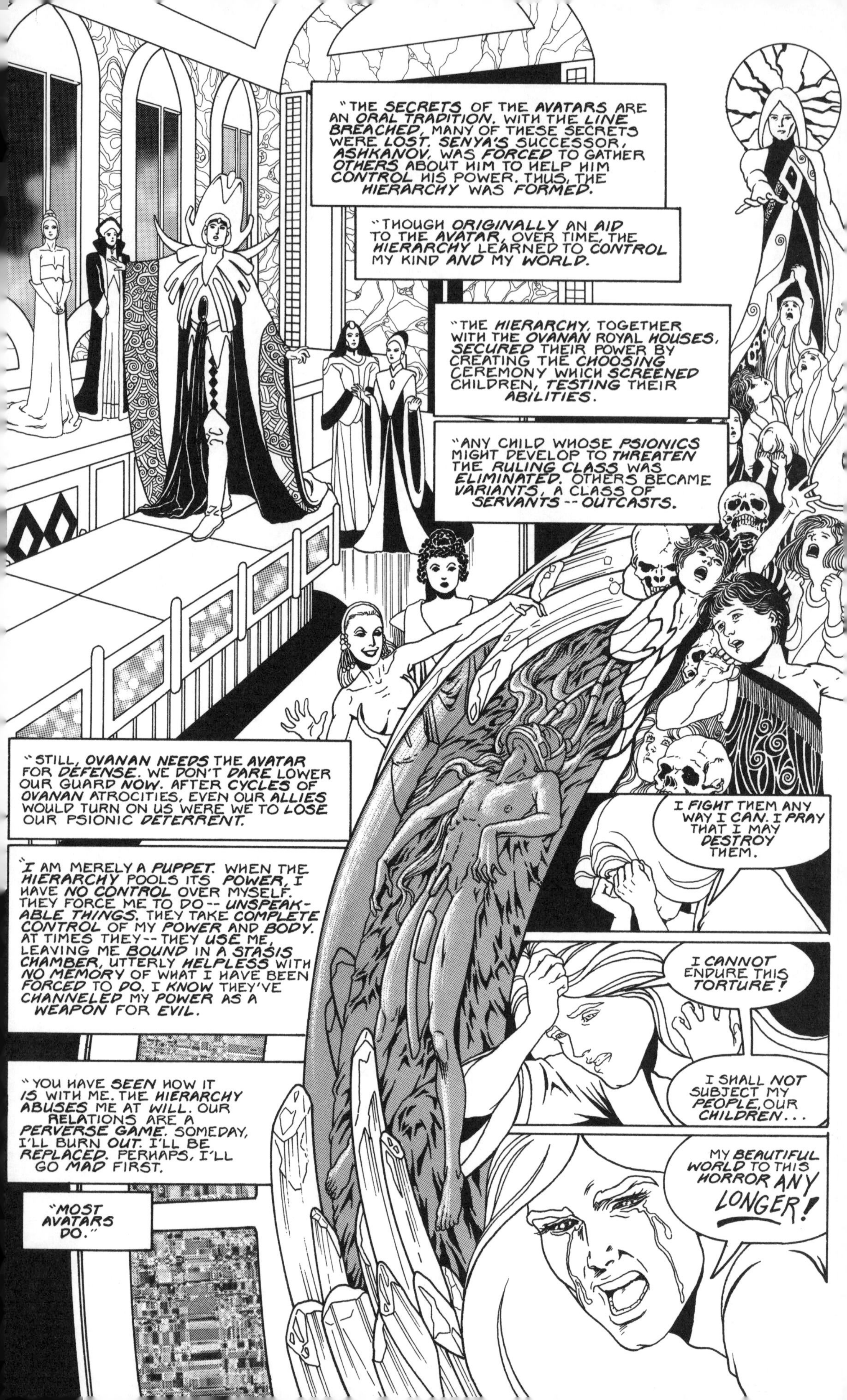

"THE SECRETS OF THE AVATARS ARE AN ORAL TRADITION. WITH THE LINE BREACHED, MANY OF THESE SECRETS WERE LOST. SENYA'S SUCCESSOR, ASHKANOV, WAS FORCED TO GATHER OTHERS ABOUT HIM TO HELP HIM CONTROL HIS POWER. THUS, THE HIERARCHY WAS FORMED.
"THOUGH ORIGINALLY AN AID TO THE AVATAR, OVER TIME, THE HIERARCHY LEARNED TO CONTROL MY KIND AND MY WORLD.
"THE HIERARCHY, TOGETHER WITH THE OVANAN ROYAL HOUSES, SECURED THEIR POWER BY CREATING THE CHOOSING CEREMONY WHICH SCREENED CHILDREN, TESTING THEIR ABILITIES.
"ANY CHILD WHOSE PSIONICS MIGHT DEVELOP TO THREATEN THE RULING CLASS WAS ELIMINATED. OTHERS BECAME VARIANTS, A CLASS OF SERVANTS -- OUTCASTS.
"STILL, OVANAN NEEDS THE AVATAR FOR DEFENSE. WE DON'T DARE LOWER OUR GUARD NOW. AFTER CYCLES OF OVANAN ATROCITIES, EVEN OUR ALLIES WOULD TURN ON US WERE WE TO LOSE OUR PSIONIC DETERRENT.
"I AM MERELY A PUPPET. WHEN THE HIERARCHY POOLS ITS POWER, I HAVE NO CONTROL OVER MYSELF. THEY FORCE ME TO DO -- UNSPEAKABLE THINGS. THEY TAKE COMPLETE CONTROL OF MY POWER AND BODY. AT TIMES THEY -- THEY USE ME, LEAVING ME BOUND IN A STASIS CHAMBER, UTTERLY HELPLESS WITH NO MEMORY OF WHAT I HAVE BEEN FORCED TO DO. I KNOW THEY'VE CHANNELED MY POWER AS A WEAPON FOR EVIL.
"YOU HAVE SEEN HOW IT IS WITH ME. THE HIERARCHY ABUSES ME AT WILL. OUR RELATIONS ARE A PERVERSE GAME. SOMEDAY, I'LL BURN OUT. I'LL BE REPLACED. PERHAPS, I'LL GO MAD FIRST.
"MOST AVATARS DO."
I FIGHT THEM ANY WAY I CAN. I PRAY THAT I MAY DESTROY THEM.
I CANNOT ENDURE THIS TORTURE!
I SHALL NOT SUBJECT MY PEOPLE, OUR CHILDREN...
MY BEAUTIFUL WORLD TO THIS HORROR ANY LONGER!

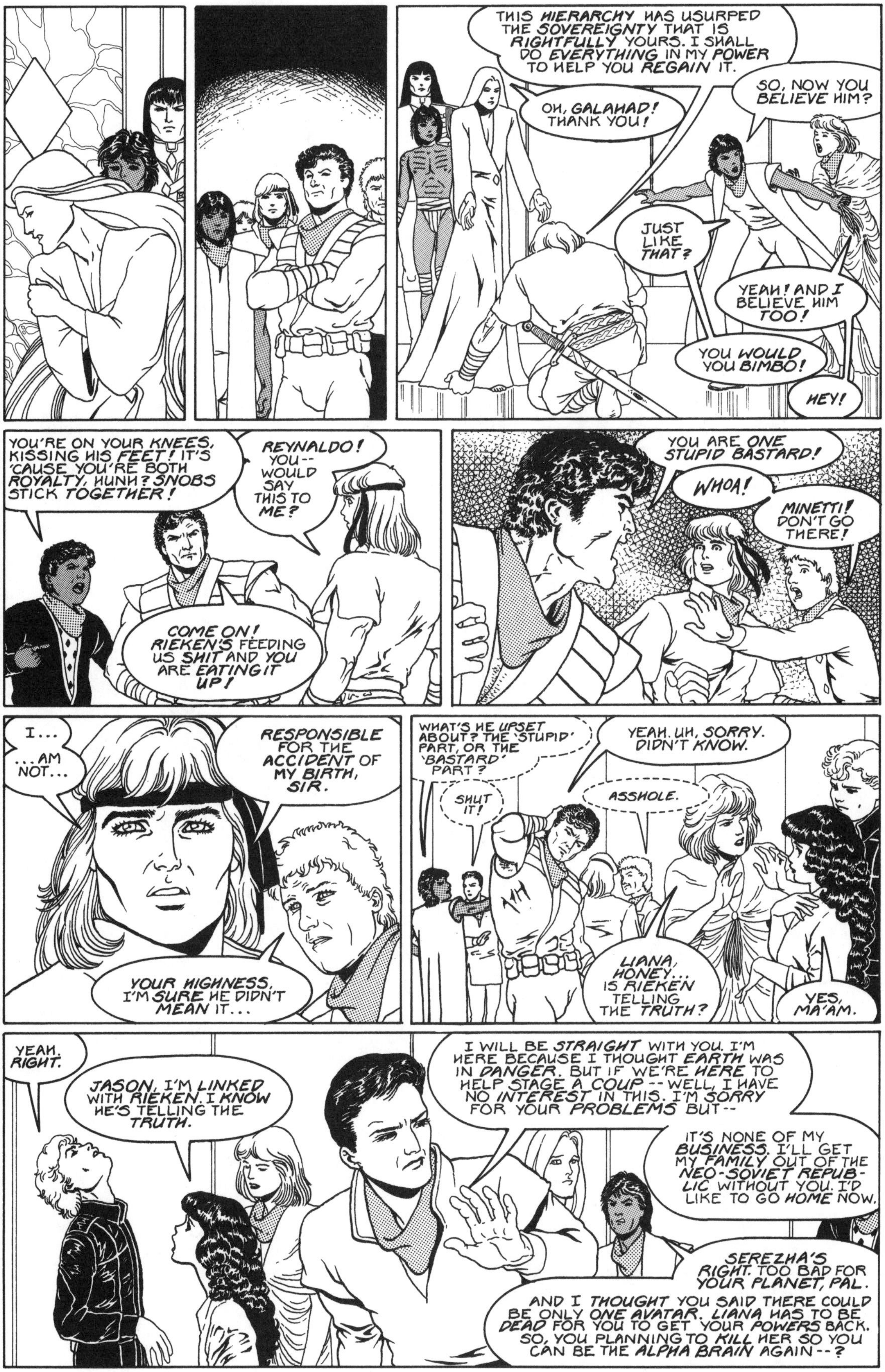
THIS HIERARCHY HAS USURPED THE SOVEREIGNTY THAT IS RIGHTFULLY YOURS. I SHALL DO EVERYTHING IN MY POWER TO HELP YOU REGAIN IT.
OH, GALAHAD! THANK YOU!
SO, NOW YOU BELIEVE HIM?
JUST LIKE THAT?
YEAH! AND I BELIEVE HIM TOO!
YOU WOULD YOU BIMBO!
HEY!
YOU'RE ON YOUR KNEES, KISSING HIS FEET! IT'S 'CAUSE YOU'RE BOTH ROYALTY, HUNH? SNOBS STICK TOGETHER!
REYNALDO! YOU-- WOULD SAY THIS TO ME?
COME ON! RIEKEN'S FEEDING US SHIT AND YOU ARE EATING IT UP!
YOU ARE ONE STUPID BASTARD!
WHOA!
MINETTI! DON'T GO THERE!
I...
...AM NOT...
RESPONSIBLE FOR THE ACCIDENT OF MY BIRTH, SIR.
YOUR HIGHNESS, I'M SURE HE DIDN'T MEAN IT...
WHAT'S HE UPSET ABOUT? THE 'STUPID' PART, OR THE 'BASTARD' PART?
SHUT IT!
YEAH. UH, SORRY. DIDN'T KNOW.
ASSHOLE.
AH
LIANA, HONEY... IS RIEKEN TELLING THE TRUTH?
YES, MA'AM.
YEAH. RIGHT.
JASON, I'M LINKED WITH RIEKEN. I KNOW HE'S TELLING THE TRUTH.
I WILL BE STRAIGHT WITH YOU. I'M HERE BECAUSE I THOUGHT EARTH WAS IN DANGER. BUT IF WE'RE HERE TO HELP STAGE A COUP -- WELL, I HAVE NO INTEREST IN THIS. I'M SORRY FOR YOUR PROBLEMS BUT--
IT'S NONE OF MY BUSINESS. I'LL GET MY FAMILY OUT OF THE NEO-SOVIET REPUB-LIC WITHOUT YOU. I'D LIKE TO GO HOME NOW.
SEREZHA'S RIGHT. TOO BAD FOR YOUR PLANET, PAL.
AND I THOUGHT YOU SAID THERE COULD BE ONLY ONE AVATAR. LIANA HAS TO BE DEAD FOR YOU TO GET YOUR POWERS BACK. SO, YOU PLANNING TO KILL HER SO YOU CAN BE THE ALPHA BRAIN AGAIN--?

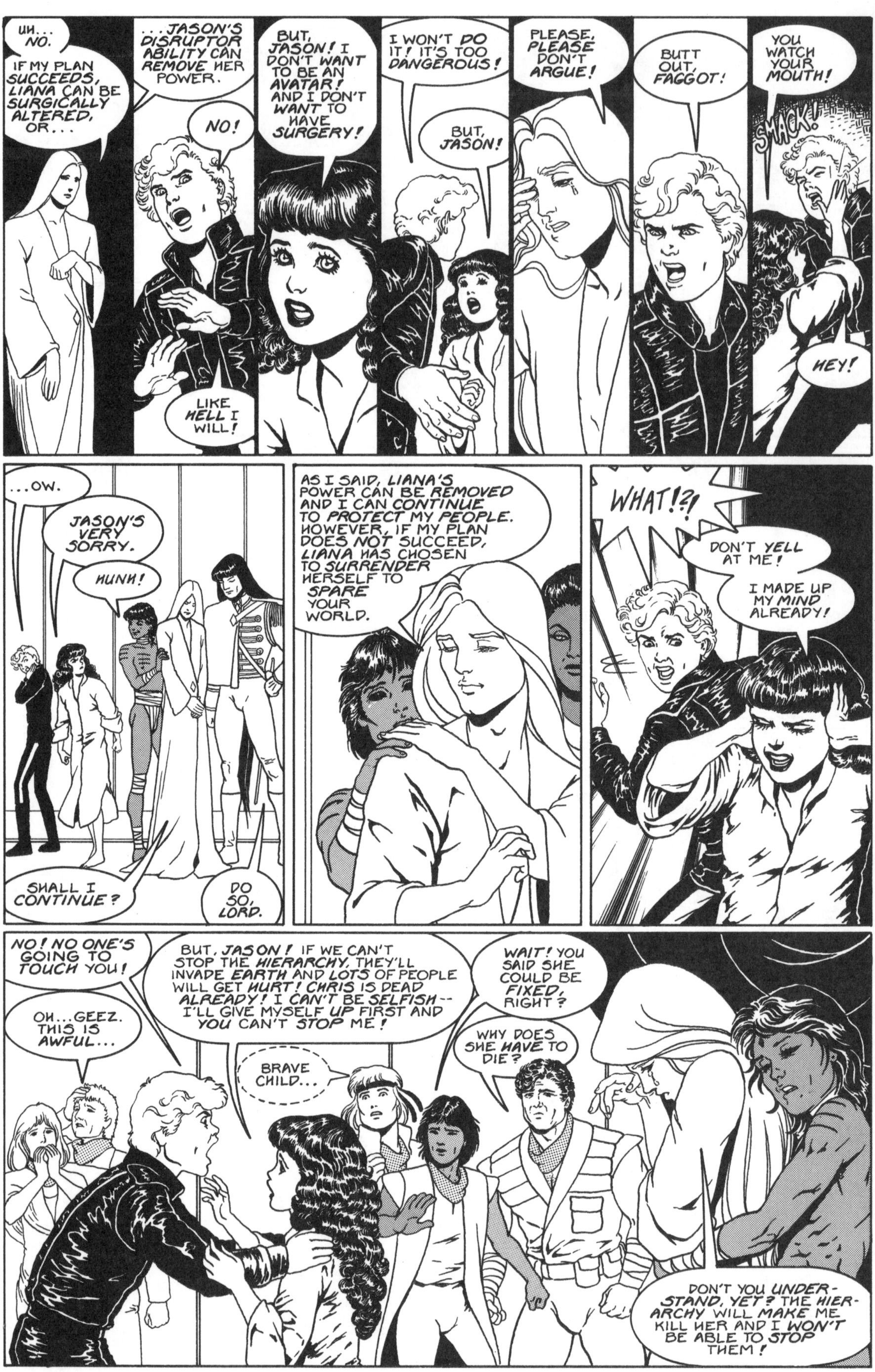
UH... NO.
IF MY PLAN SUCCEEDS, LIANA CAN BE SURGICALLY ALTERED, OR...
...JASON'S DISRUPTOR ABILITY CAN REMOVE HER POWER.
NO!
LIKE HELL I WILL!
BUT, JASON! I DON'T WANT TO BE AN AVATAR! AND I DON'T WANT TO HAVE SURGERY!
I WON'T DO IT! IT'S TOO DANGEROUS!
BUT, JASON!
PLEASE, PLEASE DON'T ARGUE!
BUTT OUT, FAGGOT!
YOU WATCH YOUR MOUTH!
SMACK!
HEY!
...OW.
JASON'S VERY SORRY.
HUNH!
SHALL I CONTINUE?
DO SO, LORD.
AS I SAID, LIANA'S POWER CAN BE REMOVED AND I CAN CONTINUE TO PROTECT MY PEOPLE. HOWEVER, IF MY PLAN DOES NOT SUCCEED, LIANA HAS CHOSEN TO SURRENDER HERSELF TO SPARE YOUR WORLD.
WHAT!?!
DON'T YELL AT ME!
I MADE UP MY MIND ALREADY!
NO! NO ONE'S GOING TO TOUCH YOU!
OH...GEEZ. THIS IS AWFUL...
BUT, JASON! IF WE CAN'T STOP THE HIERARCHY, THEY'LL INVADE EARTH AND LOTS OF PEOPLE WILL GET HURT! CHRIS IS DEAD ALREADY! I CAN'T BE SELFISH-- I'LL GIVE MYSELF UP FIRST AND YOU CAN'T STOP ME!
BRAVE CHILD...
WAIT! YOU SAID SHE COULD BE FIXED, RIGHT?
WHY DOES SHE HAVE TO DIE?
DON'T YOU UNDER-STAND, YET? THE HIER-ARCHY WILL MAKE ME KILL HER AND I WON'T BE ABLE TO STOP THEM!

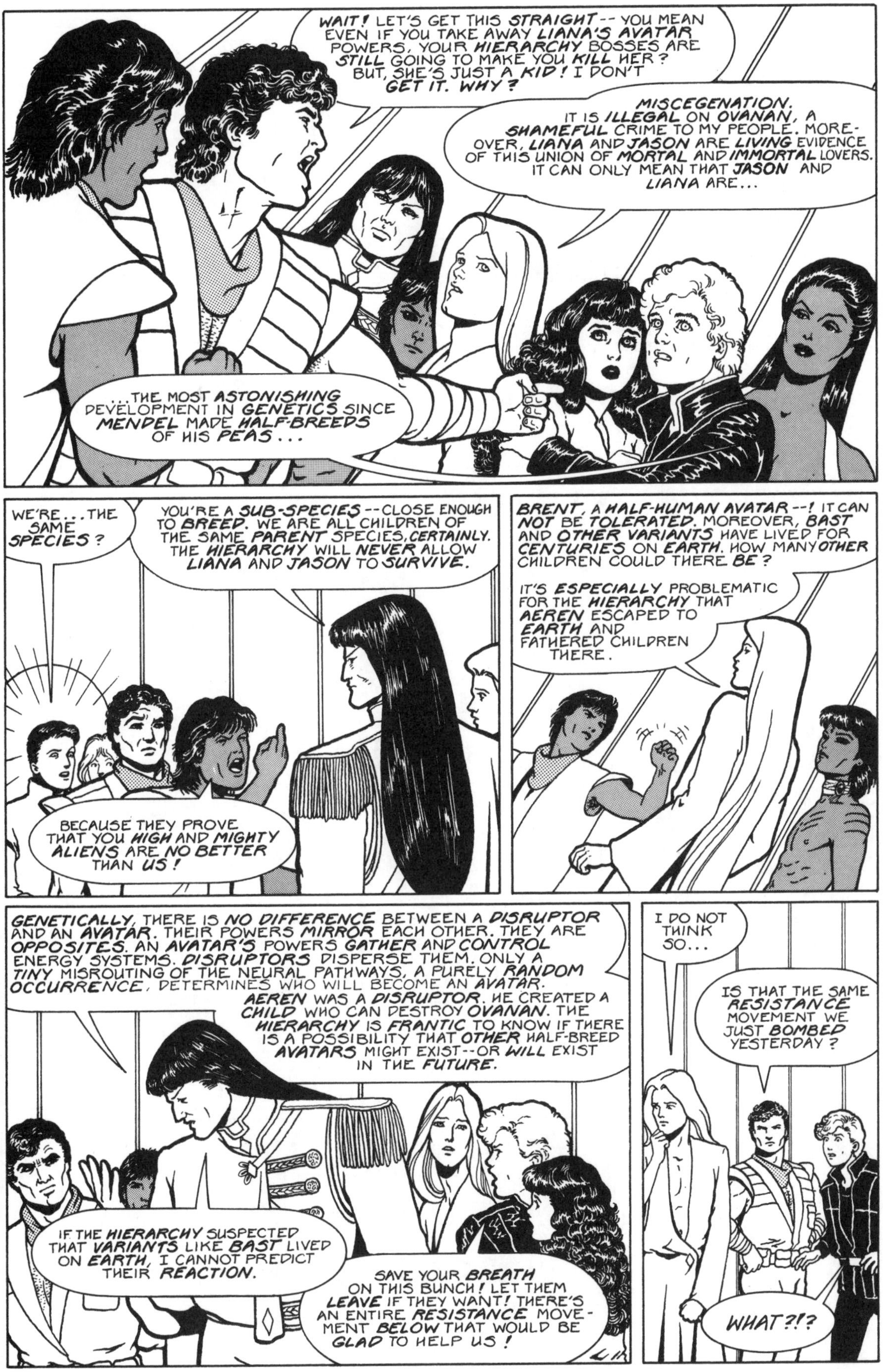
WAIT! LET'S GET THIS STRAIGHT -- YOU MEAN EVEN IF YOU TAKE AWAY LIANA'S AVATAR POWERS, YOUR HIERARCHY BOSSES ARE STILL GOING TO MAKE YOU KILL HER? BUT, SHE'S JUST A KID! I DON'T GET IT. WHY?
MISCEGENATION. IT IS ILLEGAL ON OVANAN, A SHAMEFUL CRIME TO MY PEOPLE. MOREOVER, LIANA AND JASON ARE LIVING EVIDENCE OF THIS UNION OF MORTAL AND IMMORTAL LOVERS. IT CAN ONLY MEAN THAT JASON AND LIANA ARE...
...THE MOST ASTONISHING DEVELOPMENT IN GENETICS SINCE MENDEL MADE HALF-BREEDS OF HIS PEAS...
WE'RE... THE SAME SPECIES?
YOU'RE A SUB-SPECIES -- CLOSE ENOUGH TO BREED. WE ARE ALL CHILDREN OF THE SAME PARENT SPECIES, CERTAINLY. THE HIERARCHY WILL NEVER ALLOW LIANA AND JASON TO SURVIVE.
BECAUSE THEY PROVE THAT YOU HIGH AND MIGHTY ALIENS ARE NO BETTER THAN US!
BRENT, A HALF-HUMAN AVATAR --! IT CAN NOT BE TOLERATED. MOREOVER, BAST AND OTHER VARIANTS HAVE LIVED FOR CENTURIES ON EARTH. HOW MANY OTHER CHILDREN COULD THERE BE?
IT'S ESPECIALLY PROBLEMATIC FOR THE HIERARCHY THAT AEREN ESCAPED TO EARTH AND FATHERED CHILDREN THERE.
GENETICALLY, THERE IS NO DIFFERENCE BETWEEN A DISRUPTOR AND AN AVATAR. THEIR POWERS MIRROR EACH OTHER. THEY ARE OPPOSITES. AN AVATAR'S POWERS GATHER AND CONTROL ENERGY SYSTEMS. DISRUPTORS DISPERSE THEM. ONLY A TINY MISROUTING OF THE NEURAL PATHWAYS, A PURELY RANDOM OCCURRENCE, DETERMINES WHO WILL BECOME AN AVATAR.
AEREN WAS A DISRUPTOR. HE CREATED A CHILD WHO CAN DESTROY OVANAN. THE HIERARCHY IS FRANTIC TO KNOW IF THERE IS A POSSIBILITY THAT OTHER HALF-BREED AVATARS MIGHT EXIST -- OR WILL EXIST IN THE FUTURE.
IF THE HIERARCHY SUSPECTED THAT VARIANTS LIKE BAST LIVED ON EARTH, I CANNOT PREDICT THEIR REACTION.
SAVE YOUR BREATH ON THIS BUNCH! LET THEM LEAVE IF THEY WANT! THERE'S AN ENTIRE RESISTANCE MOVEMENT BELOW THAT WOULD BE GLAD TO HELP US!
I DO NOT THINK SO...
IS THAT THE SAME RESISTANCE MOVEMENT WE JUST BOMBED YESTERDAY?
WHAT?!?

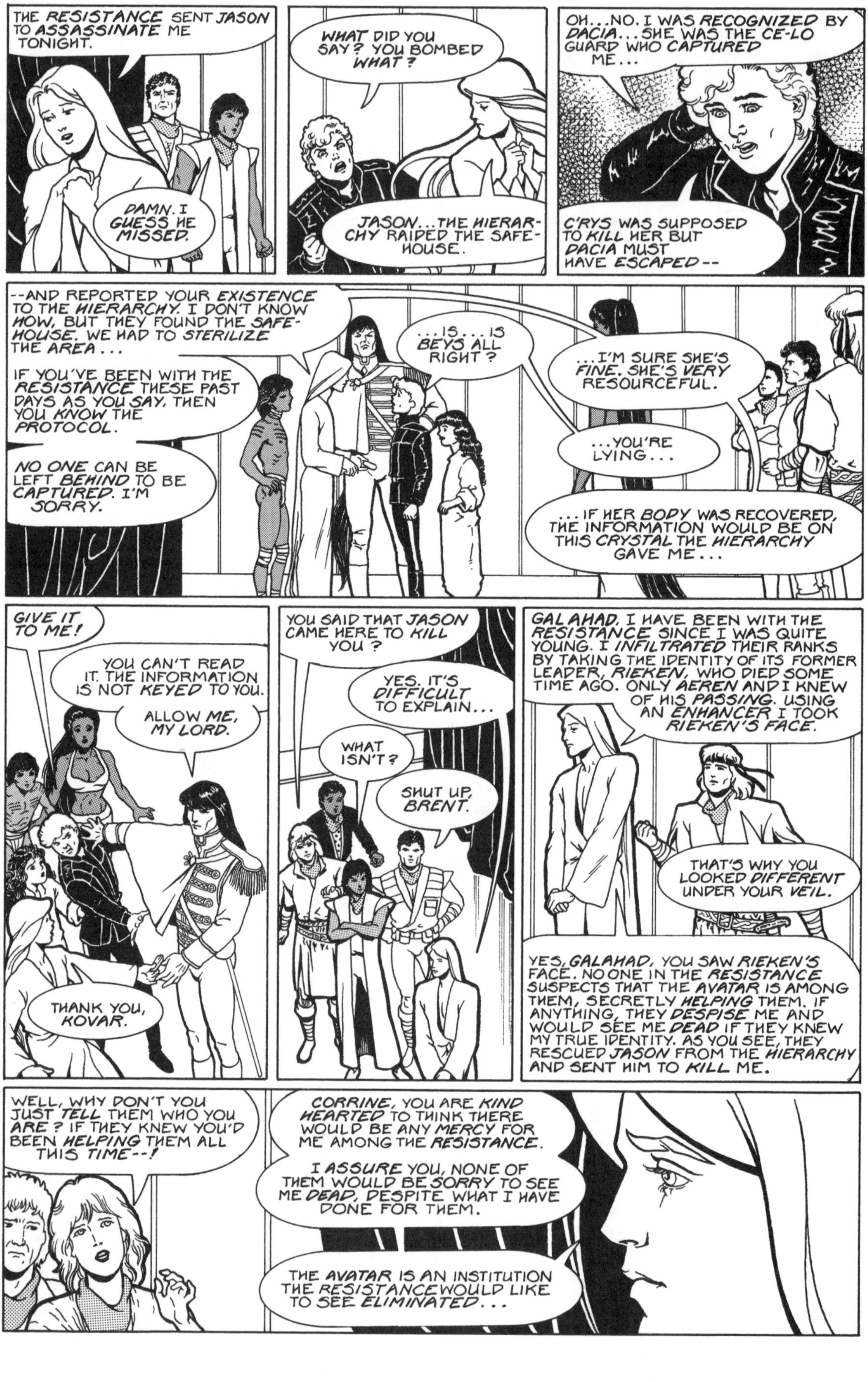
THE RESISTANCE SENT JASON TO ASSASSINATE ME TONIGHT.
DAMN. I GUESS HE MISSED.
WHAT DID YOU SAY? YOU BOMBED WHAT?
JASON...THE HIERARCHY RAIDED THE SAFE-HOUSE.
OH...NO. I WAS RECOGNIZED BY DACIA...SHE WAS THE CE-LO GUARD WHO CAPTURED ME...
C'RYS WAS SUPPOSED TO KILL HER BUT DACIA MUST HAVE ESCAPED--
--AND REPORTED YOUR EXISTENCE TO THE HIERARCHY. I DON'T KNOW HOW, BUT THEY FOUND THE SAFE-HOUSE. WE HAD TO STERILIZE THE AREA...
IF YOU'VE BEEN WITH THE RESISTANCE THESE PAST DAYS AS YOU SAY, THEN YOU KNOW THE PROTOCOL.
NO ONE CAN BE LEFT BEHIND TO BE CAPTURED. I'M SORRY.
...IS...IS BEYS ALL RIGHT?
...I'M SURE SHE'S FINE. SHE'S VERY RESOURCEFUL.
...YOU'RE LYING...
...IF HER BODY WAS RECOVERED, THE INFORMATION WOULD BE ON THIS CRYSTAL THE HIERARCHY GAVE ME...
GIVE IT TO ME!
YOU CAN'T READ IT. THE INFORMATION IS NOT KEYED TO YOU.
ALLOW ME, MY LORD.
THANK YOU, KOVAR.
YOU SAID THAT JASON CAME HERE TO KILL YOU?
YES. IT'S DIFFICULT TO EXPLAIN...
WHAT ISN'T?
SHUT UP, BRENT.
GALAHAD, I HAVE BEEN WITH THE RESISTANCE SINCE I WAS QUITE YOUNG. I INFILTRATED THEIR RANKS BY TAKING THE IDENTITY OF ITS FORMER LEADER, RIEKEN, WHO DIED SOME TIME AGO. ONLY AEREN AND I KNEW OF HIS PASSING. USING AN ENHANCER I TOOK RIEKEN'S FACE.
THAT'S WHY YOU LOOKED DIFFERENT UNDER YOUR VEIL.
YES, GALAHAD, YOU SAW RIEKEN'S FACE. NO ONE IN THE RESISTANCE SUSPECTS THAT THE AVATAR IS AMONG THEM, SECRETLY HELPING THEM. IF ANYTHING, THEY DESPISE ME AND WOULD SEE ME DEAD IF THEY KNEW MY TRUE IDENTITY. AS YOU SEE, THEY RESCUED JASON FROM THE HIERARCHY AND SENT HIM TO KILL ME.
WELL, WHY DON'T YOU JUST TELL THEM WHO YOU ARE? IF THEY KNEW YOU'D BEEN HELPING THEM ALL THIS TIME--!
CORRINE, YOU ARE KIND HEARTED TO THINK THERE WOULD BE ANY MERCY FOR ME AMONG THE RESISTANCE.
I ASSURE YOU, NONE OF THEM WOULD BE SORRY TO SEE ME DEAD, DESPITE WHAT I HAVE DONE FOR THEM.
THE AVATAR IS AN INSTITUTION THE RESISTANCE WOULD LIKE TO SEE ELIMINATED...

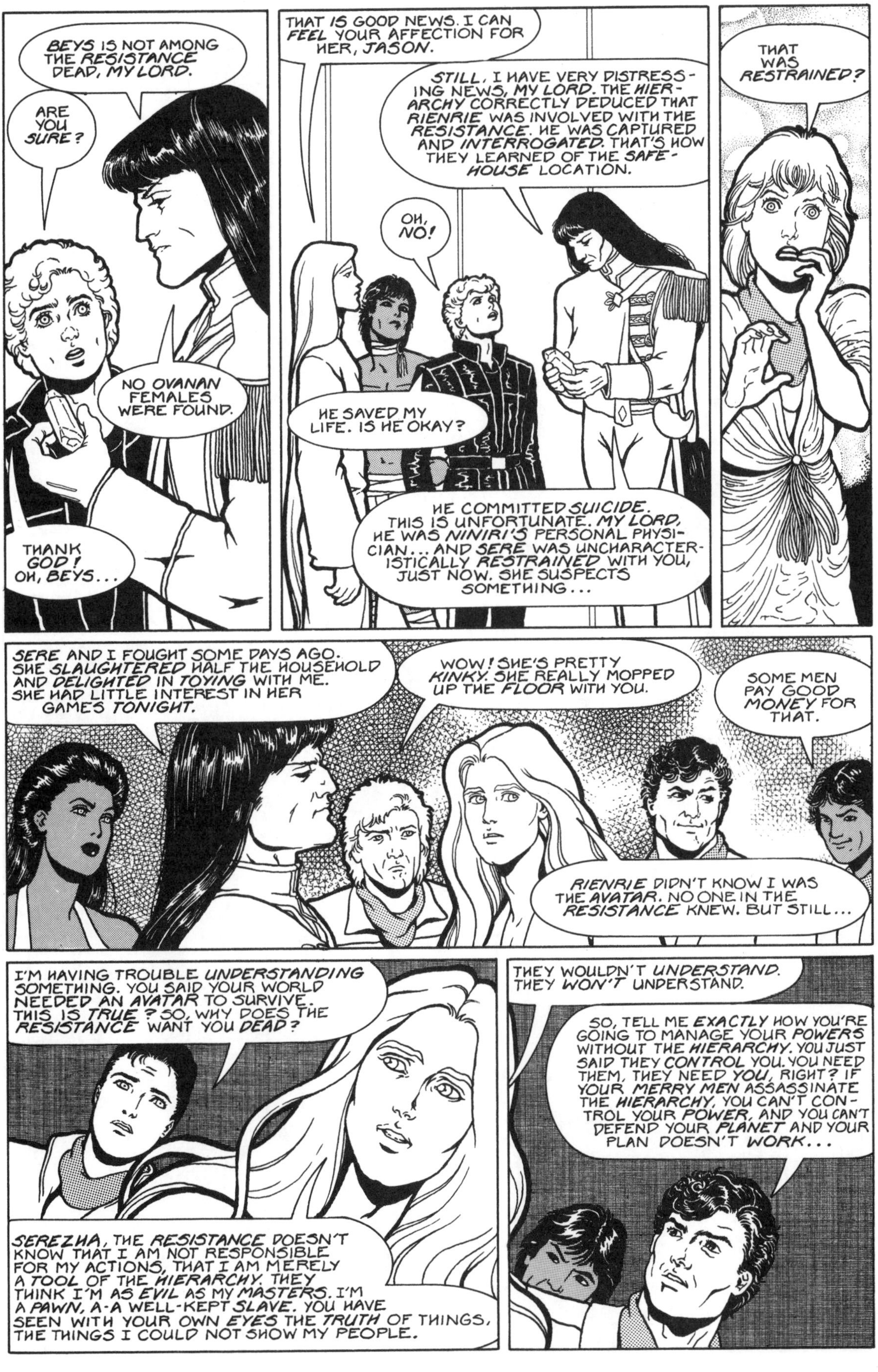
BEYS IS NOT AMONG THE RESISTANCE DEAD, MY LORD.
ARE YOU SURE?
NO OVANAN FEMALES WERE FOUND.
THANK GOD! OH, BEYS...
THAT IS GOOD NEWS. I CAN FEEL YOUR AFFECTION FOR HER, JASON.
STILL, I HAVE VERY DISTRESSING NEWS, MY LORD. THE HIERARCHY CORRECTLY DEDUCED THAT RIENRIE WAS INVOLVED WITH THE RESISTANCE. HE WAS CAPTURED AND INTERROGATED. THAT'S HOW THEY LEARNED OF THE SAFE-HOUSE LOCATION.
OH, NO!
HE SAVED MY LIFE. IS HE OKAY?
HE COMMITTED SUICIDE. THIS IS UNFORTUNATE. MY LORD, HE WAS NINIRI'S PERSONAL PHYSICIAN... AND SERE WAS UNCHARACTERISTICALLY RESTRAINED WITH YOU, JUST NOW. SHE SUSPECTS SOMETHING...
THAT WAS RESTRAINED?
SERE AND I FOUGHT SOME DAYS AGO. SHE SLAUGHTERED HALF THE HOUSEHOLD AND DELIGHTED IN TOYING WITH ME. SHE HAD LITTLE INTEREST IN HER GAMES TONIGHT.
WOW! SHE'S PRETTY KINKY. SHE REALLY MOPPED UP THE FLOOR WITH YOU.
SOME MEN PAY GOOD MONEY FOR THAT.
RIENRIE DIDN'T KNOW I WAS THE AVATAR. NO ONE IN THE RESISTANCE KNEW. BUT STILL...
I'M HAVING TROUBLE UNDERSTANDING SOMETHING. YOU SAID YOUR WORLD NEEDED AN AVATAR TO SURVIVE. THIS IS TRUE? SO, WHY DOES THE RESISTANCE WANT YOU DEAD?
SEREZHA, THE RESISTANCE DOESN'T KNOW THAT I AM NOT RESPONSIBLE FOR MY ACTIONS, THAT I AM MERELY A TOOL OF THE HIERARCHY. THEY THINK I'M AS EVIL AS MY MASTERS. I'M A PAWN, A-A WELL-KEPT SLAVE. YOU HAVE SEEN WITH YOUR OWN EYES THE TRUTH OF THINGS, THE THINGS I COULD NOT SHOW MY PEOPLE.
THEY WOULDN'T UNDERSTAND. THEY WON'T UNDERSTAND.
SO, TELL ME EXACTLY HOW YOU'RE GOING TO MANAGE YOUR POWERS WITHOUT THE HIERARCHY. YOU JUST SAID THEY CONTROL YOU. YOU NEED THEM, THEY NEED YOU, RIGHT? IF YOUR MERRY MEN ASSASSINATE THE HIERARCHY, YOU CAN'T CONTROL YOUR POWER, AND YOU CAN'T DEFEND YOUR PLANET AND YOUR PLAN DOESN'T WORK...

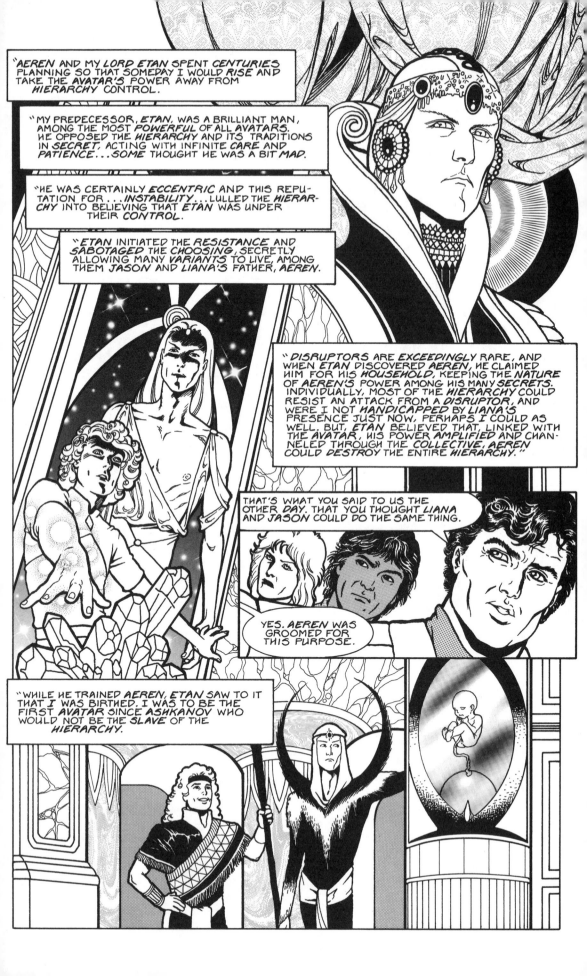

"AEREN AND MY *LORD ETAN* SPENT *CENTURIES* PLANNING SO THAT SOMEDAY I WOULD *RISE* AND TAKE THE *AVATAR'S* POWER AWAY FROM *HIERARCHY* CONTROL.

"MY PREDECESSOR, *ETAN*, WAS A BRILLIANT MAN, AMONG THE MOST *POWERFUL* OF ALL AVATARS. HE OPPOSED THE *HIERARCHY* AND ITS TRADITIONS IN *SECRET*, ACTING WITH INFINITE *CARE* AND *PATIENCE*...SOME THOUGHT HE WAS A BIT *MAD.*

"HE WAS CERTAINLY *ECCENTRIC* AND THIS REPUTATION FOR ...*INSTABILITY*...LULLED THE *HIERARCHY* INTO BELIEVING THAT *ETAN* WAS UNDER THEIR *CONTROL.*

"*ETAN* INITIATED THE *RESISTANCE* AND *SABOTAGED* THE *CHOOSING*, SECRETLY ALLOWING MANY *VARIANTS* TO LIVE, AMONG THEM *JASON* AND *LIANA'S* FATHER, *AEREN.*

" *DISRUPTORS* ARE *EXCEEDINGLY* RARE, AND WHEN *ETAN* DISCOVERED *AEREN*, HE CLAIMED HIM FOR HIS *HOUSEHOLD*, KEEPING THE *NATURE* OF *AEREN'S* POWER AMONG HIS MANY *SECRETS.* INDIVIDUALLY, MOST OF THE *HIERARCHY* COULD RESIST AN ATTACK FROM A *DISRUPTOR*, AND WERE I NOT *HANDICAPPED* BY *LIANA'S* PRESENCE JUST NOW, PERHAPS I COULD AS WELL. BUT, *ETAN* BELIEVED THAT, LINKED WITH THE *AVATAR*, HIS POWER *AMPLIFIED* AND CHANNELED THROUGH THE *COLLECTIVE*, AEREN COULD *DESTROY* THE ENTIRE *HIERARCHY.* "

THAT'S WHAT YOU SAID TO US THE OTHER *DAY.* THAT YOU THOUGHT *LIANA* AND *JASON* COULD DO THE SAME THING.

YES. AEREN WAS GROOMED FOR THIS PURPOSE.

"WHILE HE TRAINED *AEREN*, *ETAN* SAW TO IT THAT *I* WAS BIRTHED. I WAS TO BE THE FIRST *AVATAR* SINCE ASHKANOV WHO WOULD NOT BE THE *SLAVE* OF THE *HIERARCHY.*

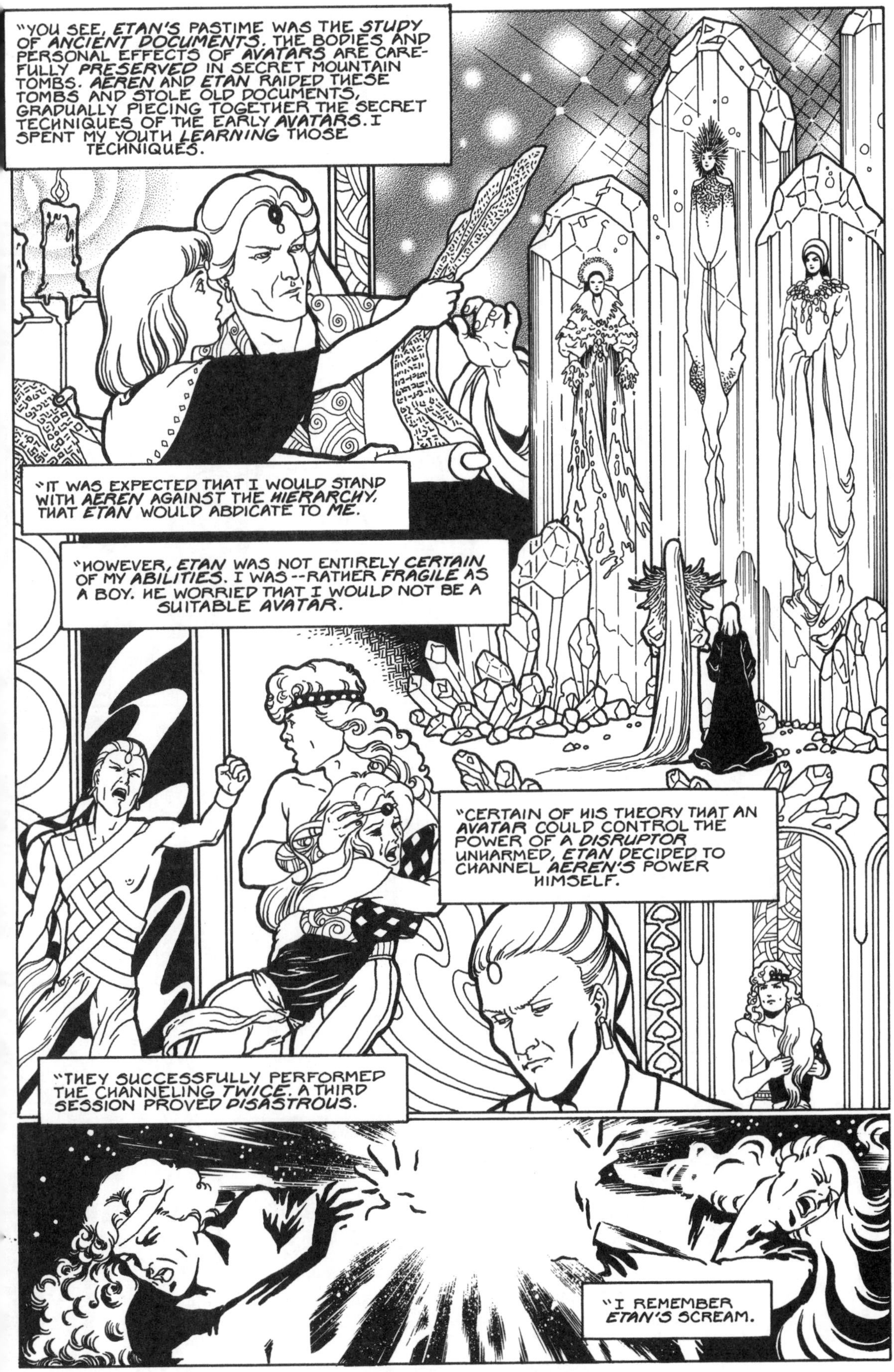
"YOU SEE, ETAN'S PASTIME WAS THE STUDY OF ANCIENT DOCUMENTS. THE BODIES AND PERSONAL EFFECTS OF AVATARS ARE CAREFULLY PRESERVED IN SECRET MOUNTAIN TOMBS. AEREN AND ETAN RAIDED THESE TOMBS AND STOLE OLD DOCUMENTS, GRADUALLY PIECING TOGETHER THE SECRET TECHNIQUES OF THE EARLY AVATARS. I SPENT MY YOUTH LEARNING THOSE TECHNIQUES.
"IT WAS EXPECTED THAT I WOULD STAND WITH AEREN AGAINST THE HIERARCHY, THAT ETAN WOULD ABDICATE TO ME.
"HOWEVER, ETAN WAS NOT ENTIRELY CERTAIN OF MY ABILITIES. I WAS--RATHER FRAGILE AS A BOY. HE WORRIED THAT I WOULD NOT BE A SUITABLE AVATAR.
"CERTAIN OF HIS THEORY THAT AN AVATAR COULD CONTROL THE POWER OF A DISRUPTOR UNHARMED, ETAN DECIDED TO CHANNEL AEREN'S POWER HIMSELF.
"THEY SUCCESSFULLY PERFORMED THE CHANNELING TWICE. A THIRD SESSION PROVED DISASTROUS.
"I REMEMBER ETAN'S SCREAM.

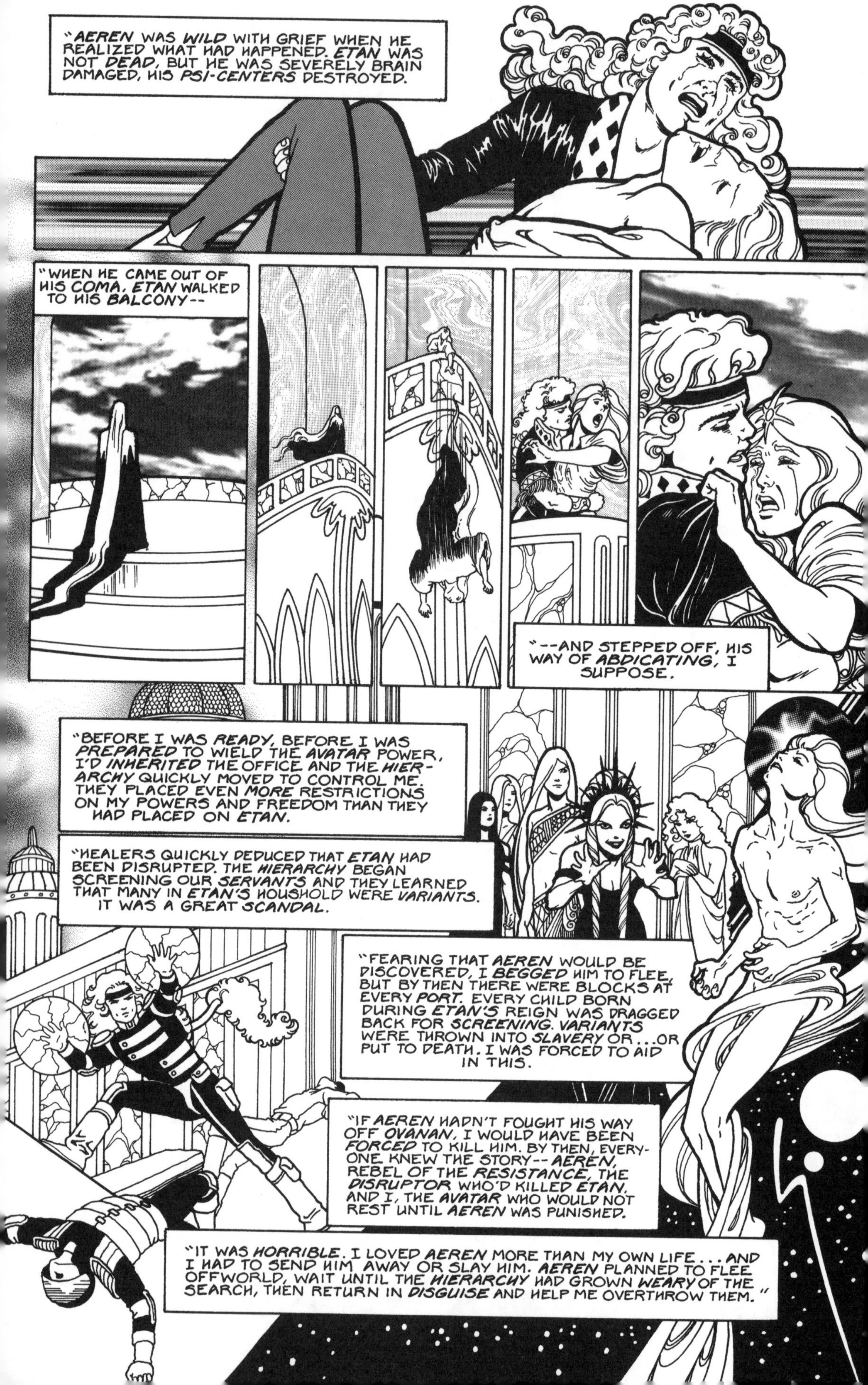
"AEREN WAS WILD WITH GRIEF WHEN HE REALIZED WHAT HAD HAPPENED. ETAN WAS NOT DEAD, BUT HE WAS SEVERELY BRAIN DAMAGED, HIS PSI-CENTERS DESTROYED.
"WHEN HE CAME OUT OF HIS COMA, ETAN WALKED TO HIS BALCONY--
"--AND STEPPED OFF, HIS WAY OF ABDICATING, I SUPPOSE.
"BEFORE I WAS READY, BEFORE I WAS PREPARED TO WIELD THE AVATAR POWER, I'D INHERITED THE OFFICE AND THE HIERARCHY QUICKLY MOVED TO CONTROL ME. THEY PLACED EVEN MORE RESTRICTIONS ON MY POWERS AND FREEDOM THAN THEY HAD PLACED ON ETAN.
"HEALERS QUICKLY DEDUCED THAT ETAN HAD BEEN DISRUPTED. THE HIERARCHY BEGAN SCREENING OUR SERVANTS AND THEY LEARNED THAT MANY IN ETAN'S HOUSHOLD WERE VARIANTS. IT WAS A GREAT SCANDAL.
"FEARING THAT AEREN WOULD BE DISCOVERED, I BEGGED HIM TO FLEE, BUT BY THEN THERE WERE BLOCKS AT EVERY PORT. EVERY CHILD BORN DURING ETAN'S REIGN WAS DRAGGED BACK FOR SCREENING. VARIANTS WERE THROWN INTO SLAVERY OR ...OR PUT TO DEATH. I WAS FORCED TO AID IN THIS.
"IF AEREN HADN'T FOUGHT HIS WAY OFF OVANAN, I WOULD HAVE BEEN FORCED TO KILL HIM. BY THEN, EVERYONE KNEW THE STORY--AEREN, REBEL OF THE RESISTANCE, THE DISRUPTOR WHO'D KILLED ETAN, AND I, THE AVATAR WHO WOULD NOT REST UNTIL AEREN WAS PUNISHED.
"IT WAS HORRIBLE. I LOVED AEREN MORE THAN MY OWN LIFE... AND I HAD TO SEND HIM AWAY OR SLAY HIM. AEREN PLANNED TO FLEE OFFWORLD, WAIT UNTIL THE HIERARCHY HAD GROWN WEARY OF THE SEARCH, THEN RETURN IN DISGUISE AND HELP ME OVERTHROW THEM."

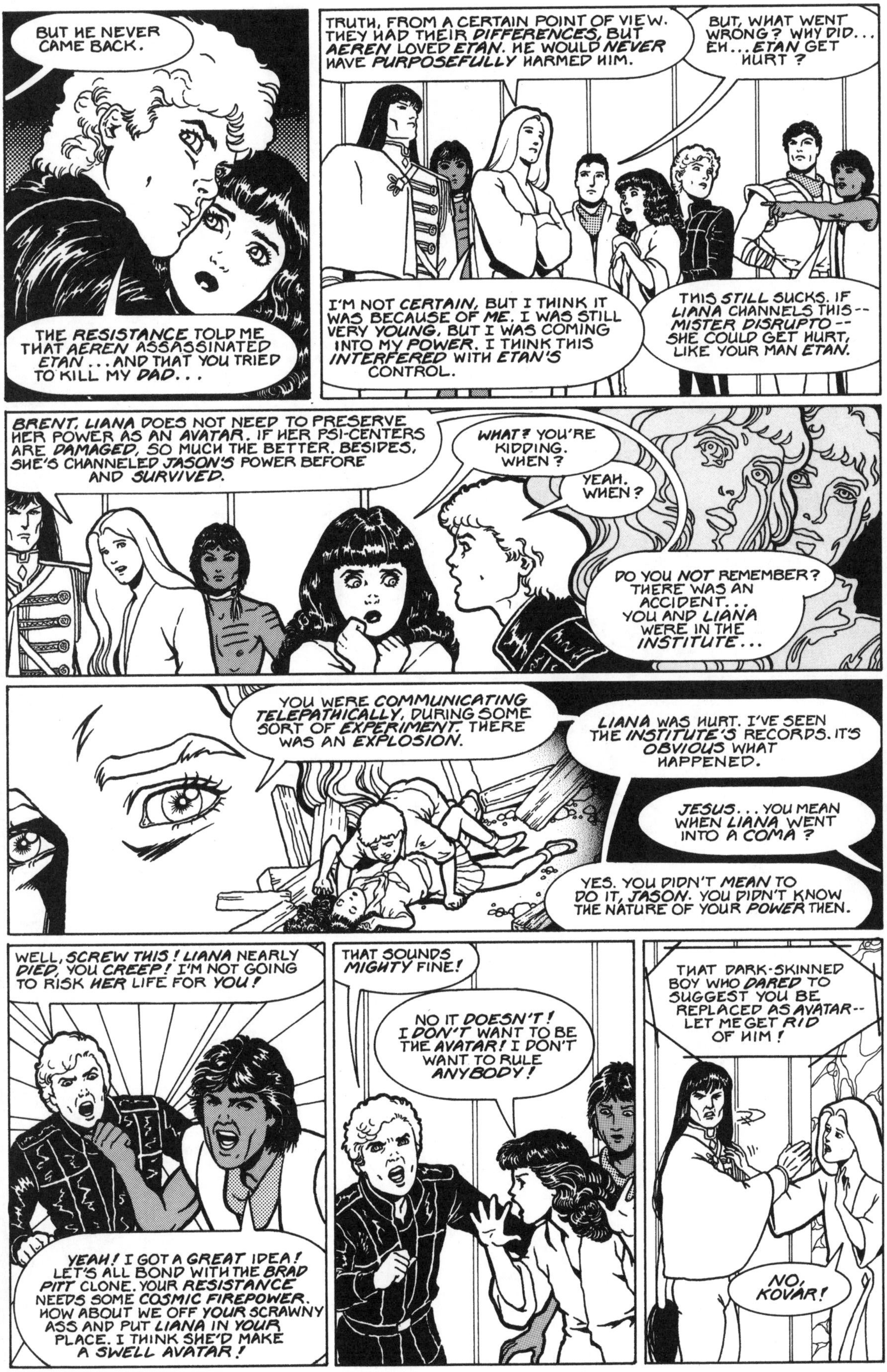
BUT HE NEVER CAME BACK.
THE RESISTANCE TOLD ME THAT AEREN ASSASSINATED ETAN . . . AND THAT YOU TRIED TO KILL MY DAD . . .
TRUTH, FROM A CERTAIN POINT OF VIEW. THEY HAD THEIR DIFFERENCES, BUT AEREN LOVED ETAN. HE WOULD NEVER HAVE PURPOSEFULLY HARMED HIM.
BUT, WHAT WENT WRONG? WHY DID . . . EH . . . ETAN GET HURT?
I'M NOT CERTAIN, BUT I THINK IT WAS BECAUSE OF ME. I WAS STILL VERY YOUNG, BUT I WAS COMING INTO MY POWER. I THINK THIS INTERFERED WITH ETAN'S CONTROL.
THIS STILL SUCKS. IF LIANA CHANNELS THIS-- MISTER DISRUPTO-- SHE COULD GET HURT, LIKE YOUR MAN ETAN.
BRENT, LIANA DOES NOT NEED TO PRESERVE HER POWER AS AN AVATAR. IF HER PSI-CENTERS ARE DAMAGED, SO MUCH THE BETTER. BESIDES, SHE'S CHANNELED JASON'S POWER BEFORE AND SURVIVED.
WHAT? YOU'RE KIDDING. WHEN?
YEAH. WHEN?
DO YOU NOT REMEMBER? THERE WAS AN ACCIDENT . . . YOU AND LIANA WERE IN THE INSTITUTE . . .
YOU WERE COMMUNICATING TELEPATHICALLY, DURING SOME SORT OF EXPERIMENT. THERE WAS AN EXPLOSION.
LIANA WAS HURT. I'VE SEEN THE INSTITUTE'S RECORDS. IT'S OBVIOUS WHAT HAPPENED.
JESUS . . . YOU MEAN WHEN LIANA WENT INTO A COMA?
YES. YOU DIDN'T MEAN TO DO IT, JASON. YOU DIDN'T KNOW THE NATURE OF YOUR POWER THEN.
WELL, SCREW THIS! LIANA NEARLY DIED, YOU CREEP! I'M NOT GOING TO RISK HER LIFE FOR YOU!
YEAH! I GOT A GREAT IDEA! LET'S ALL BOND WITH THE BRAD PITT CLONE. YOUR RESISTANCE NEEDS SOME COSMIC FIREPOWER. HOW ABOUT WE OFF YOUR SCRAWNY ASS AND PUT LIANA IN YOUR PLACE. I THINK SHE'D MAKE A SWELL AVATAR!
THAT SOUNDS MIGHTY FINE!
NO IT DOESN'T! I DON'T WANT TO BE THE AVATAR! I DON'T WANT TO RULE ANYBODY!
THAT DARK-SKINNED BOY WHO DARED TO SUGGEST YOU BE REPLACED AS AVATAR-- LET ME GET RID OF HIM!
NO, KOVAR!

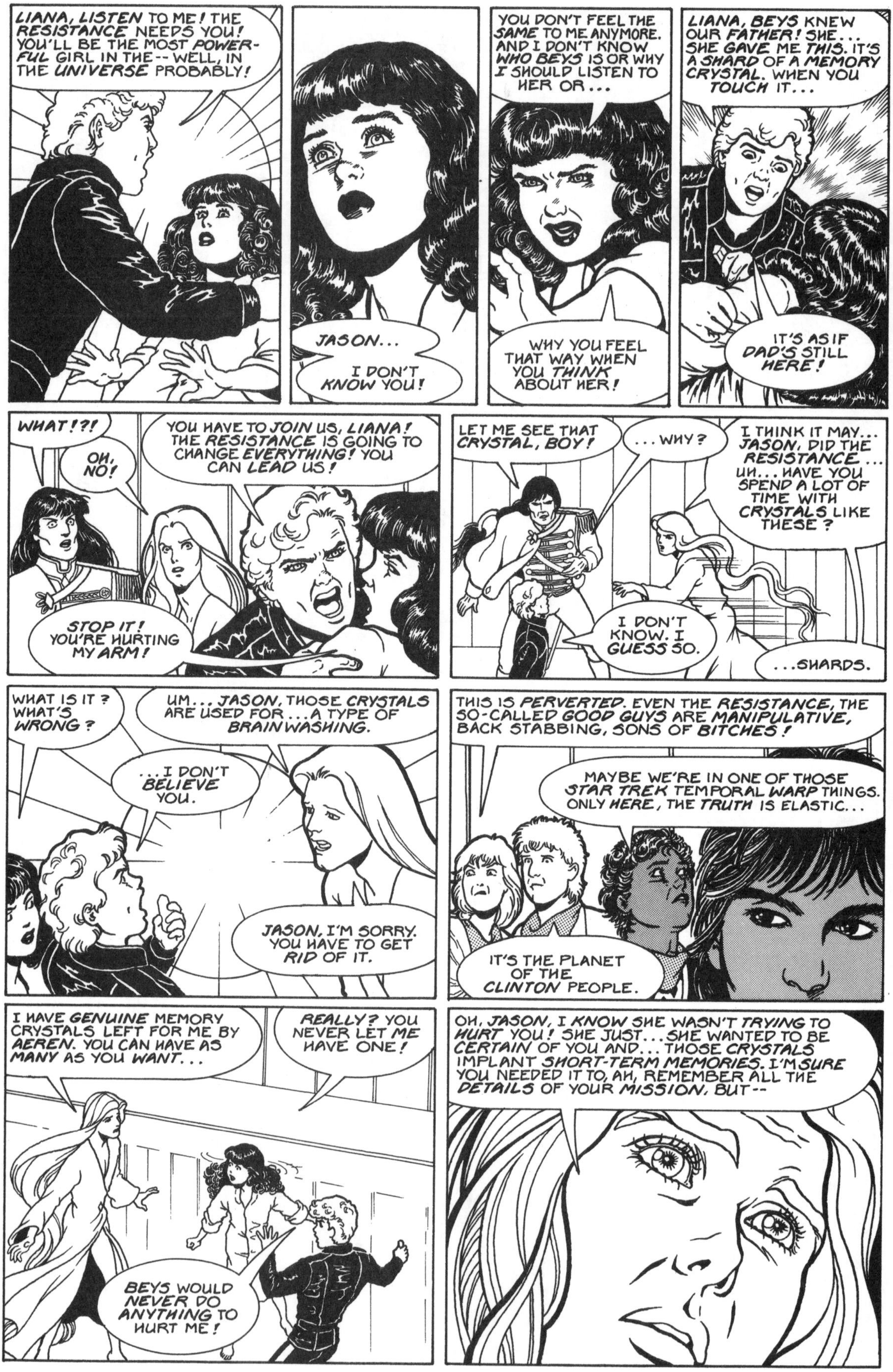
LIANA, LISTEN TO ME! THE RESISTANCE NEEDS YOU! YOU'LL BE THE MOST POWER-FUL GIRL IN THE -- WELL, IN THE UNIVERSE PROBABLY!
JASON...
I DON'T KNOW YOU!
YOU DON'T FEEL THE SAME TO ME ANYMORE. AND I DON'T KNOW WHO BEYS IS OR WHY I SHOULD LISTEN TO HER OR...
WHY YOU FEEL THAT WAY WHEN YOU THINK ABOUT HER!
LIANA, BEYS KNEW OUR FATHER! SHE... SHE GAVE ME THIS. IT'S A SHARD OF A MEMORY CRYSTAL. WHEN YOU TOUCH IT...
IT'S AS IF DAD'S STILL HERE!
WHAT!?!
OH, NO!
YOU HAVE TO JOIN US, LIANA! THE RESISTANCE IS GOING TO CHANGE EVERYTHING! YOU CAN LEAD US!
STOP IT! YOU'RE HURTING MY ARM!
LET ME SEE THAT CRYSTAL, BOY!
...WHY?
I THINK IT MAY... JASON, DID THE RESISTANCE... UH... HAVE YOU SPEND A LOT OF TIME WITH CRYSTALS LIKE THESE?
I DON'T KNOW. I GUESS SO.
...SHARDS.
WHAT IS IT? WHAT'S WRONG?
UM... JASON, THOSE CRYSTALS ARE USED FOR... A TYPE OF BRAINWASHING.
...I DON'T BELIEVE YOU.
JASON, I'M SORRY. YOU HAVE TO GET RID OF IT.
THIS IS PERVERTED. EVEN THE RESISTANCE, THE SO-CALLED GOOD GUYS ARE MANIPULATIVE, BACK STABBING, SONS OF BITCHES!
MAYBE WE'RE IN ONE OF THOSE STAR TREK TEMPORAL WARP THINGS. ONLY HERE, THE TRUTH IS ELASTIC...
IT'S THE PLANET OF THE CLINTON PEOPLE.
I HAVE GENUINE MEMORY CRYSTALS LEFT FOR ME BY AEREN. YOU CAN HAVE AS MANY AS YOU WANT...
REALLY? YOU NEVER LET ME HAVE ONE!
BEYS WOULD NEVER DO ANYTHING TO HURT ME!
OH, JASON, I KNOW SHE WASN'T TRYING TO HURT YOU! SHE JUST... SHE WANTED TO BE CERTAIN OF YOU AND... THOSE CRYSTALS IMPLANT SHORT-TERM MEMORIES. I'M SURE YOU NEEDED IT TO, AH, REMEMBER ALL THE DETAILS OF YOUR MISSION. BUT--

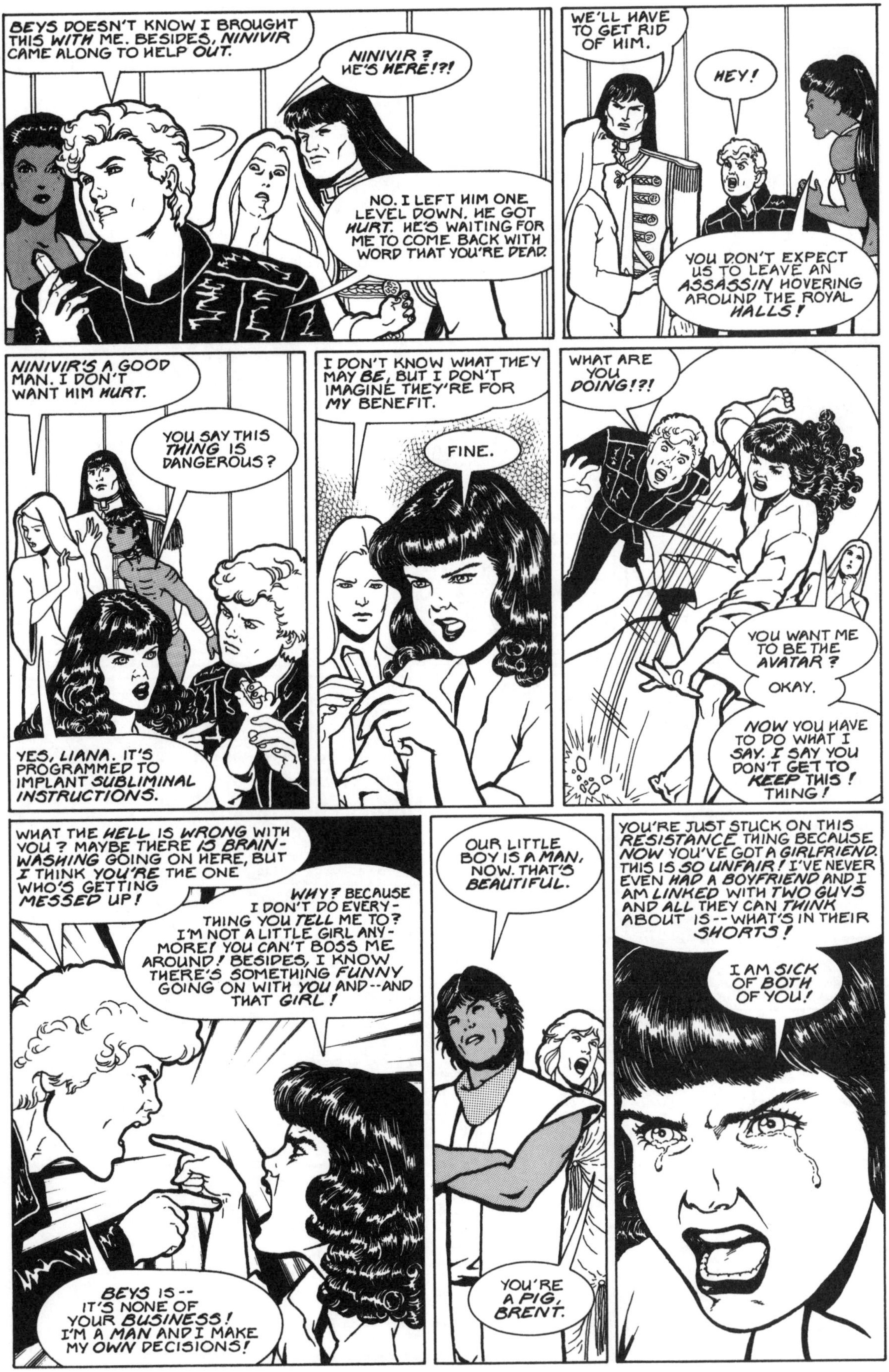
BEYS DOESN'T KNOW I BROUGHT THIS WITH ME. BESIDES, NINIVIR CAME ALONG TO HELP OUT.
NINIVIR? HE'S HERE!?!
NO. I LEFT HIM ONE LEVEL DOWN. HE GOT HURT. HE'S WAITING FOR ME TO COME BACK WITH WORD THAT YOU'RE DEAD.
WE'LL HAVE TO GET RID OF HIM.
HEY!
YOU DON'T EXPECT US TO LEAVE AN ASSASSIN HOVERING AROUND THE ROYAL HALLS!
NINIVIR'S A GOOD MAN. I DON'T WANT HIM HURT.
YOU SAY THIS THING IS DANGEROUS?
YES, LIANA. IT'S PROGRAMMED TO IMPLANT SUBLIMINAL INSTRUCTIONS.
I DON'T KNOW WHAT THEY MAY BE, BUT I DON'T IMAGINE THEY'RE FOR MY BENEFIT.
FINE.
WHAT ARE YOU DOING!?!
YOU WANT ME TO BE THE AVATAR?
OKAY.
NOW YOU HAVE TO DO WHAT I SAY. I SAY YOU DON'T GET TO KEEP THIS! THING!
WHAT THE HELL IS WRONG WITH YOU? MAYBE THERE IS BRAIN-WASHING GOING ON HERE, BUT I THINK YOU'RE THE ONE WHO'S GETTING MESSED UP!
WHY? BECAUSE I DON'T DO EVERY-THING YOU TELL ME TO? I'M NOT A LITTLE GIRL ANY-MORE! YOU CAN'T BOSS ME AROUND! BESIDES, I KNOW THERE'S SOMETHING FUNNY GOING ON WITH YOU AND--AND THAT GIRL!
BEYS IS-- IT'S NONE OF YOUR BUSINESS! I'M A MAN AND I MAKE MY OWN DECISIONS!
OUR LITTLE BOY IS A MAN, NOW. THAT'S BEAUTIFUL.
YOU'RE A PIG, BRENT.
YOU'RE JUST STUCK ON THIS RESISTANCE THING BECAUSE NOW YOU'VE GOT A GIRLFRIEND. THIS IS SO UNFAIR! I'VE NEVER EVEN HAD A BOYFRIEND AND I AM LINKED WITH TWO GUYS AND ALL THEY CAN THINK ABOUT IS--WHAT'S IN THEIR SHORTS!
I AM SICK OF BOTH OF YOU!

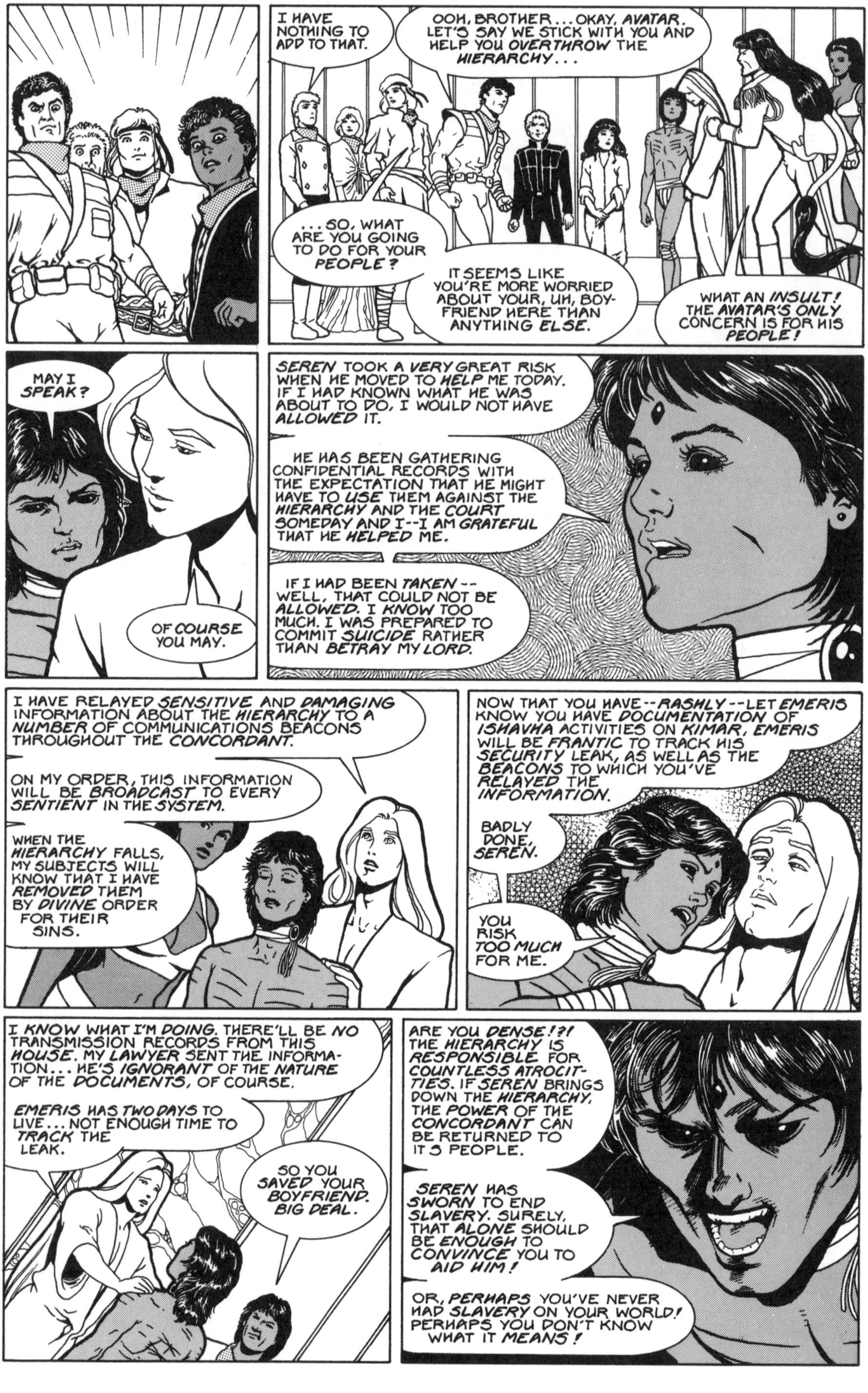
I HAVE NOTHING TO ADD TO THAT.
OOH, BROTHER... OKAY, AVATAR. LET'S SAY WE STICK WITH YOU AND HELP YOU OVERTHROW THE HIERARCHY...
...SO, WHAT ARE YOU GOING TO DO FOR YOUR PEOPLE?
IT SEEMS LIKE YOU'RE MORE WORRIED ABOUT YOUR, UH, BOY-FRIEND HERE THAN ANYTHING ELSE.
WHAT AN INSULT! THE AVATAR'S ONLY CONCERN IS FOR HIS PEOPLE!
MAY I SPEAK?
OF COURSE YOU MAY.
SEREN TOOK A VERY GREAT RISK WHEN HE MOVED TO HELP ME TODAY. IF I HAD KNOWN WHAT HE WAS ABOUT TO DO, I WOULD NOT HAVE ALLOWED IT.
HE HAS BEEN GATHERING CONFIDENTIAL RECORDS WITH THE EXPECTATION THAT HE MIGHT HAVE TO USE THEM AGAINST THE HIERARCHY AND THE COURT SOMEDAY AND I--I AM GRATEFUL THAT HE HELPED ME.
IF I HAD BEEN TAKEN--WELL, THAT COULD NOT BE ALLOWED. I KNOW TOO MUCH. I WAS PREPARED TO COMMIT SUICIDE RATHER THAN BETRAY MY LORD.
I HAVE RELAYED SENSITIVE AND DAMAGING INFORMATION ABOUT THE HIERARCHY TO A NUMBER OF COMMUNICATIONS BEACONS THROUGHOUT THE CONCORDANT.
ON MY ORDER, THIS INFORMATION WILL BE BROADCAST TO EVERY SENTIENT IN THE SYSTEM.
WHEN THE HIERARCHY FALLS, MY SUBJECTS WILL KNOW THAT I HAVE REMOVED THEM BY DIVINE ORDER FOR THEIR SINS.
NOW THAT YOU HAVE--RASHLY--LET EMERIS KNOW YOU HAVE DOCUMENTATION OF ISHAVHA ACTIVITIES ON KIMAR, EMERIS WILL BE FRANTIC TO TRACK HIS SECURITY LEAK, AS WELL AS THE BEACONS TO WHICH YOU'VE RELAYED THE INFORMATION.
BADLY DONE, SEREN.
YOU RISK TOO MUCH FOR ME.
I KNOW WHAT I'M DOING. THERE'LL BE NO TRANSMISSION RECORDS FROM THIS HOUSE. MY LAWYER SENT THE INFORMATION... HE'S IGNORANT OF THE NATURE OF THE DOCUMENTS, OF COURSE.
EMERIS HAS TWO DAYS TO LIVE... NOT ENOUGH TIME TO TRACK THE LEAK.
SO YOU SAVED YOUR BOYFRIEND. BIG DEAL.
ARE YOU DENSE!?! THE HIERARCHY IS RESPONSIBLE FOR COUNTLESS ATROCITIES. IF SEREN BRINGS DOWN THE HIERARCHY, THE POWER OF THE CONCORDANT CAN BE RETURNED TO ITS PEOPLE.
SEREN HAS SWORN TO END SLAVERY. SURELY, THAT ALONE SHOULD BE ENOUGH TO CONVINCE YOU TO AID HIM!
OR, PERHAPS YOU'VE NEVER HAD SLAVERY ON YOUR WORLD! PERHAPS YOU DON'T KNOW WHAT IT MEANS!

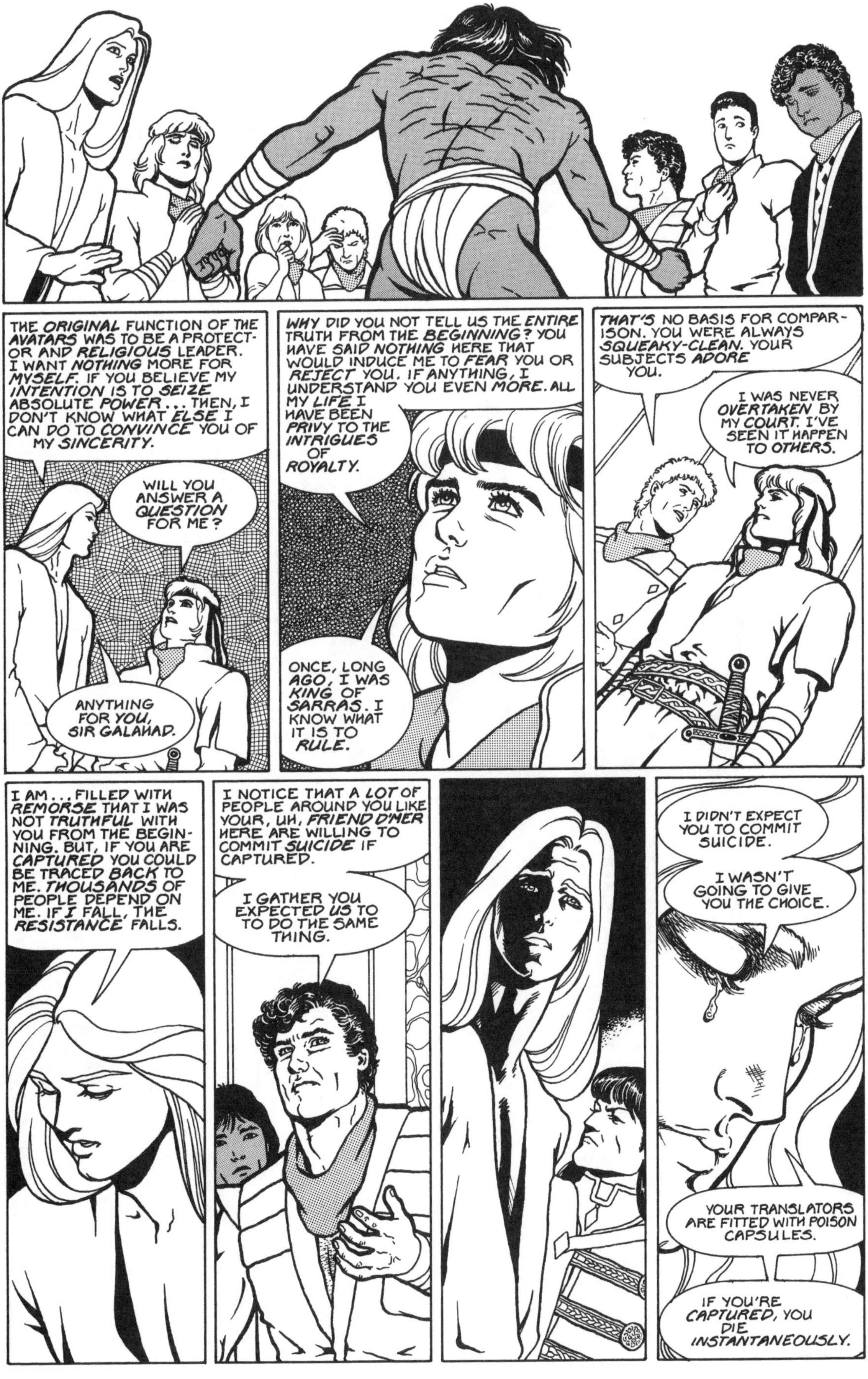
THE ORIGINAL FUNCTION OF THE AVATARS WAS TO BE A PROTECTOR AND RELIGIOUS LEADER. I WANT NOTHING MORE FOR MYSELF. IF YOU BELIEVE MY INTENTION IS TO SEIZE ABSOLUTE POWER... THEN, I DON'T KNOW WHAT ELSE I CAN DO TO CONVINCE YOU OF MY SINCERITY.
WILL YOU ANSWER A QUESTION FOR ME?
ANYTHING FOR YOU, SIR GALAHAD.
WHY DID YOU NOT TELL US THE ENTIRE TRUTH FROM THE BEGINNING? YOU HAVE SAID NOTHING HERE THAT WOULD INDUCE ME TO FEAR YOU OR REJECT YOU. IF ANYTHING, I UNDERSTAND YOU EVEN MORE. ALL MY LIFE I HAVE BEEN PRIVY TO THE INTRIGUES OF ROYALTY.
ONCE, LONG AGO, I WAS KING OF SARRAS. I KNOW WHAT IT IS TO RULE.
THAT'S NO BASIS FOR COMPARISON. YOU WERE ALWAYS SQUEAKY-CLEAN. YOUR SUBJECTS ADORE YOU.
I WAS NEVER OVERTAKEN BY MY COURT. I'VE SEEN IT HAPPEN TO OTHERS.
I AM... FILLED WITH REMORSE THAT I WAS NOT TRUTHFUL WITH YOU FROM THE BEGINNING. BUT, IF YOU ARE CAPTURED YOU COULD BE TRACED BACK TO ME. THOUSANDS OF PEOPLE DEPEND ON ME. IF I FALL, THE RESISTANCE FALLS.
I NOTICE THAT A LOT OF PEOPLE AROUND YOU LIKE YOUR, UH, FRIEND D'MER HERE ARE WILLING TO COMMIT SUICIDE IF CAPTURED.
I GATHER YOU EXPECTED US TO TO DO THE SAME THING.
I DIDN'T EXPECT YOU TO COMMIT SUICIDE.
I WASN'T GOING TO GIVE YOU THE CHOICE.
YOUR TRANSLATORS ARE FITTED WITH POISON CAPSULES.
IF YOU'RE CAPTURED, YOU DIE INSTANTANEOUSLY.

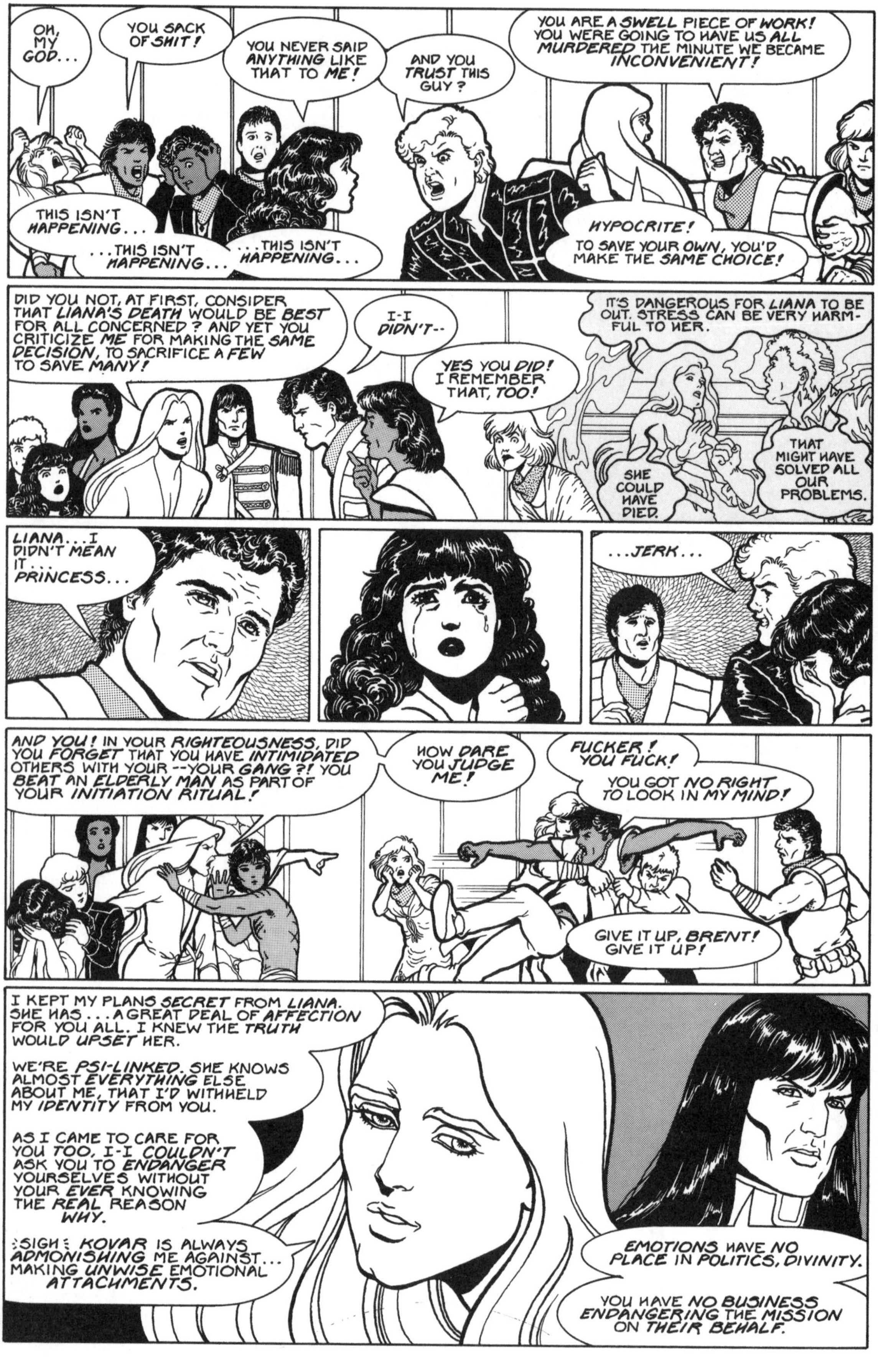

OH, MY GOD...
YOU SACK OF SHIT!
YOU NEVER SAID ANYTHING LIKE THAT TO ME!
AND YOU TRUST THIS GUY?
YOU ARE A SWELL PIECE OF WORK! YOU WERE GOING TO HAVE US ALL MURDERED THE MINUTE WE BECAME INCONVENIENT!
THIS ISN'T HAPPENING...
...THIS ISN'T HAPPENING...
...THIS ISN'T HAPPENING...
HYPOCRITE!
TO SAVE YOUR OWN, YOU'D MAKE THE SAME CHOICE!
DID YOU NOT, AT FIRST, CONSIDER THAT LIANA'S DEATH WOULD BE BEST FOR ALL CONCERNED? AND YET YOU CRITICIZE ME FOR MAKING THE SAME DECISION, TO SACRIFICE A FEW TO SAVE MANY!
I-I DIDN'T--
YES YOU DID! I REMEMBER THAT, TOO!
IT'S DANGEROUS FOR LIANA TO BE OUT. STRESS CAN BE VERY HARMFUL TO HER.
SHE COULD HAVE DIED.
THAT MIGHT HAVE SOLVED ALL OUR PROBLEMS.
LIANA... I DIDN'T MEAN IT... PRINCESS...
...JERK...
AND YOU! IN YOUR RIGHTEOUSNESS, DID YOU FORGET THAT YOU HAVE INTIMIDATED OTHERS WITH YOUR --YOUR GANG?! YOU BEAT AN ELDERLY MAN AS PART OF YOUR INITIATION RITUAL!
HOW DARE YOU JUDGE ME!
FUCKER! YOU FUCK!
YOU GOT NO RIGHT TO LOOK IN MY MIND!
GIVE IT UP, BRENT! GIVE IT UP!
I KEPT MY PLANS SECRET FROM LIANA. SHE HAS... A GREAT DEAL OF AFFECTION FOR YOU ALL. I KNEW THE TRUTH WOULD UPSET HER.
WE'RE PSI-LINKED. SHE KNOWS ALMOST EVERYTHING ELSE ABOUT ME, THAT I'D WITHHELD MY IDENTITY FROM YOU.
AS I CAME TO CARE FOR YOU TOO, I-I COULDN'T ASK YOU TO ENDANGER YOURSELVES WITHOUT YOUR EVER KNOWING THE REAL REASON WHY.
:SIGH: KOVAR IS ALWAYS ADMONISHING ME AGAINST... MAKING UNWISE EMOTIONAL ATTACHMENTS.
EMOTIONS HAVE NO PLACE IN POLITICS, DIVINITY.
YOU HAVE NO BUSINESS ENDANGERING THE MISSION ON THEIR BEHALF.

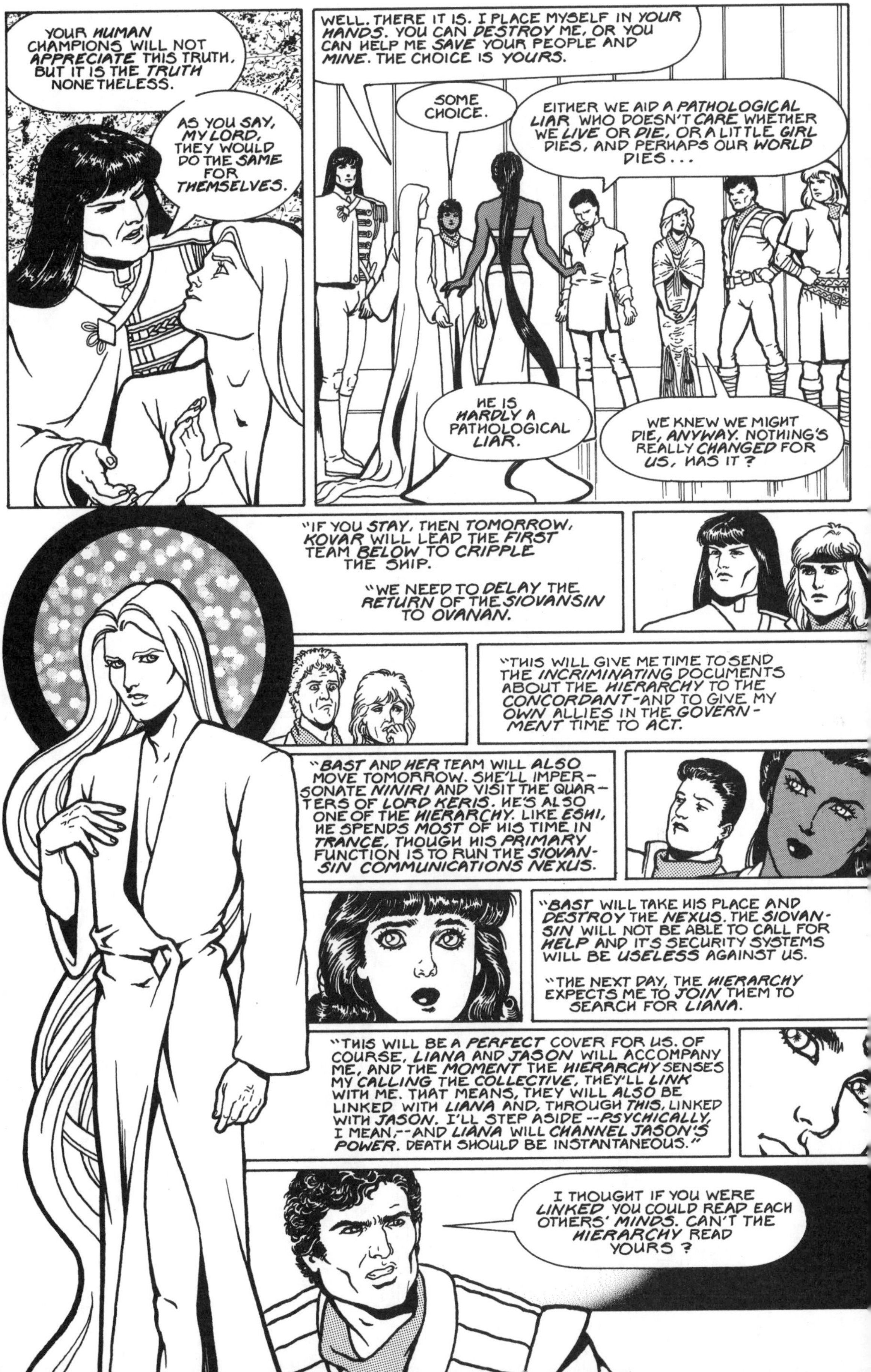

YOUR HUMAN CHAMPIONS WILL NOT APPRECIATE THIS TRUTH, BUT IT IS THE TRUTH NONETHELESS.
AS YOU SAY, MY LORD, THEY WOULD DO THE SAME FOR THEMSELVES.
WELL. THERE IT IS. I PLACE MYSELF IN YOUR HANDS. YOU CAN DESTROY ME, OR YOU CAN HELP ME SAVE YOUR PEOPLE AND MINE. THE CHOICE IS YOURS.
SOME CHOICE.
EITHER WE AID A PATHOLOGICAL LIAR WHO DOESN'T CARE WHETHER WE LIVE OR DIE, OR A LITTLE GIRL DIES, AND PERHAPS OUR WORLD DIES...
HE IS HARDLY A PATHOLOGICAL LIAR.
WE KNEW WE MIGHT DIE, ANYWAY. NOTHING'S REALLY CHANGED FOR US, HAS IT?
"IF YOU STAY, THEN TOMORROW, KOVAR WILL LEAD THE FIRST TEAM BELOW TO CRIPPLE THE SHIP.
"WE NEED TO DELAY THE RETURN OF THE SIOVANSIN TO OVANAN.
"THIS WILL GIVE ME TIME TO SEND THE INCRIMINATING DOCUMENTS ABOUT THE HIERARCHY TO THE CONCORDANT-AND TO GIVE MY OWN ALLIES IN THE GOVERN-MENT TIME TO ACT.
"BAST AND HER TEAM WILL ALSO MOVE TOMORROW. SHE'LL IMPER-SONATE NINIRI AND VISIT THE QUAR-TERS OF LORD KERIS. HE'S ALSO ONE OF THE HIERARCHY. LIKE ESHI, HE SPENDS MOST OF HIS TIME IN TRANCE, THOUGH HIS PRIMARY FUNCTION IS TO RUN THE SIOVAN-SIN COMMUNICATIONS NEXUS.
"BAST WILL TAKE HIS PLACE AND DESTROY THE NEXUS. THE SIOVAN-SIN WILL NOT BE ABLE TO CALL FOR HELP AND IT'S SECURITY SYSTEMS WILL BE USELESS AGAINST US.
"THE NEXT DAY, THE HIERARCHY EXPECTS ME TO JOIN THEM TO SEARCH FOR LIANA.
"THIS WILL BE A PERFECT COVER FOR US. OF COURSE, LIANA AND JASON WILL ACCOMPANY ME, AND THE MOMENT THE HIERARCHY SENSES MY CALLING THE COLLECTIVE, THEY'LL LINK WITH ME. THAT MEANS, THEY WILL ALSO BE LINKED WITH LIANA AND, THROUGH THIS, LINKED WITH JASON. I'LL STEP ASIDE --PSYCHICALLY, I MEAN,--AND LIANA WILL CHANNEL JASON'S POWER. DEATH SHOULD BE INSTANTANEOUS."
I THOUGHT IF YOU WERE LINKED YOU COULD READ EACH OTHERS' MINDS. CAN'T THE HIERARCHY READ YOURS?

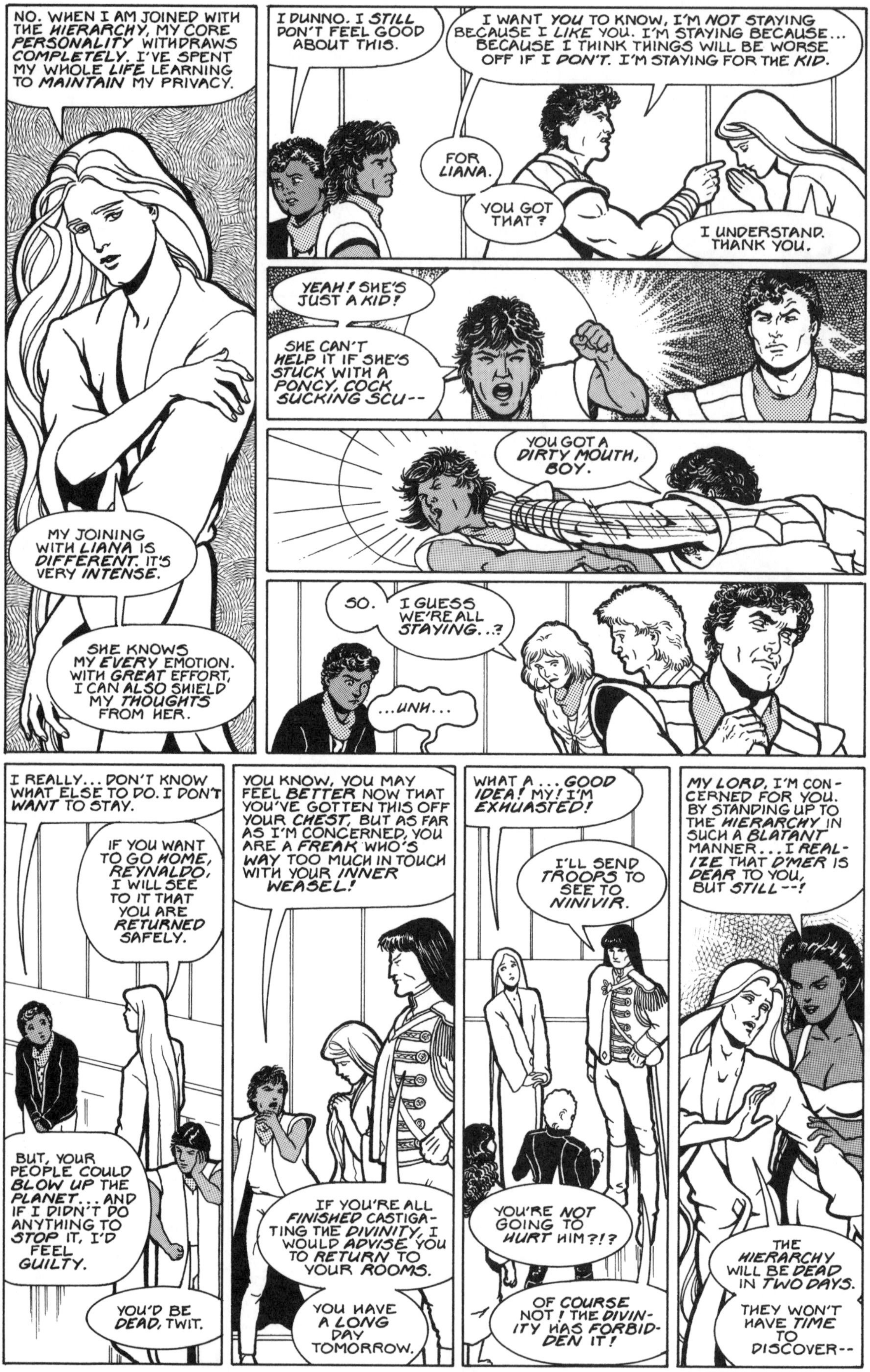

NO. WHEN I AM JOINED WITH THE HIERARCHY, MY CORE PERSONALITY WITHDRAWS COMPLETELY. I'VE SPENT MY WHOLE LIFE LEARNING TO MAINTAIN MY PRIVACY.
MY JOINING WITH LIANA IS DIFFERENT. IT'S VERY INTENSE.
SHE KNOWS MY EVERY EMOTION. WITH GREAT EFFORT, I CAN ALSO SHIELD MY THOUGHTS FROM HER.
I DUNNO. I STILL DON'T FEEL GOOD ABOUT THIS.
I WANT YOU TO KNOW, I'M NOT STAYING BECAUSE I LIKE YOU. I'M STAYING BECAUSE... BECAUSE I THINK THINGS WILL BE WORSE OFF IF I DON'T. I'M STAYING FOR THE KID.
FOR LIANA.
YOU GOT THAT?
I UNDERSTAND. THANK YOU.
YEAH! SHE'S JUST A KID!
SHE CAN'T HELP IT IF SHE'S STUCK WITH A PONCY, COCK SUCKING SCU--
YOU GOT A DIRTY MOUTH, BOY.
SO.
I GUESS WE'RE ALL STAYING...?
...UNH...
I REALLY... DON'T KNOW WHAT ELSE TO DO. I DON'T WANT TO STAY.
IF YOU WANT TO GO HOME, REYNALDO, I WILL SEE TO IT THAT YOU ARE RETURNED SAFELY.
BUT, YOUR PEOPLE COULD BLOW UP THE PLANET... AND IF I DIDN'T DO ANYTHING TO STOP IT, I'D FEEL GUILTY.
YOU'D BE DEAD, TWIT.
YOU KNOW, YOU MAY FEEL BETTER NOW THAT YOU'VE GOTTEN THIS OFF YOUR CHEST, BUT AS FAR AS I'M CONCERNED, YOU ARE A FREAK WHO'S WAY TOO MUCH IN TOUCH WITH YOUR INNER WEASEL!
IF YOU'RE ALL FINISHED CASTIGATING THE DIVINITY, I WOULD ADVISE YOU TO RETURN TO YOUR ROOMS.
YOU HAVE A LONG DAY TOMORROW.
WHAT A... GOOD IDEA! MY! I'M EXHUASTED!
I'LL SEND TROOPS TO SEE TO NINIVIR.
YOU'RE NOT GOING TO HURT HIM?!?
OF COURSE NOT! THE DIVINITY HAS FORBIDDEN IT!
MY LORD, I'M CONCERNED FOR YOU. BY STANDING UP TO THE HIERARCHY IN SUCH A BLATANT MANNER... I REALIZE THAT D'MER IS DEAR TO YOU, BUT STILL--!
THE HIERARCHY WILL BE DEAD IN TWO DAYS.
THEY WON'T HAVE TIME TO DISCOVER--

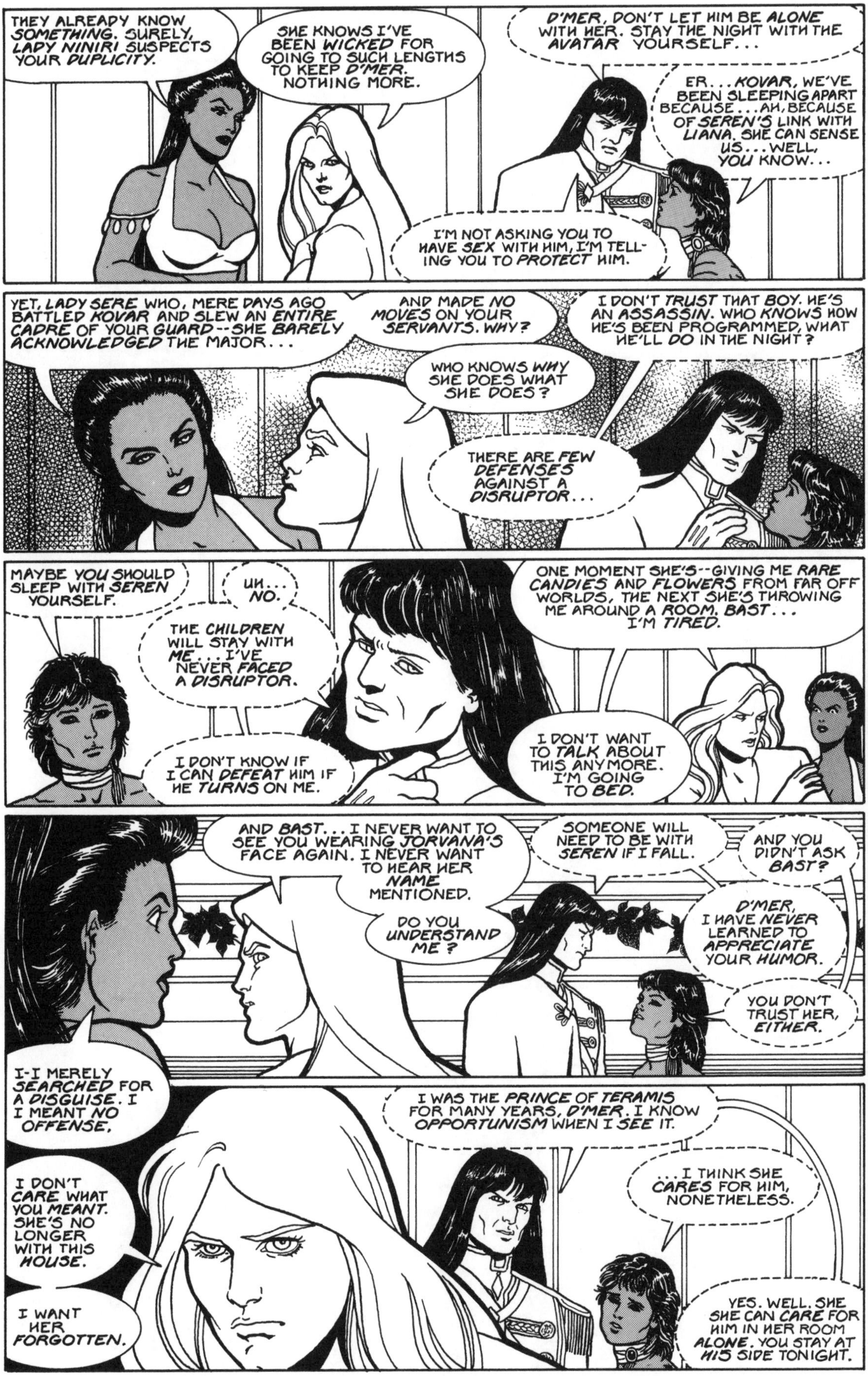

THEY ALREADY KNOW SOMETHING. SURELY, LADY NINIRI SUSPECTS YOUR DUPLICITY.
SHE KNOWS I'VE BEEN WICKED FOR GOING TO SUCH LENGTHS TO KEEP D'MER. NOTHING MORE.
D'MER, DON'T LET HIM BE ALONE WITH HER. STAY THE NIGHT WITH THE AVATAR YOURSELF...
ER... KOVAR, WE'VE BEEN SLEEPING APART BECAUSE... AH, BECAUSE OF SEREN'S LINK WITH LIANA. SHE CAN SENSE US... WELL, YOU KNOW...
I'M NOT ASKING YOU TO HAVE SEX WITH HIM, I'M TELLING YOU TO PROTECT HIM.
YET, LADY SERE WHO, MERE DAYS AGO BATTLED KOVAR AND SLEW AN ENTIRE CADRE OF YOUR GUARD--SHE BARELY ACKNOWLEDGED THE MAJOR...
AND MADE NO MOVES ON YOUR SERVANTS. WHY?
WHO KNOWS WHY SHE DOES WHAT SHE DOES?
I DON'T TRUST THAT BOY. HE'S AN ASSASSIN. WHO KNOWS HOW HE'S BEEN PROGRAMMED, WHAT HE'LL DO IN THE NIGHT?
THERE ARE FEW DEFENSES AGAINST A DISRUPTOR...
MAYBE YOU SHOULD SLEEP WITH SEREN YOURSELF.
UH... NO.
THE CHILDREN WILL STAY WITH ME... I'VE NEVER FACED A DISRUPTOR.
I DON'T KNOW IF I CAN DEFEAT HIM IF HE TURNS ON ME.
ONE MOMENT SHE'S--GIVING ME RARE CANDIES AND FLOWERS FROM FAR OFF WORLDS, THE NEXT SHE'S THROWING ME AROUND A ROOM, BAST... I'M TIRED.
I DON'T WANT TO TALK ABOUT THIS ANYMORE. I'M GOING TO BED.
AND BAST... I NEVER WANT TO SEE YOU WEARING JORVANA'S FACE AGAIN. I NEVER WANT TO HEAR HER NAME MENTIONED.
DO YOU UNDERSTAND ME?
I-I MERELY SEARCHED FOR A DISGUISE. I MEANT NO OFFENSE.
SOMEONE WILL NEED TO BE WITH SEREN IF I FALL.
AND YOU DIDN'T ASK BAST?
D'MER, I HAVE NEVER LEARNED TO APPRECIATE YOUR HUMOR.
YOU DON'T TRUST HER, EITHER.
I DON'T CARE WHAT YOU MEANT. SHE'S NO LONGER WITH THIS HOUSE.
I WANT HER FORGOTTEN.
I WAS THE PRINCE OF TERAMIS FOR MANY YEARS, D'MER. I KNOW OPPORTUNISM WHEN I SEE IT.
...I THINK SHE CARES FOR HIM, NONETHELESS.
YES. WELL. SHE SHE CAN CARE FOR HIM IN HER ROOM ALONE. YOU STAY AT HIS SIDE TONIGHT.

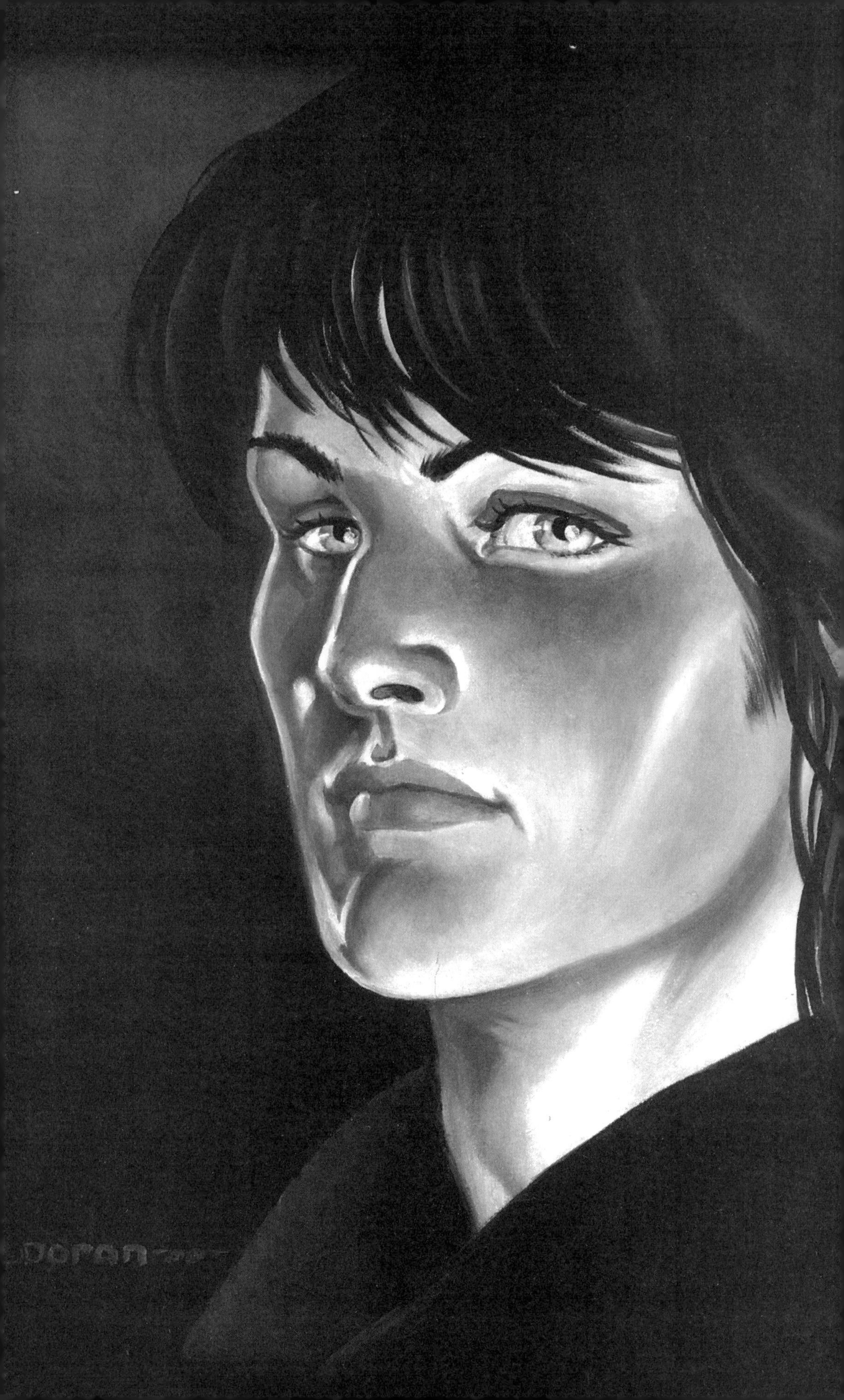
DORAN

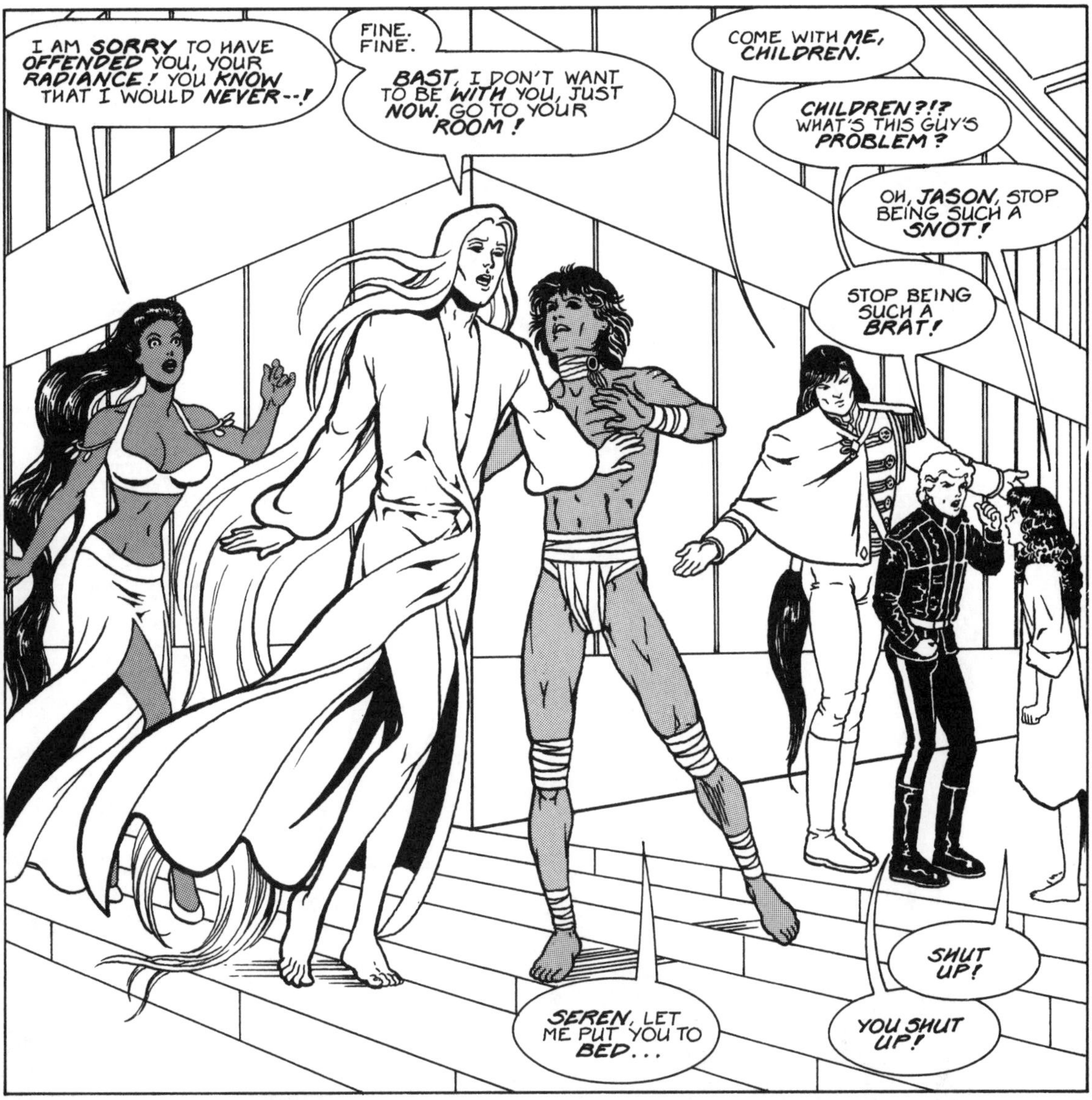
I AM SORRY TO HAVE OFFENDED YOU, YOUR RADIANCE! YOU KNOW THAT I WOULD NEVER--!
FINE. FINE.
BAST, I DON'T WANT TO BE WITH YOU, JUST NOW. GO TO YOUR ROOM!
COME WITH ME, CHILDREN.
CHILDREN?!? WHAT'S THIS GUY'S PROBLEM?
OH, JASON, STOP BEING SUCH A SNOT!
STOP BEING SUCH A BRAT!
SEREN, LET ME PUT YOU TO BED...
SHUT UP!
YOU SHUT UP!

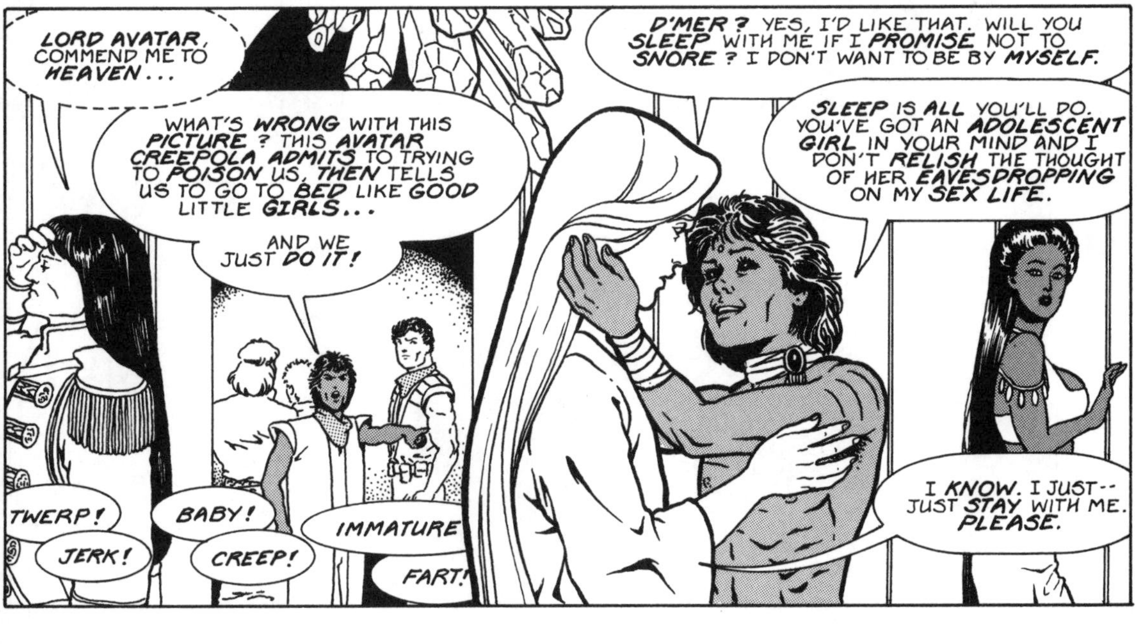
LORD AVATAR, COMMEND ME TO HEAVEN...
WHAT'S WRONG WITH THIS PICTURE? THIS AVATAR CREEPOLA ADMITS TO TRYING TO POISON US, THEN TELLS US TO GO TO BED LIKE GOOD LITTLE GIRLS...
AND WE JUST DO IT!
TWERP!
JERK!
BABY!
CREEP!
IMMATURE
FART!
D'MER? YES, I'D LIKE THAT. WILL YOU SLEEP WITH ME IF I PROMISE NOT TO SNORE? I DON'T WANT TO BE BY MYSELF.
SLEEP IS ALL YOU'LL DO. YOU'VE GOT AN ADOLESCENT GIRL IN YOUR MIND AND I DON'T RELISH THE THOUGHT OF HER EAVESDROPPING ON MY SEX LIFE.
I KNOW. I JUST-- JUST STAY WITH ME. PLEASE.

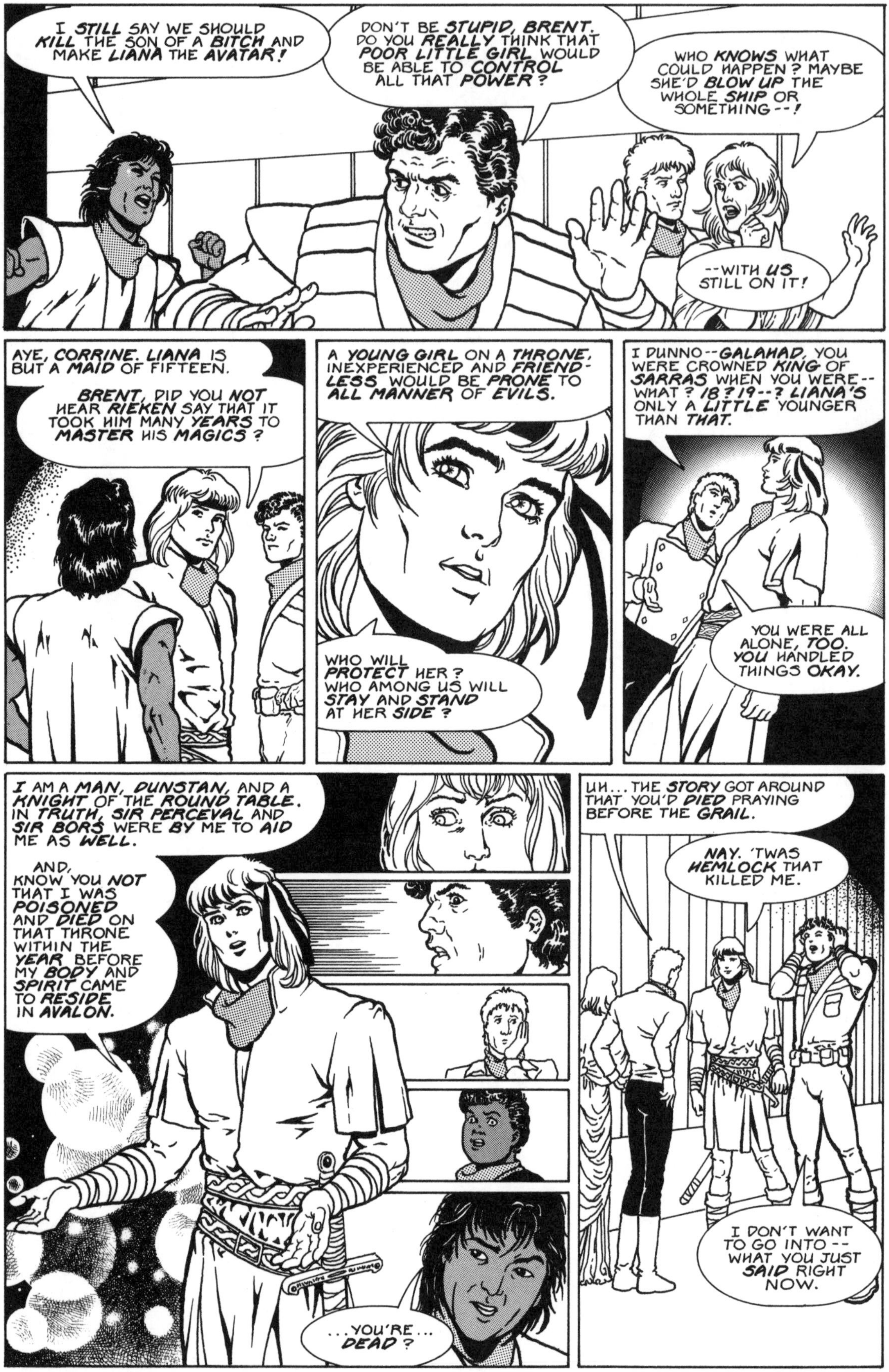
I STILL SAY WE SHOULD KILL THE SON OF A BITCH AND MAKE LIANA THE AVATAR!
DON'T BE STUPID, BRENT. DO YOU REALLY THINK THAT POOR LITTLE GIRL WOULD BE ABLE TO CONTROL ALL THAT POWER?
WHO KNOWS WHAT COULD HAPPEN? MAYBE SHE'D BLOW UP THE WHOLE SHIP OR SOMETHING--!
--WITH US STILL ON IT!
AYE, CORRINE. LIANA IS BUT A MAID OF FIFTEEN.
BRENT, DID YOU NOT HEAR RIEKEN SAY THAT IT TOOK HIM MANY YEARS TO MASTER HIS MAGICS?
A YOUNG GIRL ON A THRONE, INEXPERIENCED AND FRIENDLESS WOULD BE PRONE TO ALL MANNER OF EVILS.
WHO WILL PROTECT HER? WHO AMONG US WILL STAY AND STAND AT HER SIDE?
I DUNNO--GALAHAD, YOU WERE CROWNED KING OF SARRAS WHEN YOU WERE--WHAT? 18? 19--? LIANA'S ONLY A LITTLE YOUNGER THAN THAT.
YOU WERE ALL ALONE, TOO. YOU HANDLED THINGS OKAY.
I AM A MAN, DUNSTAN, AND A KNIGHT OF THE ROUND TABLE. IN TRUTH, SIR PERCEVAL AND SIR BORS WERE BY ME TO AID ME AS WELL.
AND, KNOW YOU NOT THAT I WAS POISONED AND DIED ON THAT THRONE WITHIN THE YEAR BEFORE MY BODY AND SPIRIT CAME TO RESIDE IN AVALON.
...YOU'RE... DEAD?
UH... THE STORY GOT AROUND THAT YOU'D DIED PRAYING BEFORE THE GRAIL.
NAY. 'TWAS HEMLOCK THAT KILLED ME.
I DON'T WANT TO GO INTO -- WHAT YOU JUST SAID RIGHT NOW.

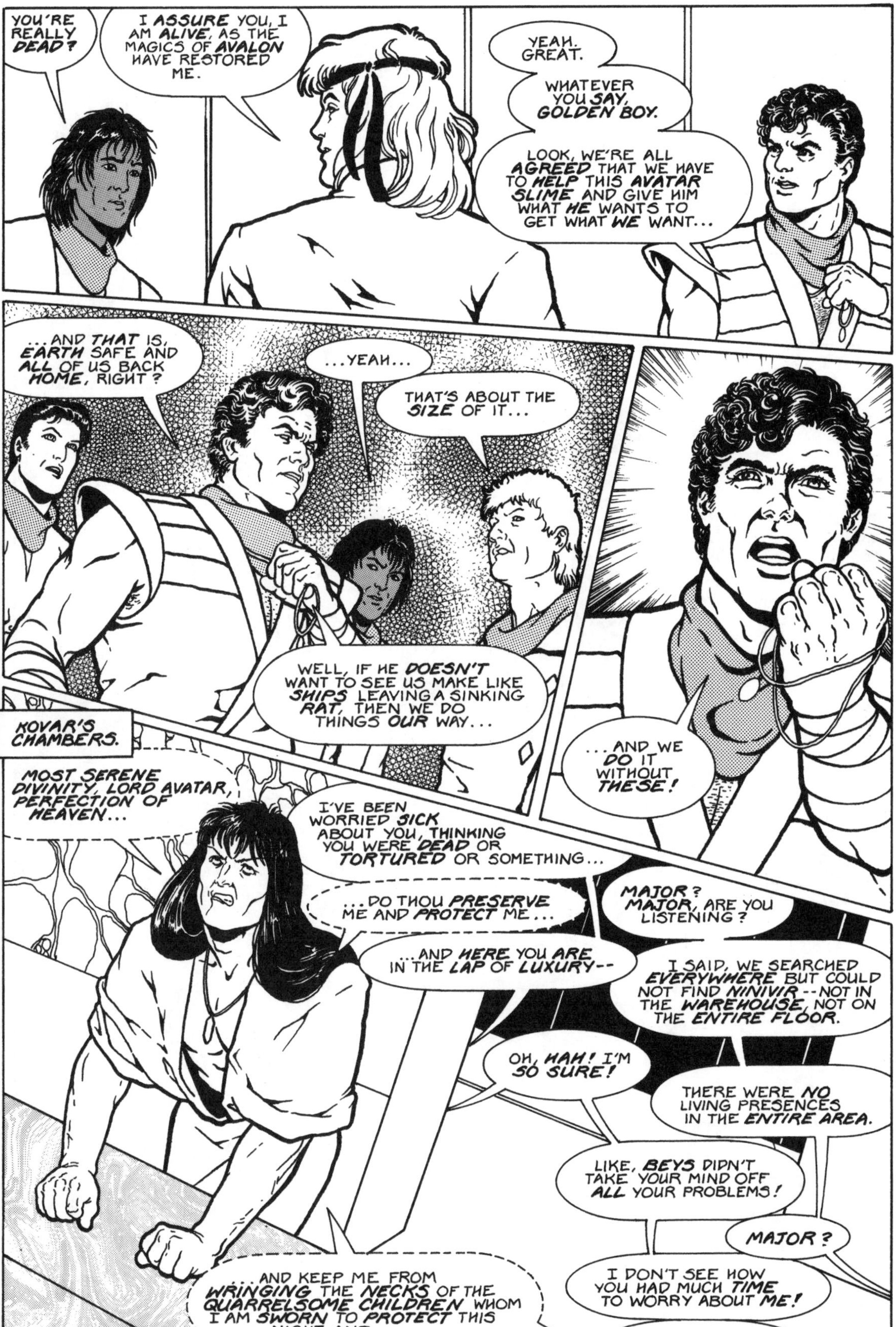
YOU'RE REALLY DEAD?
I ASSURE YOU, I AM ALIVE, AS THE MAGICS OF AVALON HAVE RESTORED ME.
YEAH. GREAT.
WHATEVER YOU SAY, GOLDEN BOY.
LOOK, WE'RE ALL AGREED THAT WE HAVE TO HELP THIS AVATAR SLIME AND GIVE HIM WHAT HE WANTS TO GET WHAT WE WANT...
...AND THAT IS, EARTH SAFE AND ALL OF US BACK HOME, RIGHT?
...YEAH...
THAT'S ABOUT THE SIZE OF IT...
WELL, IF HE DOESN'T WANT TO SEE US MAKE LIKE SHIPS LEAVING A SINKING RAT, THEN WE DO THINGS OUR WAY...
...AND WE DO IT WITHOUT THESE!
KOVAR'S CHAMBERS.
MOST SERENE DIVINITY, LORD AVATAR, PERFECTION OF HEAVEN...
I'VE BEEN WORRIED SICK ABOUT YOU, THINKING YOU WERE DEAD OR TORTURED OR SOMETHING...
...DO THOU PRESERVE ME AND PROTECT ME...
MAJOR? MAJOR, ARE YOU LISTENING?
...AND HERE YOU ARE IN THE LAP OF LUXURY--
I SAID, WE SEARCHED EVERYWHERE BUT COULD NOT FIND NINIVIR--NOT IN THE WAREHOUSE, NOT ON THE ENTIRE FLOOR.
OH, HAH! I'M SO SURE!
THERE WERE NO LIVING PRESENCES IN THE ENTIRE AREA.
LIKE, BEYS DIDN'T TAKE YOUR MIND OFF ALL YOUR PROBLEMS!
MAJOR?
I DON'T SEE HOW YOU HAD MUCH TIME TO WORRY ABOUT ME!
...AND KEEP ME FROM WRINGING THE NECKS OF THE QUARRELSOME CHILDREN WHOM I AM SWORN TO PROTECT THIS NIGHT AND...
...I HEARD YOU, LIEUTENANT.

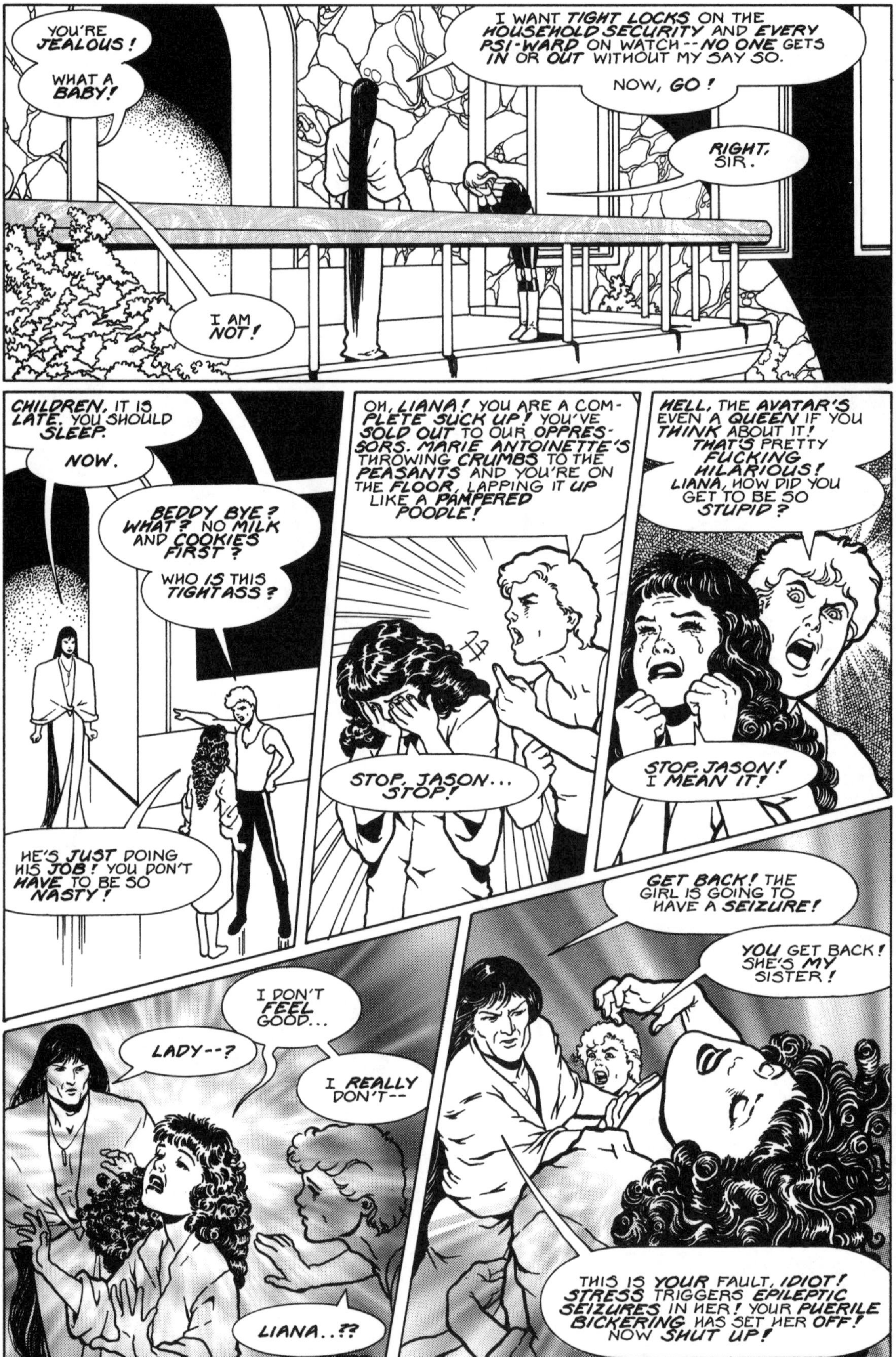

YOU'RE JEALOUS!
WHAT A BABY!
I WANT TIGHT LOCKS ON THE HOUSEHOLD SECURITY AND EVERY PSI-WARD ON WATCH--NO ONE GETS IN OR OUT WITHOUT MY SAY SO.
NOW, GO!
RIGHT, SIR.
I AM NOT!
CHILDREN, IT IS LATE. YOU SHOULD SLEEP.
NOW.
BEDDY BYE? WHAT? NO MILK AND COOKIES FIRST?
WHO IS THIS TIGHTASS?
HE'S JUST DOING HIS JOB! YOU DON'T HAVE TO BE SO NASTY!
OH, LIANA! YOU ARE A COMPLETE SUCK UP! YOU'VE SOLD OUT TO OUR OPPRESSORS. MARIE ANTOINETTE'S THROWING CRUMBS TO THE PEASANTS AND YOU'RE ON THE FLOOR, LAPPING IT UP LIKE A PAMPERED POODLE!
STOP, JASON... STOP!
HELL, THE AVATAR'S EVEN A QUEEN IF YOU THINK ABOUT IT! THAT'S PRETTY FUCKING HILARIOUS! LIANA, HOW DID YOU GET TO BE SO STUPID?
STOP, JASON! I MEAN IT!
LADY--?
I DON'T FEEL GOOD...
I REALLY DON'T--
LIANA..??
GET BACK! THE GIRL IS GOING TO HAVE A SEIZURE!
YOU GET BACK! SHE'S MY SISTER!
THIS IS YOUR FAULT, IDIOT! STRESS TRIGGERS EPILEPTIC SEIZURES IN HER! YOUR PUERILE BICKERING HAS SET HER OFF! NOW SHUT UP!

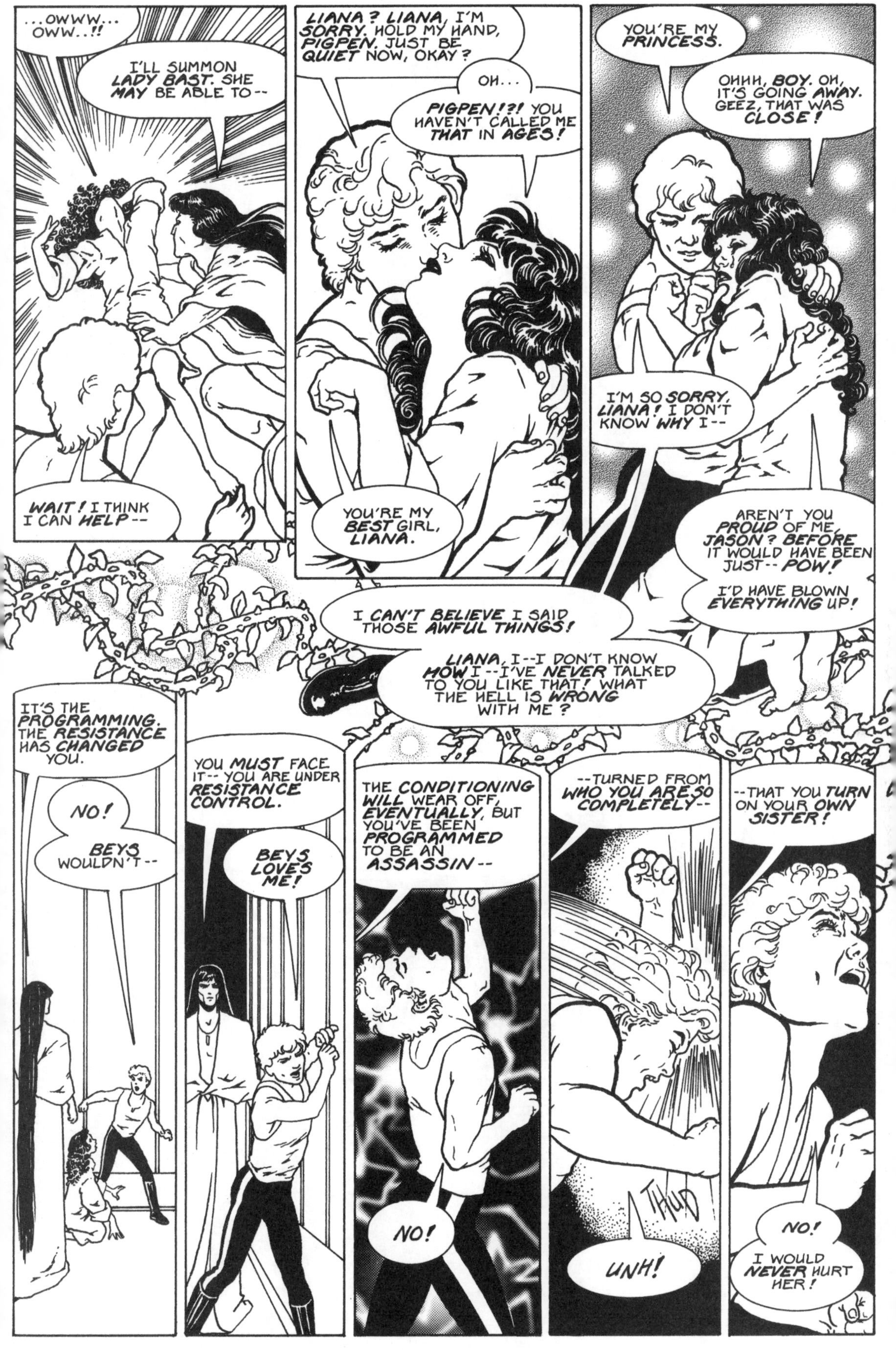
...OWWW... OWW..!!
I'LL SUMMON LADY BAST. SHE MAY BE ABLE TO--
WAIT! I THINK I CAN HELP--
LIANA? LIANA, I'M SORRY. HOLD MY HAND, PIGPEN, JUST BE QUIET NOW, OKAY?
OH...
PIGPEN!?! YOU HAVEN'T CALLED ME THAT IN AGES!
YOU'RE MY BEST GIRL, LIANA.
YOU'RE MY PRINCESS.
OHHH, BOY. OH, IT'S GOING AWAY. GEEZ, THAT WAS CLOSE!
I'M SO SORRY, LIANA! I DON'T KNOW WHY I--
AREN'T YOU PROUD OF ME, JASON? BEFORE IT WOULD HAVE BEEN JUST-- POW!
I'D HAVE BLOWN EVERYTHING UP!
I CAN'T BELIEVE I SAID THOSE AWFUL THINGS!
LIANA, I--I DON'T KNOW HOW I--I'VE NEVER TALKED TO YOU LIKE THAT! WHAT THE HELL IS WRONG WITH ME?
IT'S THE PROGRAMMING. THE RESISTANCE HAS CHANGED YOU.
NO!
BEYS WOULDN'T--
YOU MUST FACE IT-- YOU ARE UNDER RESISTANCE CONTROL.
BEYS LOVES ME!
THE CONDITIONING WILL WEAR OFF, EVENTUALLY, BUT YOU'VE BEEN PROGRAMMED TO BE AN ASSASSIN--
NO!
--TURNED FROM WHO YOU ARE SO COMPLETELY--
THUD
UNH!
--THAT YOU TURN ON YOUR OWN SISTER!
NO!
I WOULD NEVER HURT HER!

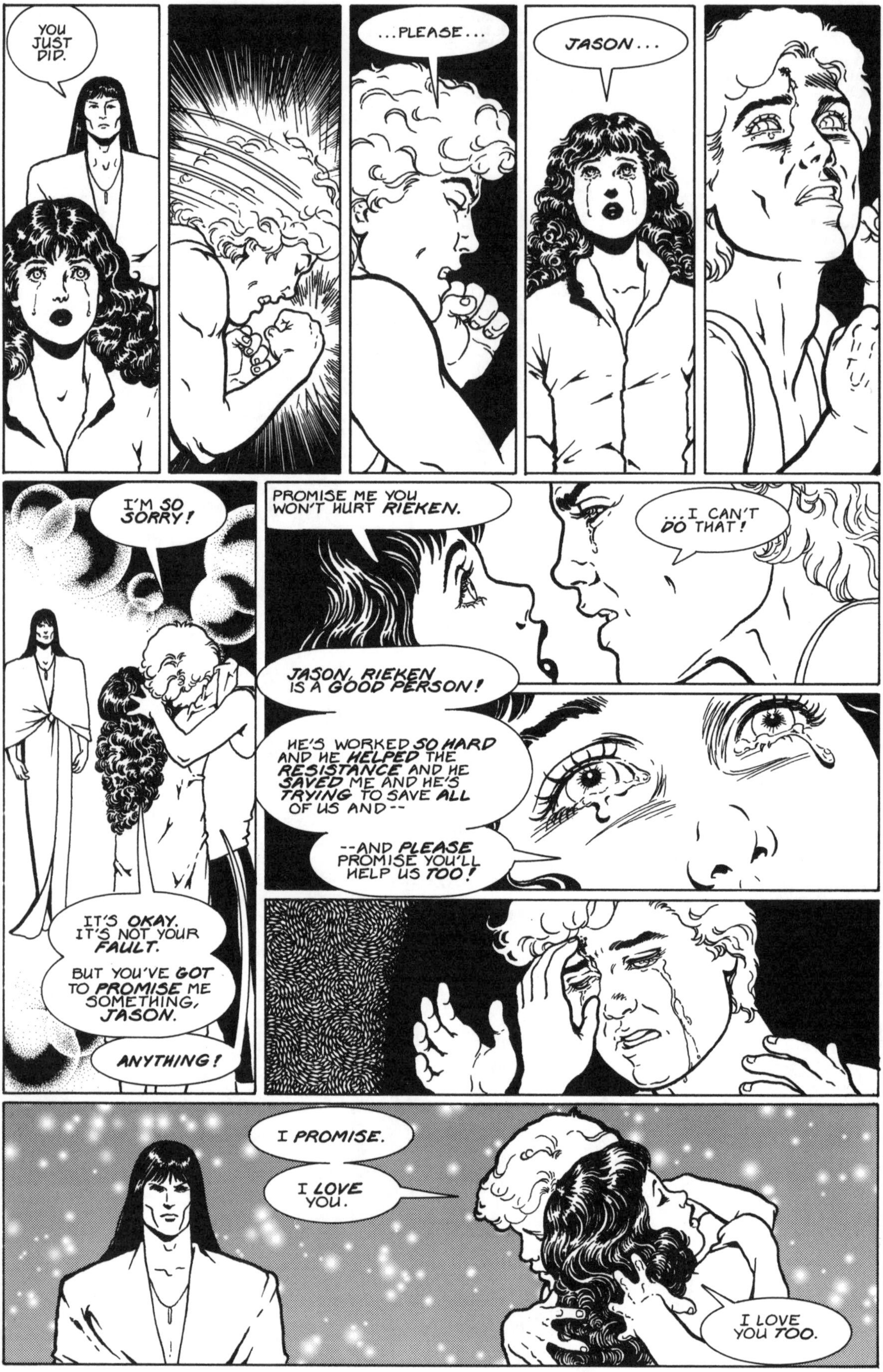
YOU JUST DID.
...PLEASE...
JASON...
I'M SO SORRY!
IT'S OKAY. IT'S NOT YOUR FAULT.
BUT YOU'VE GOT TO PROMISE ME SOMETHING, JASON.
ANYTHING!
PROMISE ME YOU WON'T HURT RIEKEN.
...I CAN'T DO THAT!
JASON, RIEKEN IS A GOOD PERSON!
HE'S WORKED SO HARD AND HE HELPED THE RESISTANCE AND HE SAVED ME AND HE'S TRYING TO SAVE ALL OF US AND --
--AND PLEASE PROMISE YOU'LL HELP US TOO!
I PROMISE.
I LOVE YOU.
I LOVE YOU TOO.

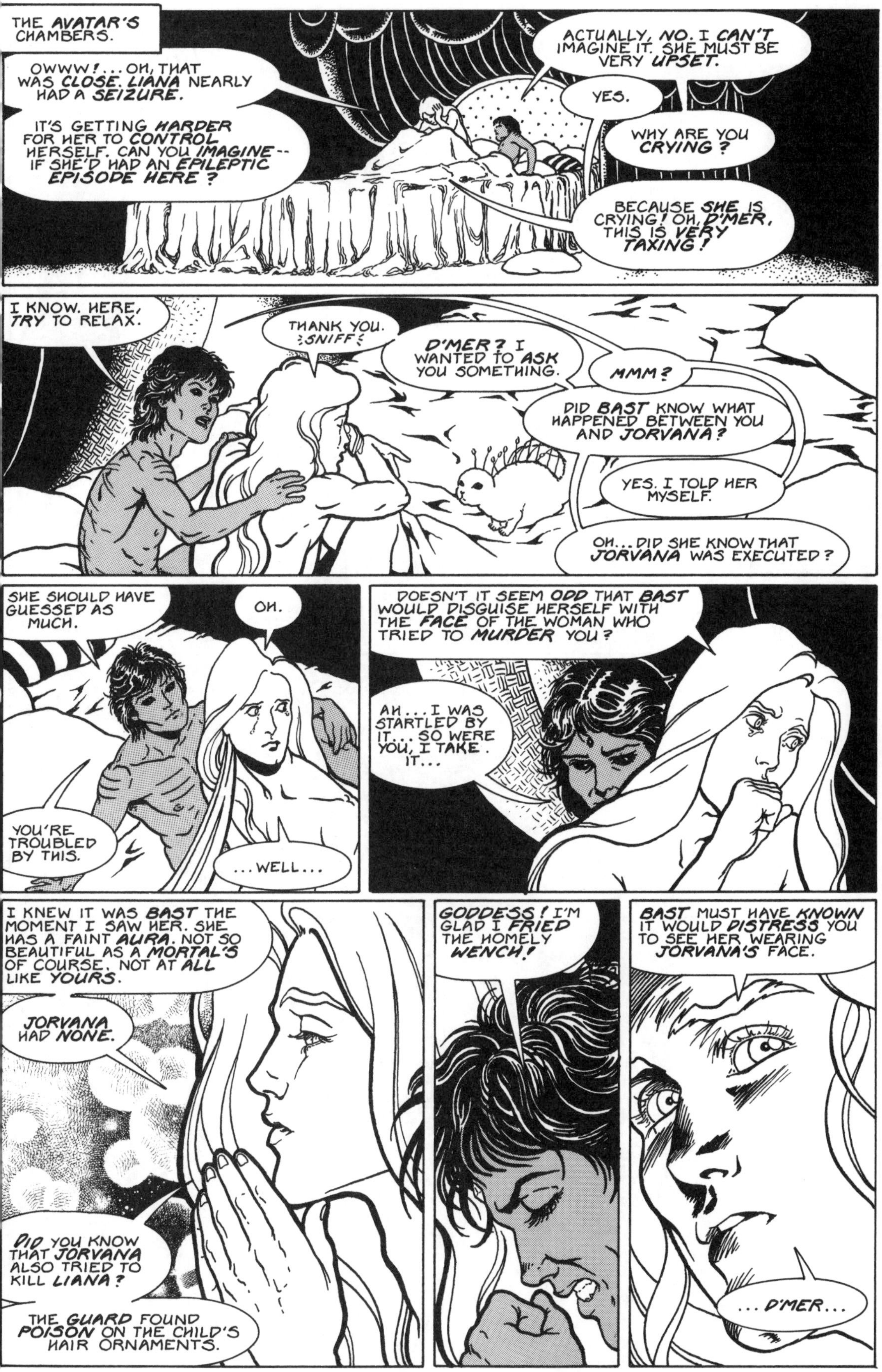
THE AVATAR'S CHAMBERS.
OWWW!... OH, THAT WAS CLOSE. LIANA NEARLY HAD A SEIZURE.
IT'S GETTING HARDER FOR HER TO CONTROL HERSELF. CAN YOU IMAGINE -- IF SHE'D HAD AN EPILEPTIC EPISODE HERE?
ACTUALLY, NO. I CAN'T IMAGINE IT. SHE MUST BE VERY UPSET.
YES.
WHY ARE YOU CRYING?
BECAUSE SHE IS CRYING! OH, D'MER, THIS IS VERY TAXING!
I KNOW. HERE, TRY TO RELAX.
THANK YOU. SNIFF
D'MER? I WANTED TO ASK YOU SOMETHING.
MMM?
DID BAST KNOW WHAT HAPPENED BETWEEN YOU AND JORVANA?
YES. I TOLD HER MYSELF.
OH... DID SHE KNOW THAT JORVANA WAS EXECUTED?
SHE SHOULD HAVE GUESSED AS MUCH.
OH.
YOU'RE TROUBLED BY THIS.
...WELL...
DOESN'T IT SEEM ODD THAT BAST WOULD DISGUISE HERSELF WITH THE FACE OF THE WOMAN WHO TRIED TO MURDER YOU?
AH... I WAS STARTLED BY IT... SO WERE YOU, I TAKE IT...
I KNEW IT WAS BAST THE MOMENT I SAW HER. SHE HAS A FAINT AURA. NOT SO BEAUTIFUL AS A MORTAL'S OF COURSE. NOT AT ALL LIKE YOURS.
JORVANA HAD NONE.
DID YOU KNOW THAT JORVANA ALSO TRIED TO KILL LIANA?
THE GUARD FOUND POISON ON THE CHILD'S HAIR ORNAMENTS.
GODDESS! I'M GLAD I FRIED THE HOMELY WENCH!
BAST MUST HAVE KNOWN IT WOULD DISTRESS YOU TO SEE HER WEARING JORVANA'S FACE.
...D'MER...

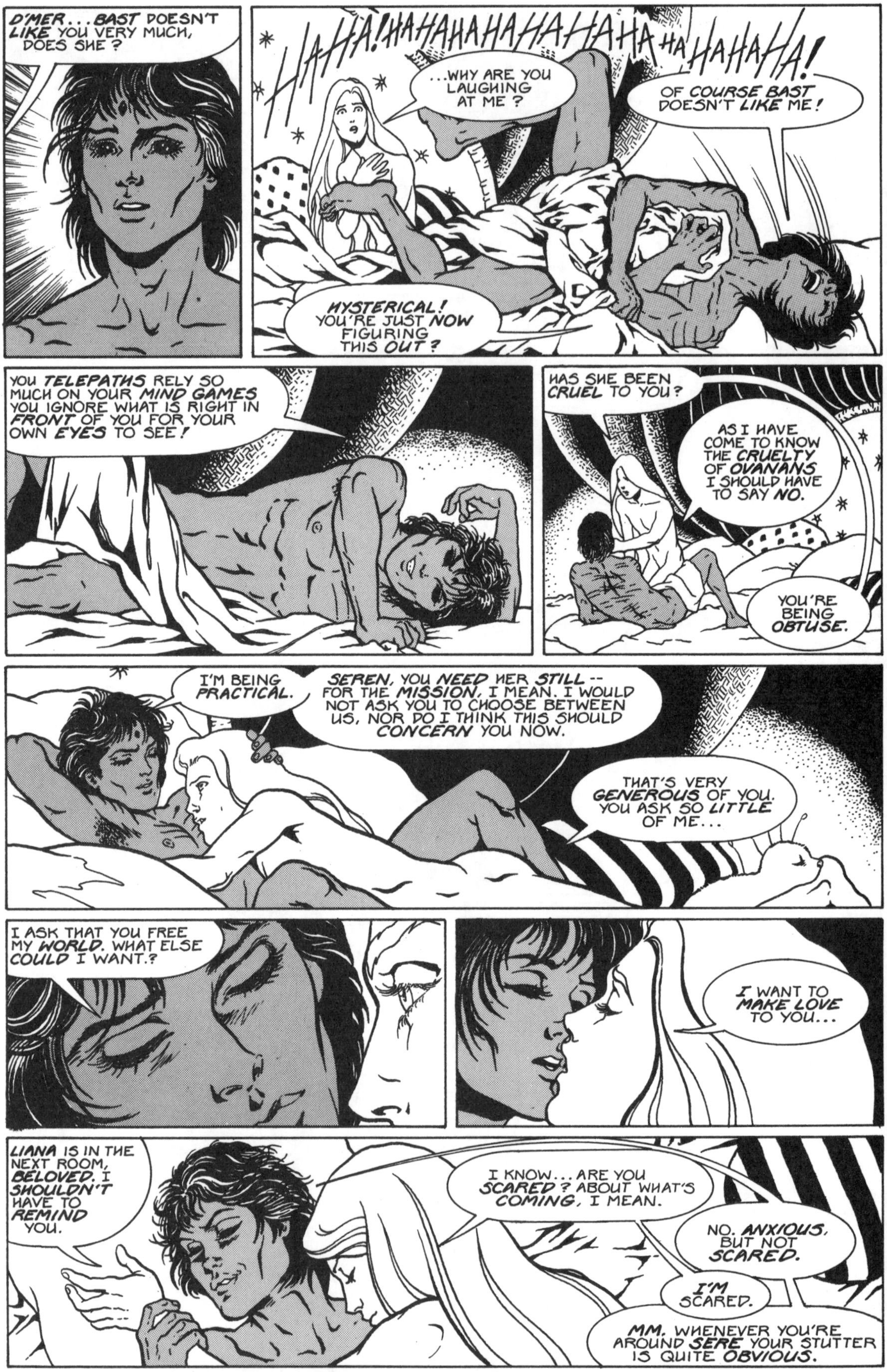
D'MER...BAST DOESN'T LIKE YOU VERY MUCH, DOES SHE?
HA HA! HAHAHAHAHAHAHAHAHA HA HAHAHA!
...WHY ARE YOU LAUGHING AT ME?
OF COURSE BAST DOESN'T LIKE ME!
HYSTERICAL! YOU'RE JUST NOW FIGURING THIS OUT?
YOU TELEPATHS RELY SO MUCH ON YOUR MIND GAMES YOU IGNORE WHAT IS RIGHT IN FRONT OF YOU FOR YOUR OWN EYES TO SEE!
HAS SHE BEEN CRUEL TO YOU?
AS I HAVE COME TO KNOW THE CRUELTY OF OVANANS I SHOULD HAVE TO SAY NO.
YOU'RE BEING OBTUSE.
I'M BEING PRACTICAL.
SEREN, YOU NEED HER STILL -- FOR THE MISSION, I MEAN. I WOULD NOT ASK YOU TO CHOOSE BETWEEN US, NOR DO I THINK THIS SHOULD CONCERN YOU NOW.
THAT'S VERY GENEROUS OF YOU. YOU ASK SO LITTLE OF ME...
I ASK THAT YOU FREE MY WORLD. WHAT ELSE COULD I WANT.?
I WANT TO MAKE LOVE TO YOU...
LIANA IS IN THE NEXT ROOM, BELOVED. I SHOULDN'T HAVE TO REMIND YOU.
I KNOW... ARE YOU SCARED? ABOUT WHAT'S COMING, I MEAN.
NO. ANXIOUS, BUT NOT SCARED.
I'M SCARED.
MM. WHENEVER YOU'RE AROUND SERE YOUR STUTTER IS QUITE OBVIOUS.

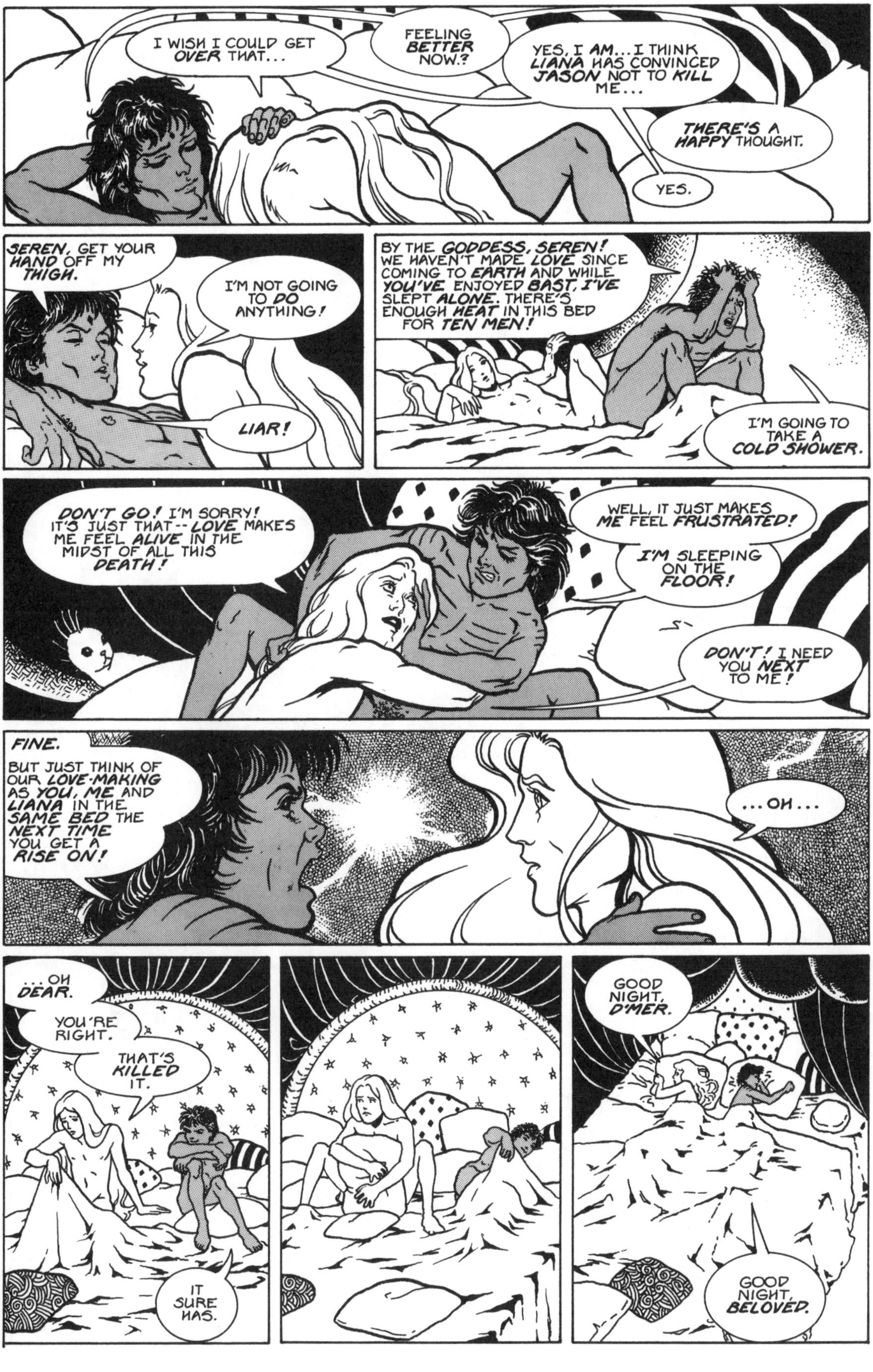
I WISH I COULD GET OVER THAT...
FEELING BETTER NOW.?
YES, I AM... I THINK LIANA HAS CONVINCED JASON NOT TO KILL ME...
THERE'S A HAPPY THOUGHT.
YES.
SEREN, GET YOUR HAND OFF MY THIGH.
I'M NOT GOING TO DO ANYTHING!
LIAR!
BY THE GODDESS, SEREN! WE HAVEN'T MADE LOVE SINCE COMING TO EARTH AND WHILE YOU'VE ENJOYED BAST, I'VE SLEPT ALONE. THERE'S ENOUGH HEAT IN THIS BED FOR TEN MEN!
I'M GOING TO TAKE A COLD SHOWER.
DON'T GO! I'M SORRY! IT'S JUST THAT--LOVE MAKES ME FEEL ALIVE IN THE MIDST OF ALL THIS DEATH!
WELL, IT JUST MAKES ME FEEL FRUSTRATED!
I'M SLEEPING ON THE FLOOR!
DON'T! I NEED YOU NEXT TO ME!
FINE.
BUT JUST THINK OF OUR LOVE-MAKING AS YOU, ME AND LIANA IN THE SAME BED THE NEXT TIME YOU GET A RISE ON!
...OH...
...OH DEAR.
YOU'RE RIGHT.
THAT'S KILLED IT.
IT SURE HAS.
GOOD NIGHT, D'MER.
GOOD NIGHT, BELOVED.

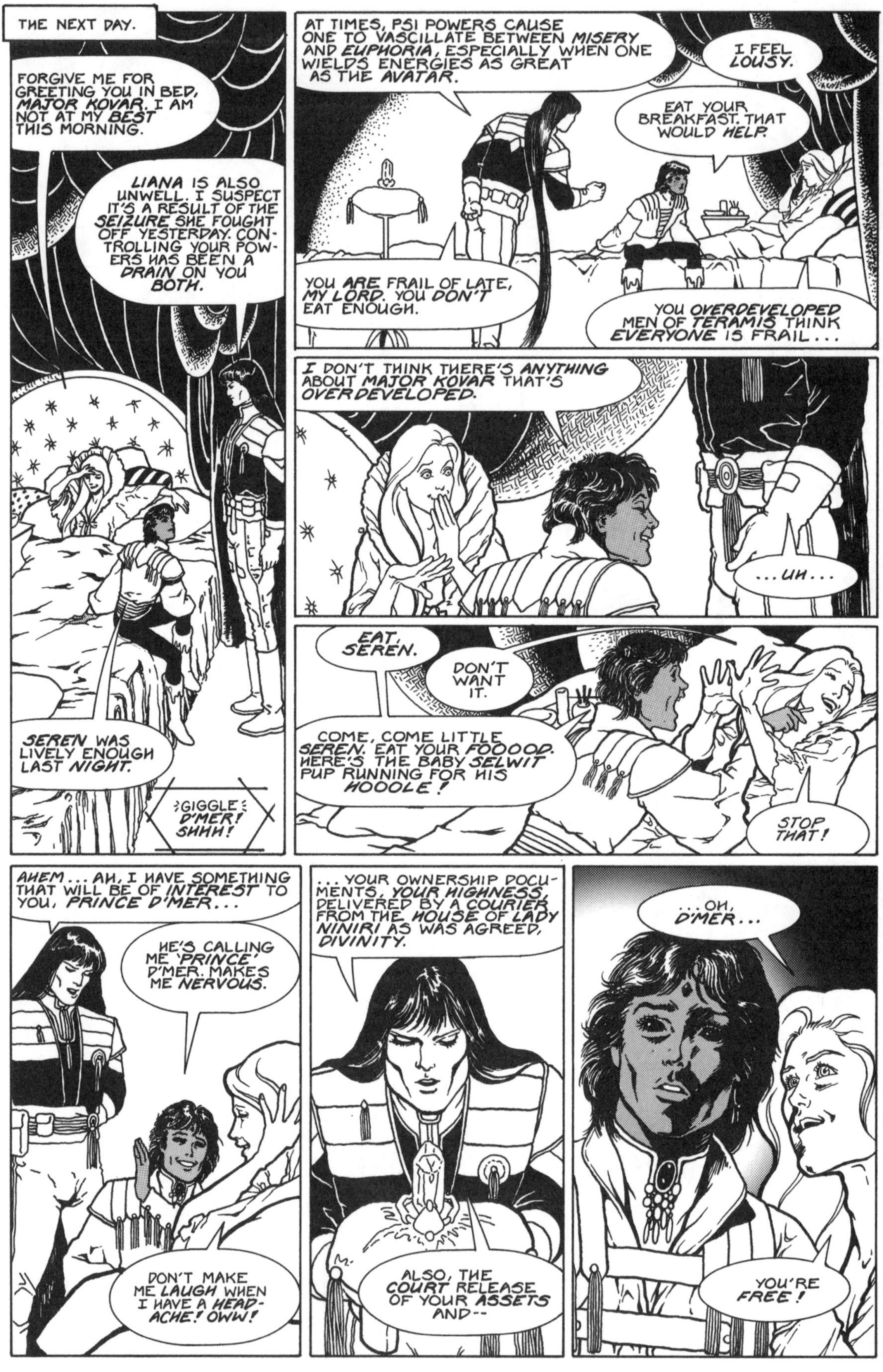
THE NEXT DAY.
FORGIVE ME FOR GREETING YOU IN BED, MAJOR KOVAR. I AM NOT AT MY BEST THIS MORNING.
LIANA IS ALSO UNWELL. I SUSPECT IT'S A RESULT OF THE SEIZURE SHE FOUGHT OFF YESTERDAY. CONTROLLING YOUR POWERS HAS BEEN A DRAIN ON YOU BOTH.
SEREN WAS LIVELY ENOUGH LAST NIGHT.
GIGGLE D'MER! SHHH!
AT TIMES, PSI POWERS CAUSE ONE TO VASCILLATE BETWEEN MISERY AND EUPHORIA, ESPECIALLY WHEN ONE WIELDS ENERGIES AS GREAT AS THE AVATAR.
I FEEL LOUSY.
EAT YOUR BREAKFAST. THAT WOULD HELP.
YOU ARE FRAIL OF LATE, MY LORD. YOU DON'T EAT ENOUGH.
YOU OVERDEVELOPED MEN OF TERAMIS THINK EVERYONE IS FRAIL...
I DON'T THINK THERE'S ANYTHING ABOUT MAJOR KOVAR THAT'S OVERDEVELOPED.
...UH...
EAT, SEREN.
DON'T WANT IT.
COME, COME LITTLE SEREN. EAT YOUR FOOOOD. HERE'S THE BABY SELWIT PUP RUNNING FOR HIS HOOOLE!
STOP THAT!
AHEM... AH, I HAVE SOMETHING THAT WILL BE OF INTEREST TO YOU, PRINCE D'MER...
HE'S CALLING ME 'PRINCE' D'MER. MAKES ME NERVOUS.
DON'T MAKE ME LAUGH WHEN I HAVE A HEAD-ACHE! OWW!
...YOUR OWNERSHIP DOCUMENTS, YOUR HIGHNESS, DELIVERED BY A COURIER FROM THE HOUSE OF LADY NINIRI AS WAS AGREED, DIVINITY.
ALSO, THE COURT RELEASE OF YOUR ASSETS AND--
...OH, D'MER...
YOU'RE FREE!

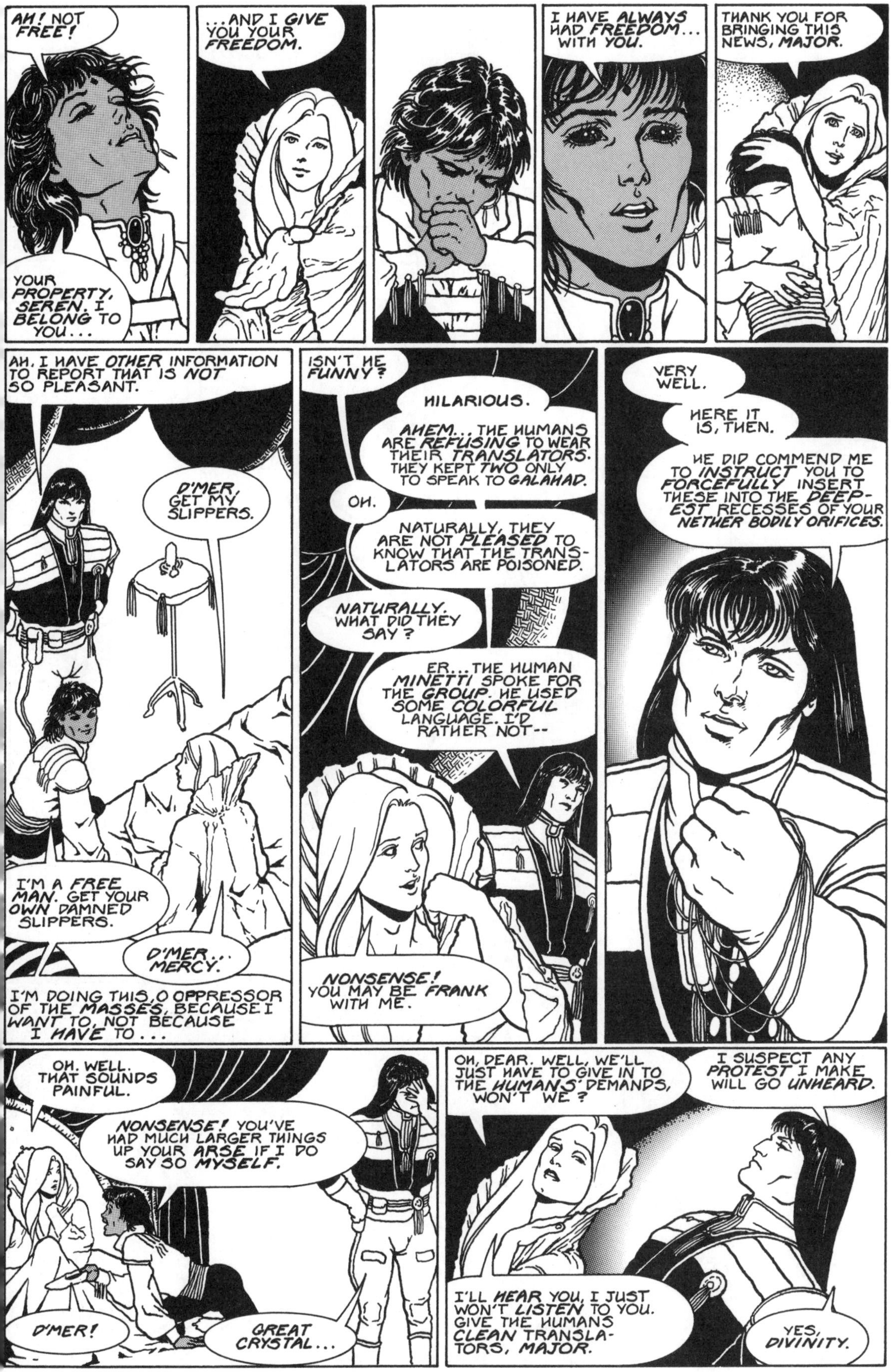
AH! NOT FREE!
YOUR PROPERTY, SEREN. I BELONG TO YOU...
...AND I GIVE YOU YOUR FREEDOM.
I HAVE ALWAYS HAD FREEDOM... WITH YOU.
THANK YOU FOR BRINGING THIS NEWS, MAJOR.
AH. I HAVE OTHER INFORMATION TO REPORT THAT IS NOT SO PLEASANT.
D'MER, GET MY SLIPPERS.
I'M A FREE MAN. GET YOUR OWN DAMNED SLIPPERS.
D'MER... MERCY.
I'M DOING THIS, O OPPRESSOR OF THE MASSES, BECAUSE I WANT TO, NOT BECAUSE I HAVE TO...
ISN'T HE FUNNY?
HILARIOUS.
AHEM... THE HUMANS ARE REFUSING TO WEAR THEIR TRANSLATORS. THEY KEPT TWO ONLY TO SPEAK TO GALAHAD.
OH.
NATURALLY, THEY ARE NOT PLEASED TO KNOW THAT THE TRANSLATORS ARE POISONED.
NATURALLY. WHAT DID THEY SAY?
ER... THE HUMAN MINETTI SPOKE FOR THE GROUP. HE USED SOME COLORFUL LANGUAGE. I'D RATHER NOT--
NONSENSE! YOU MAY BE FRANK WITH ME.
VERY WELL.
HERE IT IS, THEN.
HE DID COMMEND ME TO INSTRUCT YOU TO FORCEFULLY INSERT THESE INTO THE DEEPEST RECESSES OF YOUR NETHER BODILY ORIFICES.
OH. WELL. THAT SOUNDS PAINFUL.
NONSENSE! YOU'VE HAD MUCH LARGER THINGS UP YOUR ARSE IF I DO SAY SO MYSELF.
D'MER!
GREAT CRYSTAL...
OH, DEAR. WELL, WE'LL JUST HAVE TO GIVE IN TO THE HUMANS' DEMANDS, WON'T WE?
I SUSPECT ANY PROTEST I MAKE WILL GO UNHEARD.
I'LL HEAR YOU, I JUST WON'T LISTEN TO YOU. GIVE THE HUMANS CLEAN TRANSLATORS, MAJOR.
YES, DIVINITY.

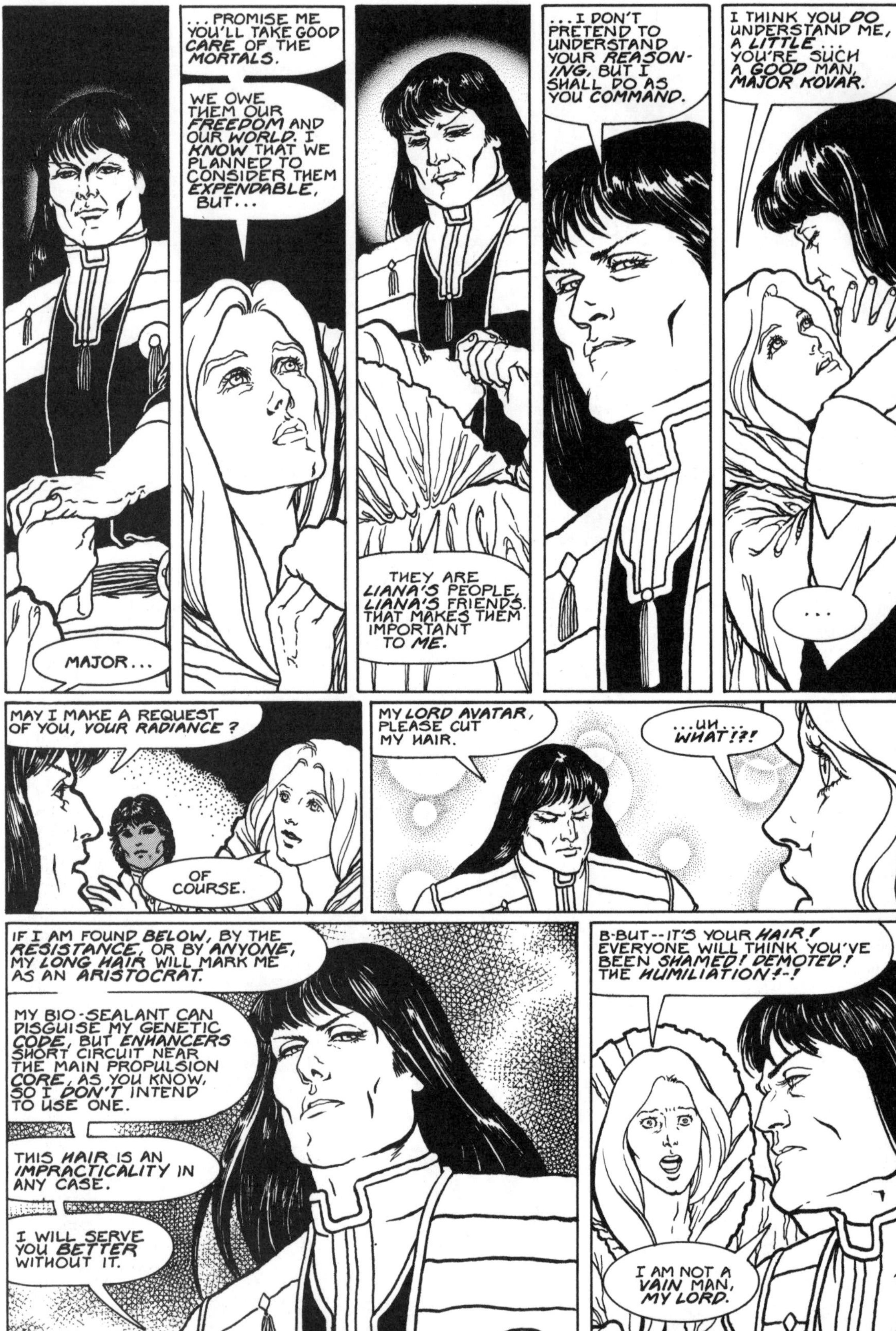
MAJOR...
...PROMISE ME YOU'LL TAKE GOOD CARE OF THE MORTALS.
WE OWE THEM OUR FREEDOM AND OUR WORLD. I KNOW THAT WE PLANNED TO CONSIDER THEM EXPENDABLE, BUT...
THEY ARE LIANA'S PEOPLE, LIANA'S FRIENDS. THAT MAKES THEM IMPORTANT TO ME.
...I DON'T PRETEND TO UNDERSTAND YOUR REASONING, BUT I SHALL DO AS YOU COMMAND.
I THINK YOU DO UNDERSTAND ME, A LITTLE... YOU'RE SUCH A GOOD MAN, MAJOR KOVAR.
...
MAY I MAKE A REQUEST OF YOU, YOUR RADIANCE?
OF COURSE.
MY LORD AVATAR, PLEASE CUT MY HAIR.
...UH... WHAT!?!
IF I AM FOUND BELOW, BY THE RESISTANCE, OR BY ANYONE, MY LONG HAIR WILL MARK ME AS AN ARISTOCRAT.
MY BIO-SEALANT CAN DISGUISE MY GENETIC CODE, BUT ENHANCERS SHORT CIRCUIT NEAR THE MAIN PROPULSION CORE, AS YOU KNOW, SO I DON'T INTEND TO USE ONE.
THIS HAIR IS AN IMPRACTICALITY IN ANY CASE.
I WILL SERVE YOU BETTER WITHOUT IT.
B-BUT--IT'S YOUR HAIR! EVERYONE WILL THINK YOU'VE BEEN SHAMED! DEMOTED! THE HUMILIATION!-!
I AM NOT A VAIN MAN, MY LORD.

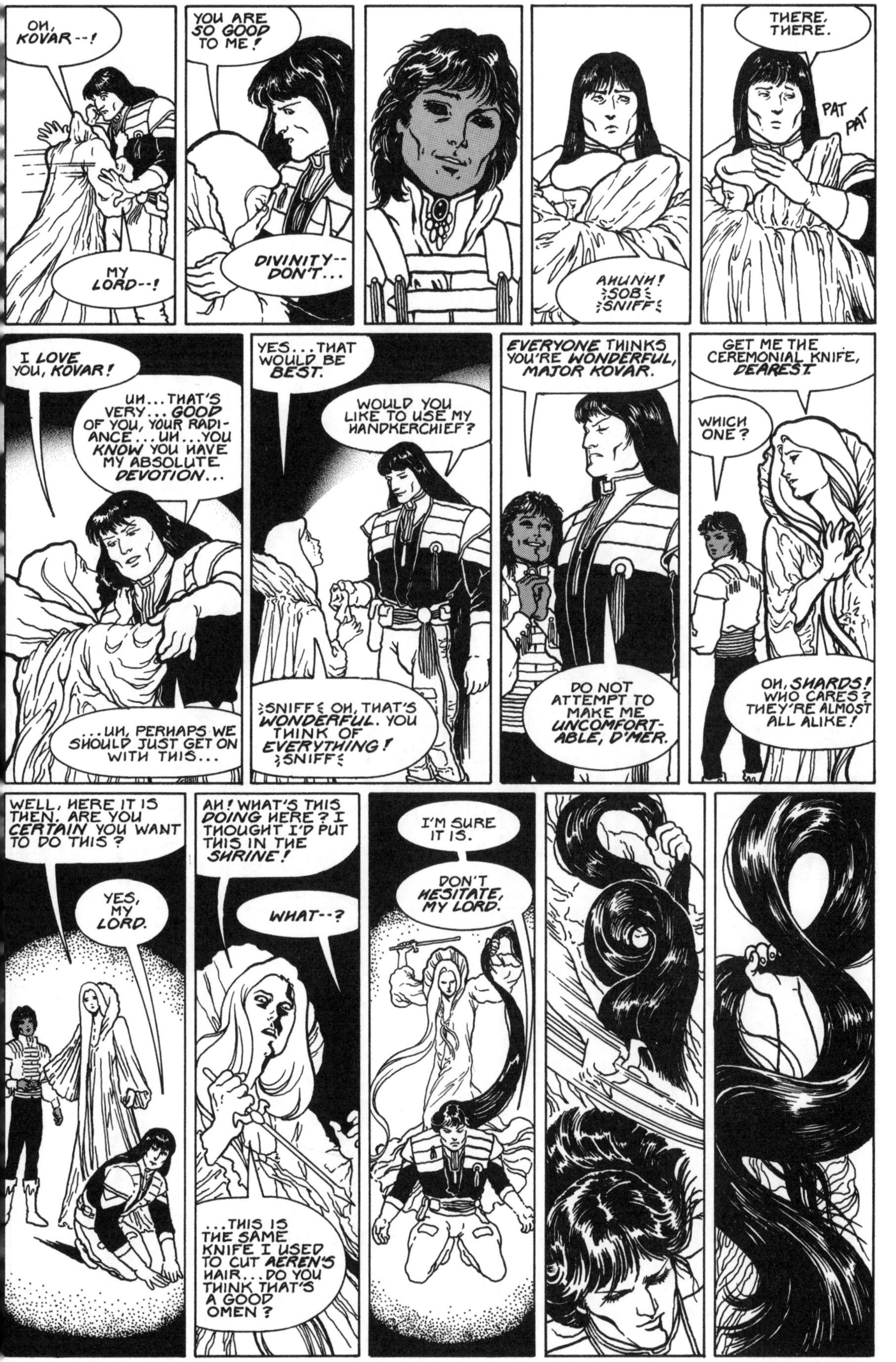
OH, KOVAR--!
MY LORD--!
YOU ARE SO GOOD TO ME!
DIVINITY-- DON'T...
AHUNH! SOB SNIFF
THERE, THERE.
PAT PAT
I LOVE YOU, KOVAR!
UH... THAT'S VERY... GOOD OF YOU, YOUR RADI-ANCE... UH... YOU KNOW YOU HAVE MY ABSOLUTE DEVOTION...
...UH, PERHAPS WE SHOULD JUST GET ON WITH THIS...
YES... THAT WOULD BE BEST.
WOULD YOU LIKE TO USE MY HANDKERCHIEF?
SNIFF OH, THAT'S WONDERFUL. YOU THINK OF EVERYTHING! SNIFF
EVERYONE THINKS YOU'RE WONDERFUL, MAJOR KOVAR.
DO NOT ATTEMPT TO MAKE ME UNCOMFORT-ABLE, D'MER.
GET ME THE CEREMONIAL KNIFE, DEAREST.
WHICH ONE?
OH, SHARDS! WHO CARES? THEY'RE ALMOST ALL ALIKE!
WELL, HERE IT IS THEN. ARE YOU CERTAIN YOU WANT TO DO THIS?
YES, MY LORD.
AH! WHAT'S THIS DOING HERE? I THOUGHT I'D PUT THIS IN THE SHRINE!
WHAT--?
...THIS IS THE SAME KNIFE I USED TO CUT AEREN'S HAIR... DO YOU THINK THAT'S A GOOD OMEN?
I'M SURE IT IS.
DON'T HESITATE, MY LORD.

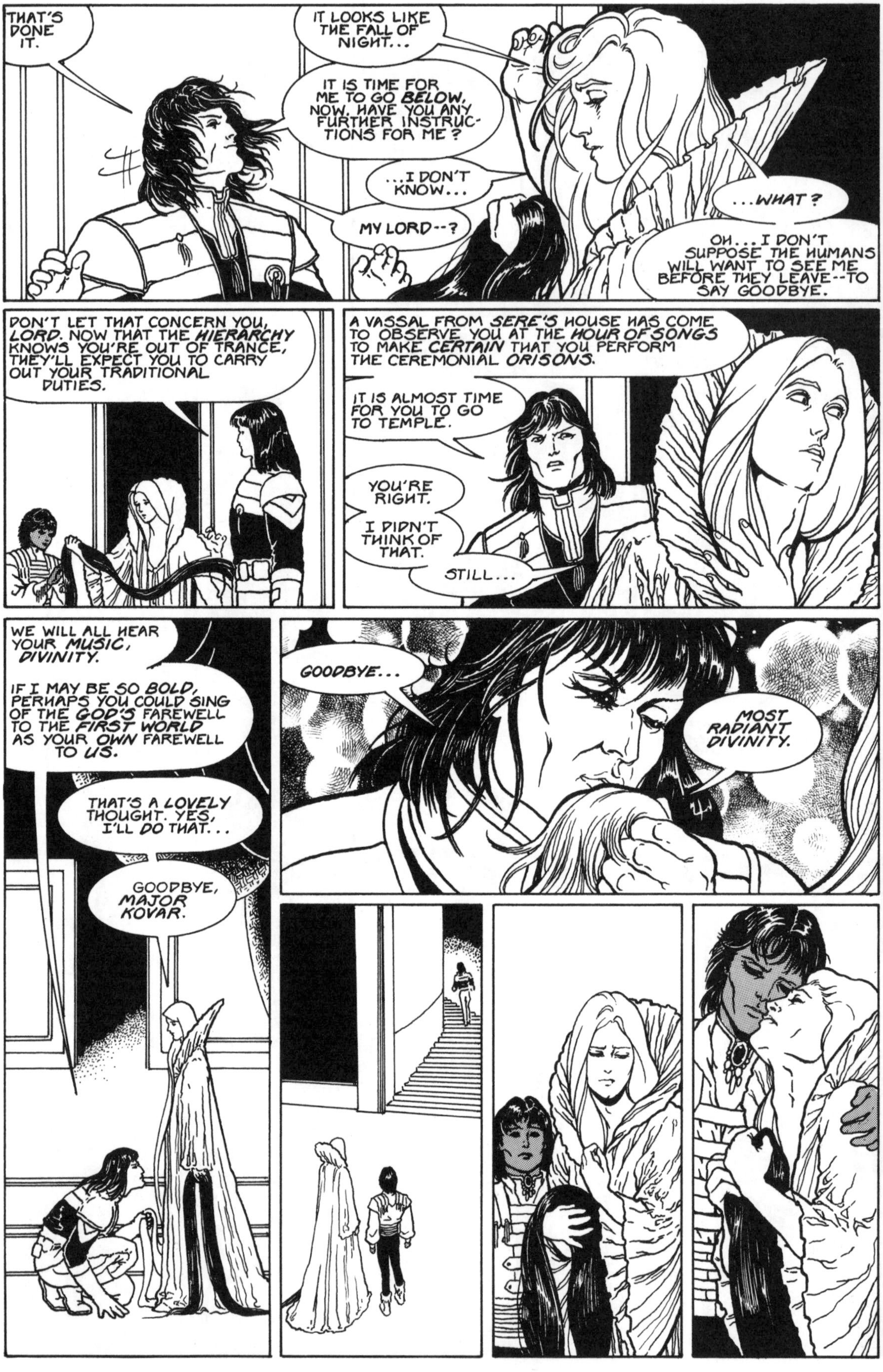
THAT'S DONE IT.
IT LOOKS LIKE THE FALL OF NIGHT...
IT IS TIME FOR ME TO GO BELOW. NOW, HAVE YOU ANY FURTHER INSTRUCTIONS FOR ME?
...I DON'T KNOW...
MY LORD--?
...WHAT?
OH... I DON'T SUPPOSE THE HUMANS WILL WANT TO SEE ME BEFORE THEY LEAVE--TO SAY GOODBYE.
DON'T LET THAT CONCERN YOU, LORD. NOW THAT THE HIERARCHY KNOWS YOU'RE OUT OF TRANCE, THEY'LL EXPECT YOU TO CARRY OUT YOUR TRADITIONAL DUTIES.
A VASSAL FROM SERE'S HOUSE HAS COME TO OBSERVE YOU AT THE HOUR OF SONGS TO MAKE CERTAIN THAT YOU PERFORM THE CEREMONIAL ORISONS.
IT IS ALMOST TIME FOR YOU TO GO TO TEMPLE.
YOU'RE RIGHT.
I DIDN'T THINK OF THAT.
STILL...
WE WILL ALL HEAR YOUR MUSIC, DIVINITY.
IF I MAY BE SO BOLD, PERHAPS YOU COULD SING OF THE GOD'S FAREWELL TO THE FIRST WORLD AS YOUR OWN FAREWELL TO US.
THAT'S A LOVELY THOUGHT. YES, I'LL DO THAT...
GOODBYE, MAJOR KOVAR.
GOODBYE...
MOST RADIANT DIVINITY.

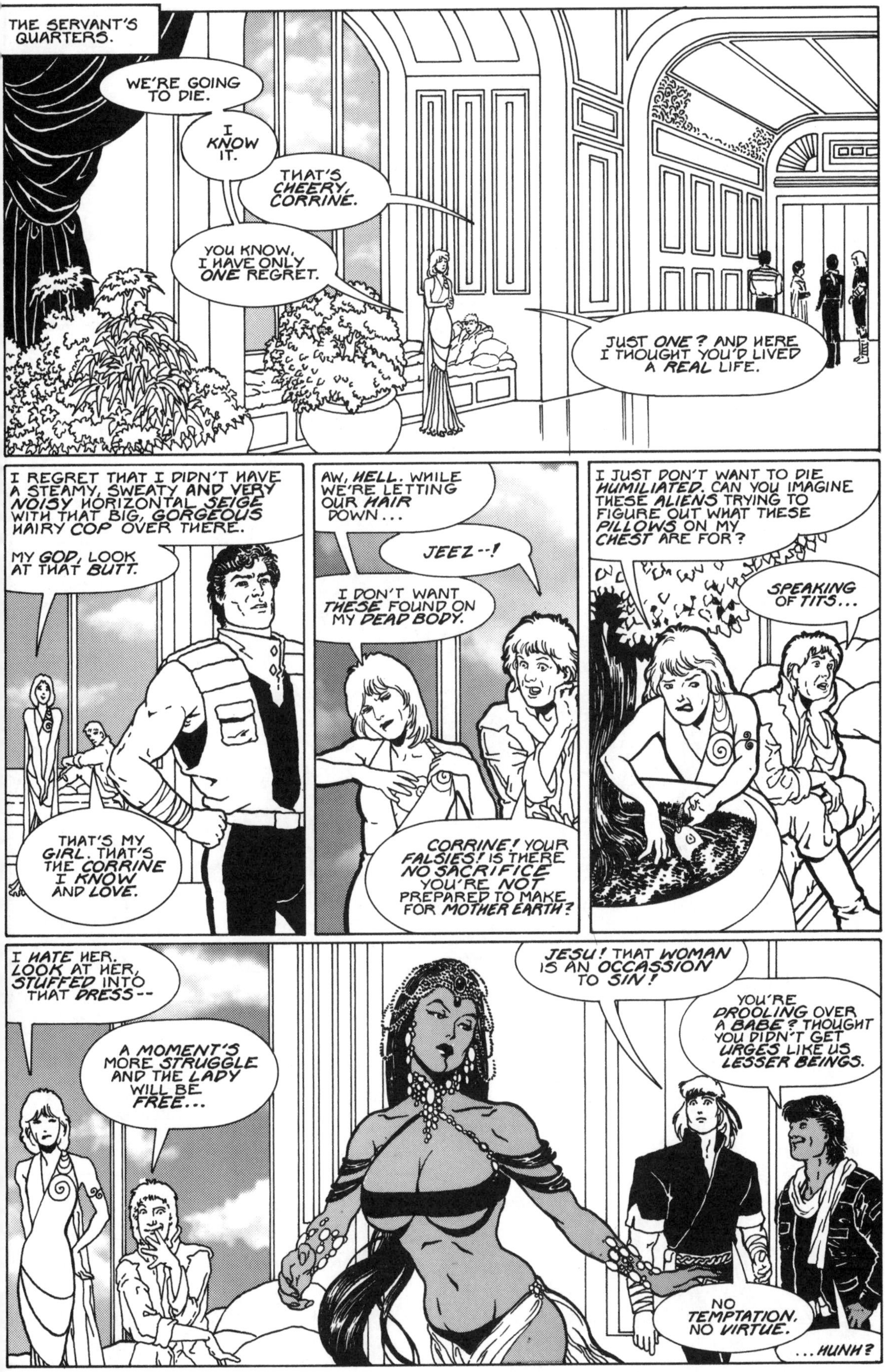
THE SERVANT'S QUARTERS.
WE'RE GOING TO DIE.
I KNOW IT.
THAT'S CHEERY, CORRINE.
YOU KNOW, I HAVE ONLY ONE REGRET.
JUST ONE? AND HERE I THOUGHT YOU'D LIVED A REAL LIFE.
I REGRET THAT I DIDN'T HAVE A STEAMY, SWEATY AND VERY NOISY HORIZONTAL SEIGE WITH THAT BIG, GORGEOUS HAIRY COP OVER THERE.
MY GOD, LOOK AT THAT BUTT.
THAT'S MY GIRL. THAT'S THE CORRINE I KNOW AND LOVE.
AW, HELL. WHILE WE'RE LETTING OUR HAIR DOWN...
JEEZ--!
I DON'T WANT THESE FOUND ON MY DEAD BODY.
CORRINE! YOUR FALSIES! IS THERE NO SACRIFICE YOU'RE NOT PREPARED TO MAKE FOR MOTHER EARTH?
I JUST DON'T WANT TO DIE HUMILIATED. CAN YOU IMAGINE THESE ALIENS TRYING TO FIGURE OUT WHAT THESE PILLOWS ON MY CHEST ARE FOR?
SPEAKING OF TITS...
I HATE HER. LOOK AT HER, STUFFED INTO THAT DRESS--
A MOMENT'S MORE STRUGGLE AND THE LADY WILL BE FREE...
JESU! THAT WOMAN IS AN OCCASSION TO SIN!
YOU'RE DROOLING OVER A BABE? THOUGHT YOU DIDN'T GET URGES LIKE US LESSER BEINGS.
NO TEMPTATION, NO VIRTUE.
...HUNH?

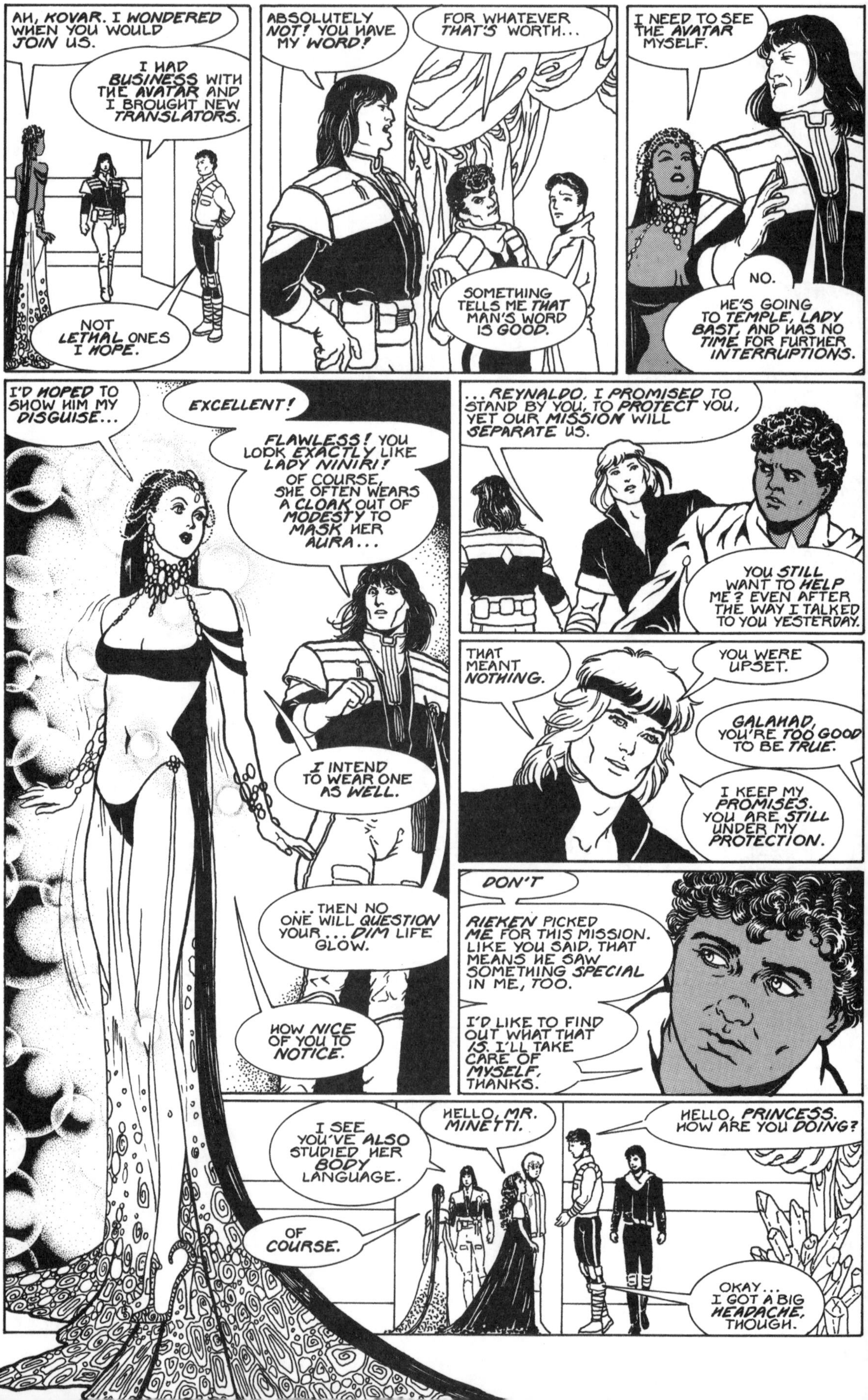
AH, KOVAR. I WONDERED WHEN YOU WOULD JOIN US.
I HAD BUSINESS WITH THE AVATAR AND I BROUGHT NEW TRANSLATORS.
NOT LETHAL ONES I HOPE.
ABSOLUTELY NOT! YOU HAVE MY WORD!
FOR WHATEVER THAT'S WORTH...
SOMETHING TELLS ME THAT MAN'S WORD IS GOOD.
I NEED TO SEE THE AVATAR MYSELF.
NO.
HE'S GOING TO TEMPLE, LADY BAST, AND HAS NO TIME FOR FURTHER INTERRUPTIONS.
I'D HOPED TO SHOW HIM MY DISGUISE...
EXCELLENT!
FLAWLESS! YOU LOOK EXACTLY LIKE LADY NINIRI! OF COURSE, SHE OFTEN WEARS A CLOAK OUT OF MODESTY TO MASK HER AURA...
I INTEND TO WEAR ONE AS WELL.
...THEN NO ONE WILL QUESTION YOUR... DIM LIFE GLOW.
HOW NICE OF YOU TO NOTICE.
...REYNALDO, I PROMISED TO STAND BY YOU, TO PROTECT YOU, YET OUR MISSION WILL SEPARATE US.
YOU STILL WANT TO HELP ME? EVEN AFTER THE WAY I TALKED TO YOU YESTERDAY.
THAT MEANT NOTHING.
YOU WERE UPSET.
GALAHAD, YOU'RE TOO GOOD TO BE TRUE.
I KEEP MY PROMISES. YOU ARE STILL UNDER MY PROTECTION.
DON'T
RIEKEN PICKED ME FOR THIS MISSION. LIKE YOU SAID, THAT MEANS HE SAW SOMETHING SPECIAL IN ME, TOO.
I'D LIKE TO FIND OUT WHAT THAT IS. I'LL TAKE CARE OF MYSELF, THANKS.
I SEE YOU'VE ALSO STUDIED HER BODY LANGUAGE.
OF COURSE.
HELLO, MR. MINETTI.
HELLO, PRINCESS. HOW ARE YOU DOING?
OKAY... I GOT A BIG HEADACHE, THOUGH.

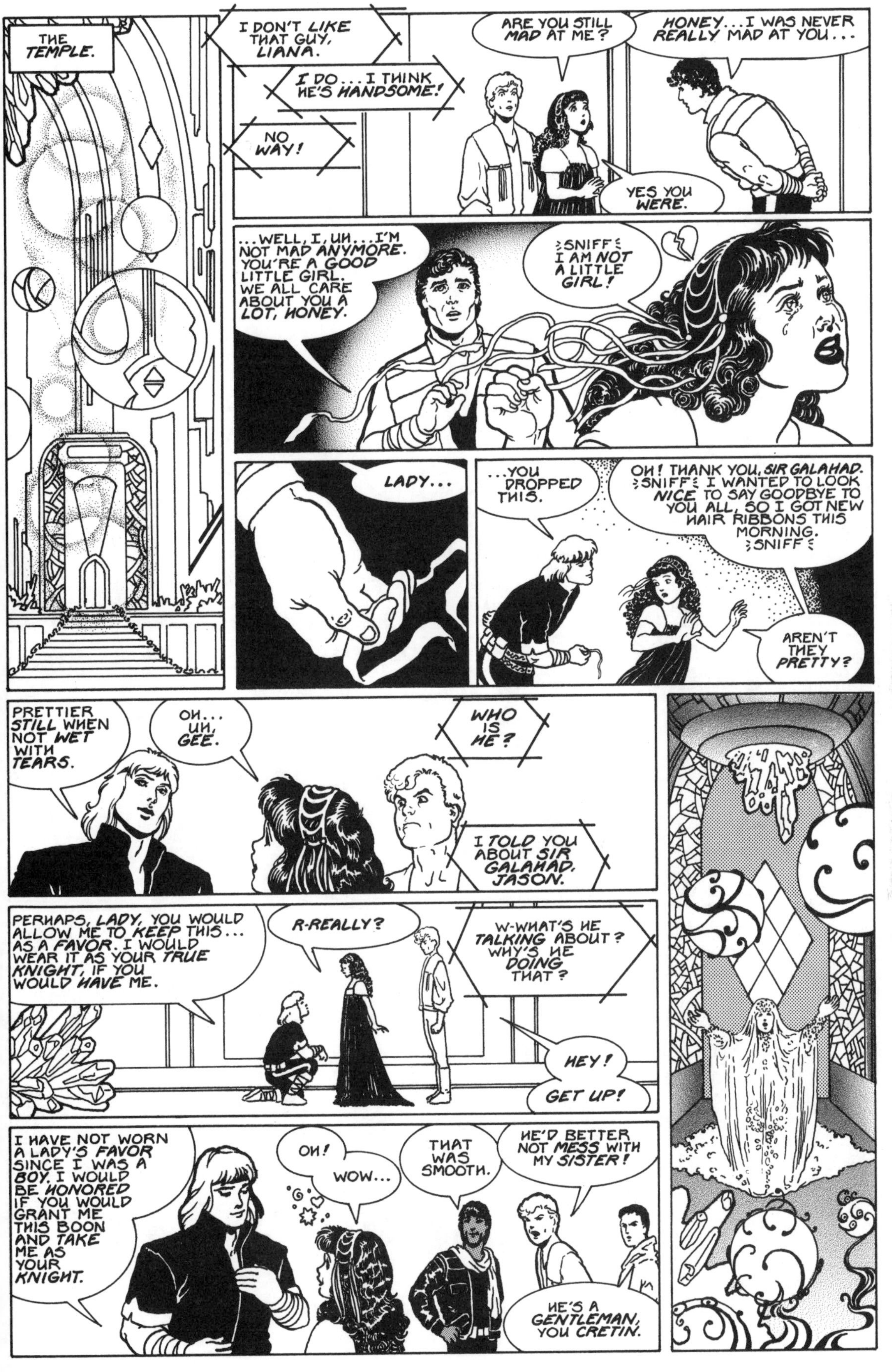
THE TEMPLE.
I DON'T LIKE THAT GUY, LIANA.
I DO... I THINK HE'S HANDSOME!
NO WAY!
ARE YOU STILL MAD AT ME?
YES YOU WERE.
HONEY... I WAS NEVER REALLY MAD AT YOU...
...WELL, I, UH... I'M NOT MAD ANYMORE. YOU'RE A GOOD LITTLE GIRL. WE ALL CARE ABOUT YOU A LOT, HONEY.
SNIFF I AM NOT A LITTLE GIRL!
LADY...
...YOU DROPPED THIS.
OH! THANK YOU, SIR GALAHAD. SNIFF I WANTED TO LOOK NICE TO SAY GOODBYE TO YOU ALL, SO I GOT NEW HAIR RIBBONS THIS MORNING. SNIFF
AREN'T THEY PRETTY?
PRETTIER STILL WHEN NOT WET WITH TEARS.
OH... UH, GEE.
WHO IS HE?
I TOLD YOU ABOUT SIR GALAHAD, JASON.
PERHAPS, LADY, YOU WOULD ALLOW ME TO KEEP THIS... AS A FAVOR. I WOULD WEAR IT AS YOUR TRUE KNIGHT, IF YOU WOULD HAVE ME.
R-REALLY?
W-WHAT'S HE TALKING ABOUT? WHY'S HE DOING THAT?
HEY!
GET UP!
I HAVE NOT WORN A LADY'S FAVOR SINCE I WAS A BOY. I WOULD BE HONORED IF YOU WOULD GRANT ME THIS BOON AND TAKE ME AS YOUR KNIGHT.
OH!
WOW...
THAT WAS SMOOTH.
HE'D BETTER NOT MESS WITH MY SISTER!
HE'S A GENTLEMAN, YOU CRETIN.

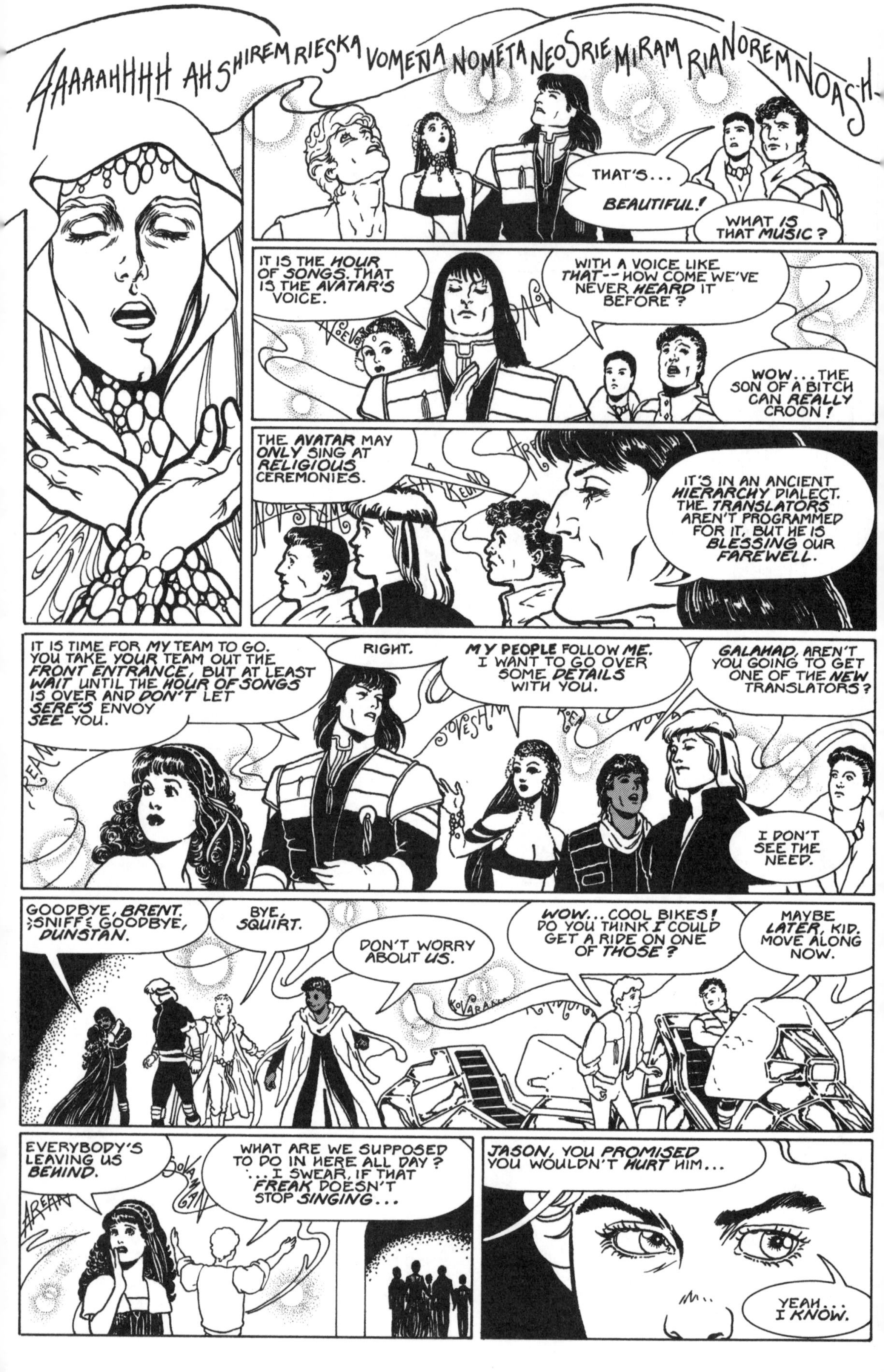
AAAAAHHHH AH SHIREM RIESKA VOMENA NOMETA NEOSRIE MIRAM RIANOREM NOASH
THAT'S... BEAUTIFUL!
WHAT IS THAT MUSIC?
IT IS THE HOUR OF SONGS. THAT IS THE AVATAR'S VOICE.
WITH A VOICE LIKE THAT-- HOW COME WE'VE NEVER HEARD IT BEFORE?
WOW... THE SON OF A BITCH CAN REALLY CROON!
THE AVATAR MAY ONLY SING AT RELIGIOUS CEREMONIES.
IT'S IN AN ANCIENT HIERARCHY DIALECT. THE TRANSLATORS AREN'T PROGRAMMED FOR IT, BUT HE IS BLESSING OUR FAREWELL.
IT IS TIME FOR MY TEAM TO GO. YOU TAKE YOUR TEAM OUT THE FRONT ENTRANCE, BUT AT LEAST WAIT UNTIL THE HOUR OF SONGS IS OVER AND DON'T LET SERE'S ENVOY SEE YOU.
RIGHT.
MY PEOPLE FOLLOW ME. I WANT TO GO OVER SOME DETAILS WITH YOU.
GALAHAD, AREN'T YOU GOING TO GET ONE OF THE NEW TRANSLATORS?
I DON'T SEE THE NEED.
GOODBYE, BRENT. ~SNIFF~ GOODBYE, DUNSTAN.
BYE, SQUIRT.
DON'T WORRY ABOUT US.
WOW... COOL BIKES! DO YOU THINK I COULD GET A RIDE ON ONE OF THOSE?
MAYBE LATER, KID. MOVE ALONG NOW.
EVERYBODY'S LEAVING US BEHIND.
WHAT ARE WE SUPPOSED TO DO IN HERE ALL DAY? ...I SWEAR, IF THAT FREAK DOESN'T STOP SINGING...
JASON, YOU PROMISED YOU WOULDN'T HURT HIM...
HM..
YEAH... I KNOW.

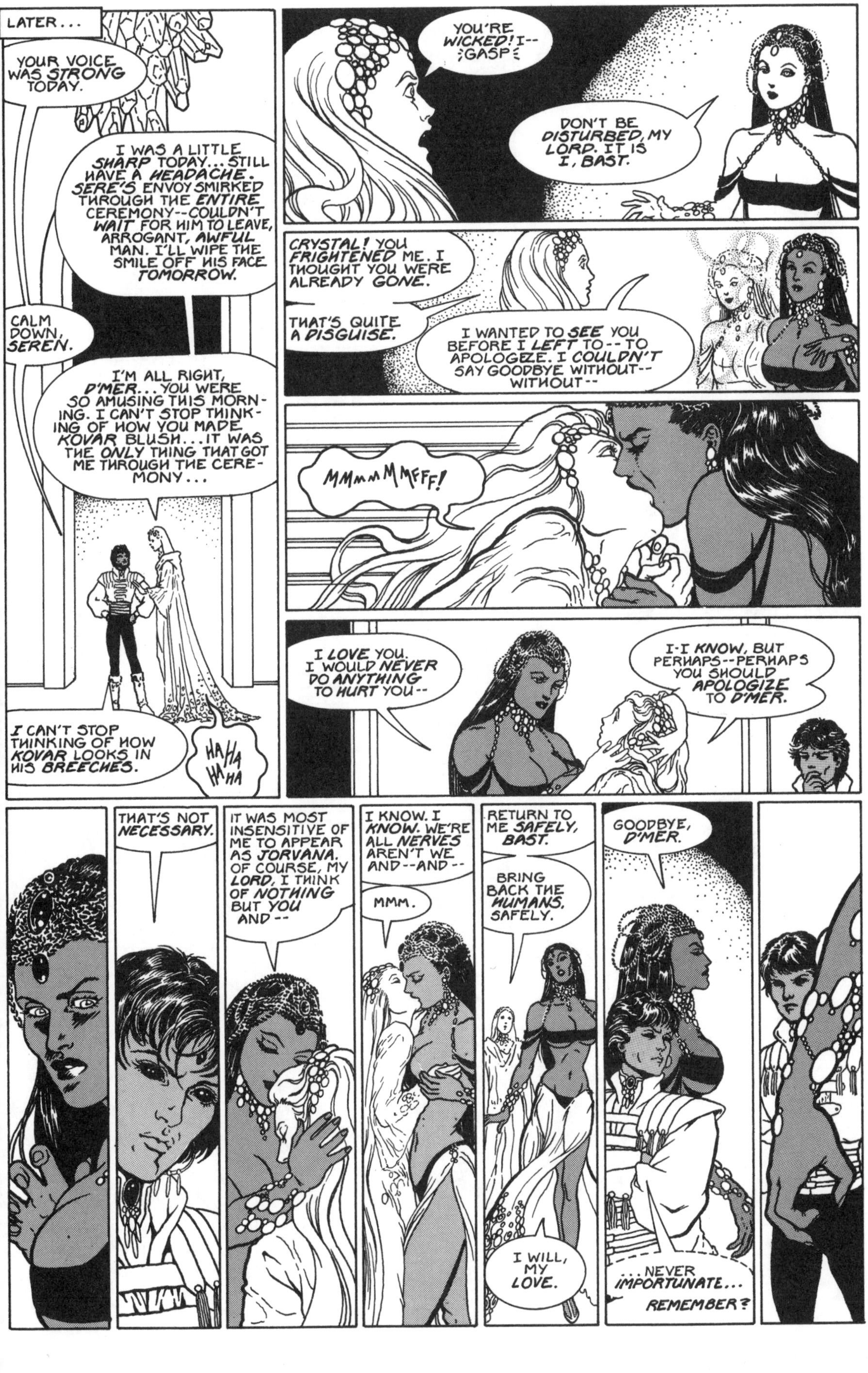
LATER...
YOUR VOICE WAS STRONG TODAY.
I WAS A LITTLE SHARP TODAY... STILL HAVE A HEADACHE. SERE'S ENVOY SMIRKED THROUGH THE ENTIRE CEREMONY--COULDN'T WAIT FOR HIM TO LEAVE, ARROGANT, AWFUL MAN. I'LL WIPE THE SMILE OFF HIS FACE TOMORROW.
CALM DOWN, SEREN.
I'M ALL RIGHT, D'MER... YOU WERE SO AMUSING THIS MORNING. I CAN'T STOP THINKING OF HOW YOU MADE KOVAR BLUSH... IT WAS THE ONLY THING THAT GOT ME THROUGH THE CEREMONY...
I CAN'T STOP THINKING OF HOW KOVAR LOOKS IN HIS BREECHES.
HA HA HA HA
YOU'RE WICKED! I-- ;GASP;
DON'T BE DISTURBED, MY LORD. IT IS I, BAST.
CRYSTAL! YOU FRIGHTENED ME. I THOUGHT YOU WERE ALREADY GONE.
THAT'S QUITE A DISGUISE.
I WANTED TO SEE YOU BEFORE I LEFT TO--TO APOLOGIZE. I COULDN'T SAY GOODBYE WITHOUT--WITHOUT--
MMmmMMFFF!
I LOVE YOU. I WOULD NEVER DO ANYTHING TO HURT YOU--
I-I KNOW, BUT PERHAPS--PERHAPS YOU SHOULD APOLOGIZE TO D'MER.
THAT'S NOT NECESSARY.
IT WAS MOST INSENSITIVE OF ME TO APPEAR AS JORVANA. OF COURSE, MY LORD, I THINK OF NOTHING BUT YOU AND--
I KNOW. I KNOW. WE'RE ALL NERVES AREN'T WE AND--AND--
MMM.
RETURN TO ME SAFELY, BAST.
BRING BACK THE HUMANS, SAFELY.
I WILL, MY LOVE.
GOODBYE, D'MER.
...NEVER IMPORTUNATE...
REMEMBER?

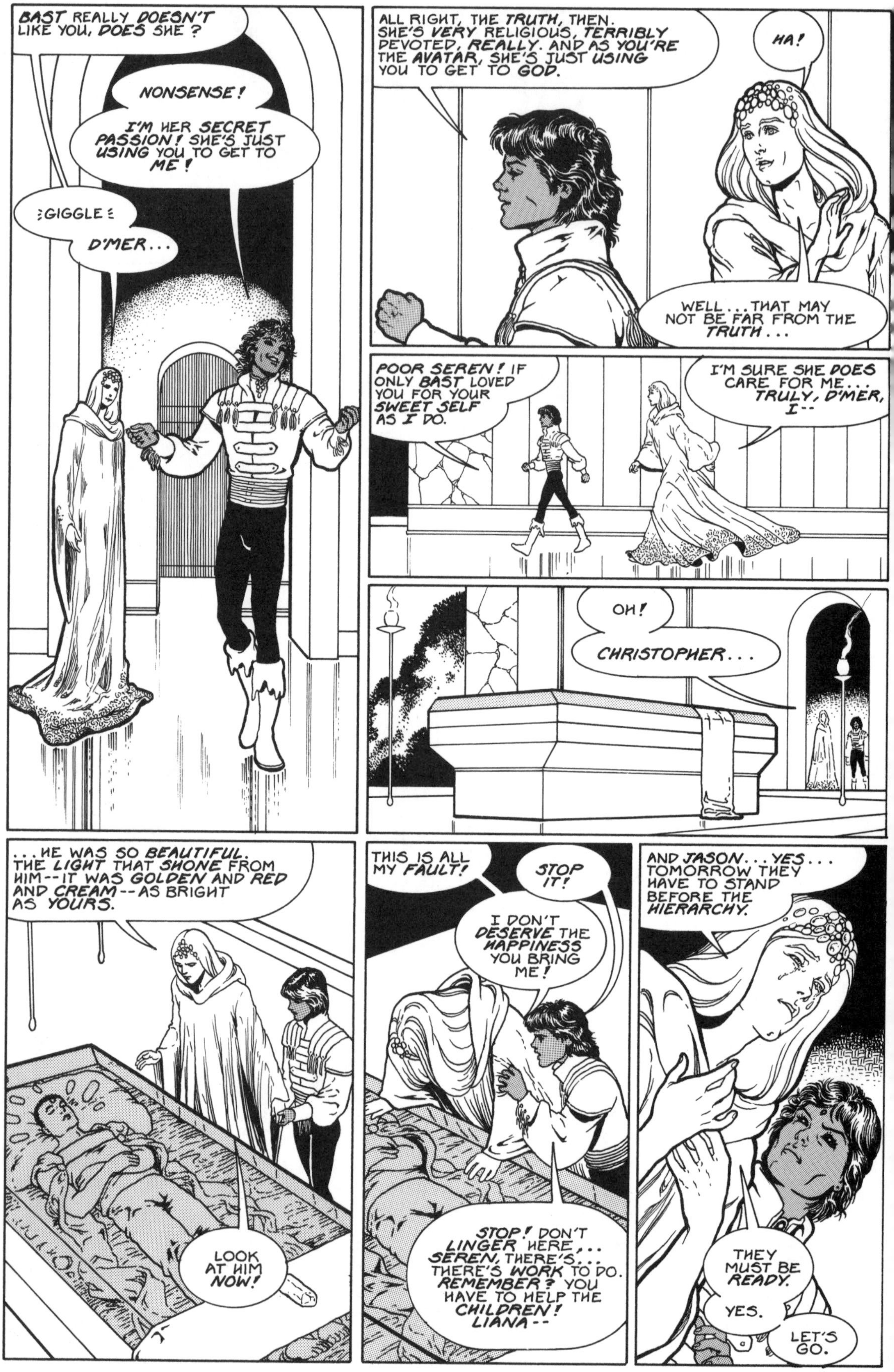
BAST REALLY DOESN'T LIKE YOU, DOES SHE?
NONSENSE!
I'M HER SECRET PASSION! SHE'S JUST USING YOU TO GET TO ME!
GIGGLE
D'MER...
ALL RIGHT, THE TRUTH, THEN. SHE'S VERY RELIGIOUS, TERRIBLY DEVOTED, REALLY. AND AS YOU'RE THE AVATAR, SHE'S JUST USING YOU TO GET TO GOD.
HA!
WELL... THAT MAY NOT BE FAR FROM THE TRUTH...
POOR SEREN! IF ONLY BAST LOVED YOU FOR YOUR SWEET SELF AS I DO.
I'M SURE SHE DOES CARE FOR ME... TRULY, D'MER, I--
OH!
CHRISTOPHER...
...HE WAS SO BEAUTIFUL. THE LIGHT THAT SHONE FROM HIM--IT WAS GOLDEN AND RED AND CREAM--AS BRIGHT AS YOURS.
LOOK AT HIM NOW!
THIS IS ALL MY FAULT!
STOP IT!
I DON'T DESERVE THE HAPPINESS YOU BRING ME!
STOP! DON'T LINGER HERE... SEREN, THERE'S... THERE'S WORK TO DO. REMEMBER? YOU HAVE TO HELP THE CHILDREN! LIANA--
AND JASON... YES... TOMORROW THEY HAVE TO STAND BEFORE THE HIERARCHY.
THEY MUST BE READY.
YES.
LET'S GO.

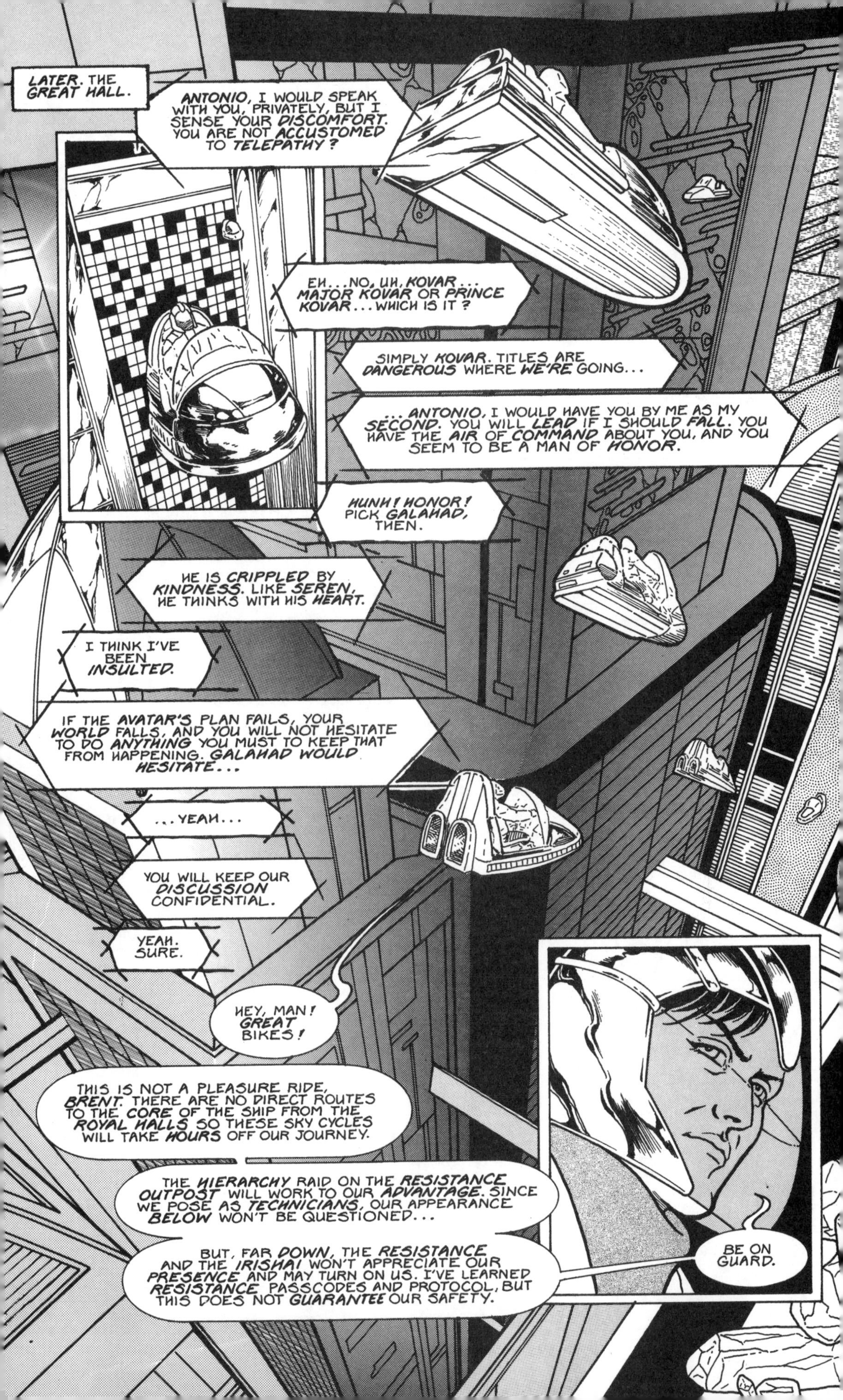
LATER. THE GREAT HALL.
ANTONIO, I WOULD SPEAK WITH YOU, PRIVATELY, BUT I SENSE YOUR DISCOMFORT. YOU ARE NOT ACCUSTOMED TO TELEPATHY?
EH...NO, UH, KOVAR... MAJOR KOVAR OR PRINCE KOVAR...WHICH IS IT?
SIMPLY KOVAR. TITLES ARE DANGEROUS WHERE WE'RE GOING...
...ANTONIO, I WOULD HAVE YOU BY ME AS MY SECOND. YOU WILL LEAD IF I SHOULD FALL. YOU HAVE THE AIR OF COMMAND ABOUT YOU, AND YOU SEEM TO BE A MAN OF HONOR.
HUNH! HONOR! PICK GALAHAD, THEN.
HE IS CRIPPLED BY KINDNESS. LIKE SEREN, HE THINKS WITH HIS HEART.
I THINK I'VE BEEN INSULTED.
IF THE AVATAR'S PLAN FAILS, YOUR WORLD FALLS, AND YOU WILL NOT HESITATE TO DO ANYTHING YOU MUST TO KEEP THAT FROM HAPPENING. GALAHAD WOULD HESITATE...
...YEAH...
YOU WILL KEEP OUR DISCUSSION CONFIDENTIAL.
YEAH. SURE.
HEY, MAN! GREAT BIKES!
THIS IS NOT A PLEASURE RIDE, BRENT. THERE ARE NO DIRECT ROUTES TO THE CORE OF THE SHIP FROM THE ROYAL HALLS SO THESE SKY CYCLES WILL TAKE HOURS OFF OUR JOURNEY.
THE HIERARCHY RAID ON THE RESISTANCE OUTPOST WILL WORK TO OUR ADVANTAGE. SINCE WE POSE AS TECHNICIANS, OUR APPEARANCE BELOW WON'T BE QUESTIONED...
BUT, FAR DOWN, THE RESISTANCE AND THE IRISHAI WON'T APPRECIATE OUR PRESENCE AND MAY TURN ON US. I'VE LEARNED RESISTANCE PASSCODES AND PROTOCOL, BUT THIS DOES NOT GUARANTEE OUR SAFETY.
BE ON GUARD.

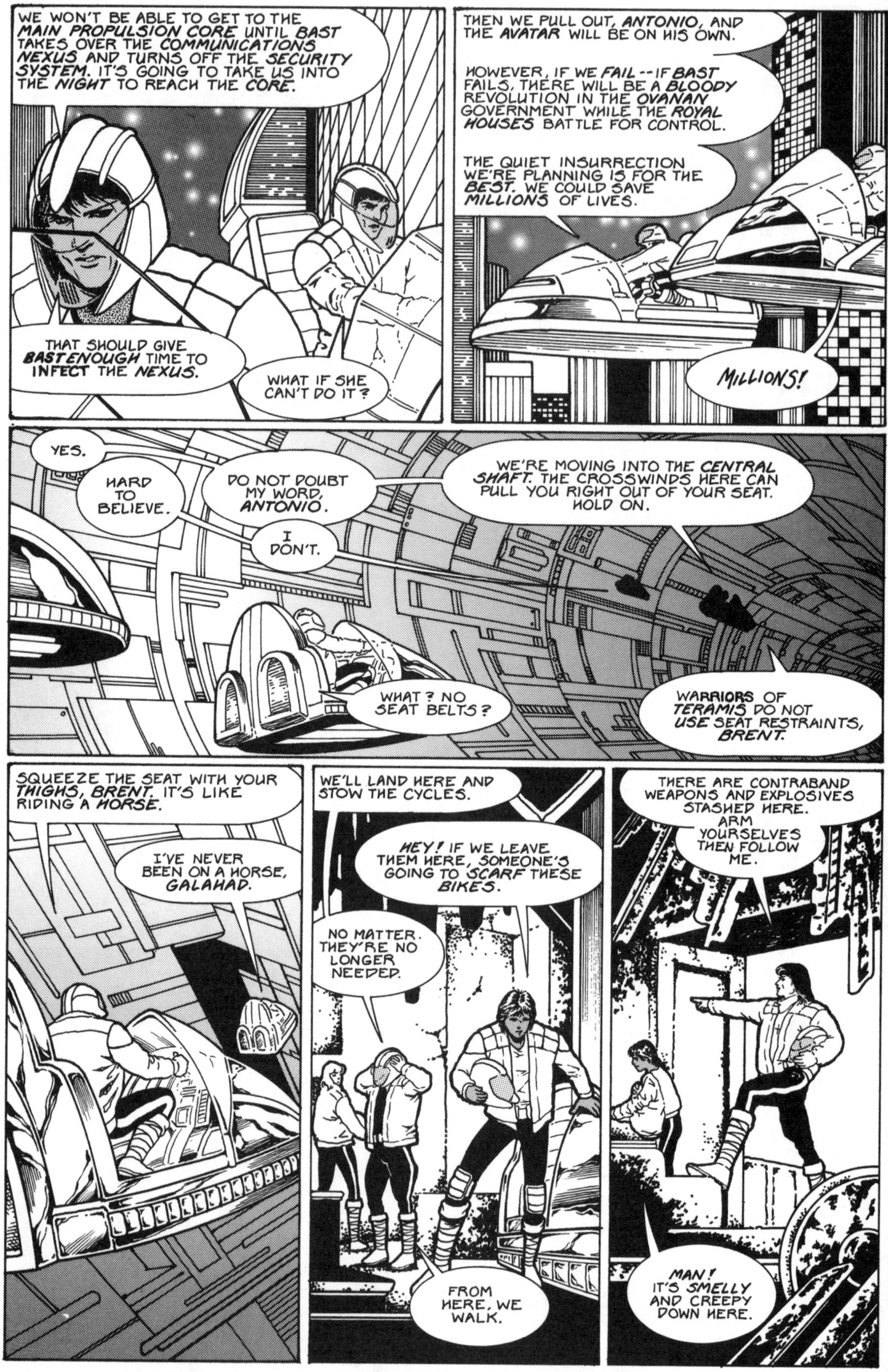
WE WON'T BE ABLE TO GET TO THE MAIN PROPULSION CORE UNTIL BAST TAKES OVER THE COMMUNICATIONS NEXUS AND TURNS OFF THE SECURITY SYSTEM. IT'S GOING TO TAKE US INTO THE NIGHT TO REACH THE CORE.
THAT SHOULD GIVE BAST ENOUGH TIME TO INFECT THE NEXUS.
WHAT IF SHE CAN'T DO IT?
THEN WE PULL OUT, ANTONIO, AND THE AVATAR WILL BE ON HIS OWN.
HOWEVER, IF WE FAIL--IF BAST FAILS, THERE WILL BE A BLOODY REVOLUTION IN THE OVANAN GOVERNMENT WHILE THE ROYAL HOUSES BATTLE FOR CONTROL.
THE QUIET INSURRECTION WE'RE PLANNING IS FOR THE BEST. WE COULD SAVE MILLIONS OF LIVES.
MILLIONS!
YES.
HARD TO BELIEVE.
DO NOT DOUBT MY WORD, ANTONIO.
I DON'T.
WE'RE MOVING INTO THE CENTRAL SHAFT. THE CROSSWINDS HERE CAN PULL YOU RIGHT OUT OF YOUR SEAT. HOLD ON.
WHAT? NO SEAT BELTS?
WARRIORS OF TERAMIS DO NOT USE SEAT RESTRAINTS, BRENT.
SQUEEZE THE SEAT WITH YOUR THIGHS, BRENT. IT'S LIKE RIDING A HORSE.
I'VE NEVER BEEN ON A HORSE, GALAHAD.
WE'LL LAND HERE AND STOW THE CYCLES.
HEY! IF WE LEAVE THEM HERE, SOMEONE'S GOING TO SCARF THESE BIKES.
NO MATTER. THEY'RE NO LONGER NEEDED.
FROM HERE, WE WALK.
THERE ARE CONTRABAND WEAPONS AND EXPLOSIVES STASHED HERE.
ARM YOURSELVES THEN FOLLOW ME.
MAN! IT'S SMELLY AND CREEPY DOWN HERE.

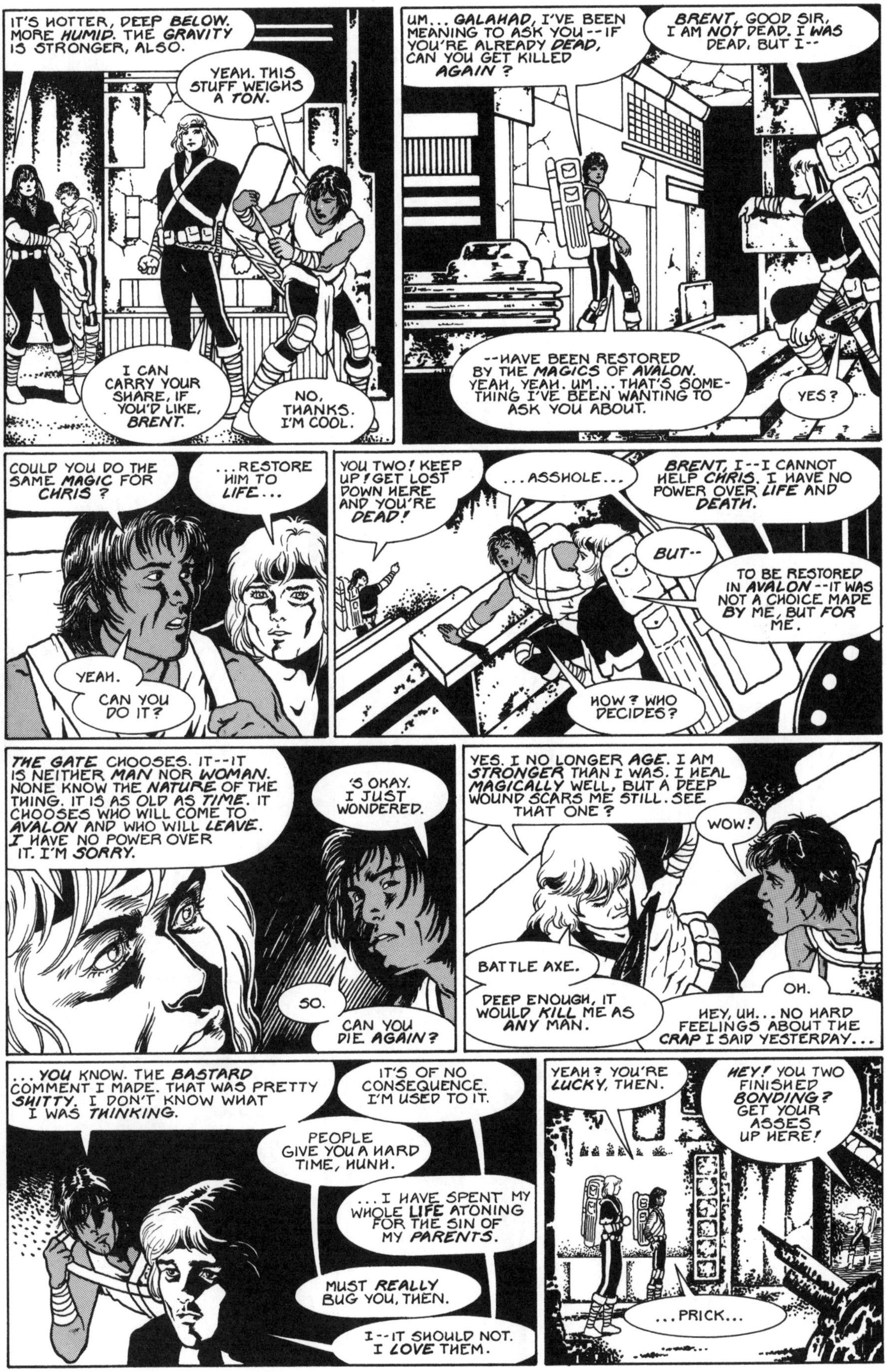
IT'S HOTTER, DEEP BELOW. MORE HUMID. THE GRAVITY IS STRONGER, ALSO.
YEAH. THIS STUFF WEIGHS A TON.
I CAN CARRY YOUR SHARE, IF YOU'D LIKE, BRENT.
NO, THANKS. I'M COOL.
UM... GALAHAD, I'VE BEEN MEANING TO ASK YOU--IF YOU'RE ALREADY DEAD, CAN YOU GET KILLED AGAIN?
BRENT, GOOD SIR, I AM NOT DEAD. I WAS DEAD. BUT I--
--HAVE BEEN RESTORED BY THE MAGICS OF AVALON. YEAH, YEAH. UM... THAT'S SOMETHING I'VE BEEN WANTING TO ASK YOU ABOUT.
YES?
COULD YOU DO THE SAME MAGIC FOR CHRIS?
...RESTORE HIM TO LIFE...
YEAH.
CAN YOU DO IT?
YOU TWO! KEEP UP! GET LOST DOWN HERE AND YOU'RE DEAD!
...ASSHOLE...
BRENT, I--I CANNOT HELP CHRIS. I HAVE NO POWER OVER LIFE AND DEATH.
BUT--
TO BE RESTORED IN AVALON--IT WAS NOT A CHOICE MADE BY ME, BUT FOR ME.
HOW? WHO DECIDES?
THE GATE CHOOSES. IT--IT IS NEITHER MAN NOR WOMAN. NONE KNOW THE NATURE OF THE THING. IT IS AS OLD AS TIME. IT CHOOSES WHO WILL COME TO AVALON AND WHO WILL LEAVE. I HAVE NO POWER OVER IT. I'M SORRY.
'S OKAY. I JUST WONDERED.
SO.
CAN YOU DIE AGAIN?
YES. I NO LONGER AGE. I AM STRONGER THAN I WAS. I HEAL MAGICALLY WELL, BUT A DEEP WOUND SCARS ME STILL. SEE THAT ONE?
WOW!
BATTLE AXE.
DEEP ENOUGH, IT WOULD KILL ME AS ANY MAN.
OH.
HEY, UH... NO HARD FEELINGS ABOUT THE CRAP I SAID YESTERDAY...
...YOU KNOW. THE BASTARD COMMENT I MADE. THAT WAS PRETTY SHITTY. I DON'T KNOW WHAT I WAS THINKING.
IT'S OF NO CONSEQUENCE. I'M USED TO IT.
PEOPLE GIVE YOU A HARD TIME, HUNH.
...I HAVE SPENT MY WHOLE LIFE ATONING FOR THE SIN OF MY PARENTS.
MUST REALLY BUG YOU, THEN.
I--IT SHOULD NOT. I LOVE THEM.
YEAH? YOU'RE LUCKY, THEN.
HEY! YOU TWO FINISHED BONDING? GET YOUR ASSES UP HERE!
...PRICK...

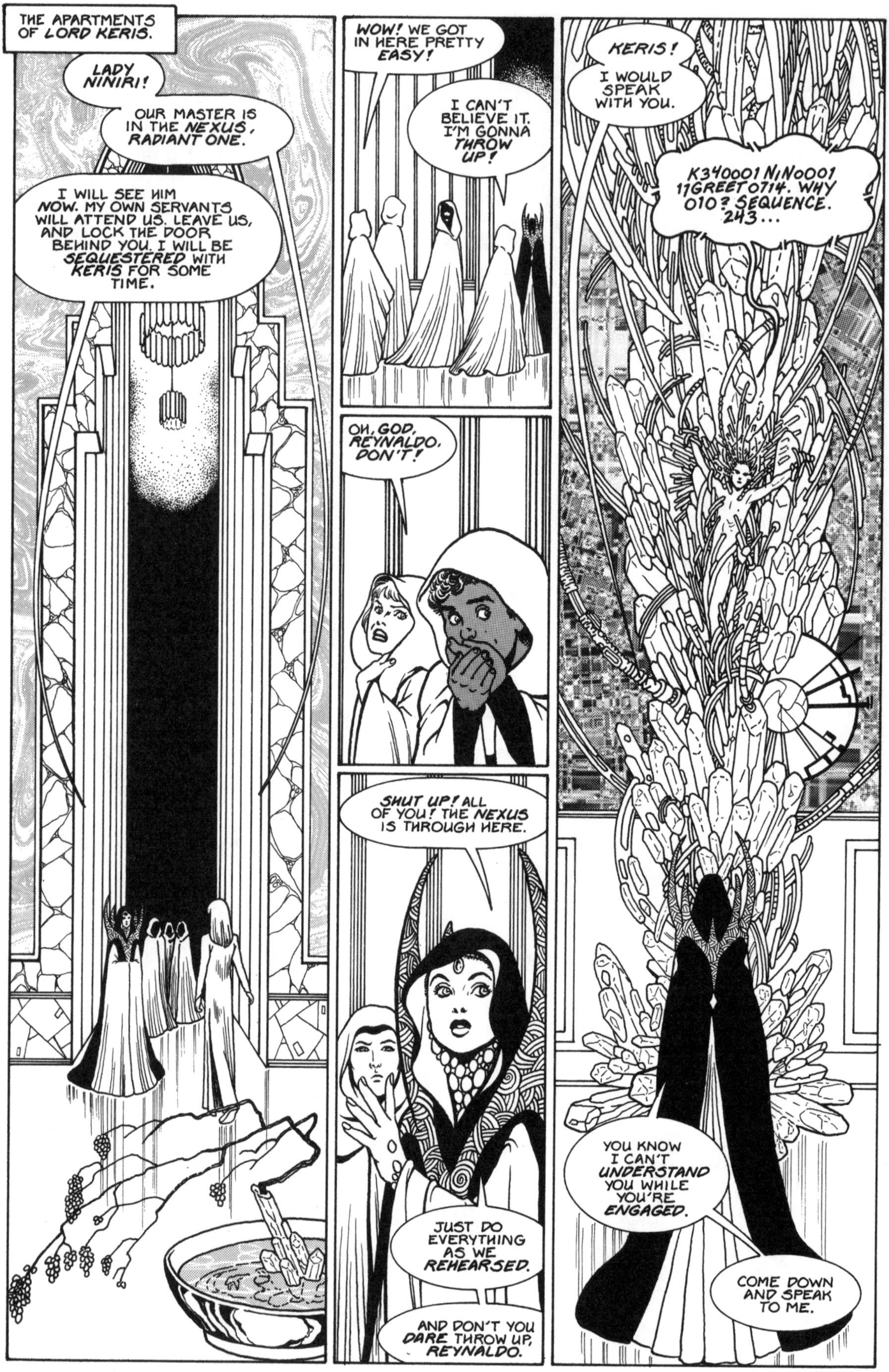
THE APARTMENTS OF LORD KERIS.
LADY NINIRI!
OUR MASTER IS IN THE NEXUS, RADIANT ONE.
I WILL SEE HIM NOW. MY OWN SERVANTS WILL ATTEND US. LEAVE US, AND LOCK THE DOOR BEHIND YOU. I WILL BE SEQUESTERED WITH KERIS FOR SOME TIME.
WOW! WE GOT IN HERE PRETTY EASY!
I CAN'T BELIEVE IT. I'M GONNA THROW UP!
OH, GOD, REYNALDO, DON'T!
SHUT UP! ALL OF YOU! THE NEXUS IS THROUGH HERE.
JUST DO EVERYTHING AS WE REHEARSED.
AND DON'T YOU DARE THROW UP, REYNALDO.
KERIS! I WOULD SPEAK WITH YOU.
K340001 NiN0001 11GREET 0714. WHY 010? SEQUENCE. 243...
YOU KNOW I CAN'T UNDERSTAND YOU WHILE YOU'RE ENGAGED.
COME DOWN AND SPEAK TO ME.

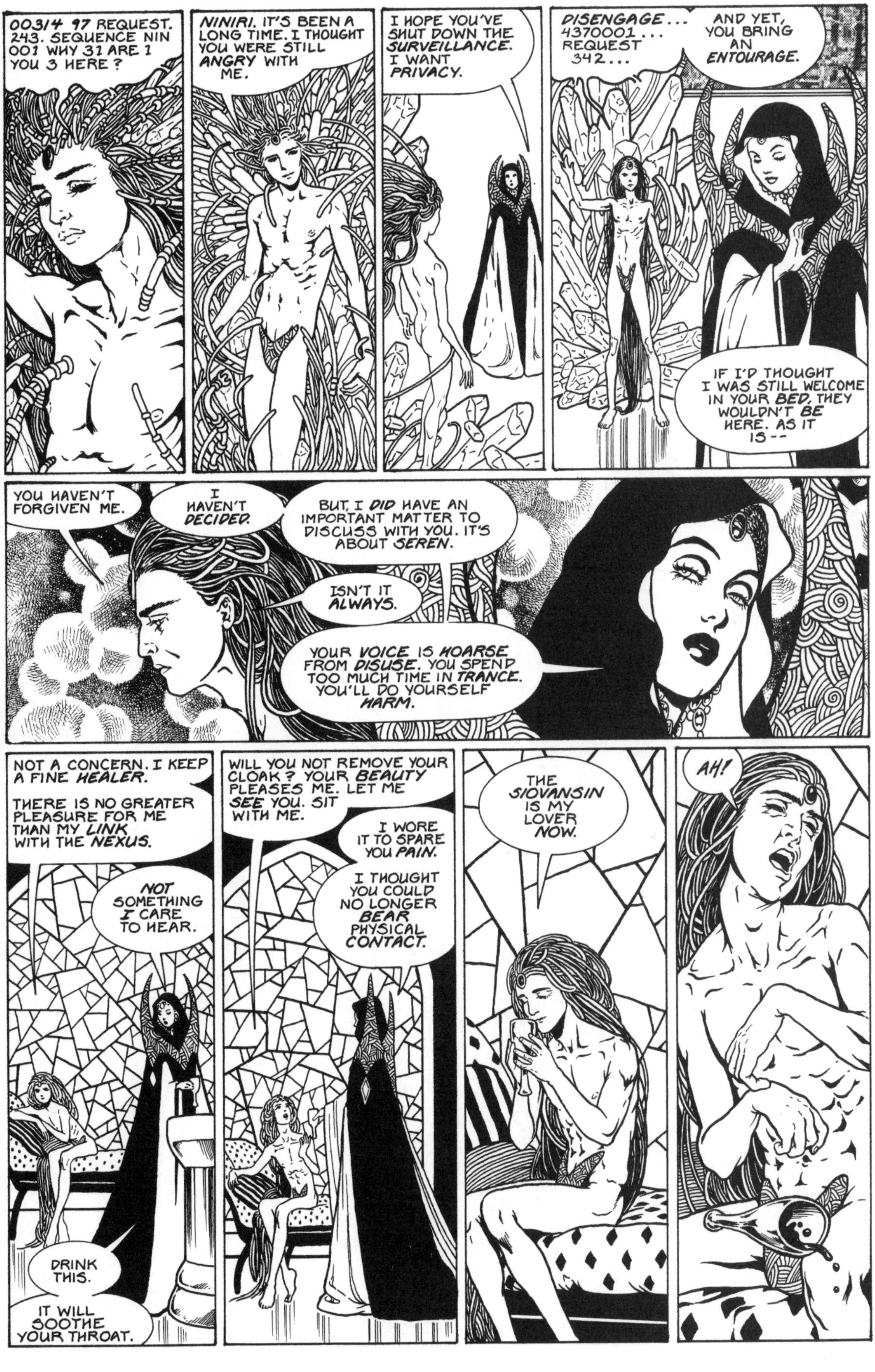

003/4 97 REQUEST. 243. SEQUENCE NIN 001 WHY 31 ARE 1 YOU 3 HERE?
NINIRI. IT'S BEEN A LONG TIME. I THOUGHT YOU WERE STILL ANGRY WITH ME.
I HOPE YOU'VE SHUT DOWN THE SURVEILLANCE. I WANT PRIVACY.
DISENGAGE... 4370001... REQUEST 342...
AND YET, YOU BRING AN ENTOURAGE.
IF I'D THOUGHT I WAS STILL WELCOME IN YOUR BED, THEY WOULDN'T BE HERE. AS IT IS --
YOU HAVEN'T FORGIVEN ME.
I HAVEN'T DECIDED.
BUT, I DID HAVE AN IMPORTANT MATTER TO DISCUSS WITH YOU. IT'S ABOUT SEREN.
ISN'T IT ALWAYS.
YOUR VOICE IS HOARSE FROM DISUSE. YOU SPEND TOO MUCH TIME IN TRANCE. YOU'LL DO YOURSELF HARM.
NOT A CONCERN. I KEEP A FINE HEALER.
THERE IS NO GREATER PLEASURE FOR ME THAN MY LINK WITH THE NEXUS.
NOT SOMETHING I CARE TO HEAR.
DRINK THIS.
IT WILL SOOTHE YOUR THROAT.
WILL YOU NOT REMOVE YOUR CLOAK? YOUR BEAUTY PLEASES ME. LET ME SEE YOU. SIT WITH ME.
I WORE IT TO SPARE YOU PAIN.
I THOUGHT YOU COULD NO LONGER BEAR PHYSICAL CONTACT.
THE SIOVANSIN IS MY LOVER NOW.
AH!

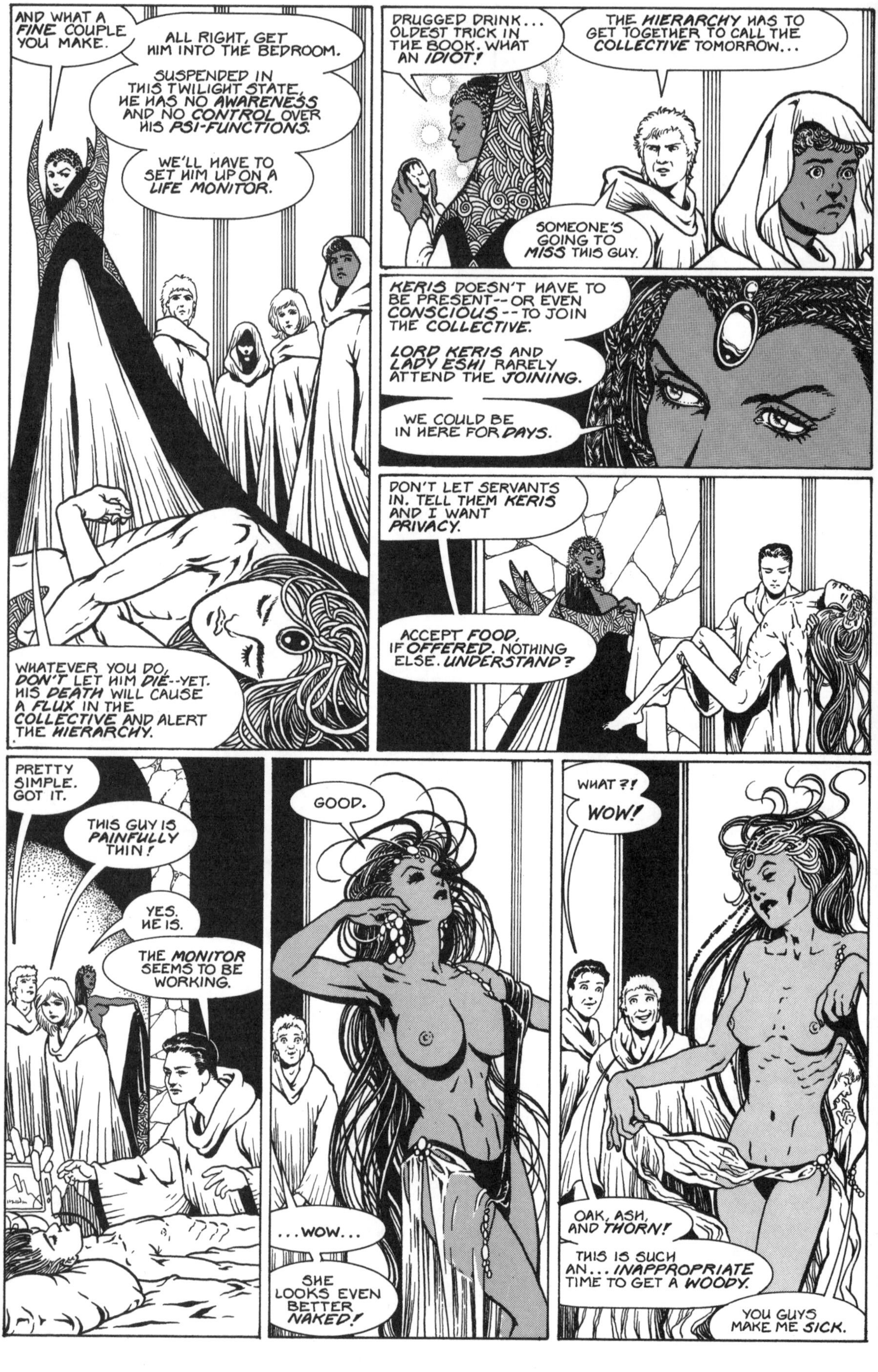
AND WHAT A FINE COUPLE YOU MAKE.
ALL RIGHT, GET HIM INTO THE BEDROOM.
SUSPENDED IN THIS TWILIGHT STATE, HE HAS NO AWARENESS AND NO CONTROL OVER HIS PSI-FUNCTIONS.
WE'LL HAVE TO SET HIM UP ON A LIFE MONITOR.
WHATEVER YOU DO, DON'T LET HIM DIE--YET. HIS DEATH WILL CAUSE A FLUX IN THE COLLECTIVE AND ALERT THE HIERARCHY.
DRUGGED DRINK... OLDEST TRICK IN THE BOOK. WHAT AN IDIOT!
THE HIERARCHY HAS TO GET TOGETHER TO CALL THE COLLECTIVE TOMORROW...
SOMEONE'S GOING TO MISS THIS GUY.
KERIS DOESN'T HAVE TO BE PRESENT--OR EVEN CONSCIOUS--TO JOIN THE COLLECTIVE.
LORD KERIS AND LADY ESHI RARELY ATTEND THE JOINING.
WE COULD BE IN HERE FOR DAYS.
DON'T LET SERVANTS IN. TELL THEM KERIS AND I WANT PRIVACY.
ACCEPT FOOD, IF OFFERED. NOTHING ELSE. UNDERSTAND?
PRETTY SIMPLE. GOT IT.
THIS GUY IS PAINFULLY THIN!
YES. HE IS.
THE MONITOR SEEMS TO BE WORKING.
GOOD.
...WOW...
SHE LOOKS EVEN BETTER NAKED!
WHAT?!
WOW!
OAK, ASH, AND THORN!
THIS IS SUCH AN... INAPPROPRIATE TIME TO GET A WOODY.
YOU GUYS MAKE ME SICK.

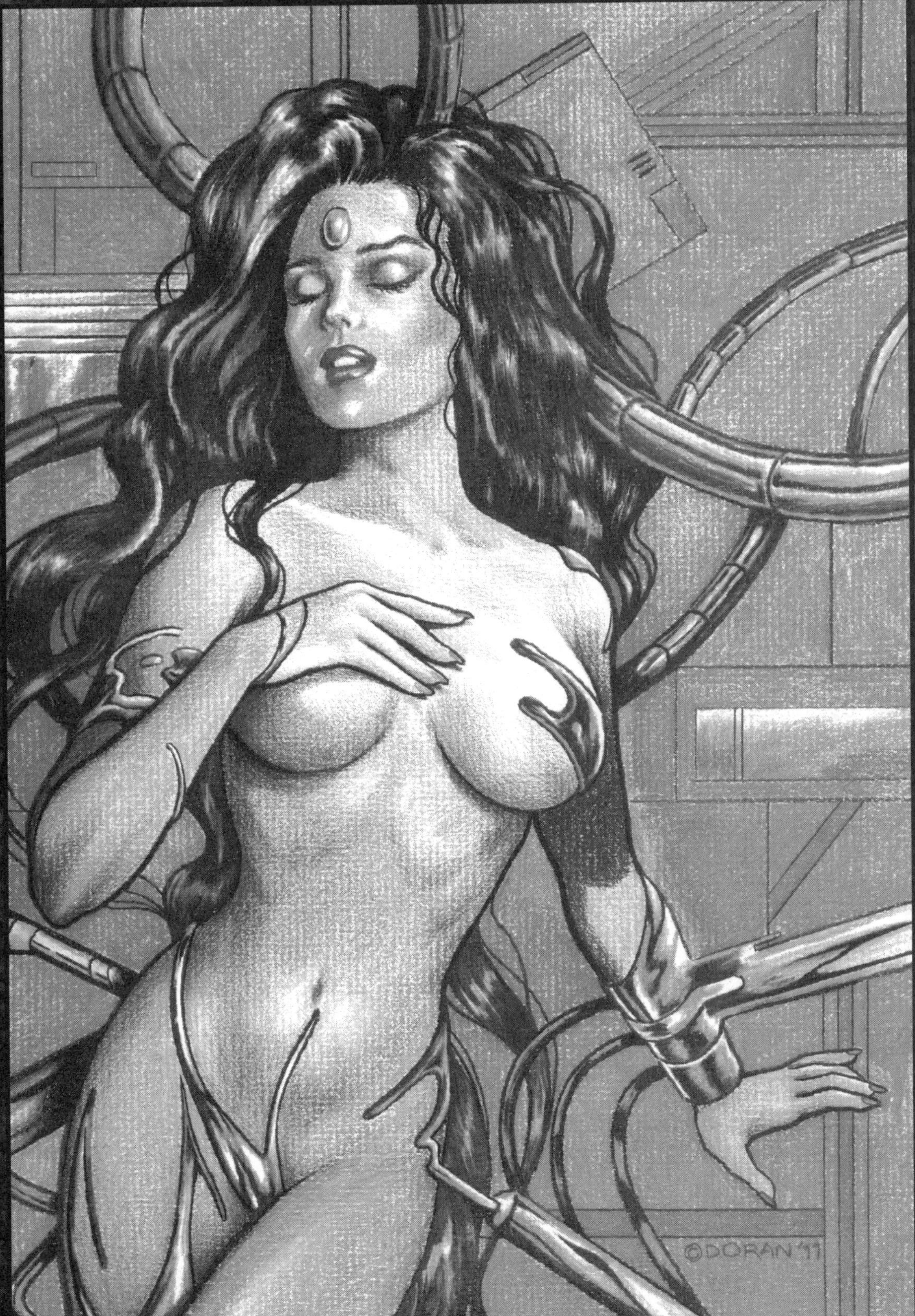
©DORAN

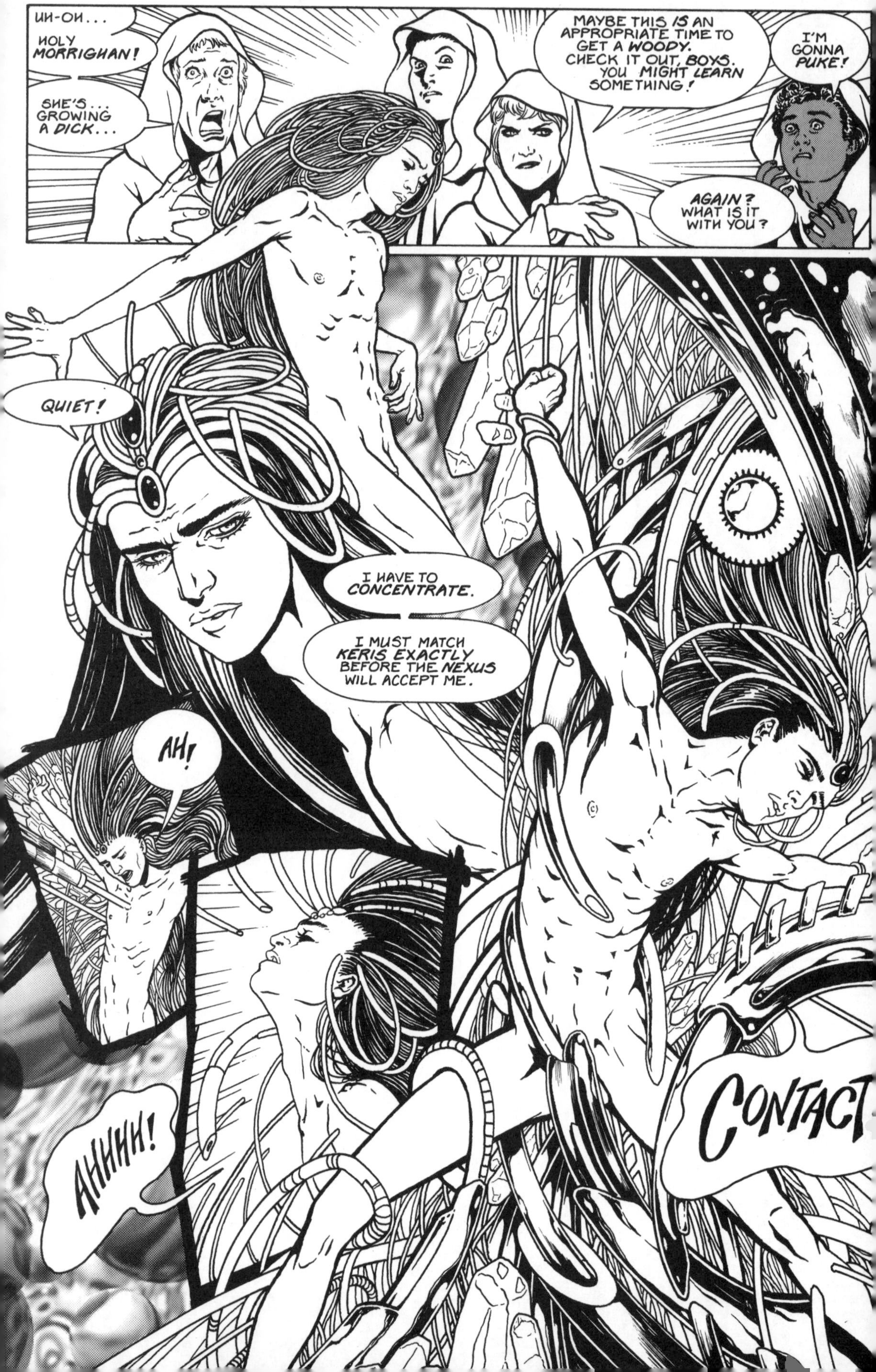
UH-OH...
HOLY MORRIGHAN!
SHE'S... GROWING A DICK...
MAYBE THIS IS AN APPROPRIATE TIME TO GET A WOODY. CHECK IT OUT, BOYS. YOU MIGHT LEARN SOMETHING!
I'M GONNA PUKE!
AGAIN? WHAT IS IT WITH YOU?
QUIET!
I HAVE TO CONCENTRATE.
I MUST MATCH KERIS EXACTLY BEFORE THE NEXUS WILL ACCEPT ME.
AH!
AHHHH!
CONTACT

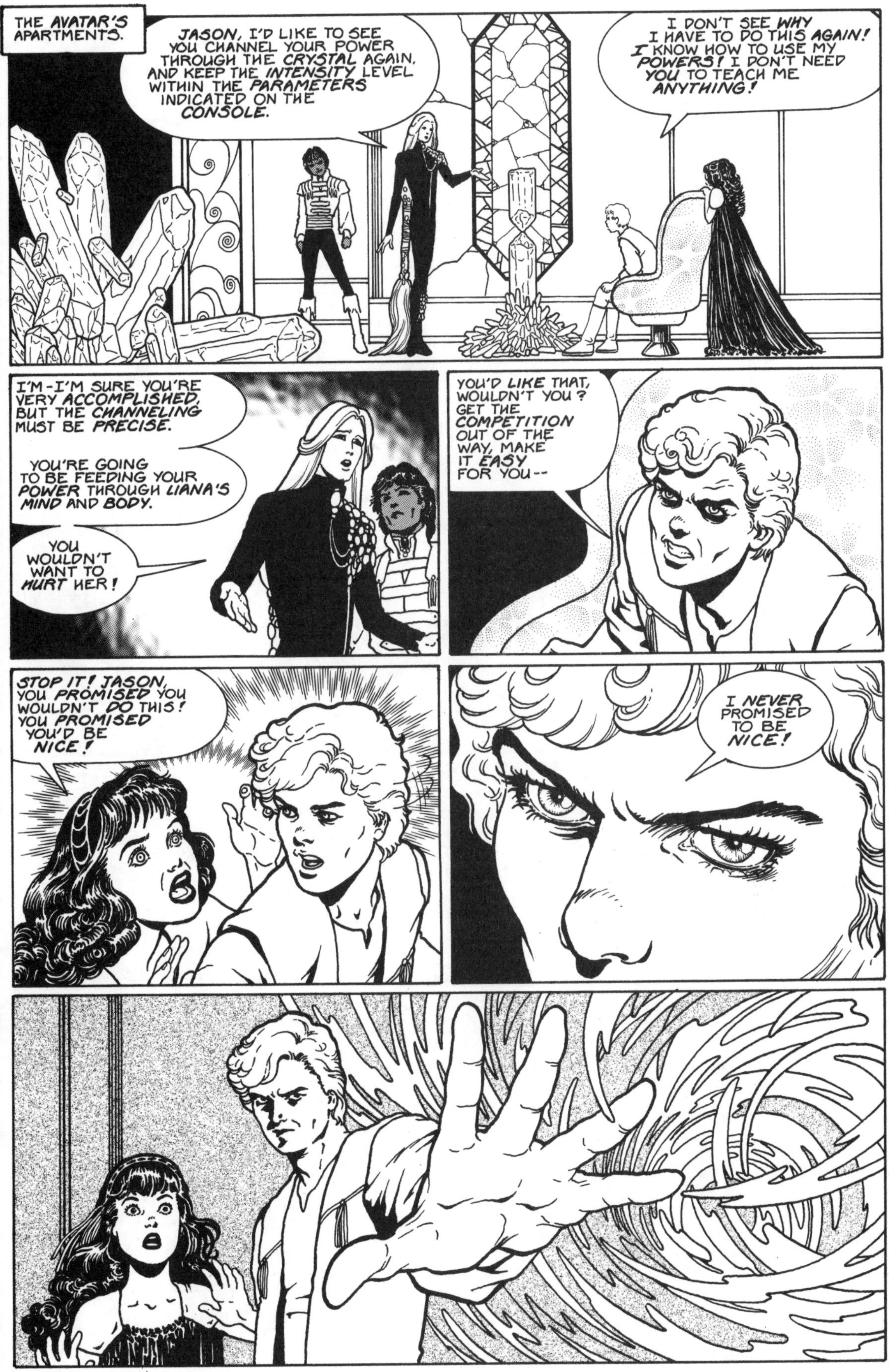

THE AVATAR'S APARTMENTS.
JASON, I'D LIKE TO SEE YOU CHANNEL YOUR POWER THROUGH THE CRYSTAL AGAIN, AND KEEP THE INTENSITY LEVEL WITHIN THE PARAMETERS INDICATED ON THE CONSOLE.
I DON'T SEE WHY I HAVE TO DO THIS AGAIN! I KNOW HOW TO USE MY POWERS! I DON'T NEED YOU TO TEACH ME ANYTHING!
I'M-I'M SURE YOU'RE VERY ACCOMPLISHED, BUT THE CHANNELING MUST BE PRECISE.
YOU'RE GOING TO BE FEEDING YOUR POWER THROUGH LIANA'S MIND AND BODY.
YOU WOULDN'T WANT TO HURT HER!
YOU'D LIKE THAT, WOULDN'T YOU? GET THE COMPETITION OUT OF THE WAY, MAKE IT EASY FOR YOU--
STOP IT! JASON, YOU PROMISED YOU WOULDN'T DO THIS! YOU PROMISED YOU'D BE NICE!
I NEVER PROMISED TO BE NICE!

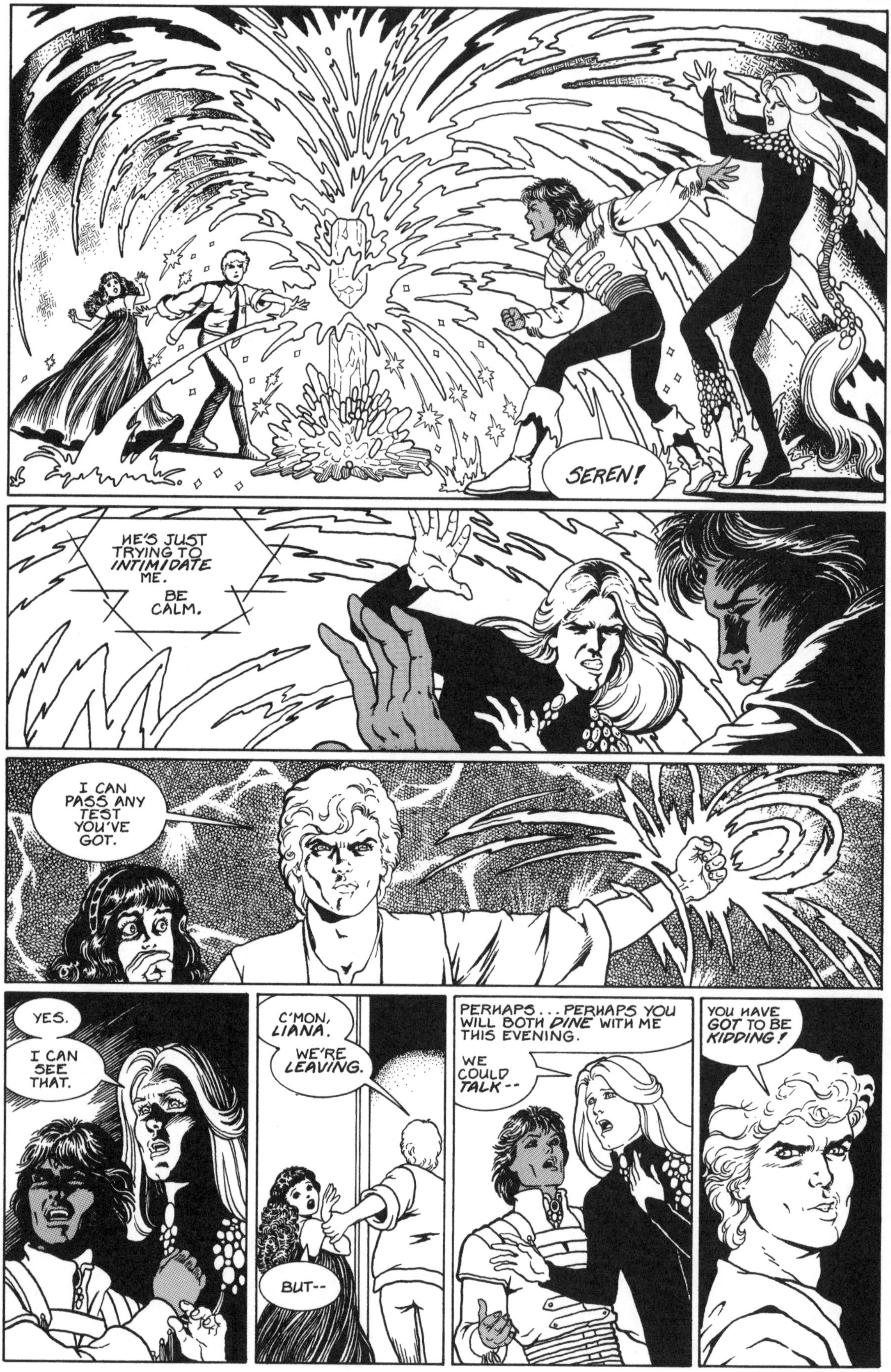
SEREN!
HE'S JUST TRYING TO *INTIMIDATE* ME.
BE CALM.
I CAN PASS ANY *TEST* YOU'VE GOT.
YES.
I CAN SEE THAT.
C'MON, *LIANA*.
WE'RE *LEAVING*.
BUT--
PERHAPS . . . PERHAPS YOU WILL BOTH *DINE* WITH ME THIS EVENING.
WE COULD *TALK* --
YOU HAVE *GOT* TO BE *KIDDING!*

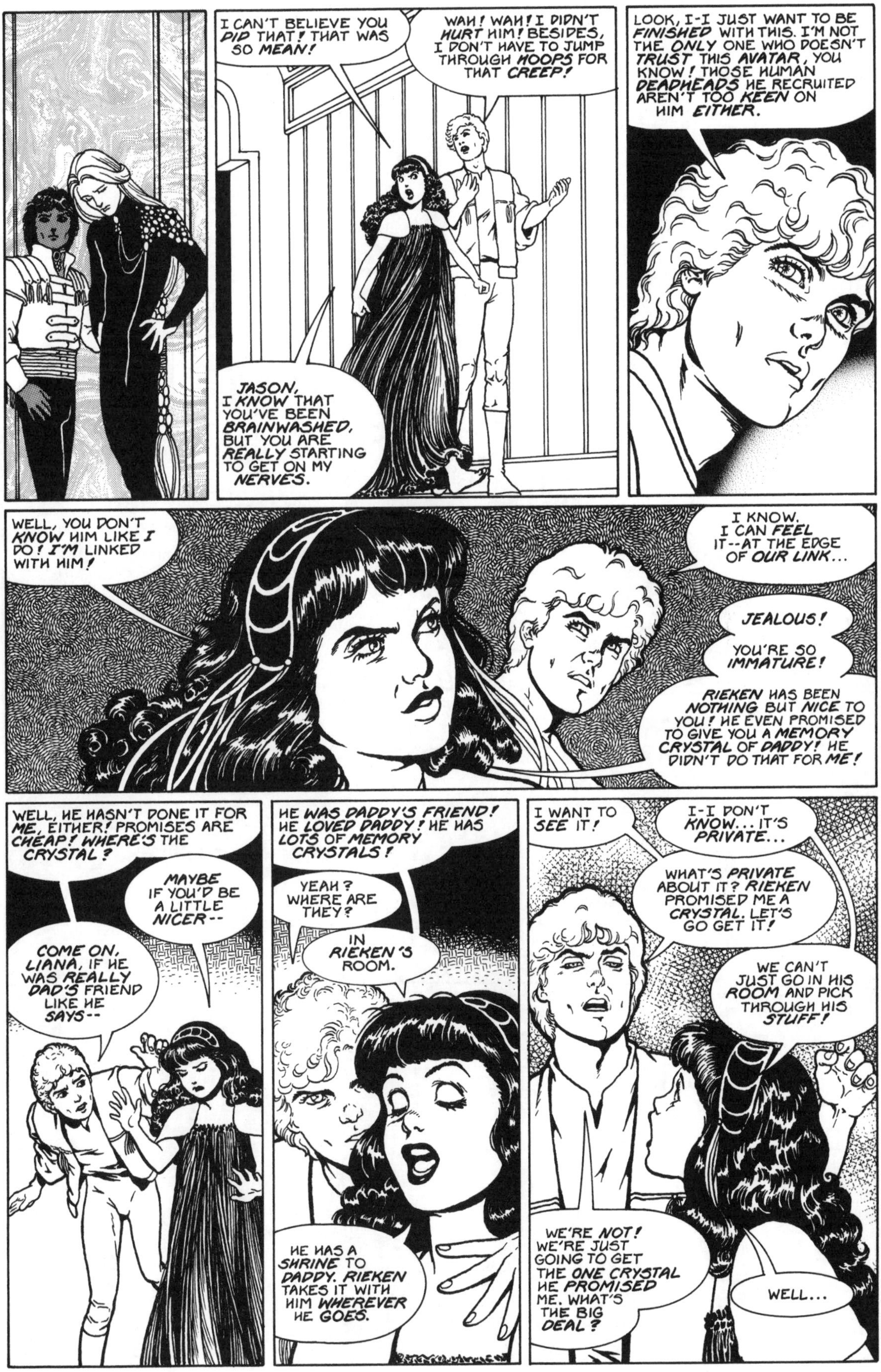
I CAN'T BELIEVE YOU DID THAT! THAT WAS SO MEAN!
WAH! WAH! I DIDN'T HURT HIM! BESIDES, I DON'T HAVE TO JUMP THROUGH HOOPS FOR THAT CREEP!
JASON, I KNOW THAT YOU'VE BEEN BRAINWASHED, BUT YOU ARE REALLY STARTING TO GET ON MY NERVES.
LOOK, I-I JUST WANT TO BE FINISHED WITH THIS. I'M NOT THE ONLY ONE WHO DOESN'T TRUST THIS AVATAR, YOU KNOW! THOSE HUMAN DEADHEADS HE RECRUITED AREN'T TOO KEEN ON HIM EITHER.
WELL, YOU DON'T KNOW HIM LIKE I DO! I'M LINKED WITH HIM!
I KNOW. I CAN FEEL IT--AT THE EDGE OF OUR LINK...
JEALOUS!
YOU'RE SO IMMATURE!
RIEKEN HAS BEEN NOTHING BUT NICE TO YOU! HE EVEN PROMISED TO GIVE YOU A MEMORY CRYSTAL OF DADDY! HE DIDN'T DO THAT FOR ME!
WELL, HE HASN'T DONE IT FOR ME, EITHER! PROMISES ARE CHEAP! WHERE'S THE CRYSTAL?
MAYBE IF YOU'D BE A LITTLE NICER--
COME ON, LIANA, IF HE WAS REALLY DAD'S FRIEND LIKE HE SAYS--
HE WAS DADDY'S FRIEND! HE LOVED DADDY! HE HAS LOTS OF MEMORY CRYSTALS!
YEAH? WHERE ARE THEY?
IN RIEKEN'S ROOM.
HE HAS A SHRINE TO DADDY. RIEKEN TAKES IT WITH HIM WHEREVER HE GOES.
I WANT TO SEE IT!
I-I DON'T KNOW... IT'S PRIVATE...
WHAT'S PRIVATE ABOUT IT? RIEKEN PROMISED ME A CRYSTAL. LET'S GO GET IT!
WE CAN'T JUST GO IN HIS ROOM AND PICK THROUGH HIS STUFF!
WE'RE NOT! WE'RE JUST GOING TO GET THE ONE CRYSTAL HE PROMISED ME. WHAT'S THE BIG DEAL?
WELL...

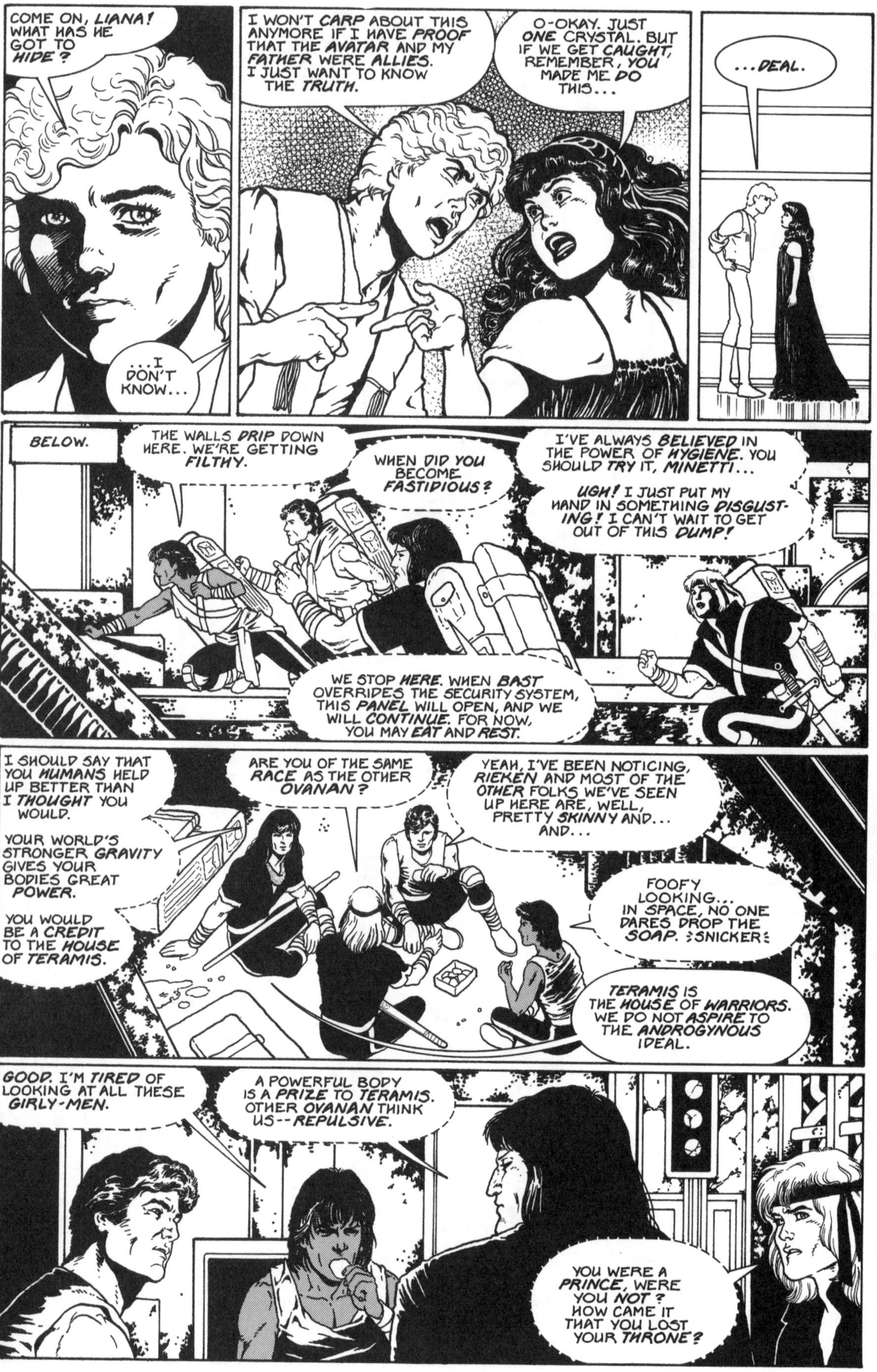
COME ON, LIANA! WHAT HAS HE GOT TO HIDE?
...I DON'T KNOW...
I WON'T CARP ABOUT THIS ANYMORE IF I HAVE PROOF THAT THE AVATAR AND MY FATHER WERE ALLIES. I JUST WANT TO KNOW THE TRUTH.
O-OKAY. JUST ONE CRYSTAL. BUT IF WE GET CAUGHT, REMEMBER, YOU MADE ME DO THIS...
...DEAL.
BELOW.
THE WALLS DRIP DOWN HERE. WE'RE GETTING FILTHY.
WHEN DID YOU BECOME FASTIDIOUS?
I'VE ALWAYS BELIEVED IN THE POWER OF HYGIENE. YOU SHOULD TRY IT, MINETTI...
UGH! I JUST PUT MY HAND IN SOMETHING DISGUSTING! I CAN'T WAIT TO GET OUT OF THIS DUMP!
WE STOP HERE. WHEN BAST OVERRIDES THE SECURITY SYSTEM, THIS PANEL WILL OPEN, AND WE WILL CONTINUE. FOR NOW, YOU MAY EAT AND REST.
I SHOULD SAY THAT YOU HUMANS HELD UP BETTER THAN I THOUGHT YOU WOULD.
YOUR WORLD'S STRONGER GRAVITY GIVES YOUR BODIES GREAT POWER.
YOU WOULD BE A CREDIT TO THE HOUSE OF TERAMIS.
ARE YOU OF THE SAME RACE AS THE OTHER OVANAN?
YEAH, I'VE BEEN NOTICING, RIEKEN AND MOST OF THE OTHER FOLKS WE'VE SEEN UP HERE ARE, WELL, PRETTY SKINNY AND... AND...
FOOFY LOOKING... IN SPACE, NO ONE DARES DROP THE SOAP. :SNICKER:
TERAMIS IS THE HOUSE OF WARRIORS. WE DO NOT ASPIRE TO THE ANDROGYNOUS IDEAL.
GOOD. I'M TIRED OF LOOKING AT ALL THESE GIRLY-MEN.
A POWERFUL BODY IS A PRIZE TO TERAMIS. OTHER OVANAN THINK US--REPULSIVE.
YOU WERE A PRINCE, WERE YOU NOT? HOW CAME IT THAT YOU LOST YOUR THRONE?

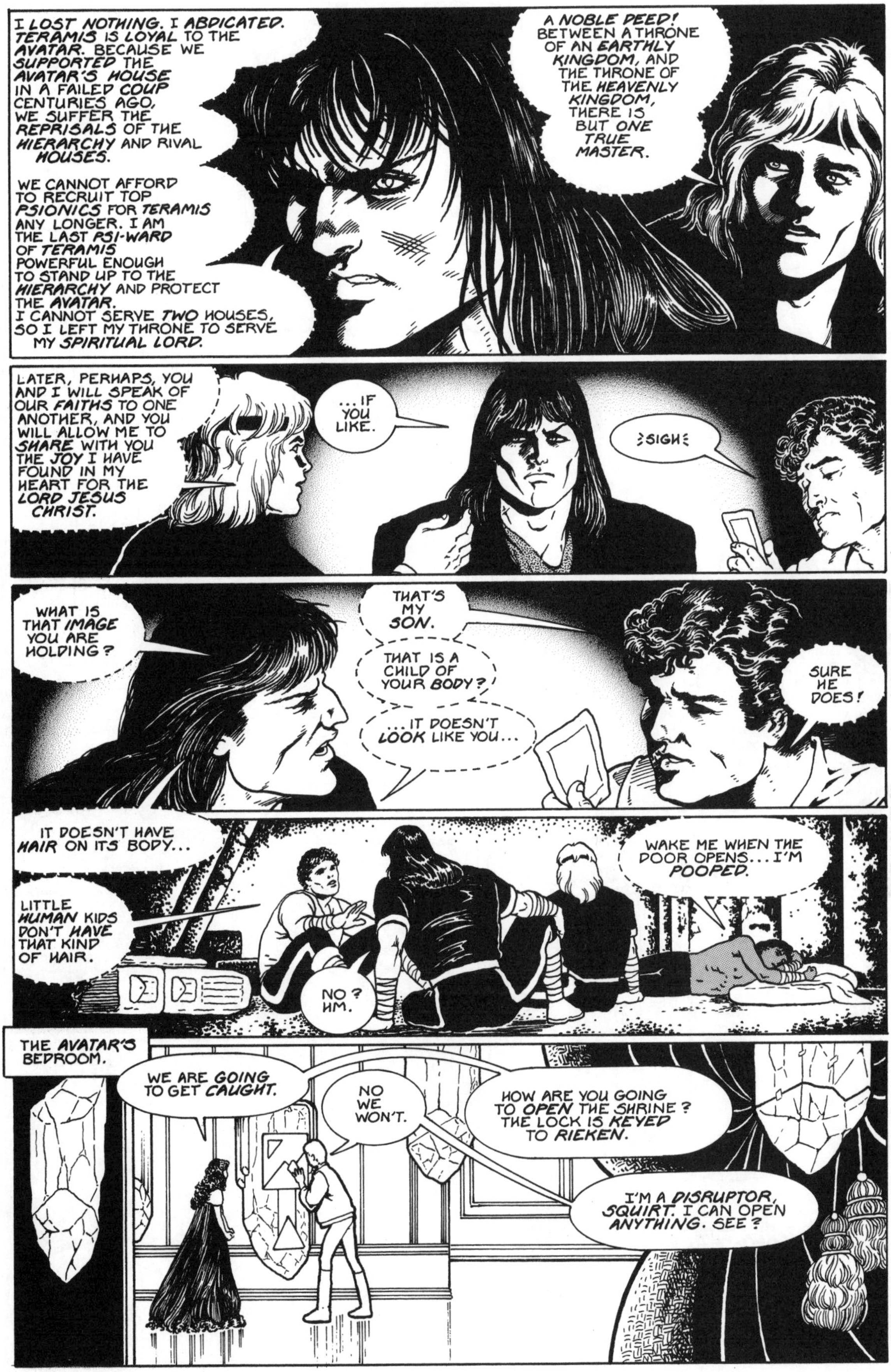
I LOST NOTHING. I ABDICATED. TERAMIS IS LOYAL TO THE AVATAR. BECAUSE WE SUPPORTED THE AVATAR'S HOUSE IN A FAILED COUP CENTURIES AGO, WE SUFFER THE REPRISALS OF THE HIERARCHY AND RIVAL HOUSES.
WE CANNOT AFFORD TO RECRUIT TOP PSIONICS FOR TERAMIS ANY LONGER. I AM THE LAST PSI-WARD OF TERAMIS POWERFUL ENOUGH TO STAND UP TO THE HIERARCHY AND PROTECT THE AVATAR. I CANNOT SERVE TWO HOUSES, SO I LEFT MY THRONE TO SERVE MY SPIRITUAL LORD.
A NOBLE DEED! BETWEEN A THRONE OF AN EARTHLY KINGDOM, AND THE THRONE OF THE HEAVENLY KINGDOM, THERE IS BUT ONE TRUE MASTER.
LATER, PERHAPS, YOU AND I WILL SPEAK OF OUR FAITHS TO ONE ANOTHER, AND YOU WILL ALLOW ME TO SHARE WITH YOU THE JOY I HAVE FOUND IN MY HEART FOR THE LORD JESUS CHRIST.
...IF YOU LIKE.
SIGH
WHAT IS THAT IMAGE YOU ARE HOLDING?
THAT'S MY SON.
THAT IS A CHILD OF YOUR BODY?
...IT DOESN'T LOOK LIKE YOU...
SURE HE DOES!
IT DOESN'T HAVE HAIR ON ITS BODY...
LITTLE HUMAN KIDS DON'T HAVE THAT KIND OF HAIR.
NO? HM.
WAKE ME WHEN THE DOOR OPENS...I'M POOPED.
THE AVATAR'S BEDROOM.
WE ARE GOING TO GET CAUGHT.
NO WE WON'T.
HOW ARE YOU GOING TO OPEN THE SHRINE? THE LOCK IS KEYED TO RIEKEN.
I'M A DISRUPTOR, SQUIRT. I CAN OPEN ANYTHING. SEE?

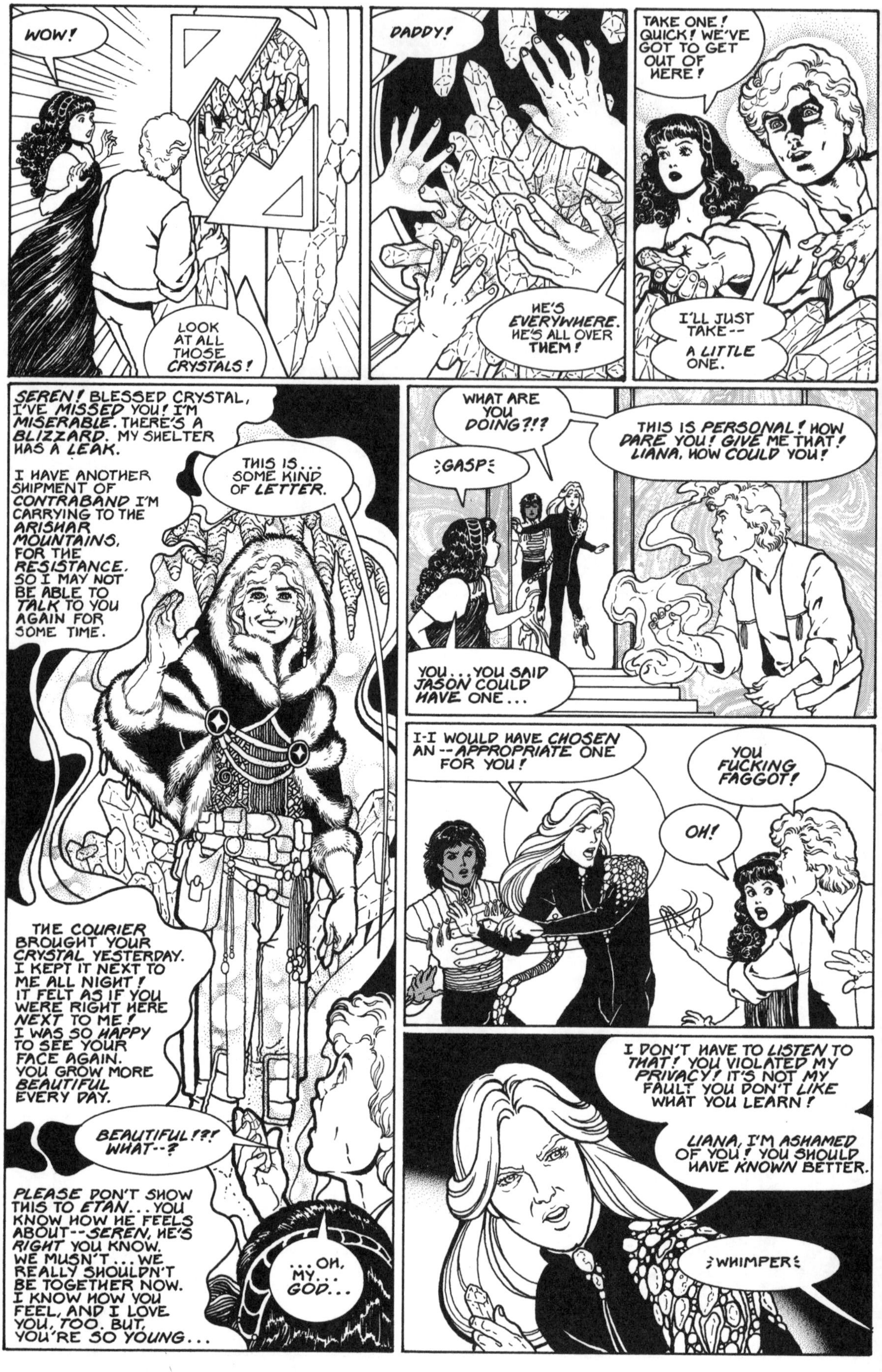
WOW!
LOOK AT ALL THOSE CRYSTALS!
DADDY!
HE'S EVERYWHERE. HE'S ALL OVER THEM!
TAKE ONE! QUICK! WE'VE GOT TO GET OUT OF HERE!
I'LL JUST TAKE--
A LITTLE ONE.
SEREN! BLESSED CRYSTAL, I'VE MISSED YOU! I'M MISERABLE. THERE'S A BLIZZARD. MY SHELTER HAS A LEAK.
I HAVE ANOTHER SHIPMENT OF CONTRABAND I'M CARRYING TO THE ARISHAR MOUNTAINS, FOR THE RESISTANCE. SO I MAY NOT BE ABLE TO TALK TO YOU AGAIN FOR SOME TIME.
THIS IS... SOME KIND OF LETTER.
THE COURIER BROUGHT YOUR CRYSTAL YESTERDAY. I KEPT IT NEXT TO ME ALL NIGHT! IT FELT AS IF YOU WERE RIGHT HERE NEXT TO ME! I WAS SO HAPPY TO SEE YOUR FACE AGAIN. YOU GROW MORE BEAUTIFUL EVERY DAY.
BEAUTIFUL!?! WHAT--?
PLEASE DON'T SHOW THIS TO ETAN... YOU KNOW HOW HE FEELS ABOUT--SEREN, HE'S RIGHT YOU KNOW. WE MUSN'T... WE REALLY SHOULDN'T BE TOGETHER NOW. I KNOW HOW YOU FEEL, AND I LOVE YOU, TOO. BUT, YOU'RE SO YOUNG...
...OH, MY... GOD...
WHAT ARE YOU DOING?!?
GASP
THIS IS PERSONAL! HOW DARE YOU! GIVE ME THAT! LIANA, HOW COULD YOU!
YOU... YOU SAID JASON COULD HAVE ONE...
I-I WOULD HAVE CHOSEN AN--APPROPRIATE ONE FOR YOU!
YOU FUCKING FAGGOT!
OH!
I DON'T HAVE TO LISTEN TO THAT! YOU VIOLATED MY PRIVACY! IT'S NOT MY FAULT YOU DON'T LIKE WHAT YOU LEARN!
LIANA, I'M ASHAMED OF YOU! YOU SHOULD HAVE KNOWN BETTER.
WHIMPER

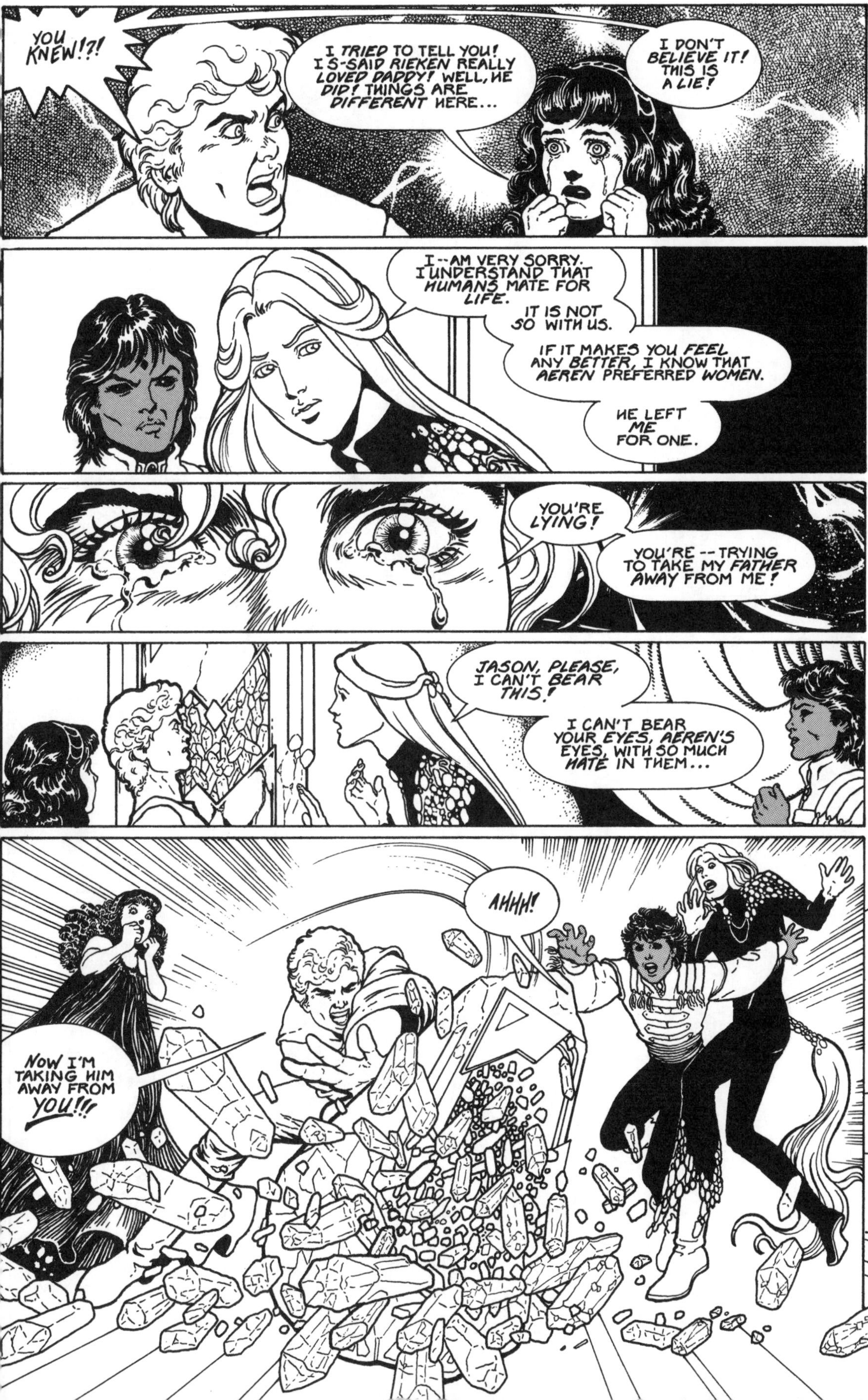
YOU KNEW!?!
I TRIED TO TELL YOU! I S-SAID RIEKEN REALLY LOVED DADDY! WELL, HE DID! THINGS ARE DIFFERENT HERE...
I DON'T BELIEVE IT! THIS IS A LIE!
I--AM VERY SORRY. I UNDERSTAND THAT HUMANS MATE FOR LIFE.
IT IS NOT SO WITH US.
IF IT MAKES YOU FEEL ANY BETTER, I KNOW THAT AEREN PREFERRED WOMEN.
HE LEFT ME FOR ONE.
YOU'RE LYING!
YOU'RE --TRYING TO TAKE MY FATHER AWAY FROM ME!
JASON, PLEASE, I CAN'T BEAR THIS!
I CAN'T BEAR YOUR EYES, AEREN'S EYES, WITH SO MUCH HATE IN THEM...
AHHH!
NOW I'M TAKING HIM AWAY FROM YOU!!!

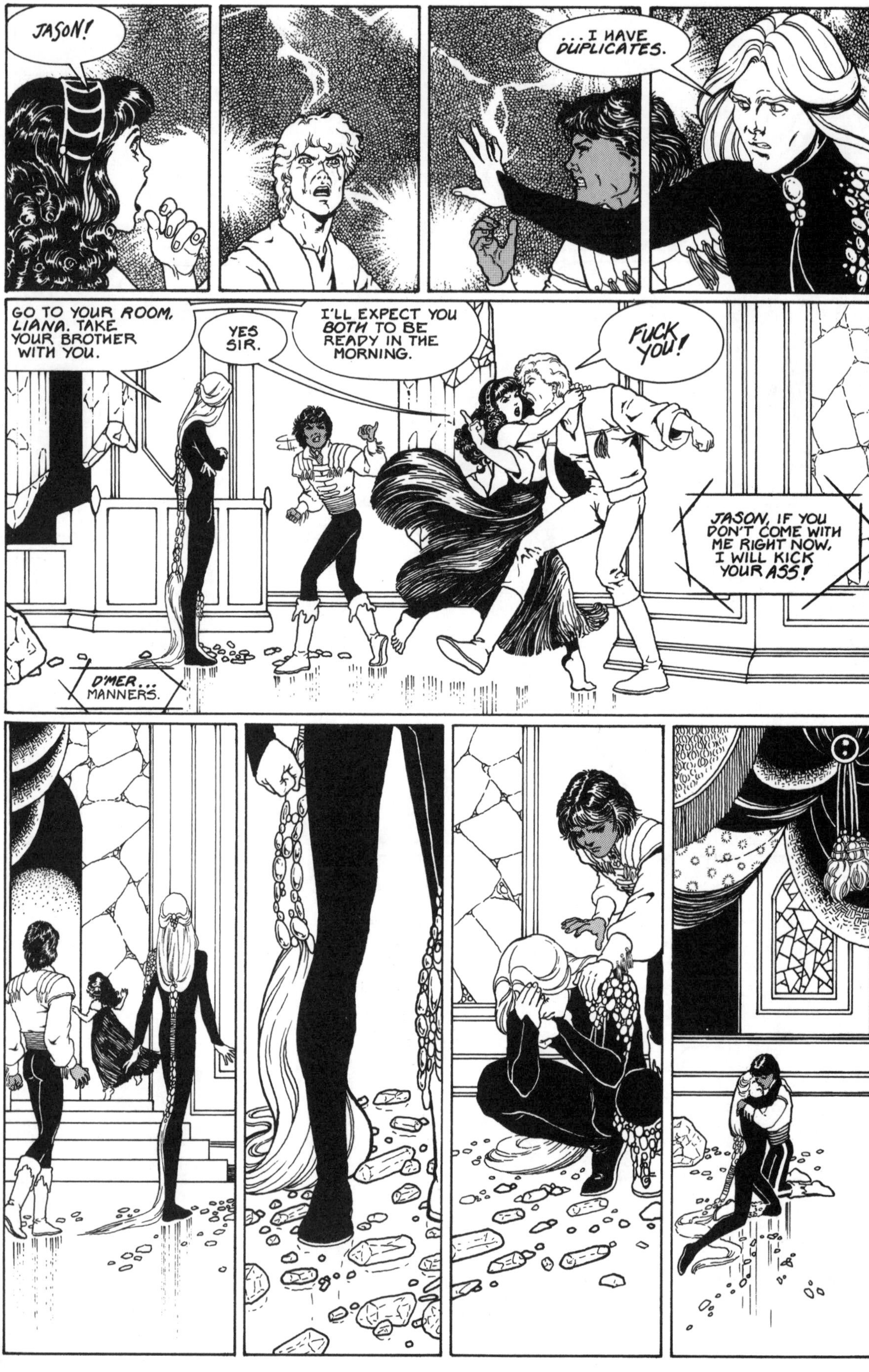
JASON!
...I HAVE DUPLICATES.
GO TO YOUR ROOM, LIANA. TAKE YOUR BROTHER WITH YOU.
YES SIR.
I'LL EXPECT YOU BOTH TO BE READY IN THE MORNING.
FUCK YOU!
JASON, IF YOU DON'T COME WITH ME RIGHT NOW, I WILL KICK YOUR ASS!
D'MER... MANNERS.

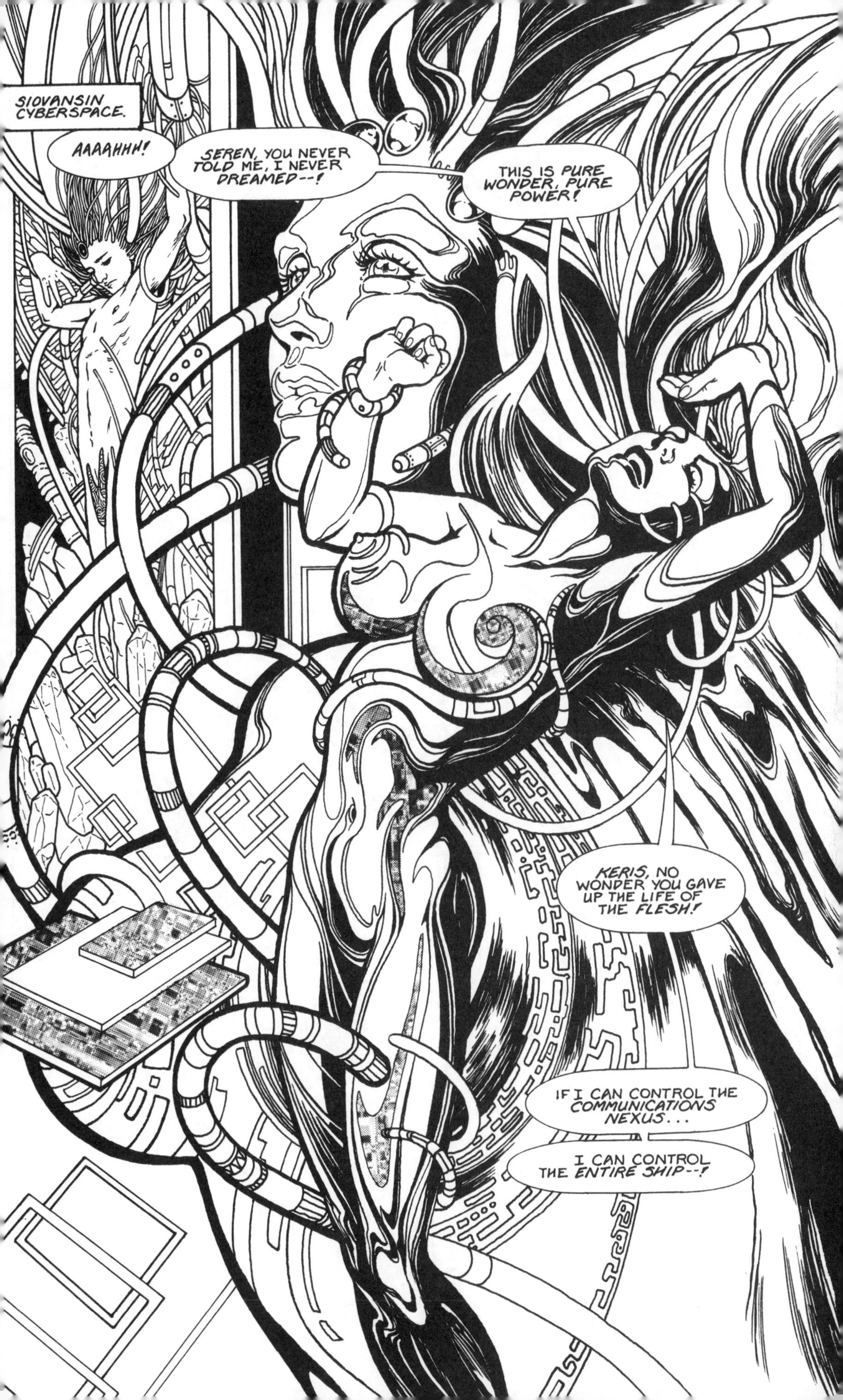
SIOVANSIN CYBERSPACE.
AAAAHHH!
SEREN, YOU NEVER TOLD ME, I NEVER DREAMED--!
THIS IS PURE WONDER, PURE POWER!
KERIS, NO WONDER YOU GAVE UP THE LIFE OF THE FLESH!
IF I CAN CONTROL THE COMMUNICATIONS NEXUS...
I CAN CONTROL THE ENTIRE SHIP--!

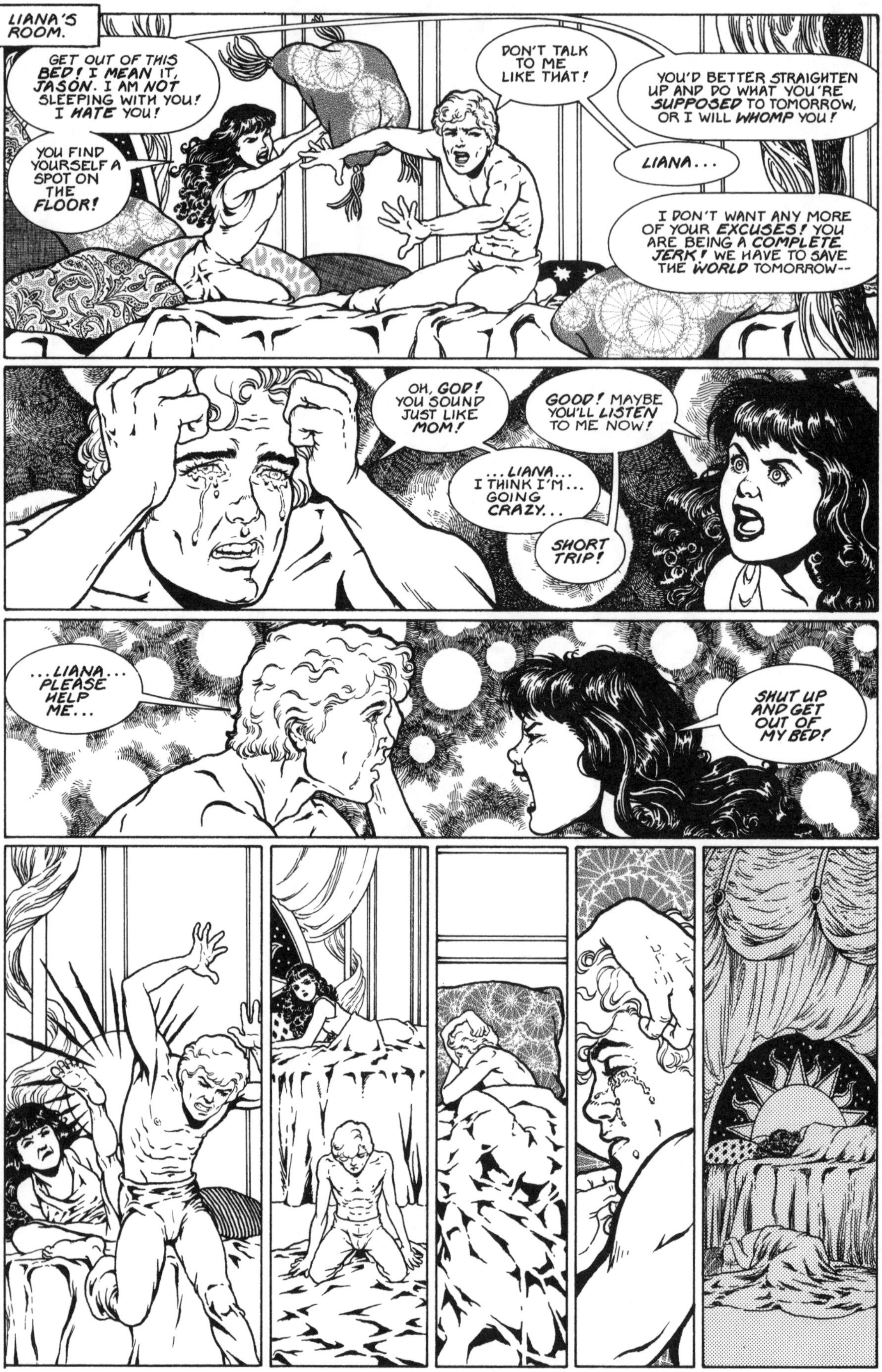
LIANA'S ROOM.
GET OUT OF THIS BED! I MEAN IT, JASON. I AM NOT SLEEPING WITH YOU! I HATE YOU!
YOU FIND YOURSELF A SPOT ON THE FLOOR!
DON'T TALK TO ME LIKE THAT!
LIANA...
YOU'D BETTER STRAIGHTEN UP AND DO WHAT YOU'RE SUPPOSED TO TOMORROW, OR I WILL WHOMP YOU!
I DON'T WANT ANY MORE OF YOUR EXCUSES! YOU ARE BEING A COMPLETE JERK! WE HAVE TO SAVE THE WORLD TOMORROW--
OH, GOD! YOU SOUND JUST LIKE MOM!
...LIANA... I THINK I'M... GOING CRAZY...
GOOD! MAYBE YOU'LL LISTEN TO ME NOW!
SHORT TRIP!
...LIANA... PLEASE HELP ME...
SHUT UP AND GET OUT OF MY BED!

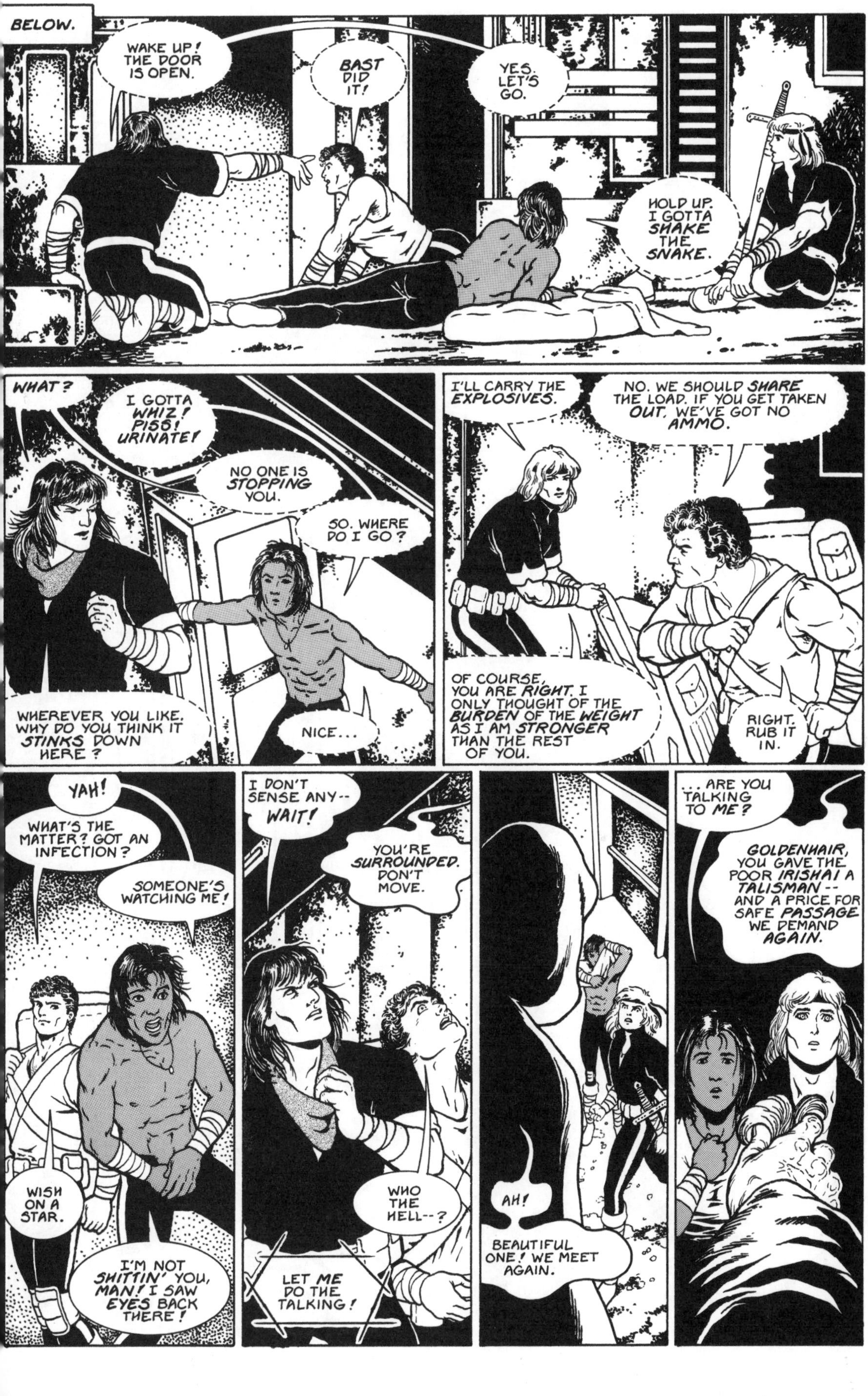
BELOW.
WAKE UP! THE DOOR IS OPEN.
BAST DID IT!
YES. LET'S GO.
HOLD UP. I GOTTA SHAKE THE SNAKE.
WHAT?
I GOTTA WHIZ! PISS! URINATE!
NO ONE IS STOPPING YOU.
SO. WHERE DO I GO?
WHEREVER YOU LIKE. WHY DO YOU THINK IT STINKS DOWN HERE?
NICE...
I'LL CARRY THE EXPLOSIVES.
NO. WE SHOULD SHARE THE LOAD. IF YOU GET TAKEN OUT, WE'VE GOT NO AMMO.
OF COURSE, YOU ARE RIGHT. I ONLY THOUGHT OF THE BURDEN OF THE WEIGHT AS I AM STRONGER THAN THE REST OF YOU.
RIGHT. RUB IT IN.
YAH!
WHAT'S THE MATTER? GOT AN INFECTION?
SOMEONE'S WATCHING ME!
WISH ON A STAR.
I'M NOT SHITTIN' YOU, MAN! I SAW EYES BACK THERE!
I DON'T SENSE ANY-- WAIT!
YOU'RE SURROUNDED. DON'T MOVE.
WHO THE HELL--?
LET ME DO THE TALKING!
AH!
BEAUTIFUL ONE! WE MEET AGAIN.
...ARE YOU TALKING TO ME?
GOLDENHAIR, YOU GAVE THE POOR IRISHAI A TALISMAN -- AND A PRICE FOR SAFE PASSAGE WE DEMAND AGAIN.

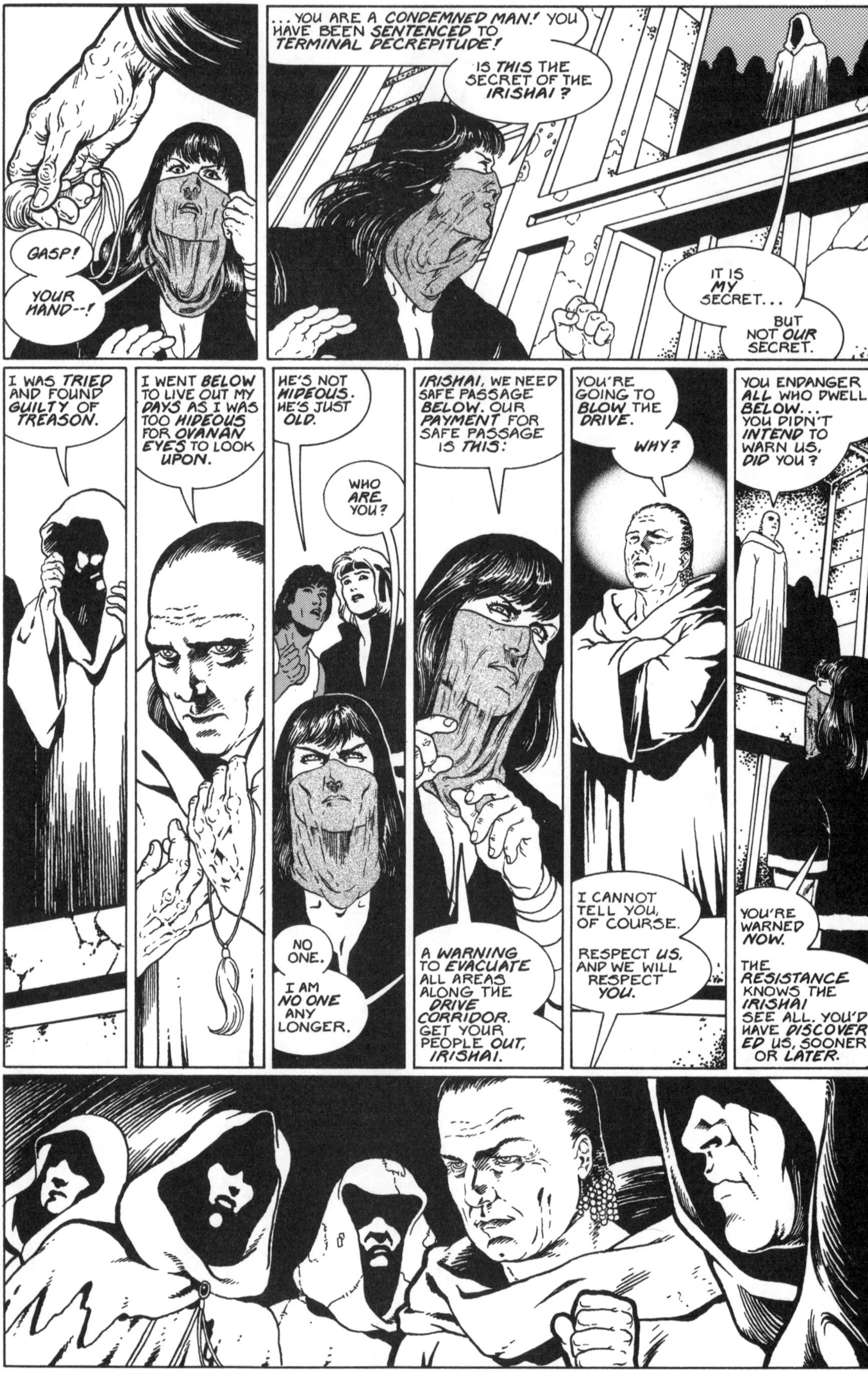
GASP!
YOUR HAND--!
...YOU ARE A CONDEMNED MAN! YOU HAVE BEEN SENTENCED TO TERMINAL DECREPITUDE!
IS THIS THE SECRET OF THE IRISHAI?
IT IS MY SECRET...
BUT NOT OUR SECRET.
I WAS TRIED AND FOUND GUILTY OF TREASON.
I WENT BELOW TO LIVE OUT MY DAYS AS I WAS TOO HIDEOUS FOR OVANAN EYES TO LOOK UPON.
HE'S NOT HIDEOUS. HE'S JUST OLD.
WHO ARE YOU?
NO ONE.
I AM NO ONE ANY LONGER.
IRISHAI, WE NEED SAFE PASSAGE BELOW. OUR PAYMENT FOR SAFE PASSAGE IS THIS:
A WARNING TO EVACUATE ALL AREAS ALONG THE DRIVE CORRIDOR. GET YOUR PEOPLE OUT, IRISHAI.
YOU'RE GOING TO BLOW THE DRIVE.
WHY?
I CANNOT TELL YOU, OF COURSE.
RESPECT US, AND WE WILL RESPECT YOU.
YOU ENDANGER ALL WHO DWELL BELOW... YOU DIDN'T INTEND TO WARN US, DID YOU?
YOU'RE WARNED NOW.
THE RESISTANCE KNOWS THE IRISHAI SEE ALL. YOU'D HAVE DISCOVERED US, SOONER OR LATER.

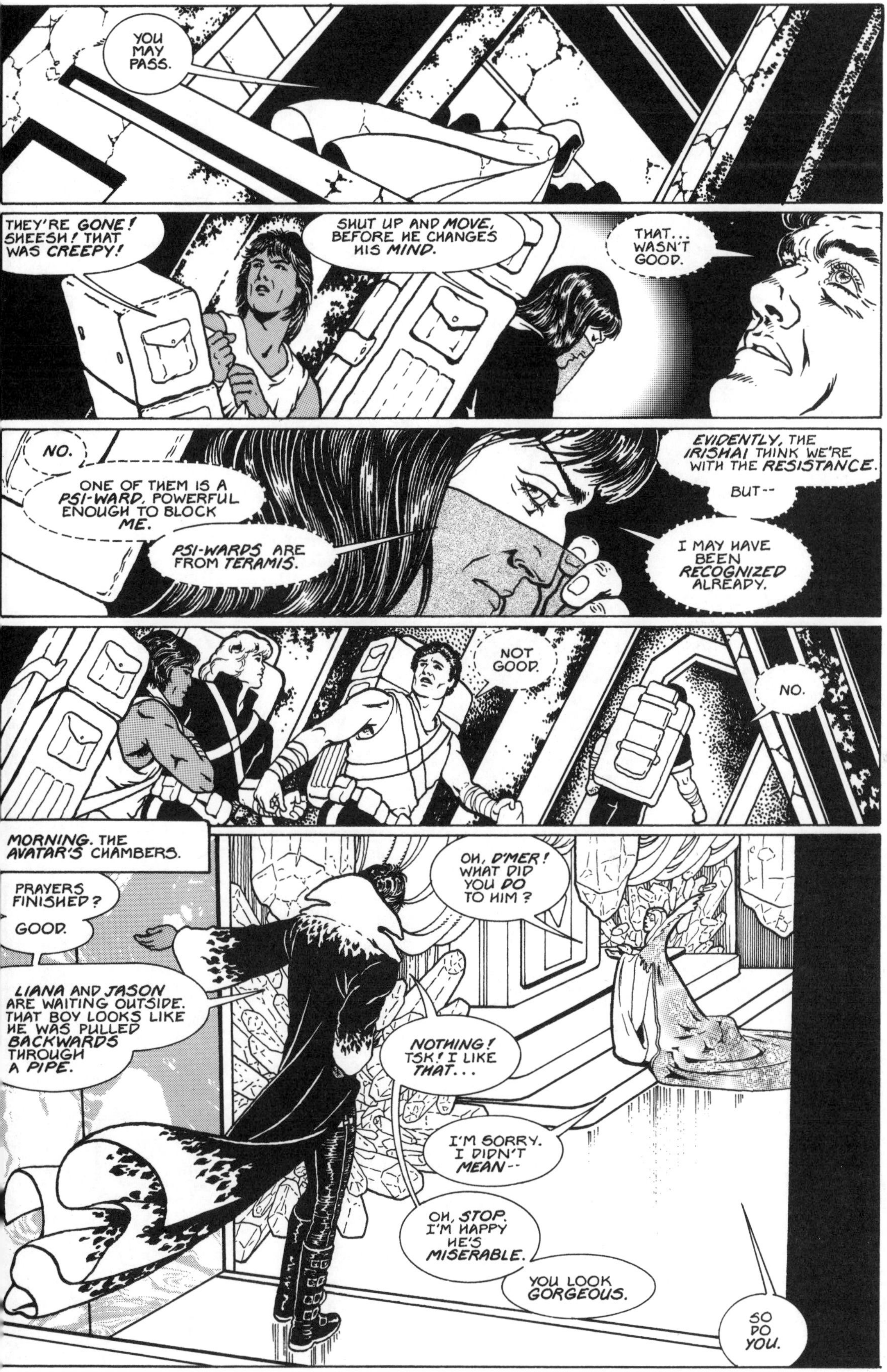
YOU MAY PASS.
THEY'RE GONE! SHEESH! THAT WAS CREEPY!
SHUT UP AND MOVE, BEFORE HE CHANGES HIS MIND.
THAT... WASN'T GOOD.
NO.
ONE OF THEM IS A PSI-WARD, POWERFUL ENOUGH TO BLOCK ME.
PSI-WARDS ARE FROM TERAMIS.
EVIDENTLY, THE IRISHAI THINK WE'RE WITH THE RESISTANCE.
BUT--
I MAY HAVE BEEN RECOGNIZED ALREADY.
NOT GOOD.
NO.
MORNING. THE AVATAR'S CHAMBERS.
PRAYERS FINISHED?
GOOD.
LIANA AND JASON ARE WAITING OUTSIDE. THAT BOY LOOKS LIKE HE WAS PULLED BACKWARDS THROUGH A PIPE.
OH, D'MER! WHAT DID YOU DO TO HIM?
NOTHING! TSK! I LIKE THAT...
I'M SORRY. I DIDN'T MEAN--
OH, STOP. I'M HAPPY HE'S MISERABLE.
YOU LOOK GORGEOUS.
SO DO YOU.

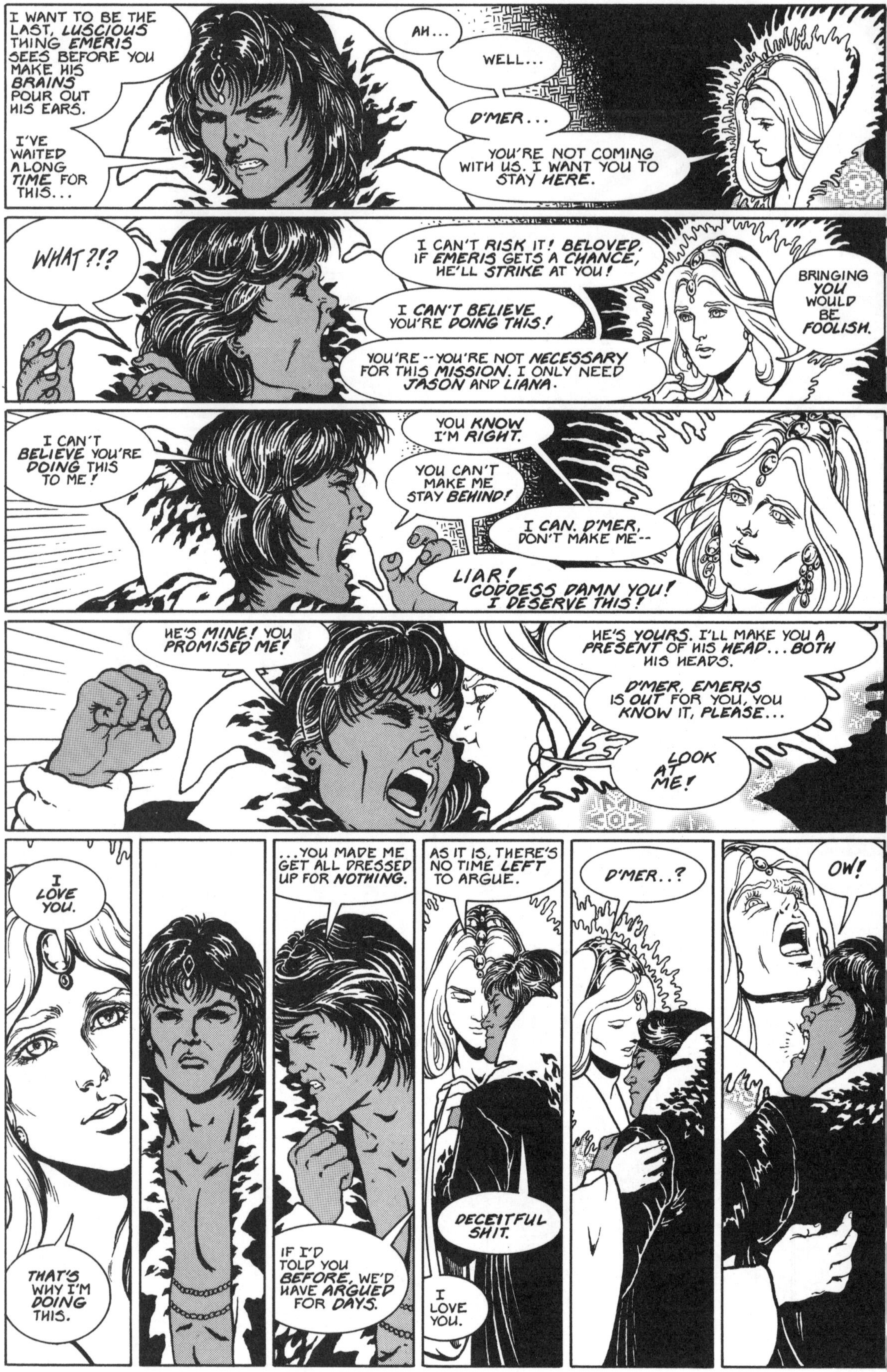
I WANT TO BE THE LAST, LUSCIOUS THING EMERIS SEES BEFORE YOU MAKE HIS BRAINS POUR OUT HIS EARS.
I'VE WAITED A LONG TIME FOR THIS...
AH...
WELL...
D'MER...
YOU'RE NOT COMING WITH US. I WANT YOU TO STAY HERE.
WHAT?!?
I CAN'T RISK IT! BELOVED, IF EMERIS GETS A CHANCE, HE'LL STRIKE AT YOU!
I CAN'T BELIEVE YOU'RE DOING THIS!
YOU'RE--YOU'RE NOT NECESSARY FOR THIS MISSION. I ONLY NEED JASON AND LIANA.
BRINGING YOU WOULD BE FOOLISH.
I CAN'T BELIEVE YOU'RE DOING THIS TO ME!
YOU KNOW I'M RIGHT.
YOU CAN'T MAKE ME STAY BEHIND!
I CAN, D'MER, DON'T MAKE ME--
LIAR! GODDESS DAMN YOU! I DESERVE THIS!
HE'S MINE! YOU PROMISED ME!
HE'S YOURS. I'LL MAKE YOU A PRESENT OF HIS HEAD... BOTH HIS HEADS.
D'MER, EMERIS IS OUT FOR YOU, YOU KNOW IT, PLEASE...
LOOK AT ME!
I LOVE YOU.
THAT'S WHY I'M DOING THIS.
...YOU MADE ME GET ALL DRESSED UP FOR NOTHING.
IF I'D TOLD YOU BEFORE, WE'D HAVE ARGUED FOR DAYS.
AS IT IS, THERE'S NO TIME LEFT TO ARGUE.
DECEITFUL SHIT.
I LOVE YOU.
D'MER..?
OW!

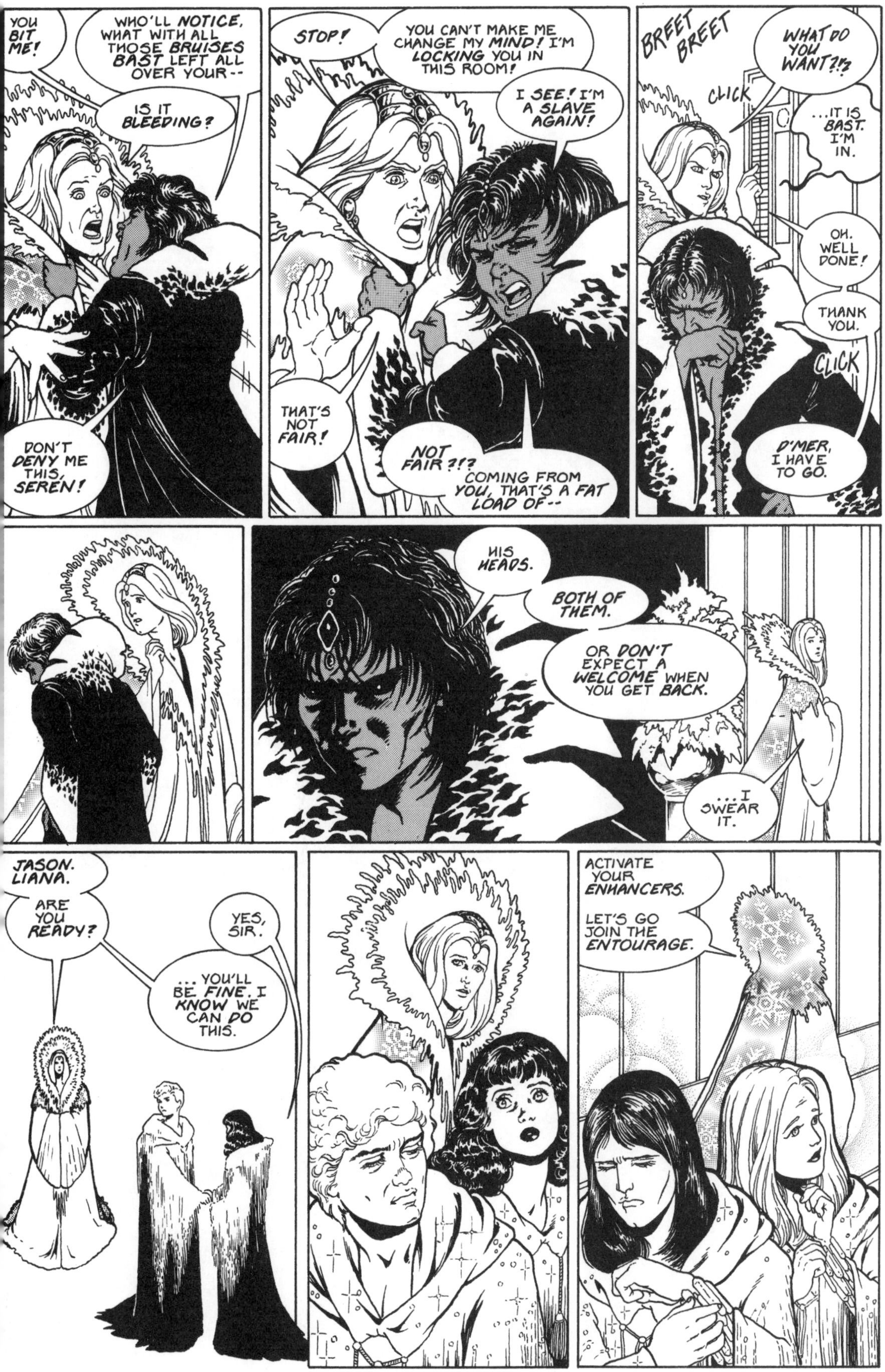
YOU BIT ME!
WHO'LL NOTICE, WHAT WITH ALL THOSE BRUISES BAST LEFT ALL OVER YOUR--
IS IT BLEEDING?
DON'T DENY ME THIS, SEREN!
STOP!
YOU CAN'T MAKE ME CHANGE MY MIND! I'M LOCKING YOU IN THIS ROOM!
I SEE! I'M A SLAVE AGAIN!
THAT'S NOT FAIR!
NOT FAIR?!? COMING FROM YOU, THAT'S A FAT LOAD OF--
BREET BREET
WHAT DO YOU WANT?!?
CLICK
...IT IS BAST. I'M IN.
OH. WELL DONE!
THANK YOU.
CLICK
D'MER, I HAVE TO GO.
HIS HEADS.
BOTH OF THEM.
OR DON'T EXPECT A WELCOME WHEN YOU GET BACK.
...I SWEAR IT.
JASON. LIANA.
ARE YOU READY?
YES, SIR.
...YOU'LL BE FINE. I KNOW WE CAN DO THIS.
ACTIVATE YOUR ENHANCERS.
LET'S GO JOIN THE ENTOURAGE.

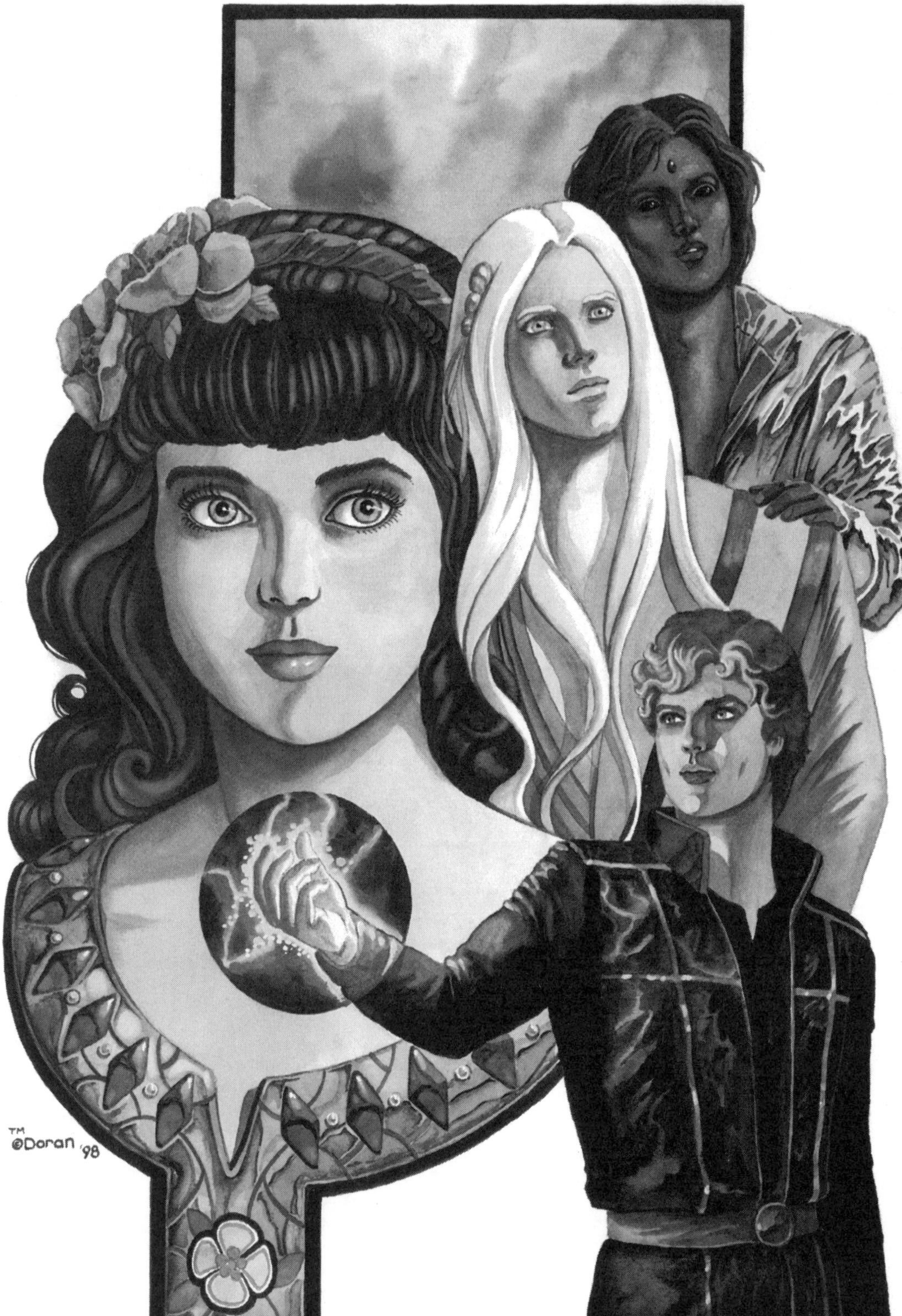
TM
©Doran '98

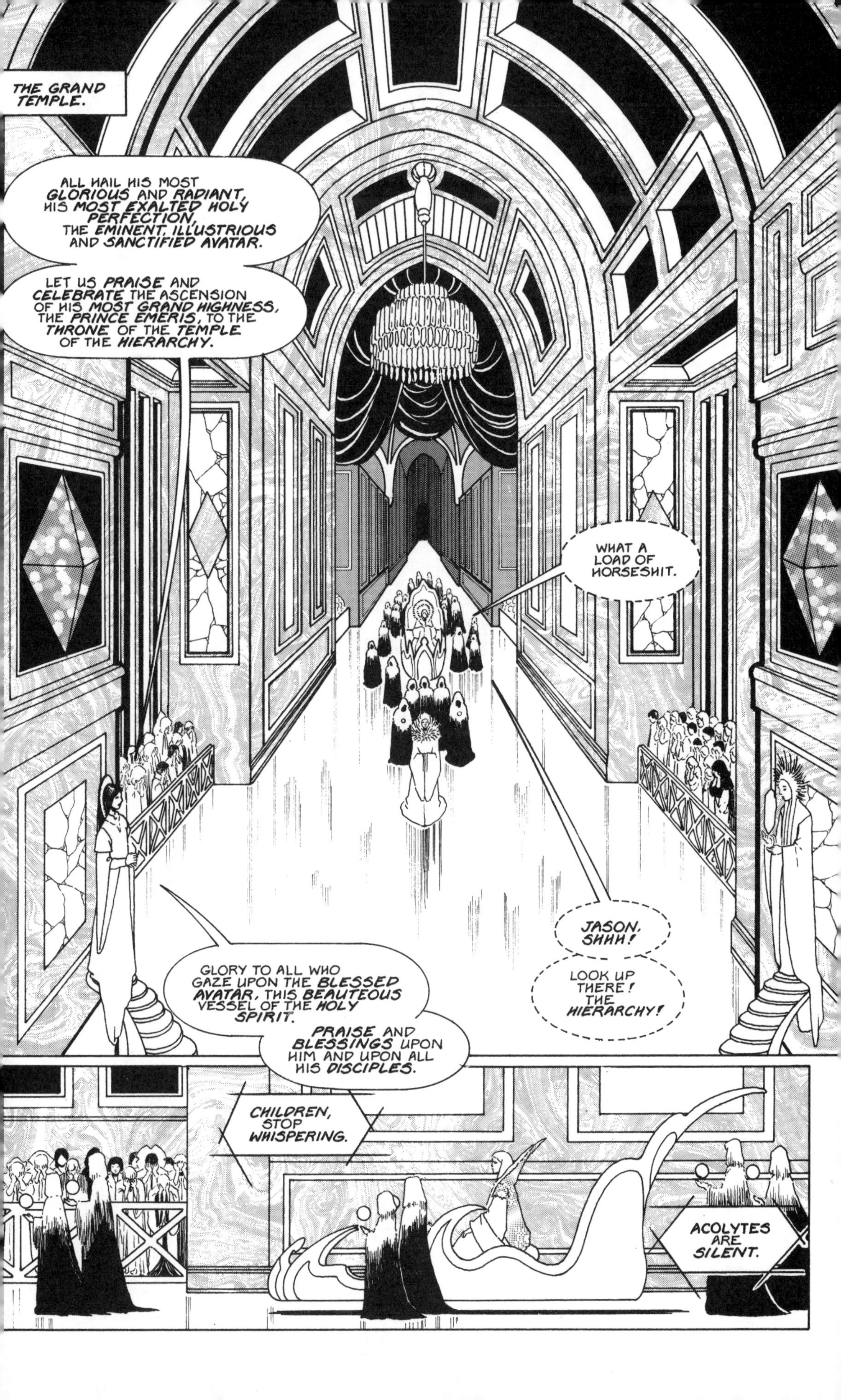
THE GRAND TEMPLE.
ALL HAIL HIS MOST GLORIOUS AND RADIANT, HIS MOST EXALTED HOLY PERFECTION, THE EMINENT, ILLUSTRIOUS AND SANCTIFIED AVATAR.
LET US PRAISE AND CELEBRATE THE ASCENSION OF HIS MOST GRAND HIGHNESS, THE PRINCE EMERIS, TO THE THRONE OF THE TEMPLE OF THE HIERARCHY.
WHAT A LOAD OF HORSESHIT.
JASON, SHHH!
LOOK UP THERE! THE HIERARCHY!
GLORY TO ALL WHO GAZE UPON THE BLESSED AVATAR, THIS BEAUTEOUS VESSEL OF THE HOLY SPIRIT.
PRAISE AND BLESSINGS UPON HIM AND UPON ALL HIS DISCIPLES.
CHILDREN, STOP WHISPERING.
ACOLYTES ARE SILENT.

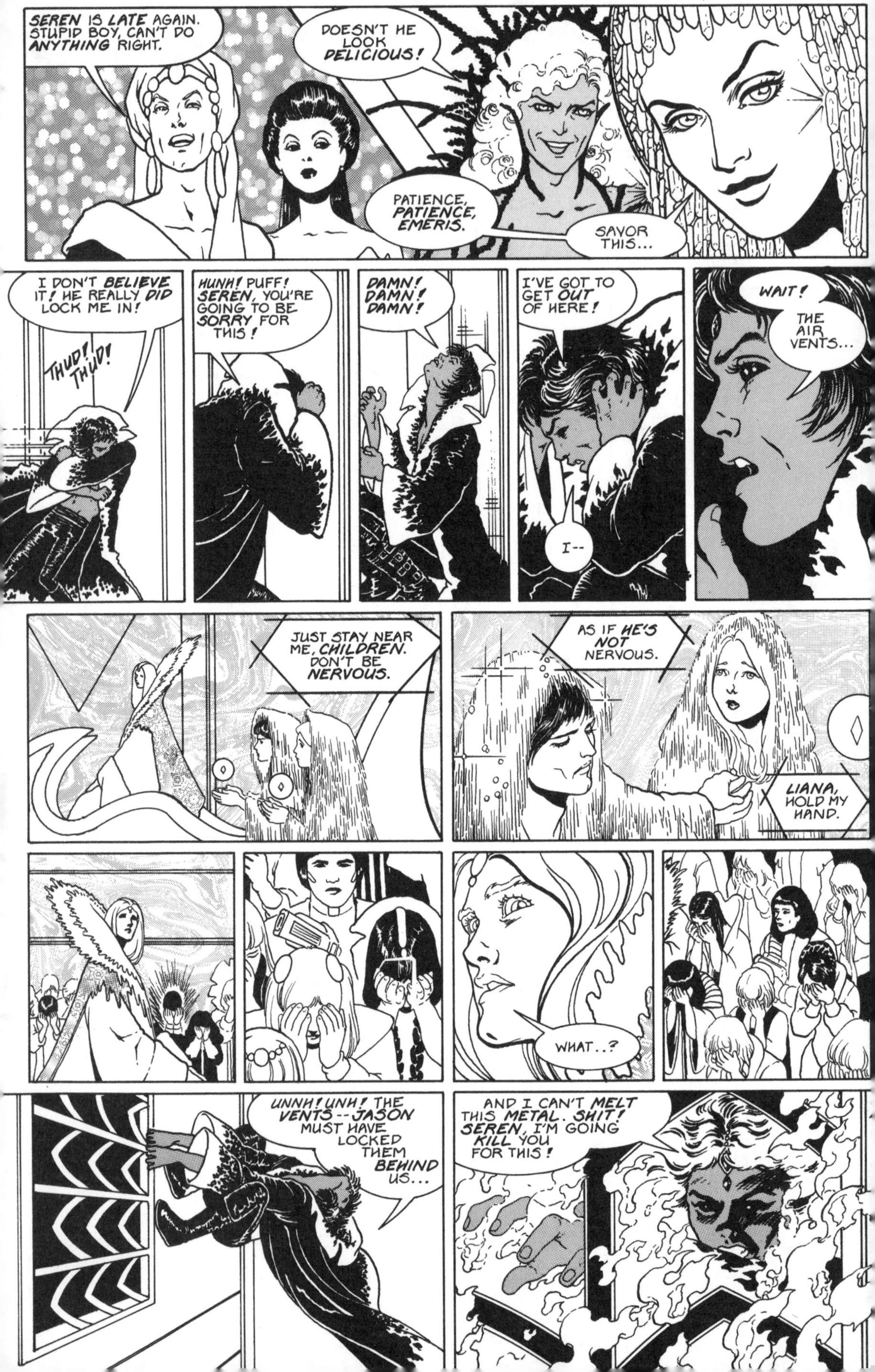
SEREN IS LATE AGAIN. STUPID BOY, CAN'T DO ANYTHING RIGHT.
DOESN'T HE LOOK DELICIOUS!
PATIENCE, PATIENCE, EMERIS.
SAVOR THIS...
I DON'T BELIEVE IT! HE REALLY DID LOCK ME IN!
THUD! THUD!
HUNH! PUFF! SEREN, YOU'RE GOING TO BE SORRY FOR THIS!
DAMN! DAMN! DAMN!
I'VE GOT TO GET OUT OF HERE!
I--
WAIT!
THE AIR VENTS...
JUST STAY NEAR ME, CHILDREN. DON'T BE NERVOUS.
AS IF HE'S NOT NERVOUS.
LIANA, HOLD MY HAND.
WHAT..?
UNNH! UNH! THE VENTS--JASON MUST HAVE LOCKED THEM BEHIND US...
AND I CAN'T MELT THIS METAL. SHIT! SEREN, I'M GOING KILL YOU FOR THIS!

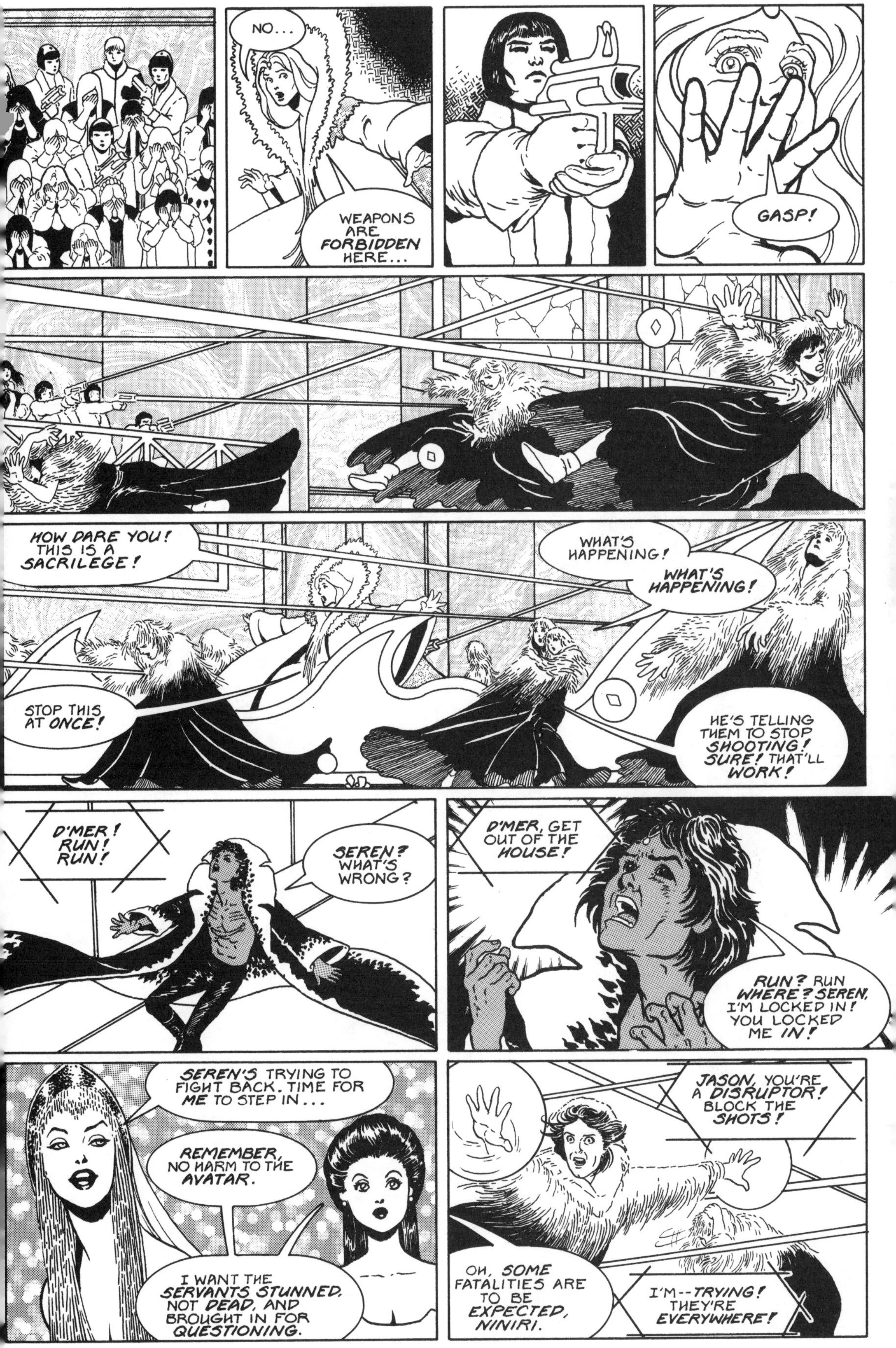
NO...
WEAPONS ARE FORBIDDEN HERE...
GASP!
HOW DARE YOU! THIS IS A SACRILEGE!
STOP THIS AT ONCE!
WHAT'S HAPPENING! WHAT'S HAPPENING!
HE'S TELLING THEM TO STOP SHOOTING! SURE! THAT'LL WORK!
D'MER! RUN! RUN!
SEREN? WHAT'S WRONG?
D'MER, GET OUT OF THE HOUSE!
RUN? RUN WHERE? SEREN, I'M LOCKED IN! YOU LOCKED ME IN!
SEREN'S TRYING TO FIGHT BACK. TIME FOR ME TO STEP IN...
REMEMBER, NO HARM TO THE AVATAR.
I WANT THE SERVANTS STUNNED, NOT DEAD, AND BROUGHT IN FOR QUESTIONING.
JASON, YOU'RE A DISRUPTOR! BLOCK THE SHOTS!
OH, SOME FATALITIES ARE TO BE EXPECTED, NINIRI.
I'M--TRYING! THEY'RE EVERYWHERE!

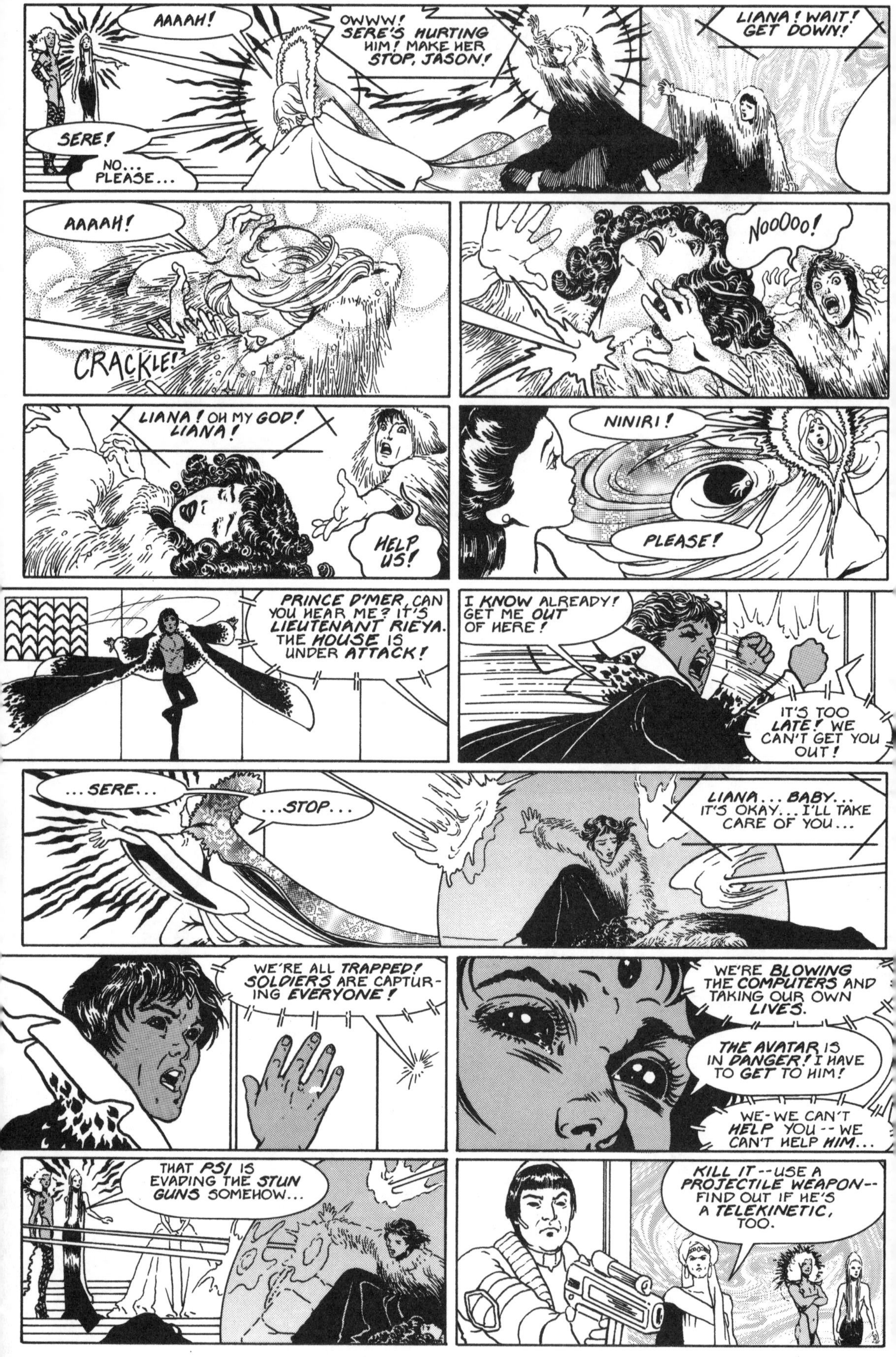

AAAAH!
SERE!
NO... PLEASE...
OWWW! SERE'S HURTING HIM! MAKE HER STOP, JASON!
LIANA! WAIT! GET DOWN!
AAAAH!
CRACKLE!
NoOOoo!
LIANA! OH MY GOD! LIANA!
HELP US!
NINIRI!
PLEASE!
PRINCE D'MER, CAN YOU HEAR ME? IT'S LIEUTENANT RIEYA. THE HOUSE IS UNDER ATTACK!
I KNOW ALREADY! GET ME OUT OF HERE!
IT'S TOO LATE! WE CAN'T GET YOU OUT!
...SERE...
...STOP...
LIANA... BABY... IT'S OKAY... I'LL TAKE CARE OF YOU...
WE'RE ALL TRAPPED! SOLDIERS ARE CAPTURING EVERYONE!
WE'RE BLOWING THE COMPUTERS AND TAKING OUR OWN LIVES.
THE AVATAR IS IN DANGER! I HAVE TO GET TO HIM!
WE-WE CAN'T HELP YOU -- WE CAN'T HELP HIM...
THAT PSI IS EVADING THE STUN GUNS SOMEHOW...
KILL IT -- USE A PROJECTILE WEAPON -- FIND OUT IF HE'S A TELEKINETIC, TOO.

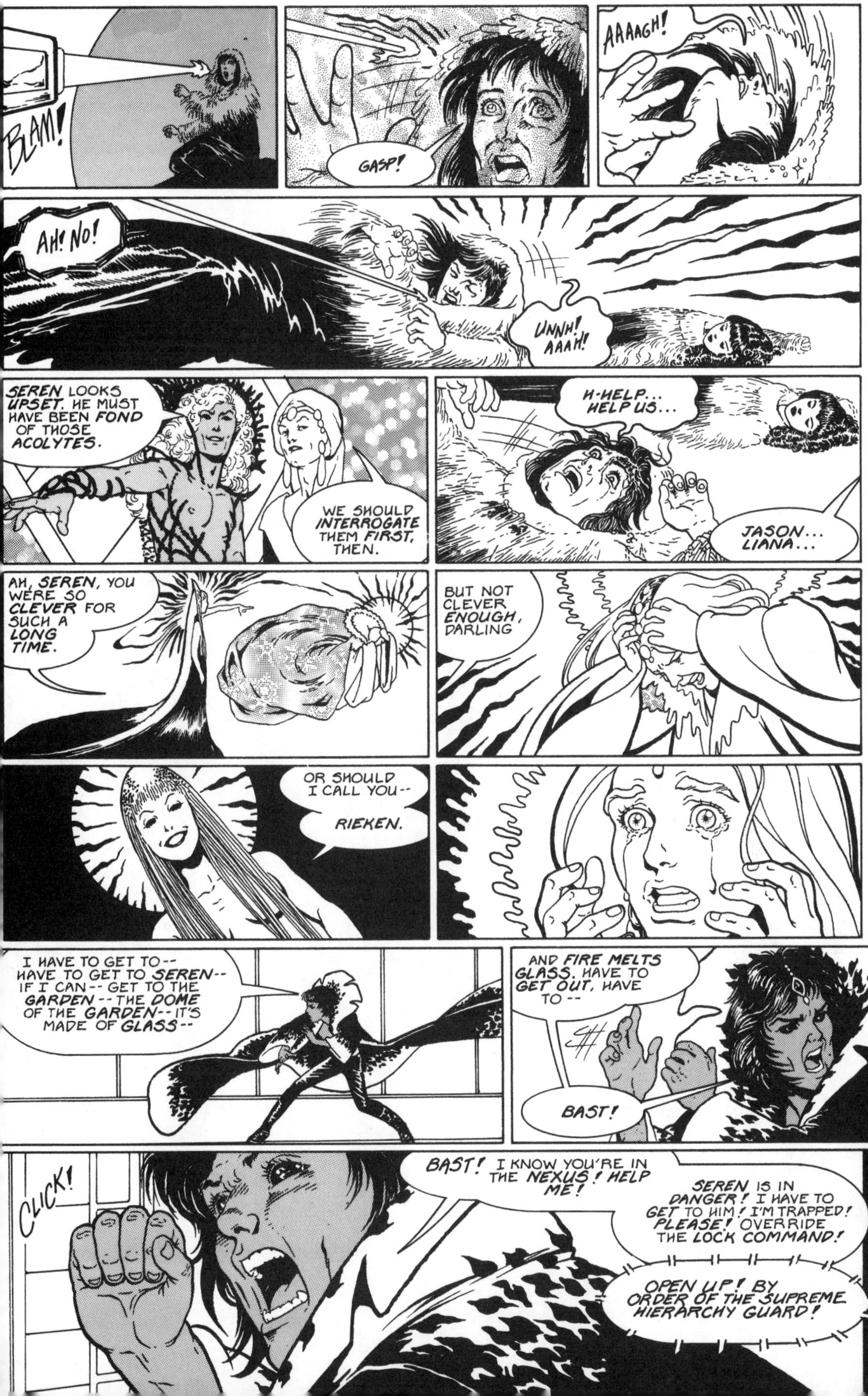
BLAM!
GASP!
AAAAGH!
AH! NO!
UNNH! AAAH!
SEREN LOOKS UPSET. HE MUST HAVE BEEN FOND OF THOSE ACOLYTES.
WE SHOULD INTERROGATE THEM FIRST, THEN.
H-HELP... HELP US...
JASON... LIANA...
AH, SEREN, YOU WERE SO CLEVER FOR SUCH A LONG TIME.
BUT NOT CLEVER ENOUGH, DARLING
OR SHOULD I CALL YOU--
RIEKEN.
I HAVE TO GET TO-- HAVE TO GET TO SEREN-- IF I CAN-- GET TO THE GARDEN--THE DOME OF THE GARDEN--IT'S MADE OF GLASS--
AND FIRE MELTS GLASS. HAVE TO GET OUT. HAVE TO--
BAST!
CLICK!
BAST! I KNOW YOU'RE IN THE NEXUS! HELP ME!
SEREN IS IN DANGER! I HAVE TO GET TO HIM! I'M TRAPPED! PLEASE! OVERRIDE THE LOCK COMMAND!
OPEN UP! BY ORDER OF THE SUPREME HIERARCHY GUARD!

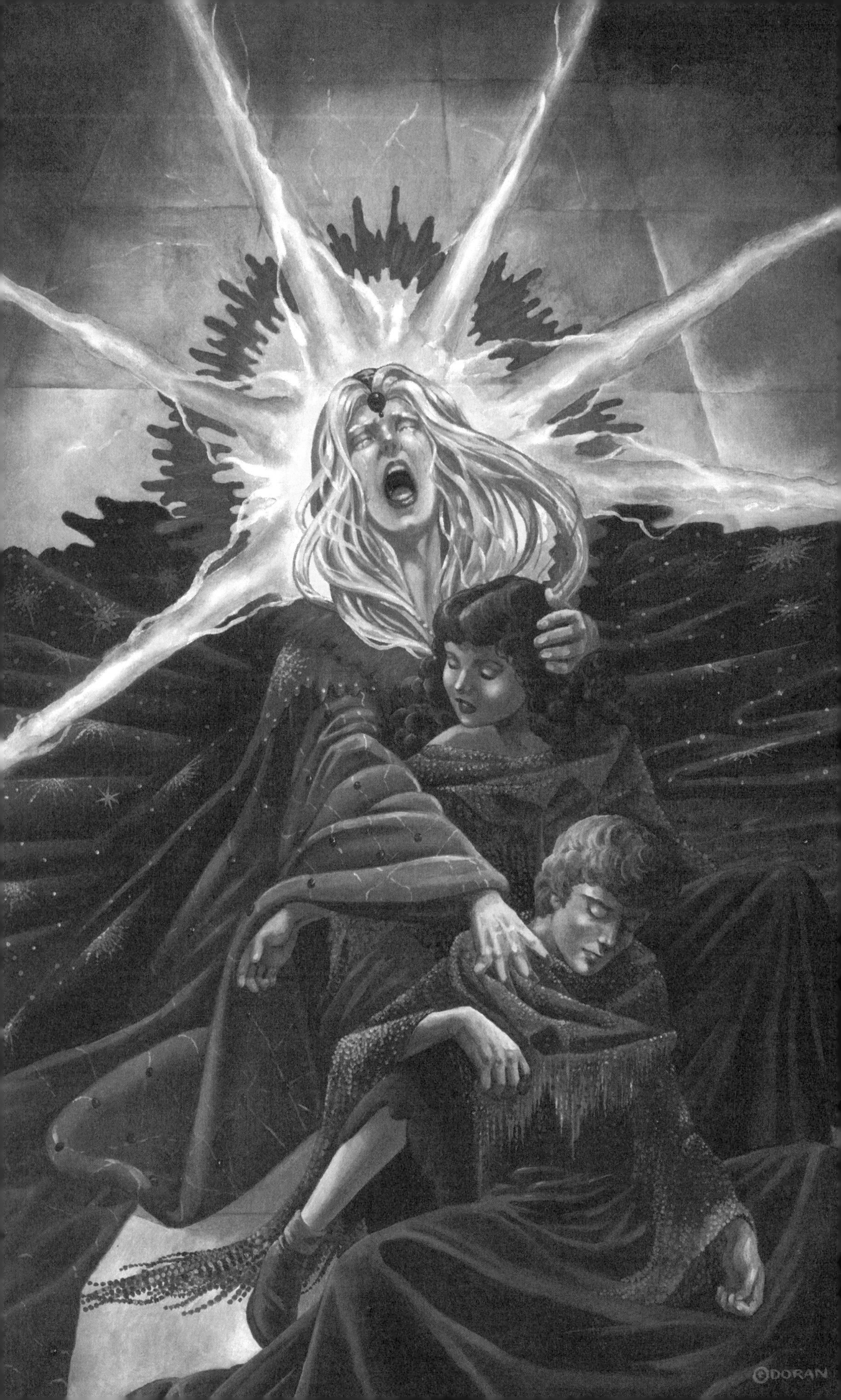
©DORAN

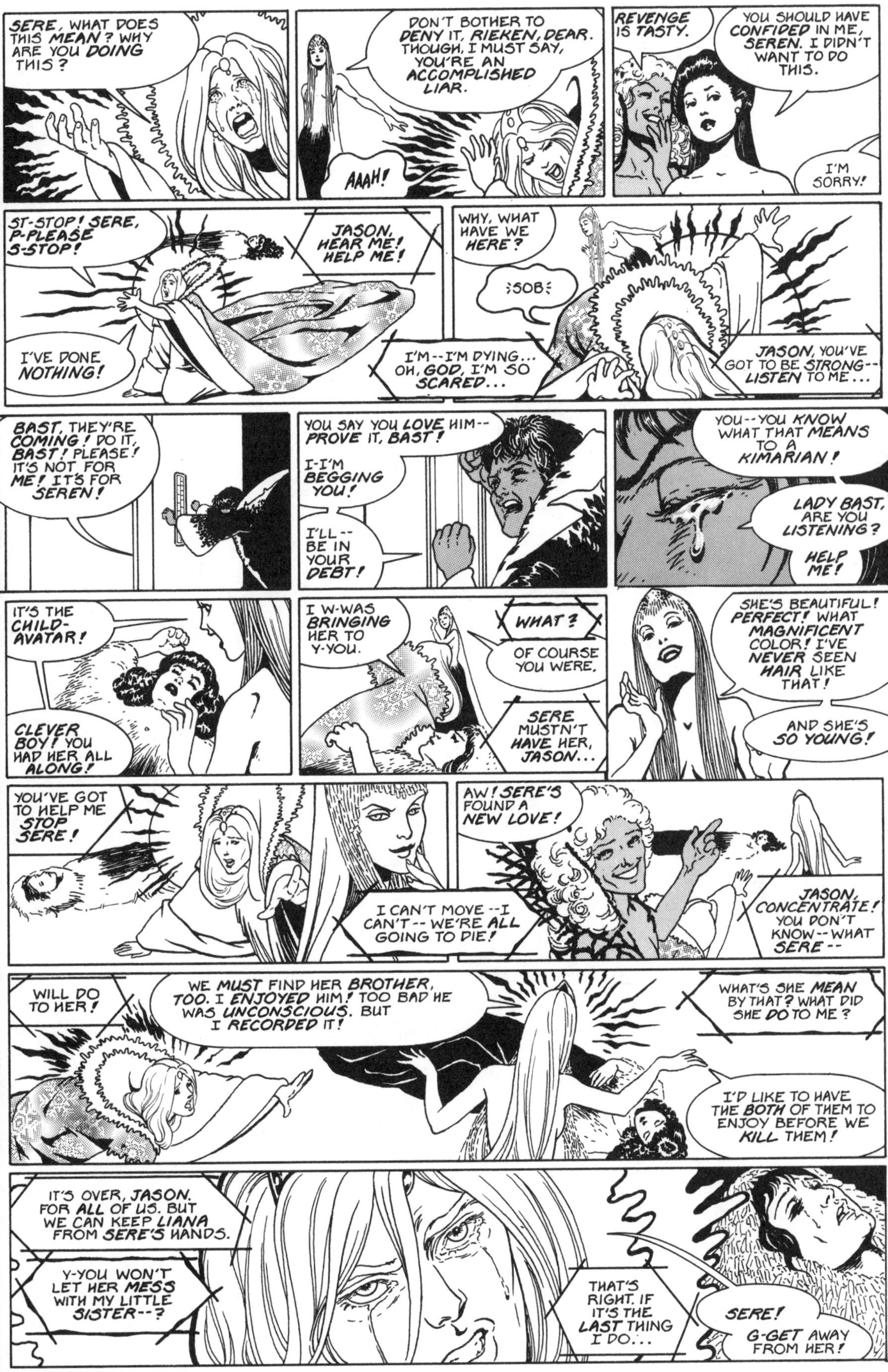

SERE, WHAT DOES THIS MEAN? WHY ARE YOU DOING THIS?
DON'T BOTHER TO DENY IT, RIEKEN, DEAR. THOUGH, I MUST SAY, YOU'RE AN ACCOMPLISHED LIAR.
AAAH!
REVENGE IS TASTY.
YOU SHOULD HAVE CONFIDED IN ME, SEREN. I DIDN'T WANT TO DO THIS.
I'M SORRY!
ST-STOP! SERE, P-PLEASE S-STOP!
JASON, HEAR ME! HELP ME!
I'VE DONE NOTHING!
WHY, WHAT HAVE WE HERE?
SOB
I'M--I'M DYING... OH, GOD, I'M SO SCARED...
JASON, YOU'VE GOT TO BE STRONG-- LISTEN TO ME...
BAST, THEY'RE COMING! DO IT, BAST! PLEASE! IT'S NOT FOR ME! IT'S FOR SEREN!
YOU SAY YOU LOVE HIM-- PROVE IT, BAST!
I-I'M BEGGING YOU!
I'LL-- BE IN YOUR DEBT!
YOU--YOU KNOW WHAT THAT MEANS TO A KIMARIAN!
LADY BAST, ARE YOU LISTENING?
HELP ME!
IT'S THE CHILD-AVATAR!
CLEVER BOY! YOU HAD HER ALL ALONG!
I W-WAS BRINGING HER TO Y-YOU.
WHAT?
OF COURSE YOU WERE.
SERE MUSTN'T HAVE HER, JASON...
SHE'S BEAUTIFUL! PERFECT! WHAT MAGNIFICENT COLOR! I'VE NEVER SEEN HAIR LIKE THAT!
AND SHE'S SO YOUNG!
YOU'VE GOT TO HELP ME STOP SERE!
I CAN'T MOVE--I CAN'T-- WE'RE ALL GOING TO DIE!
AW! SERE'S FOUND A NEW LOVE!
JASON, CONCENTRATE! YOU DON'T KNOW--WHAT SERE--
WILL DO TO HER!
WE MUST FIND HER BROTHER, TOO. I ENJOYED HIM! TOO BAD HE WAS UNCONSCIOUS. BUT I RECORDED IT!
WHAT'S SHE MEAN BY THAT? WHAT DID SHE DO TO ME?
I'D LIKE TO HAVE THE BOTH OF THEM TO ENJOY BEFORE WE KILL THEM!
IT'S OVER, JASON. FOR ALL OF US. BUT WE CAN KEEP LIANA FROM SERE'S HANDS.
Y-YOU WON'T LET HER MESS WITH MY LITTLE SISTER--?
THAT'S RIGHT. IF IT'S THE LAST THING I DO...
SERE!
G-GET AWAY FROM HER!

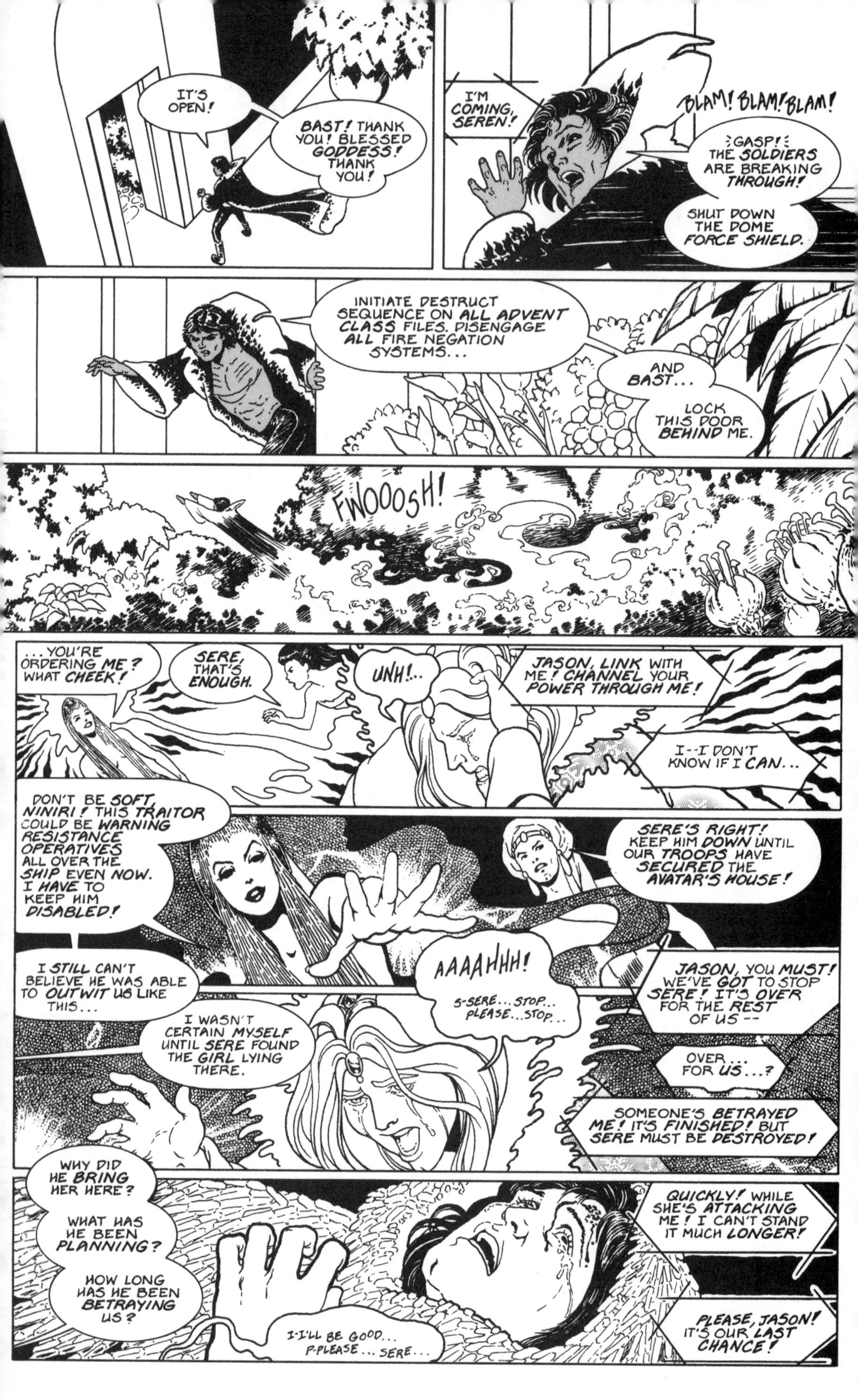
IT'S OPEN!
BAST! THANK YOU! BLESSED GODDESS! THANK YOU!
I'M COMING, SEREN!
BLAM! BLAM! BLAM!
GASP! THE SOLDIERS ARE BREAKING THROUGH!
SHUT DOWN THE DOME FORCE SHIELD.
INITIATE DESTRUCT SEQUENCE ON ALL ADVENT CLASS FILES. DISENGAGE ALL FIRE NEGATION SYSTEMS...
AND BAST...
LOCK THIS DOOR BEHIND ME.
FWOOOSH!
...YOU'RE ORDERING ME? WHAT CHEEK!
SERE, THAT'S ENOUGH.
UNH!..
JASON, LINK WITH ME! CHANNEL YOUR POWER THROUGH ME!
I--I DON'T KNOW IF I CAN...
DON'T BE SOFT, NINIRI! THIS TRAITOR COULD BE WARNING RESISTANCE OPERATIVES ALL OVER THE SHIP EVEN NOW. I HAVE TO KEEP HIM DISABLED!
SERE'S RIGHT! KEEP HIM DOWN UNTIL OUR TROOPS HAVE SECURED THE AVATAR'S HOUSE!
I STILL CAN'T BELIEVE HE WAS ABLE TO OUTWIT US LIKE THIS...
AAAAHHH!
S-SERE... STOP... PLEASE... STOP...
JASON, YOU MUST! WE'VE GOT TO STOP SERE! IT'S OVER FOR THE REST OF US --
I WASN'T CERTAIN MYSELF UNTIL SERE FOUND THE GIRL LYING THERE.
OVER... FOR US...?
SOMEONE'S BETRAYED ME! IT'S FINISHED! BUT SERE MUST BE DESTROYED!
WHY DID HE BRING HER HERE?
WHAT HAS HE BEEN PLANNING?
HOW LONG HAS HE BEEN BETRAYING US?
I-I'LL BE GOOD... P-PLEASE... SERE...
QUICKLY! WHILE SHE'S ATTACKING ME! I CAN'T STAND IT MUCH LONGER!
PLEASE, JASON! IT'S OUR LAST CHANCE!

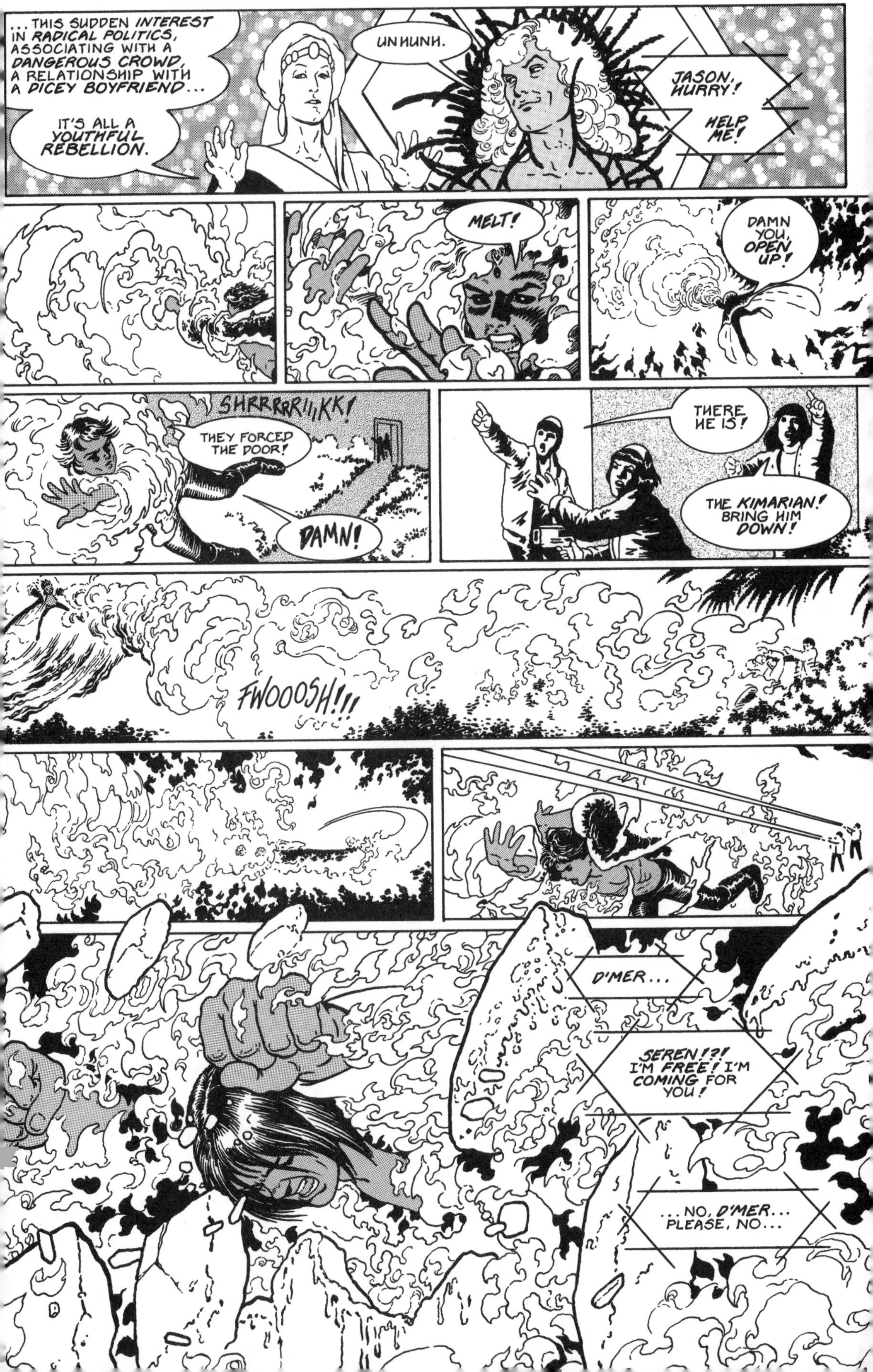

...THIS SUDDEN INTEREST IN RADICAL POLITICS, ASSOCIATING WITH A DANGEROUS CROWD, A RELATIONSHIP WITH A DICEY BOYFRIEND...
IT'S ALL A YOUTHFUL REBELLION.
UNHUNH.
JASON, HURRY!
HELP ME!
MELT!
DAMN YOU, OPEN UP!
SHRRRRRIIIKK!
THEY FORCED THE DOOR!
DAMN!
THERE HE IS!
THE KIMARIAN! BRING HIM DOWN!
FWOOOSH!!!
D'MER...
SEREN!?! I'M FREE! I'M COMING FOR YOU!
...NO, D'MER... PLEASE, NO...

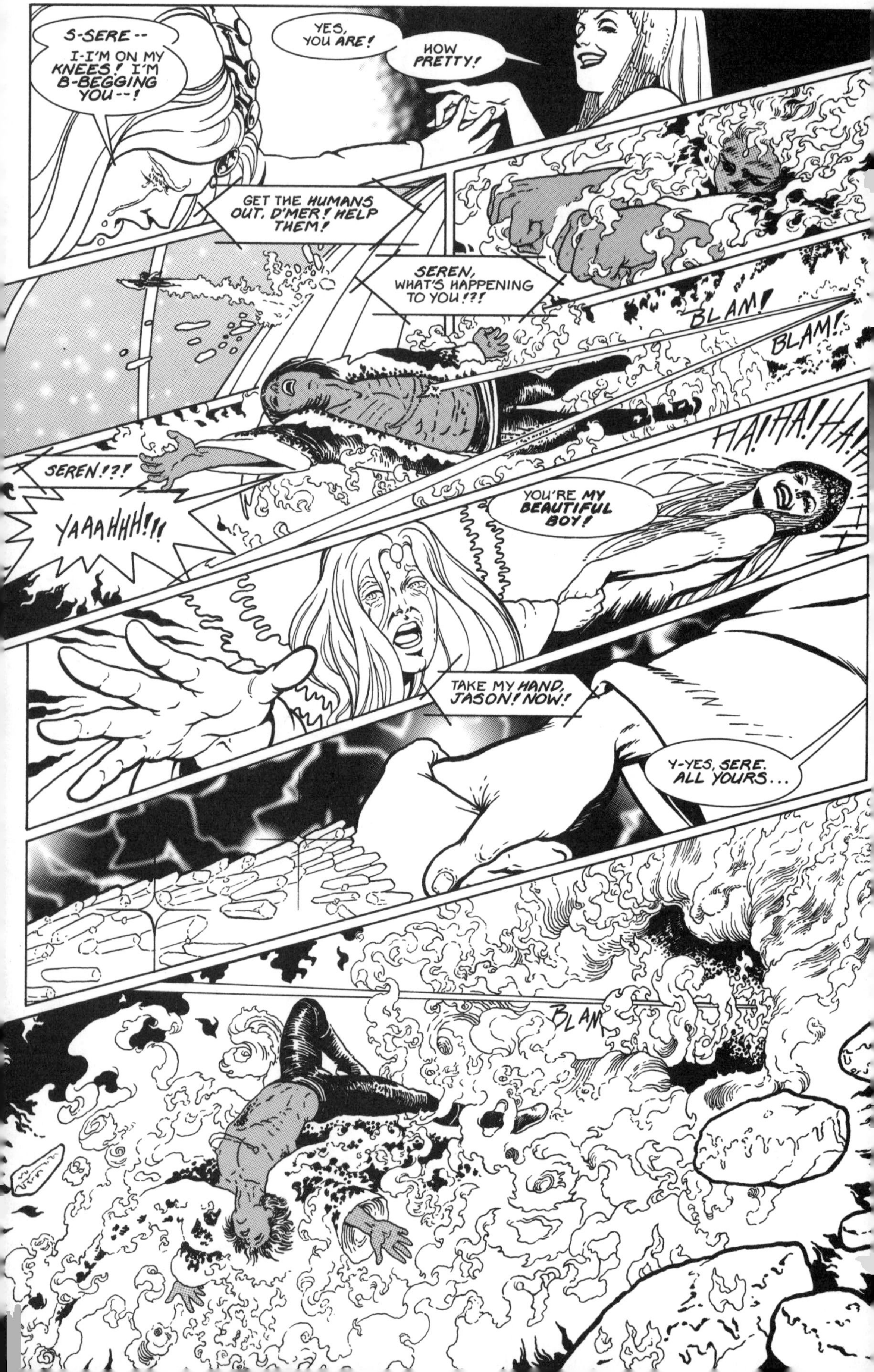

S-SERE -- I-I'M ON MY KNEES! I'M B-BEGGING YOU--!
YES, YOU ARE!
HOW PRETTY!
GET THE HUMANS OUT, D'MER! HELP THEM!
SEREN, WHAT'S HAPPENING TO YOU!?!
BLAM!
BLAM!
SEREN!?!
YAAAHHH!!!
HA!HA!HA!
YOU'RE MY BEAUTIFUL BOY!
TAKE MY HAND, JASON! NOW!
Y-YES, SERE. ALL YOURS...
BLAM

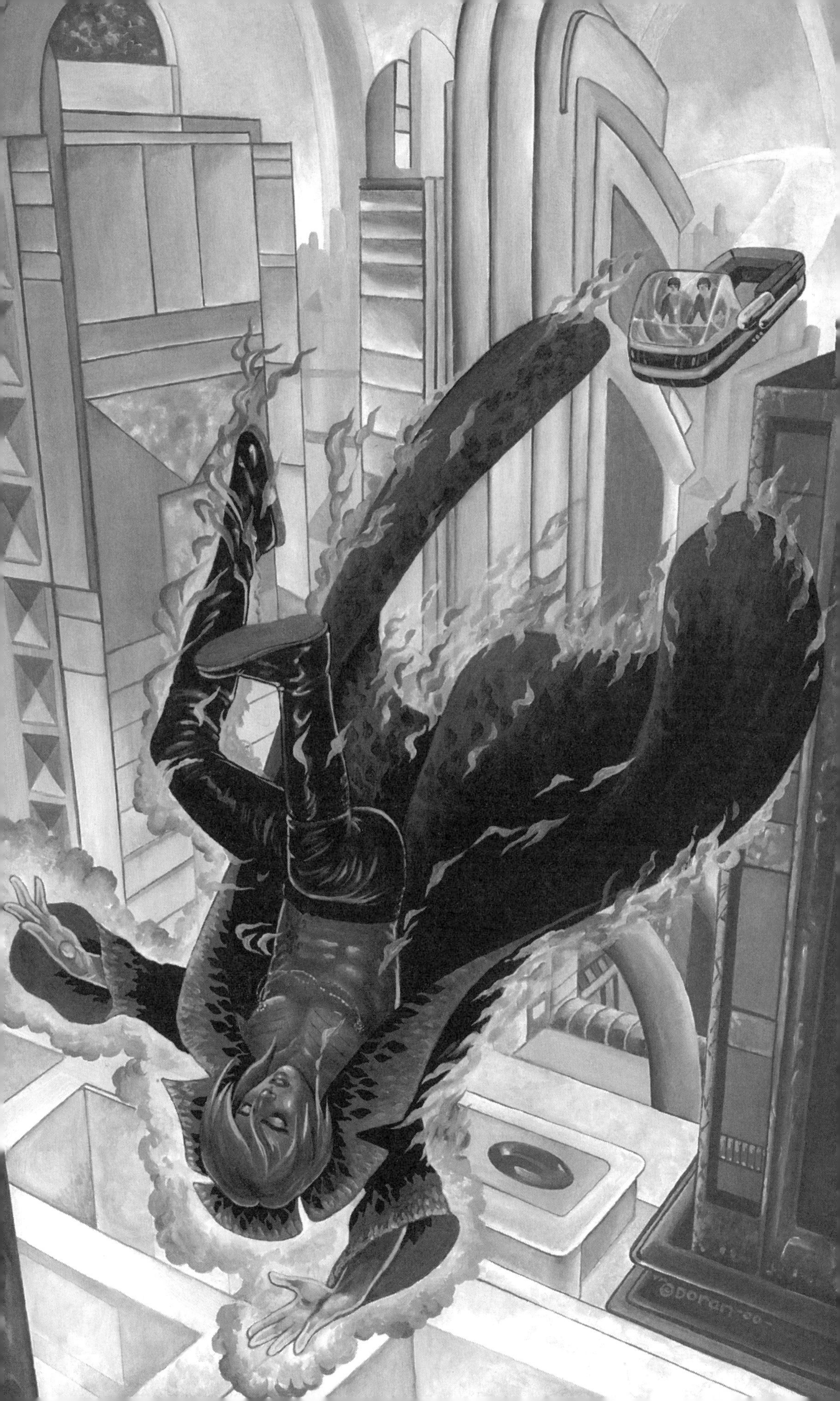

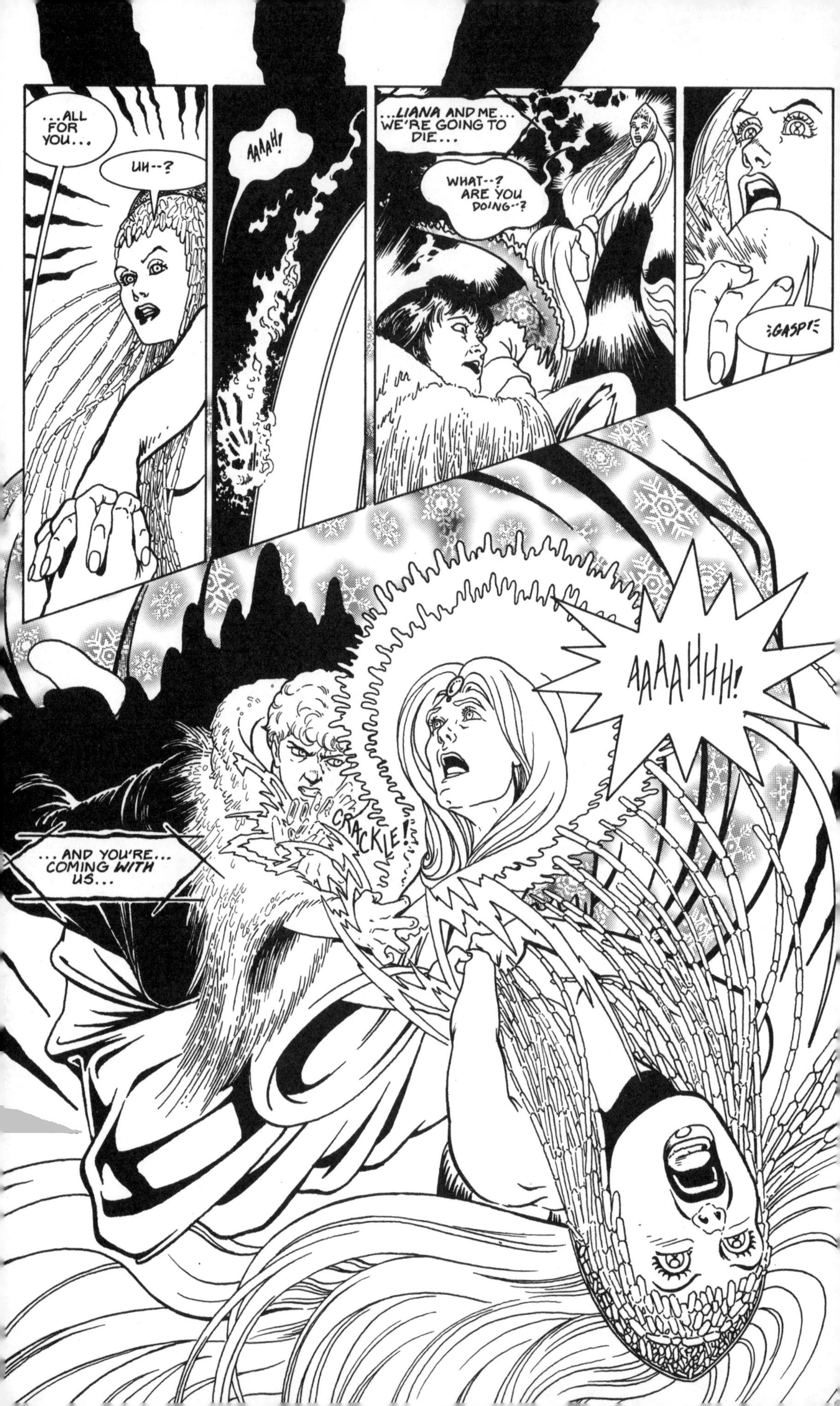
...ALL FOR YOU...
UH--?
AAAAH!
...LIANA AND ME... WE'RE GOING TO DIE...
WHAT--? ARE YOU DOING--?
GASP!
AAAAHHH!
...AND YOU'RE... COMING WITH US...
CRACKLE!

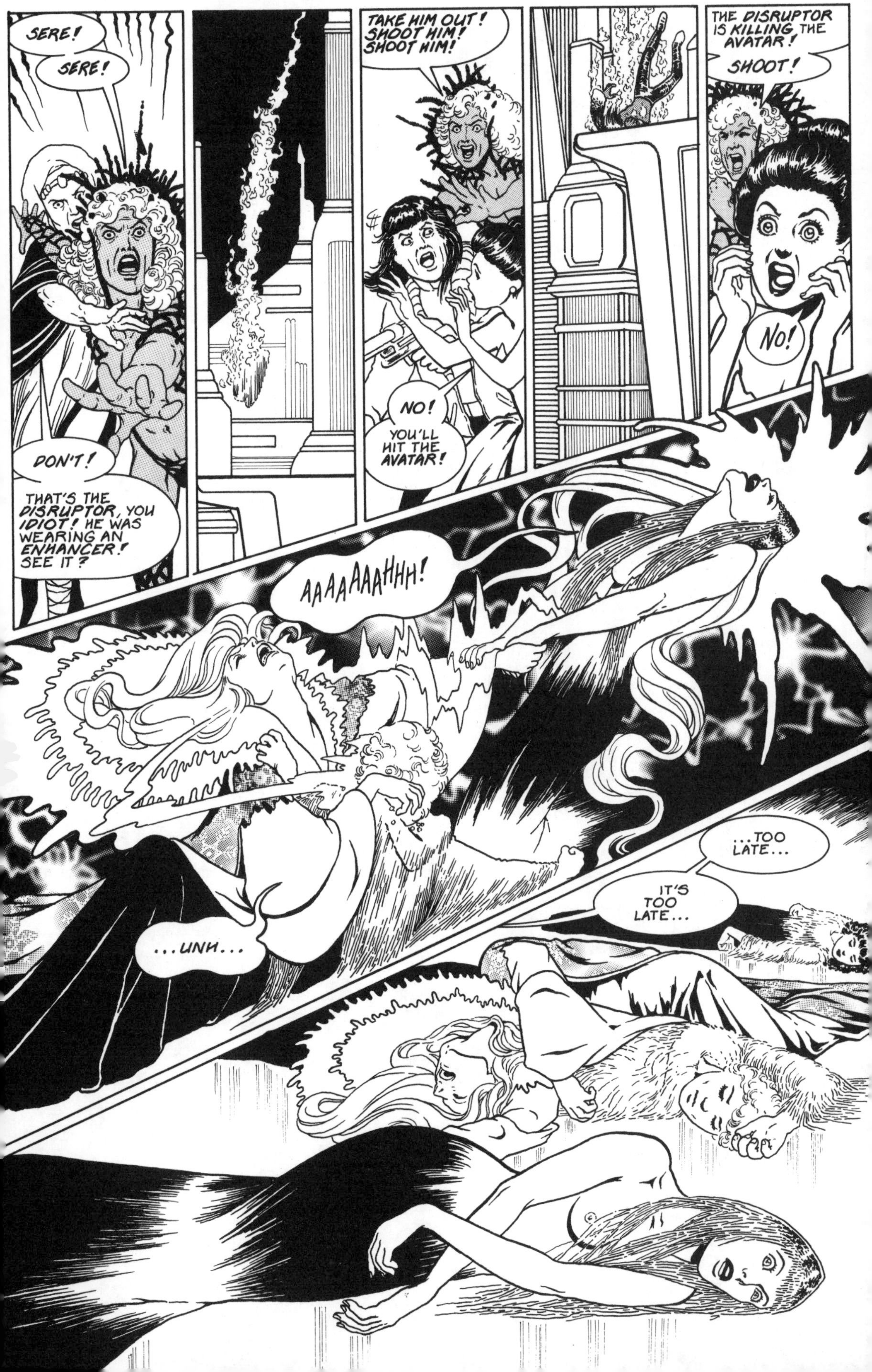
SERE!
SERE!
DON'T!
THAT'S THE DISRUPTOR, YOU IDIOT! HE WAS WEARING AN ENHANCER! SEE IT?
TAKE HIM OUT! SHOOT HIM! SHOOT HIM!
NO!
YOU'LL HIT THE AVATAR!
THE DISRUPTOR IS KILLING THE AVATAR!
SHOOT!
NO!
AAAAAAAHHH!
...UNH...
...TOO LATE...
IT'S TOO LATE...

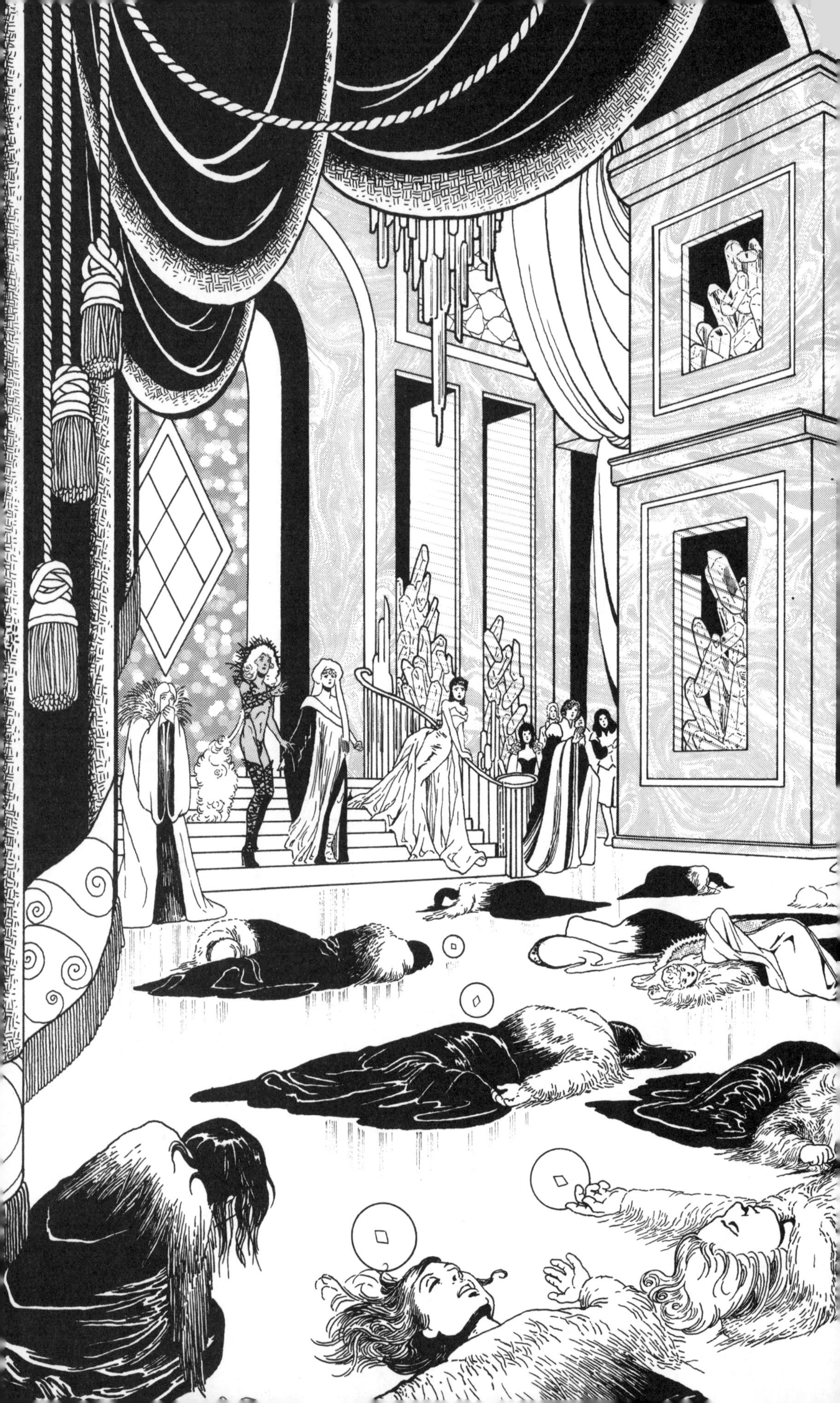

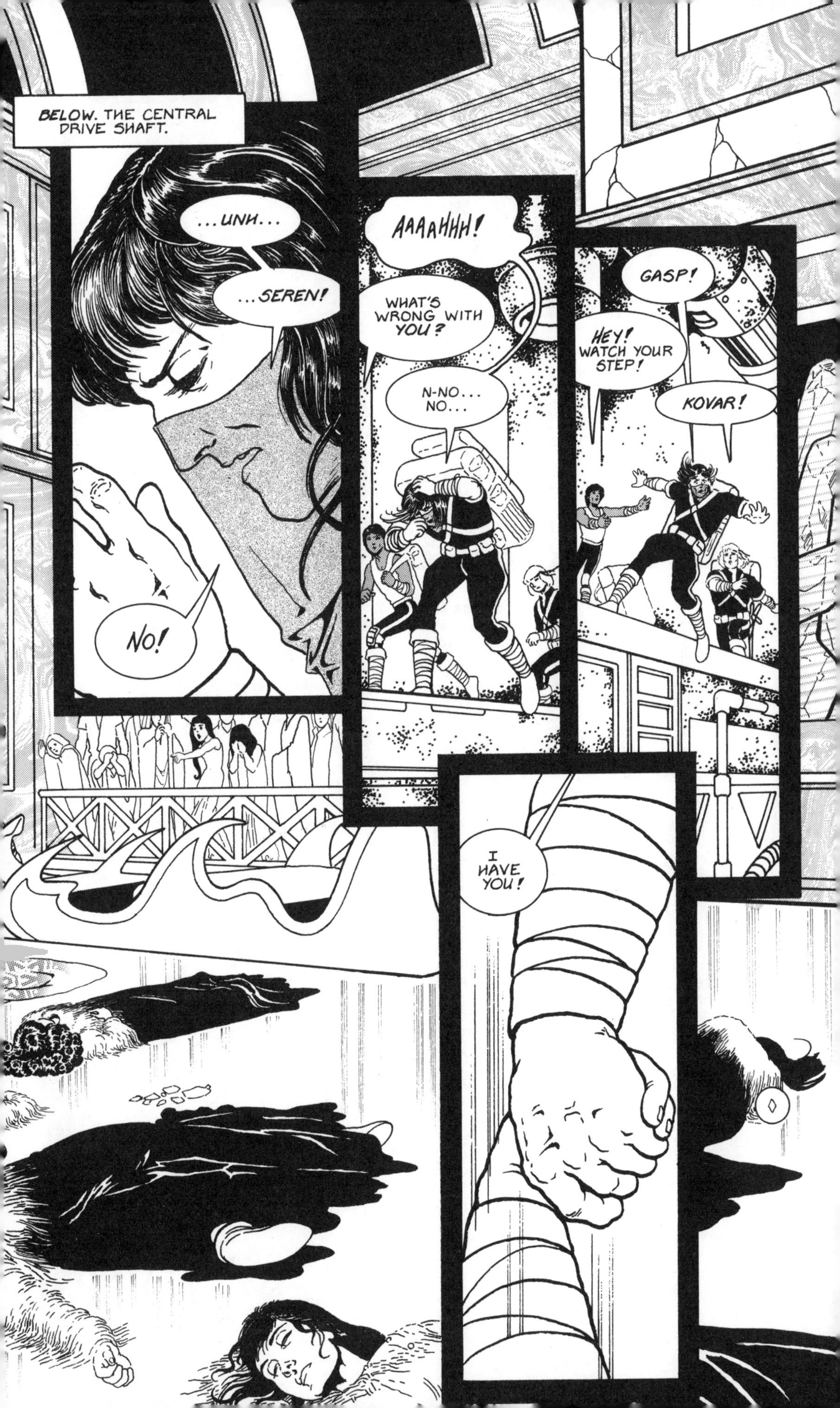
BELOW. THE CENTRAL DRIVE SHAFT.
...UNH...
...SEREN!
NO!
AAAAHHH!
WHAT'S WRONG WITH YOU?
N-NO... NO...
GASP!
HEY! WATCH YOUR STEP!
KOVAR!
I HAVE YOU!

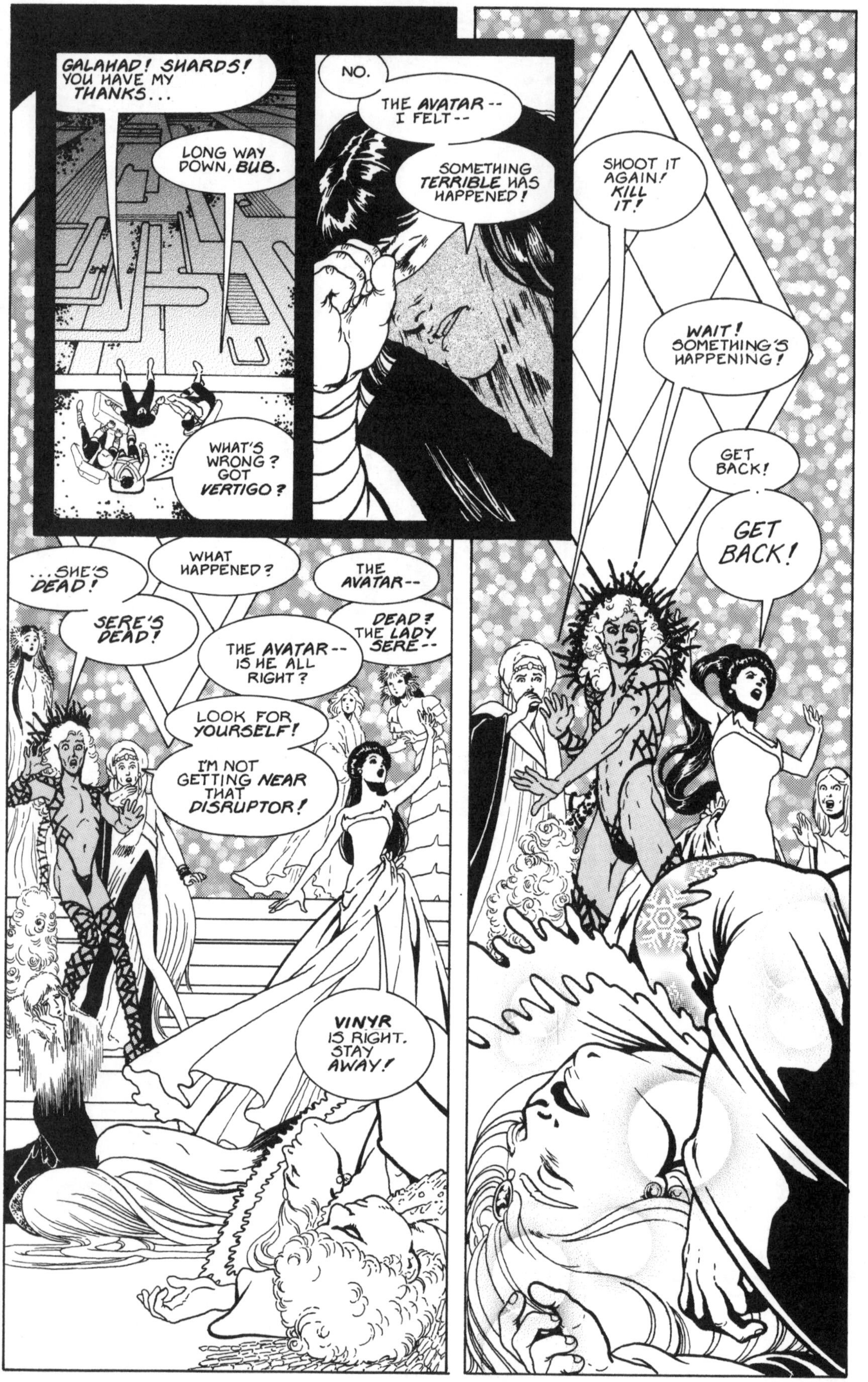
GALAHAD! SHARDS! YOU HAVE MY THANKS...
LONG WAY DOWN, BUB.
WHAT'S WRONG? GOT VERTIGO?
NO.
THE AVATAR-- I FELT--
SOMETHING TERRIBLE HAS HAPPENED!
...SHE'S DEAD!
WHAT HAPPENED?
SERE'S DEAD!
THE AVATAR--
DEAD? THE LADY SERE--
THE AVATAR-- IS HE ALL RIGHT?
LOOK FOR YOURSELF!
I'M NOT GETTING NEAR THAT DISRUPTOR!
VINYR IS RIGHT. STAY AWAY!
SHOOT IT AGAIN! KILL IT!
WAIT! SOMETHING'S HAPPENING!
GET BACK!
GET BACK!

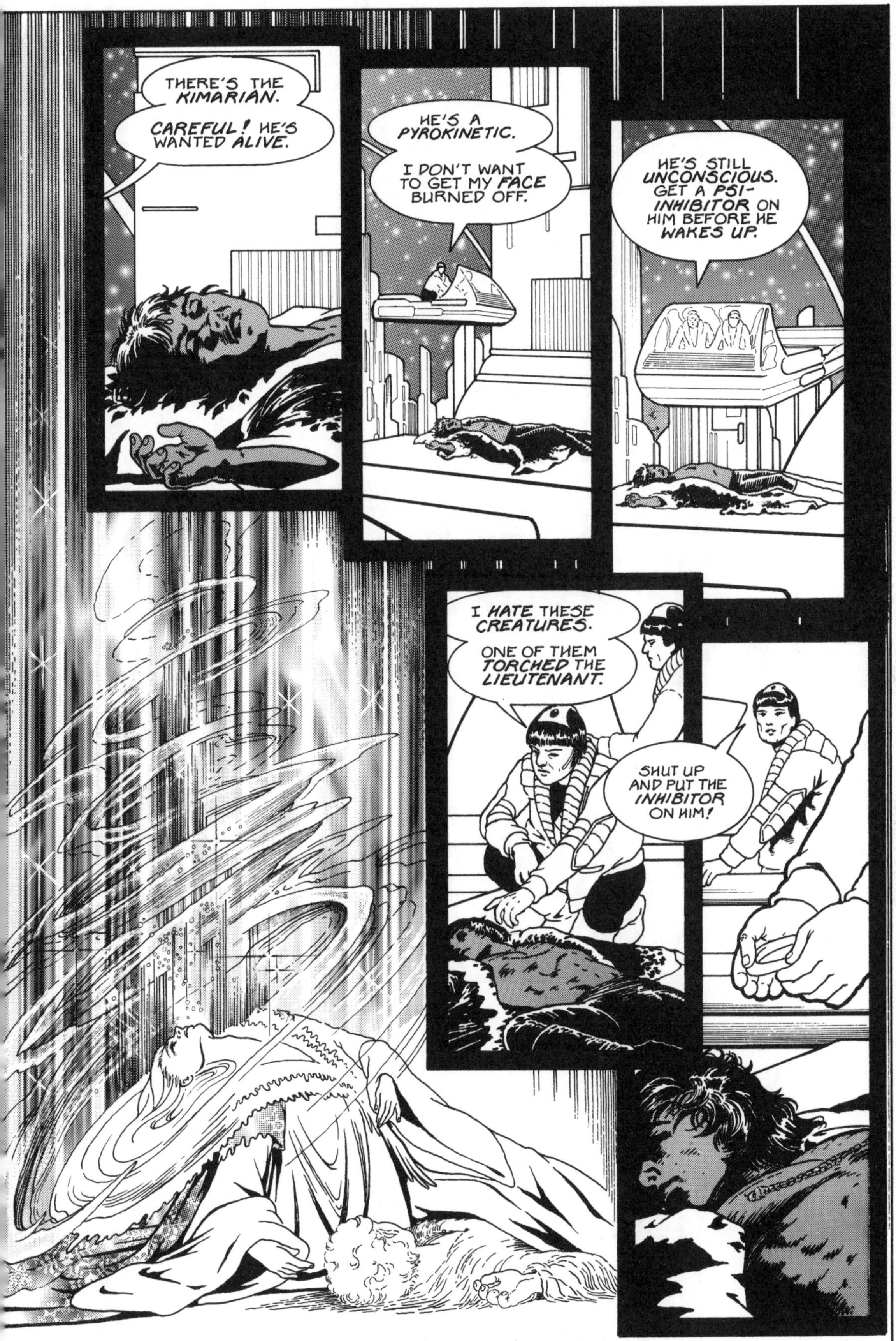
THERE'S THE KIMARIAN.
CAREFUL! HE'S WANTED ALIVE.
HE'S A PYROKINETIC.
I DON'T WANT TO GET MY FACE BURNED OFF.
HE'S STILL UNCONSCIOUS. GET A PSI-INHIBITOR ON HIM BEFORE HE WAKES UP.
I HATE THESE CREATURES.
ONE OF THEM TORCHED THE LIEUTENANT.
SHUT UP AND PUT THE INHIBITOR ON HIM!

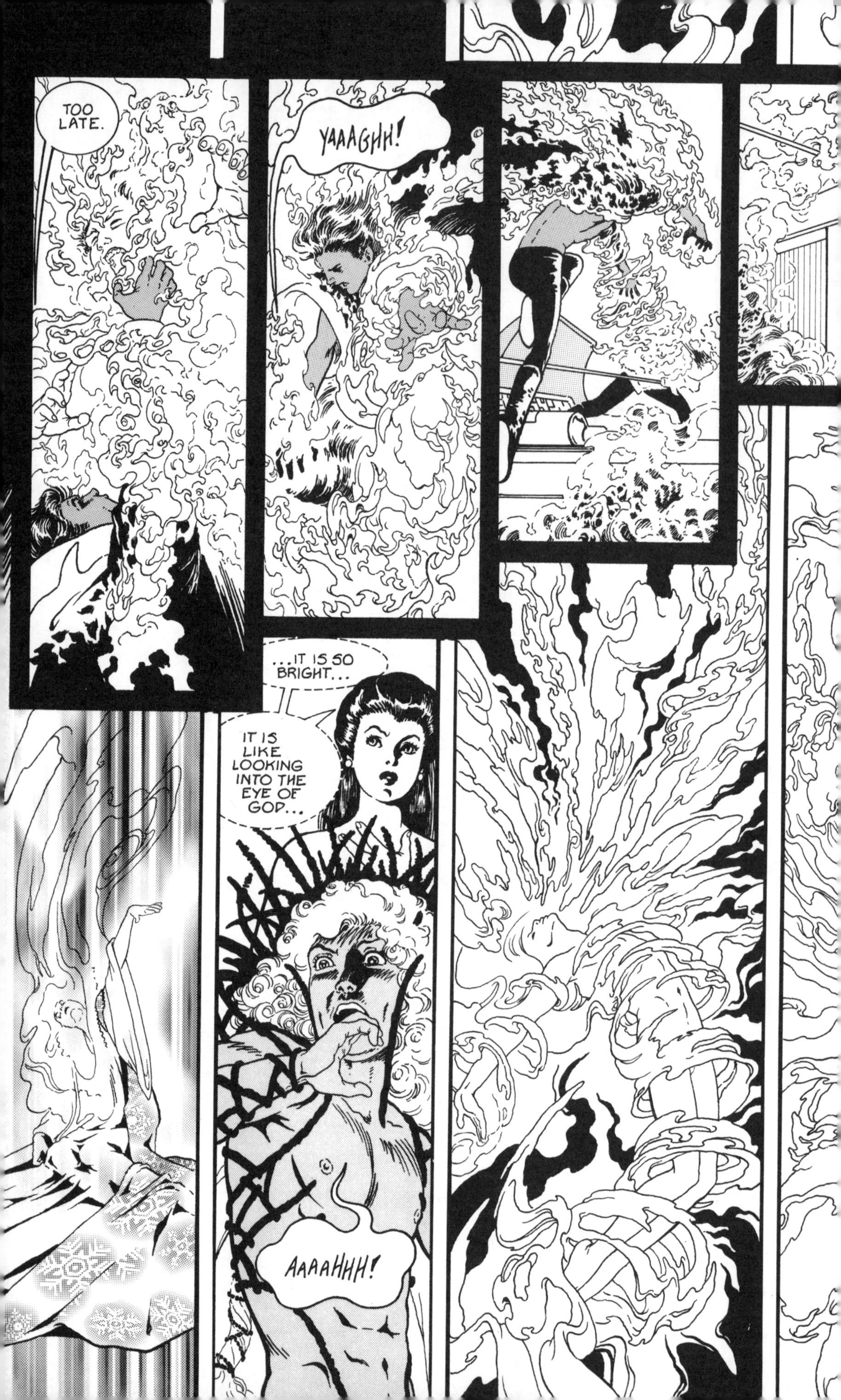
TOO LATE.
YAAAGHH!
...IT IS SO BRIGHT...
IT IS LIKE LOOKING INTO THE EYE OF GOD...
AAAAHHH!

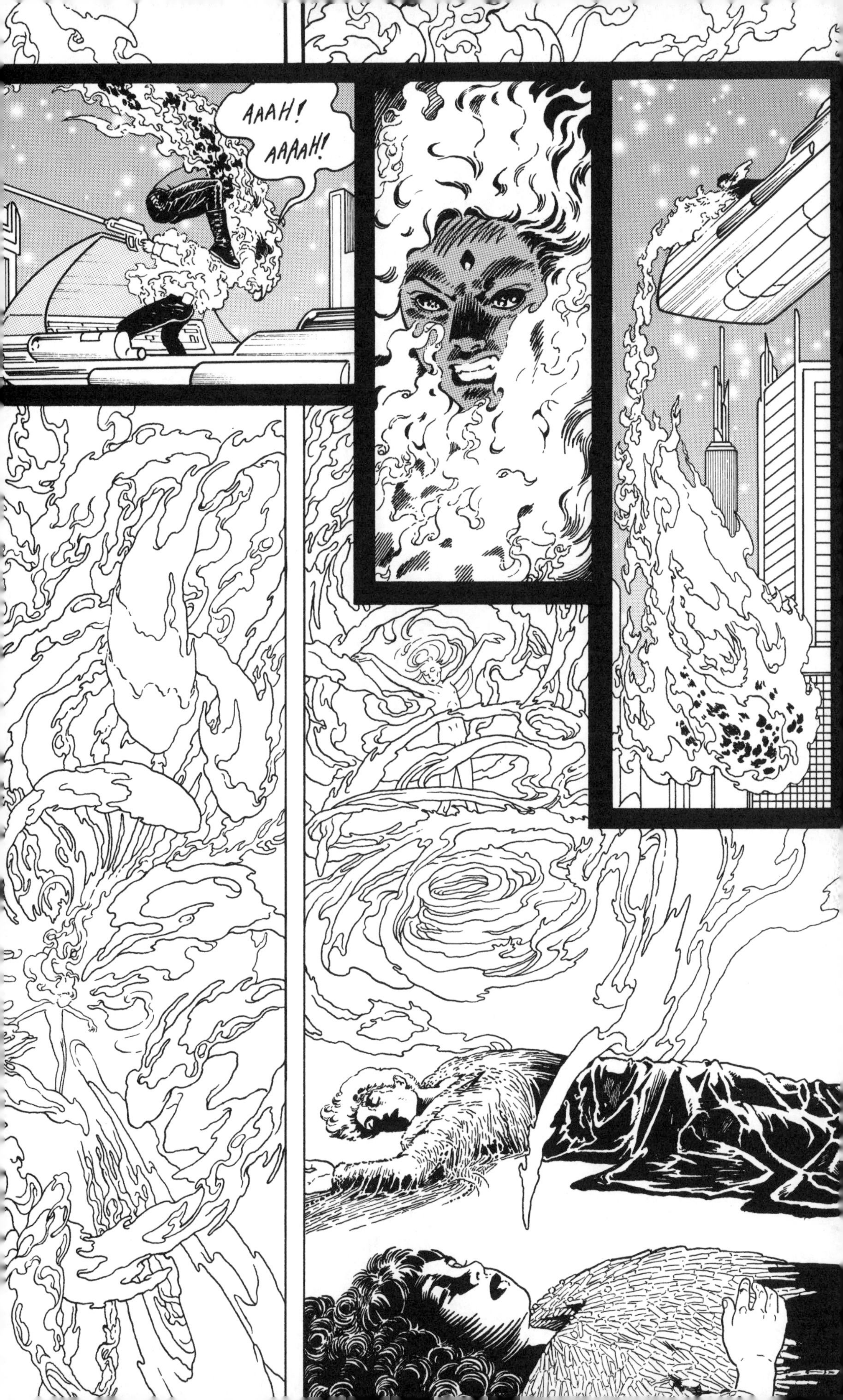
AAAH! AAAAH!

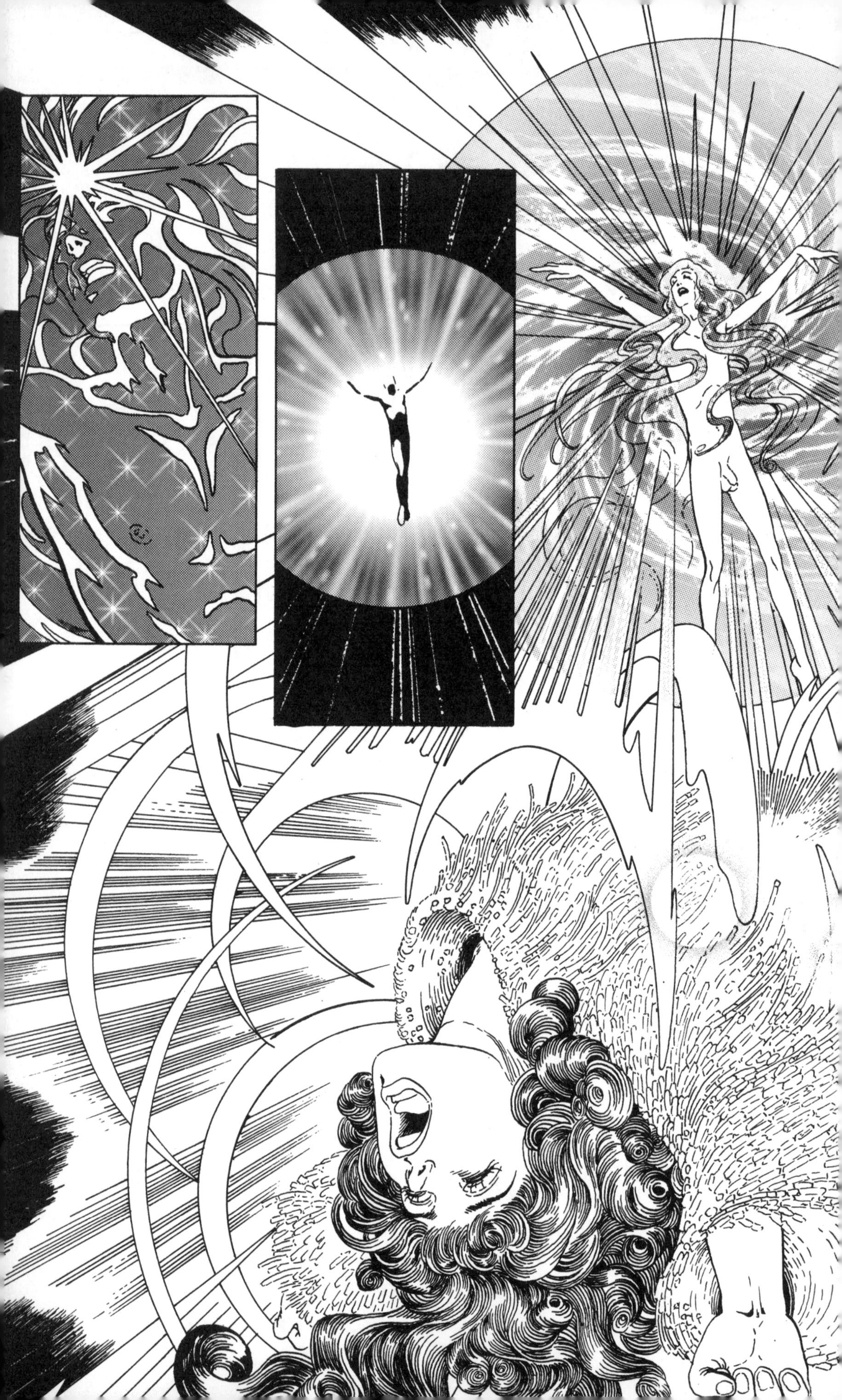

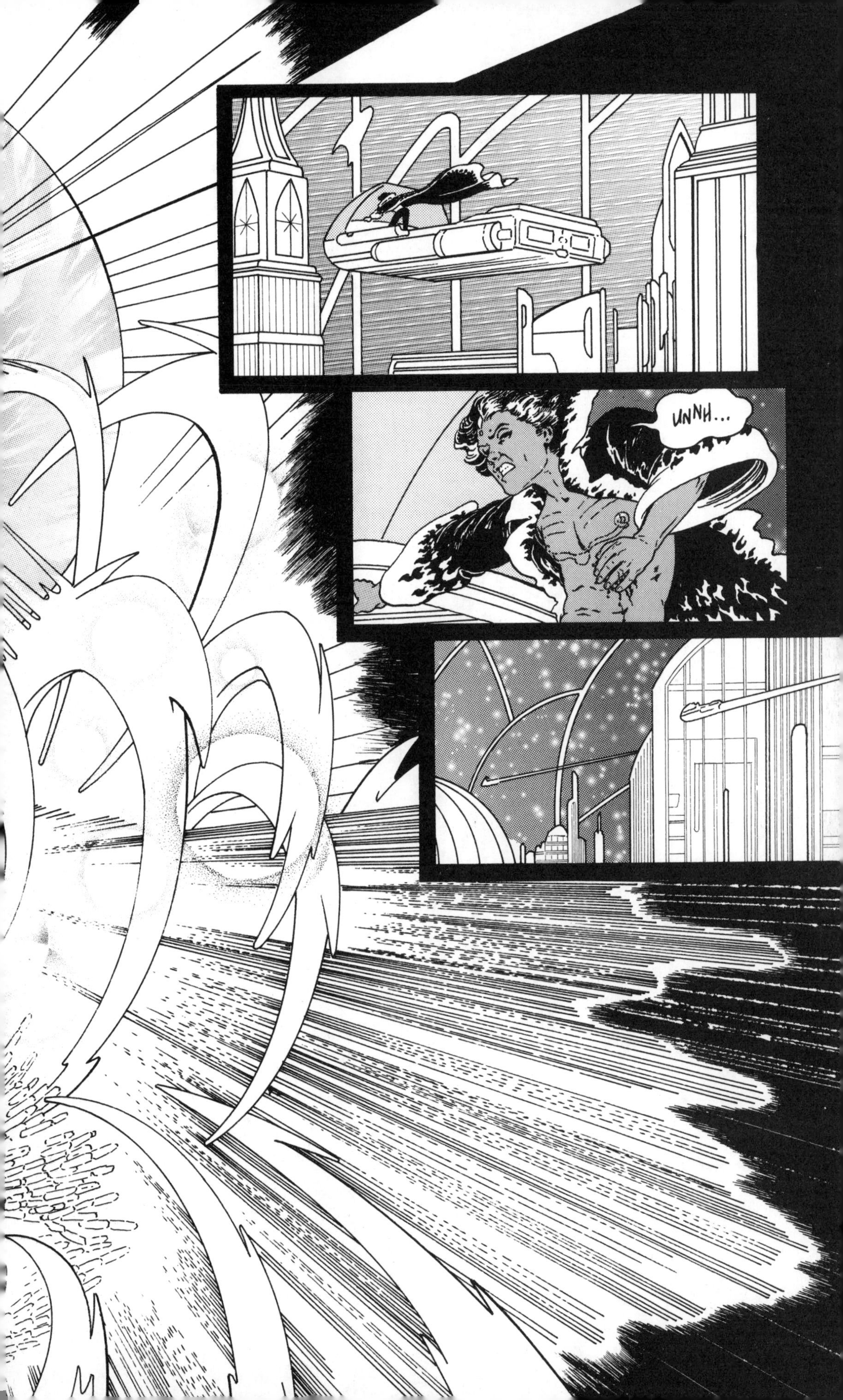
UNNH...

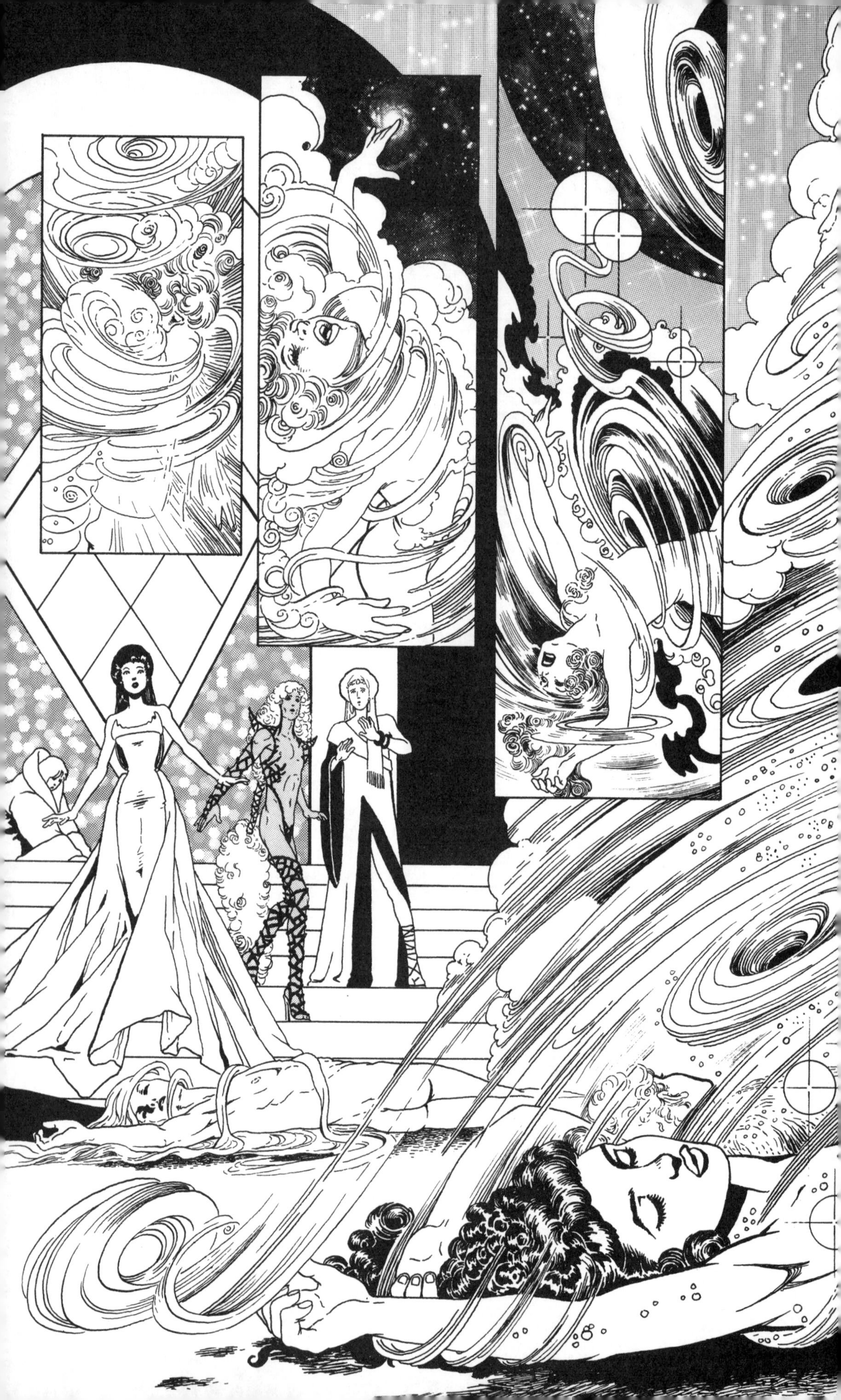

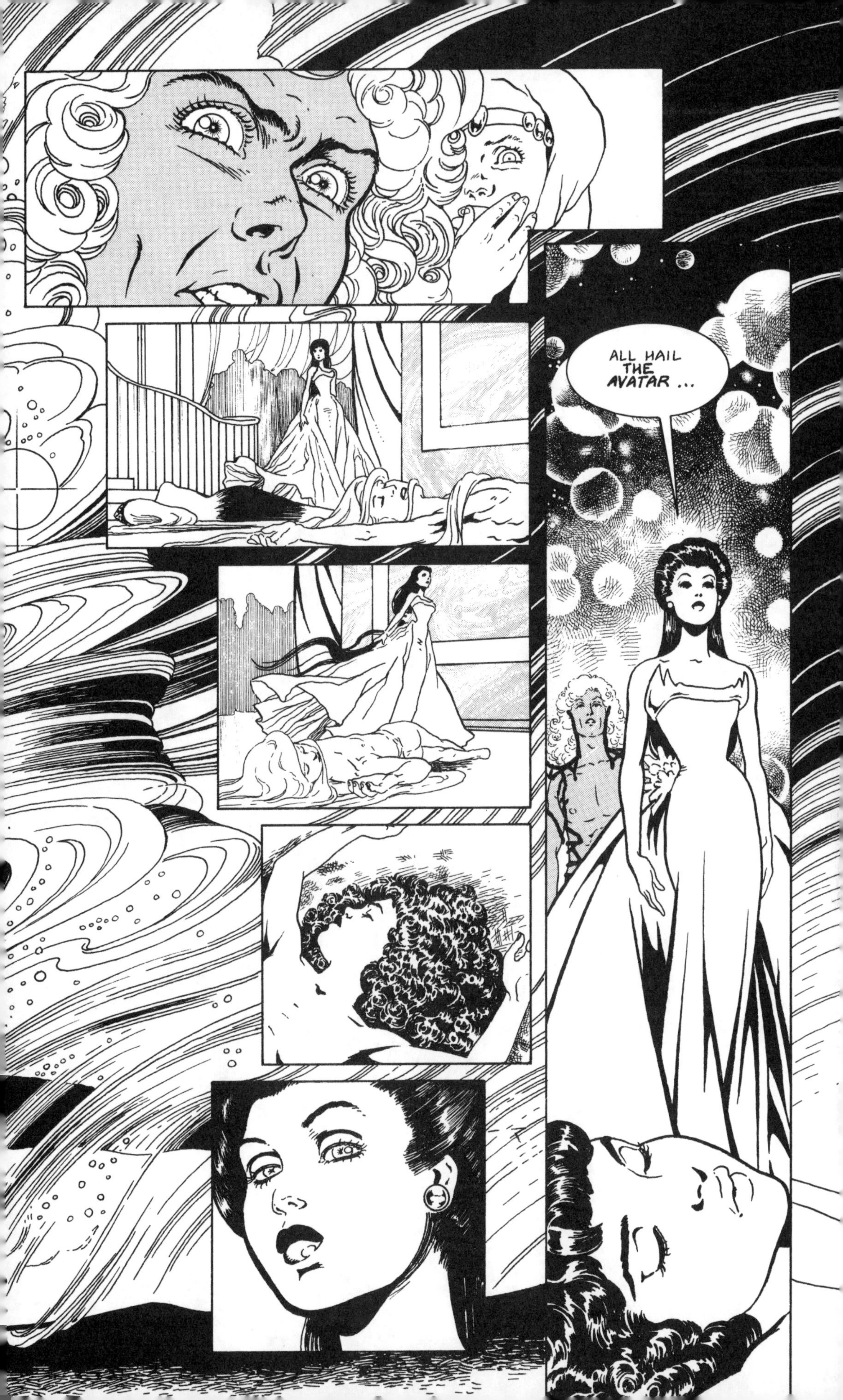
ALL HAIL THE AVATAR ...

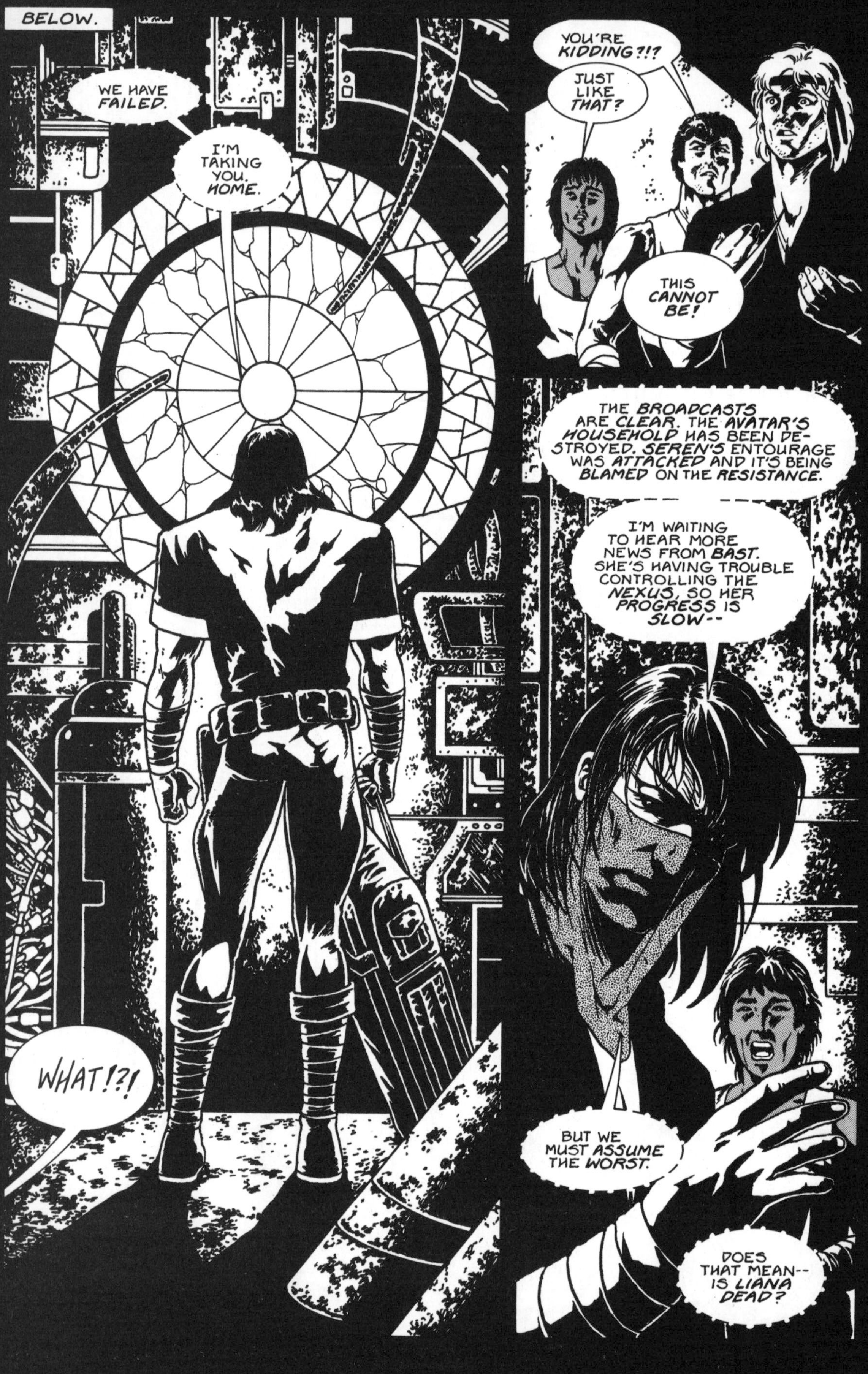
BELOW.
WE HAVE FAILED.
I'M TAKING YOU. HOME.
WHAT!?!
YOU'RE KIDDING?!?
JUST LIKE THAT?
THIS CANNOT BE!
THE BROADCASTS ARE CLEAR. THE AVATAR'S HOUSEHOLD HAS BEEN DE-STROYED. SEREN'S ENTOURAGE WAS ATTACKED AND IT'S BEING BLAMED ON THE RESISTANCE.
I'M WAITING TO HEAR MORE NEWS FROM BAST. SHE'S HAVING TROUBLE CONTROLLING THE NEXUS, SO HER PROGRESS IS SLOW--
BUT WE MUST ASSUME THE WORST.
DOES THAT MEAN-- IS LIANA DEAD?

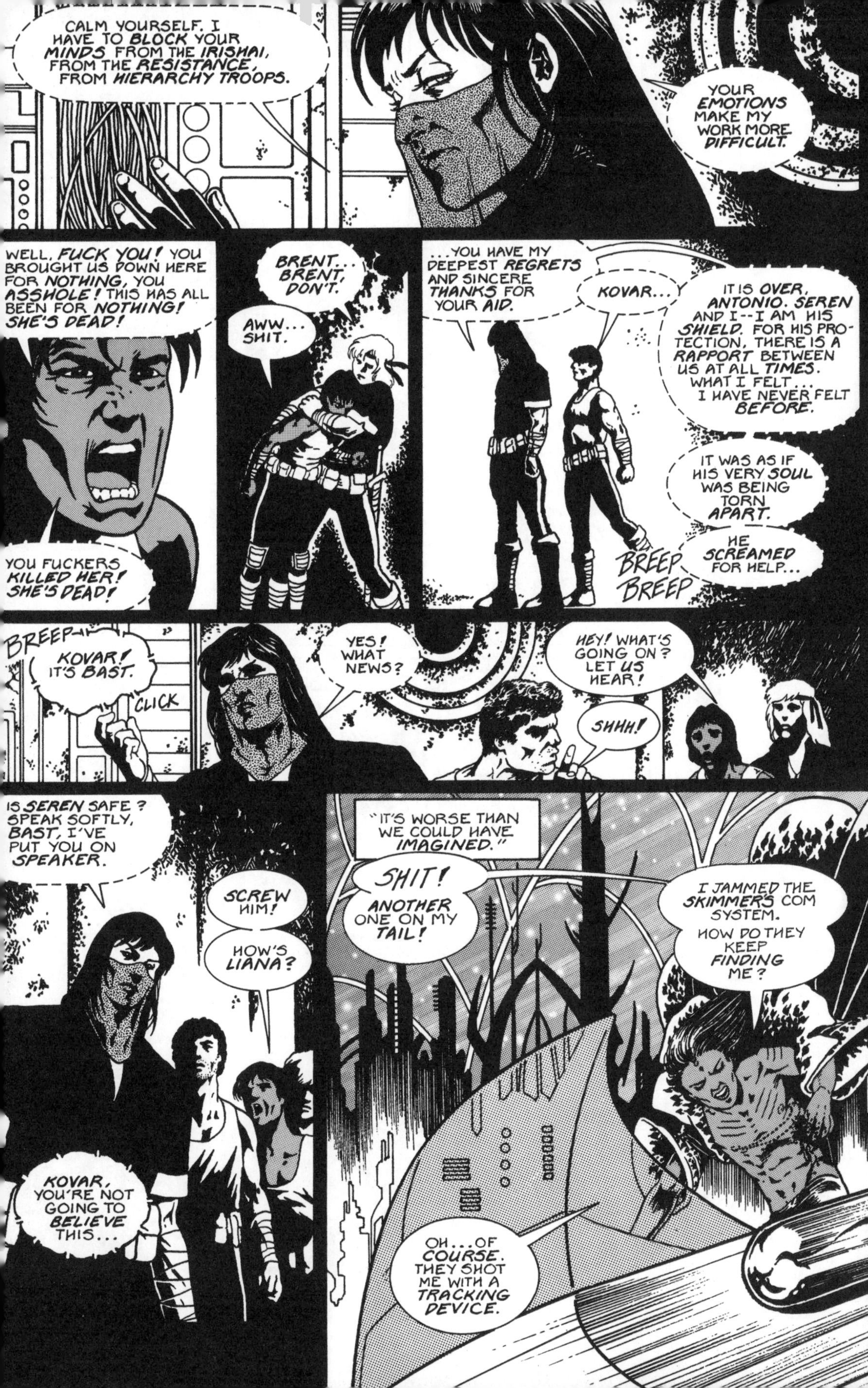
CALM YOURSELF. I HAVE TO BLOCK YOUR MINDS FROM THE IRISHAI, FROM THE RESISTANCE, FROM HIERARCHY TROOPS.
YOUR EMOTIONS MAKE MY WORK MORE DIFFICULT.
WELL, FUCK YOU! YOU BROUGHT US DOWN HERE FOR NOTHING, YOU ASSHOLE! THIS HAS ALL BEEN FOR NOTHING! SHE'S DEAD!
YOU FUCKERS KILLED HER! SHE'S DEAD!
BRENT... BRENT, DON'T.
AWW... SHIT.
...YOU HAVE MY DEEPEST REGRETS AND SINCERE THANKS FOR YOUR AID.
KOVAR...
IT IS OVER, ANTONIO. SEREN AND I--I AM HIS SHIELD. FOR HIS PROTECTION, THERE IS A RAPPORT BETWEEN US AT ALL TIMES. WHAT I FELT... I HAVE NEVER FELT BEFORE.
IT WAS AS IF HIS VERY SOUL WAS BEING TORN APART.
HE SCREAMED FOR HELP...
BREEP BREEP
BREEP
KOVAR! IT'S BAST.
CLICK
YES! WHAT NEWS?
HEY! WHAT'S GOING ON? LET US HEAR!
SHHH!
IS SEREN SAFE? SPEAK SOFTLY, BAST, I'VE PUT YOU ON SPEAKER.
SCREW HIM!
HOW'S LIANA?
KOVAR, YOU'RE NOT GOING TO BELIEVE THIS...
"IT'S WORSE THAN WE COULD HAVE IMAGINED."
SHIT! ANOTHER ONE ON MY TAIL!
I JAMMED THE SKIMMER'S COM SYSTEM.
HOW DO THEY KEEP FINDING ME?
OH... OF COURSE. THEY SHOT ME WITH A TRACKING DEVICE.

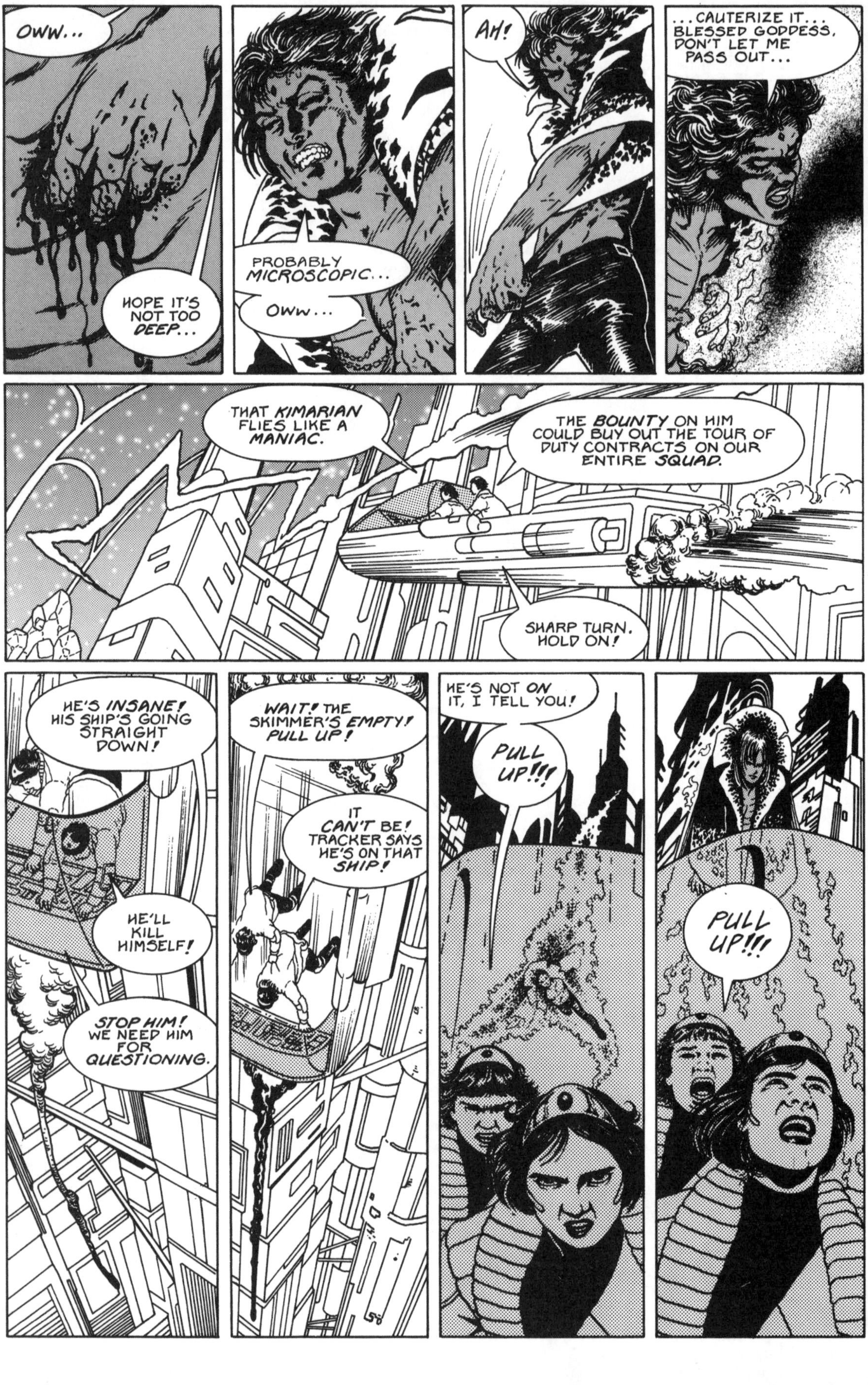
OWW...
HOPE IT'S NOT TOO DEEP...
PROBABLY MICROSCOPIC...
OWW...
AH!
...CAUTERIZE IT... BLESSED GODDESS, DON'T LET ME PASS OUT...
THAT KIMARIAN FLIES LIKE A MANIAC.
THE BOUNTY ON HIM COULD BUY OUT THE TOUR OF DUTY CONTRACTS ON OUR ENTIRE SQUAD.
SHARP TURN. HOLD ON!
HE'S INSANE! HIS SHIP'S GOING STRAIGHT DOWN!
HE'LL KILL HIMSELF!
STOP HIM! WE NEED HIM FOR QUESTIONING.
WAIT! THE SKIMMER'S EMPTY! PULL UP!
IT CAN'T BE! TRACKER SAYS HE'S ON THAT SHIP!
HE'S NOT ON IT, I TELL YOU!
PULL UP!!!
PULL UP!!!

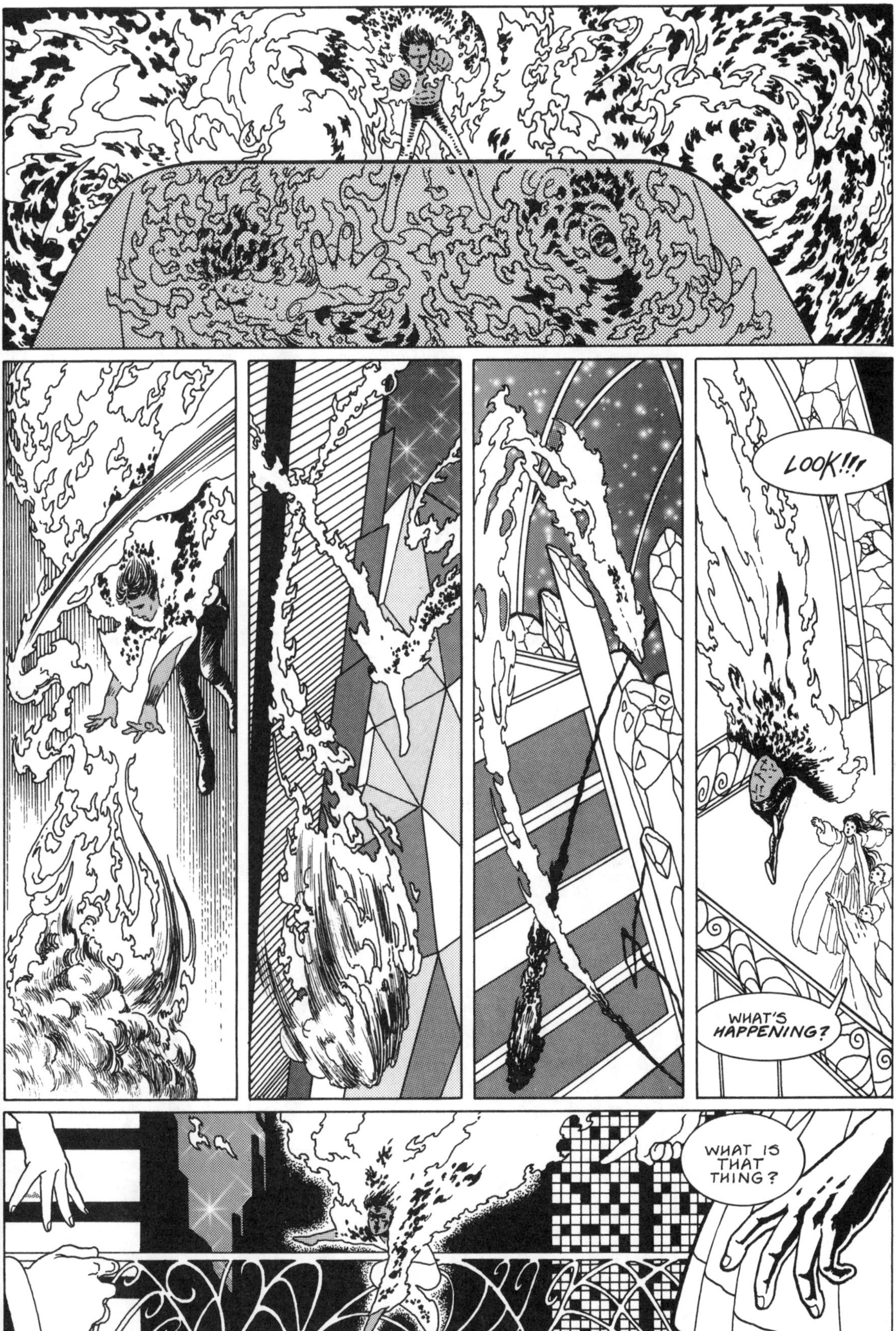
LOOK!!!
WHAT'S HAPPENING?
WHAT IS THAT THING?

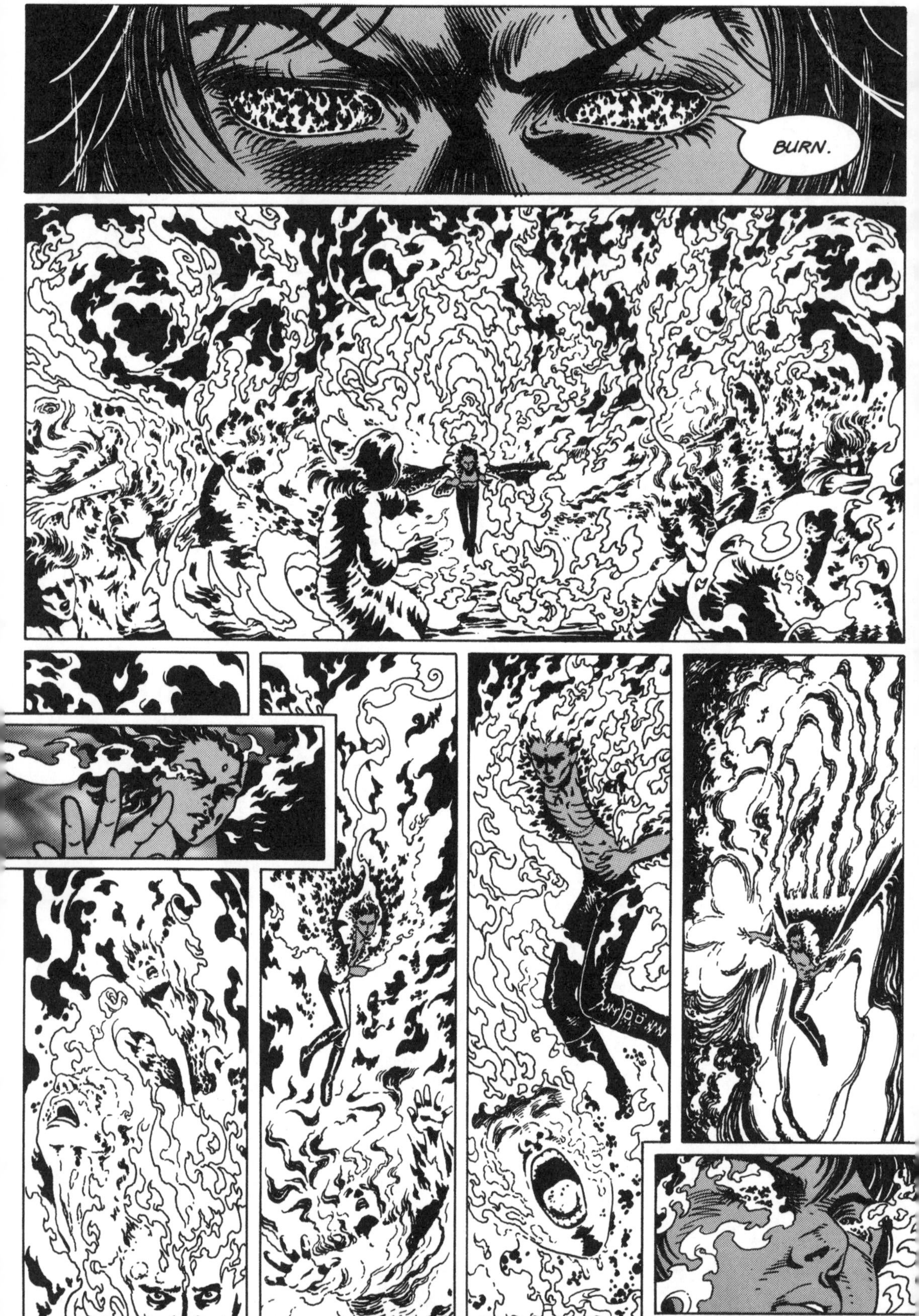
BURN.

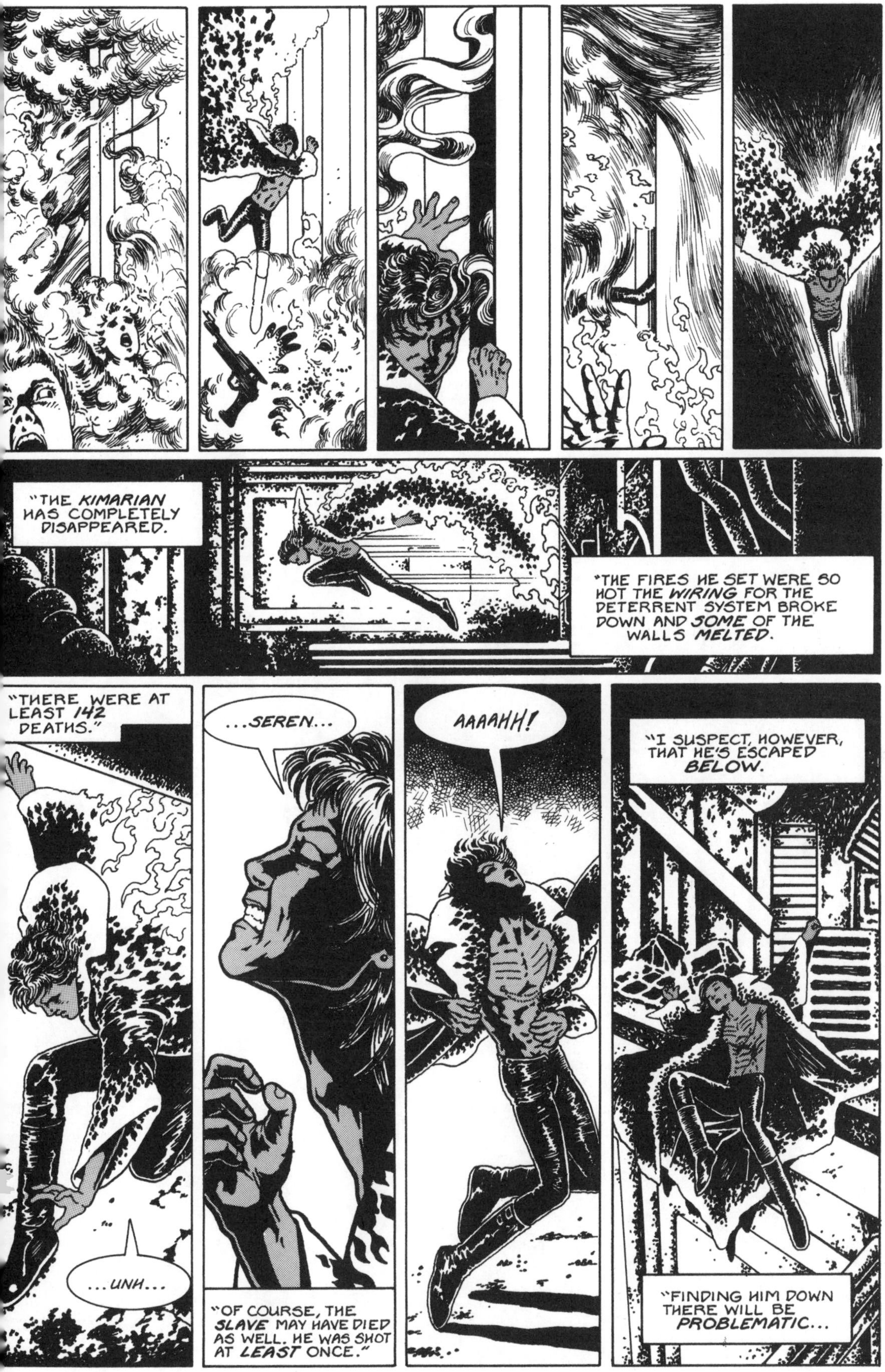
"THE KIMARIAN HAS COMPLETELY DISAPPEARED.
"THE FIRES HE SET WERE SO HOT THE WIRING FOR THE DETERRENT SYSTEM BROKE DOWN AND SOME OF THE WALLS MELTED.
"THERE WERE AT LEAST 142 DEATHS."
...UNH...
...SEREN...
"OF COURSE, THE SLAVE MAY HAVE DIED AS WELL. HE WAS SHOT AT LEAST ONCE."
AAAAHH!
"I SUSPECT, HOWEVER, THAT HE'S ESCAPED BELOW.
"FINDING HIM DOWN THERE WILL BE PROBLEMATIC...

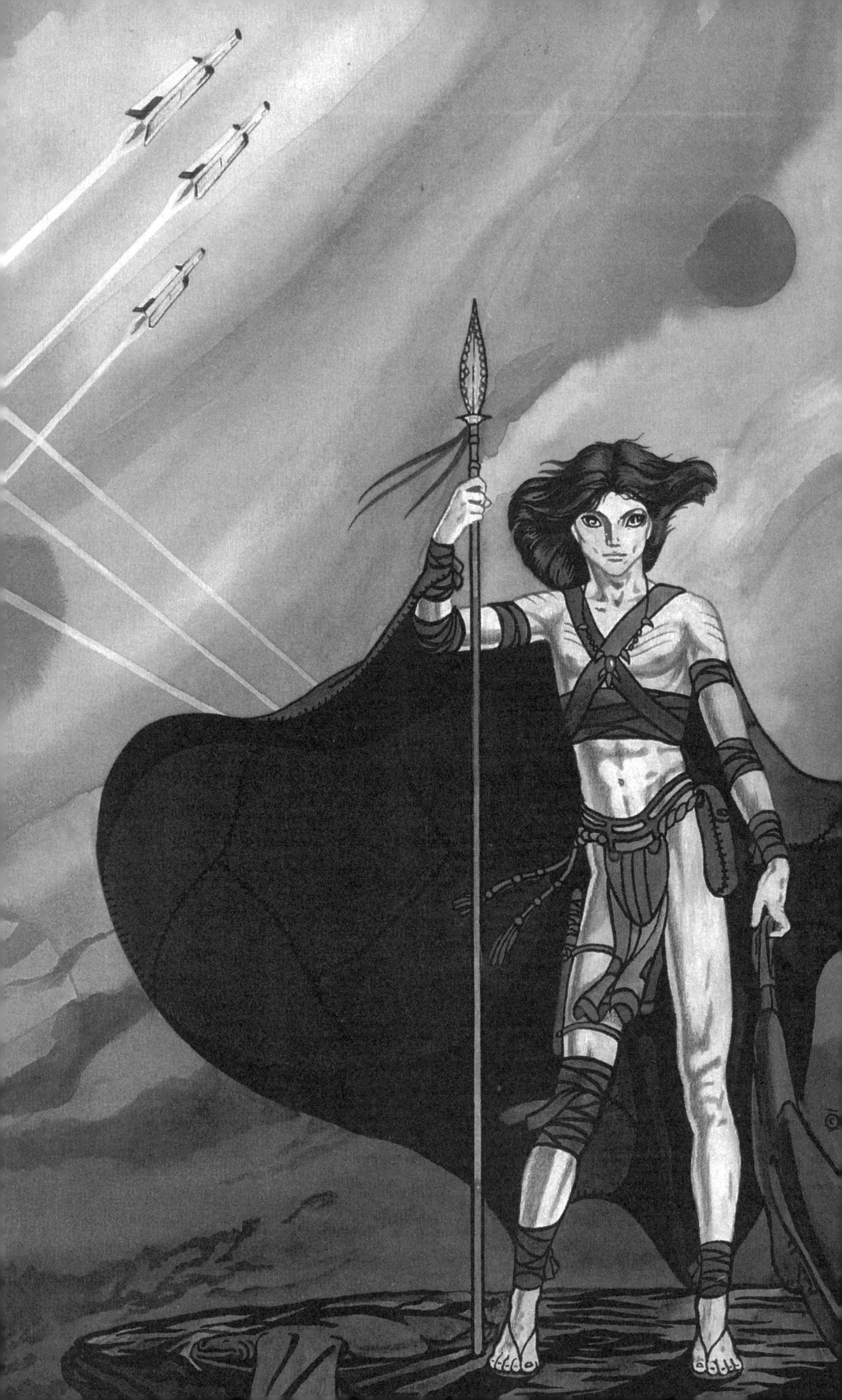

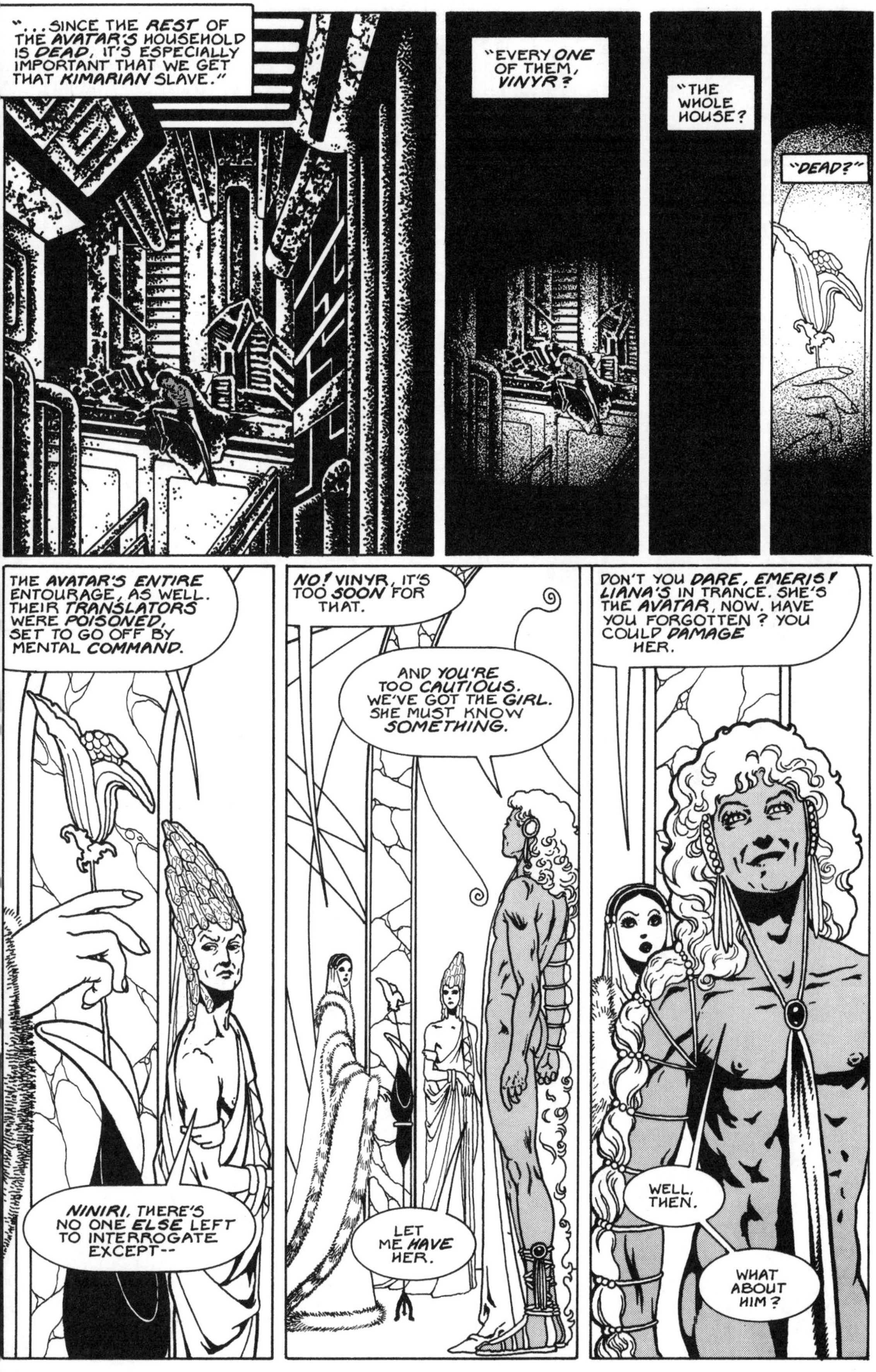
"...SINCE THE REST OF THE AVATAR'S HOUSEHOLD IS DEAD, IT'S ESPECIALLY IMPORTANT THAT WE GET THAT KIMARIAN SLAVE."
"EVERY ONE OF THEM, VINYR?
"THE WHOLE HOUSE?
"DEAD?"
THE AVATAR'S ENTIRE ENTOURAGE, AS WELL. THEIR TRANSLATORS WERE POISONED, SET TO GO OFF BY MENTAL COMMAND.
NINIRI, THERE'S NO ONE ELSE LEFT TO INTERROGATE EXCEPT--
NO! VINYR, IT'S TOO SOON FOR THAT.
AND YOU'RE TOO CAUTIOUS. WE'VE GOT THE GIRL. SHE MUST KNOW SOMETHING.
LET ME HAVE HER.
DON'T YOU DARE, EMERIS! LIANA'S IN TRANCE. SHE'S THE AVATAR, NOW. HAVE YOU FORGOTTEN? YOU COULD DAMAGE HER.
WELL, THEN.
WHAT ABOUT HIM?

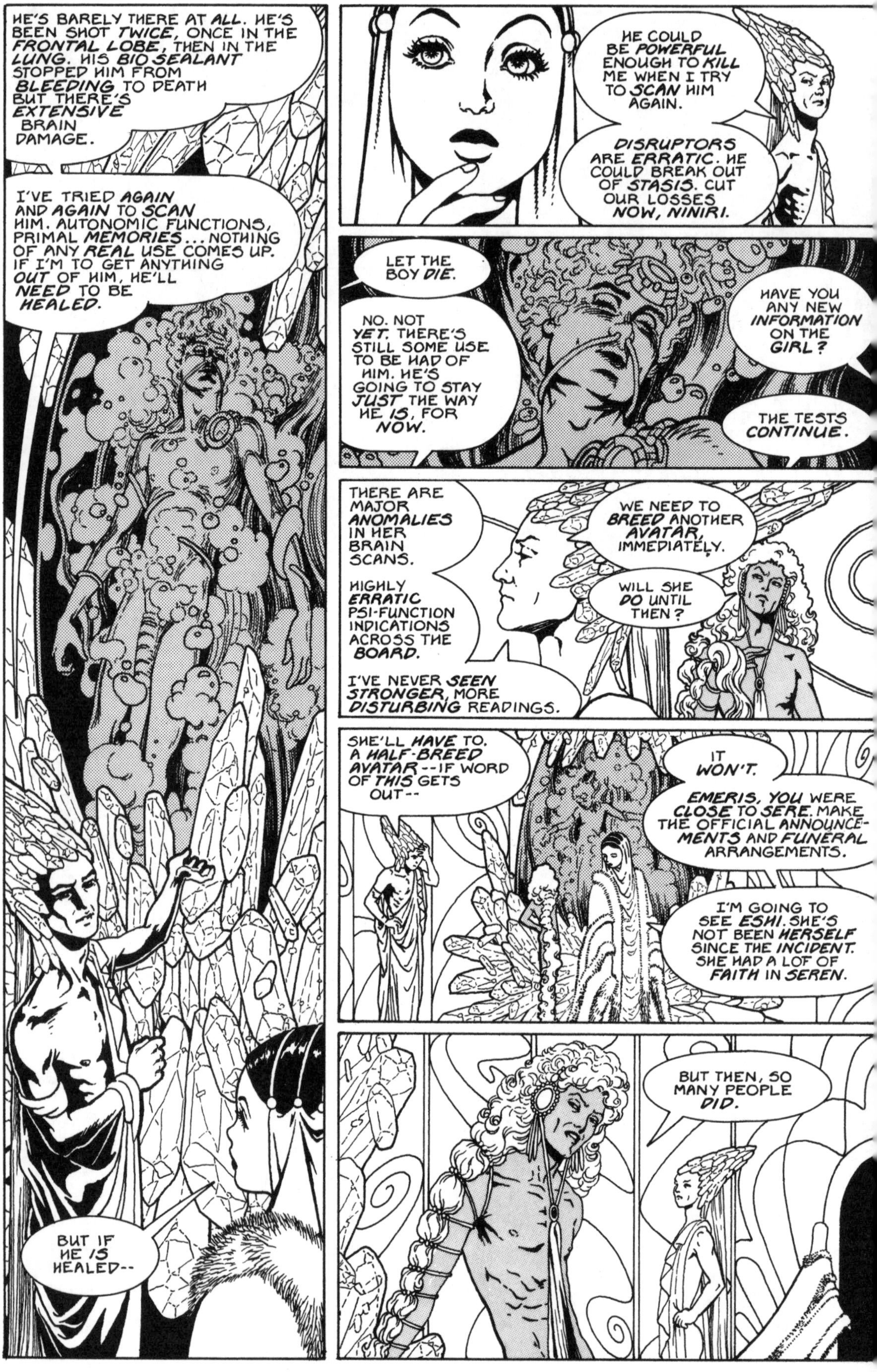
HE'S BARELY THERE AT ALL. HE'S BEEN SHOT TWICE, ONCE IN THE FRONTAL LOBE, THEN IN THE LUNG. HIS BIO SEALANT STOPPED HIM FROM BLEEDING TO DEATH BUT THERE'S EXTENSIVE BRAIN DAMAGE.
I'VE TRIED AGAIN AND AGAIN TO SCAN HIM. AUTONOMIC FUNCTIONS, PRIMAL MEMORIES... NOTHING OF ANY REAL USE COMES UP. IF I'M TO GET ANYTHING OUT OF HIM, HE'LL NEED TO BE HEALED.
BUT IF HE IS HEALED--
HE COULD BE POWERFUL ENOUGH TO KILL ME WHEN I TRY TO SCAN HIM AGAIN.
DISRUPTORS ARE ERRATIC. HE COULD BREAK OUT OF STASIS. CUT OUR LOSSES NOW, NINIRI.
LET THE BOY DIE.
NO. NOT YET. THERE'S STILL SOME USE TO BE HAD OF HIM. HE'S GOING TO STAY JUST THE WAY HE IS, FOR NOW.
HAVE YOU ANY NEW INFORMATION ON THE GIRL?
THE TESTS CONTINUE.
THERE ARE MAJOR ANOMALIES IN HER BRAIN SCANS.
HIGHLY ERRATIC PSI-FUNCTION INDICATIONS ACROSS THE BOARD.
I'VE NEVER SEEN STRONGER, MORE DISTURBING READINGS.
WE NEED TO BREED ANOTHER AVATAR, IMMEDIATELY.
WILL SHE DO UNTIL THEN?
SHE'LL HAVE TO. A HALF-BREED AVATAR--IF WORD OF THIS GETS OUT--
IT WON'T.
EMERIS, YOU WERE CLOSE TO SERE. MAKE THE OFFICIAL ANNOUNCEMENTS AND FUNERAL ARRANGEMENTS.
I'M GOING TO SEE ESHI. SHE'S NOT BEEN HERSELF SINCE THE INCIDENT. SHE HAD A LOT OF FAITH IN SEREN.
BUT THEN, SO MANY PEOPLE DID.

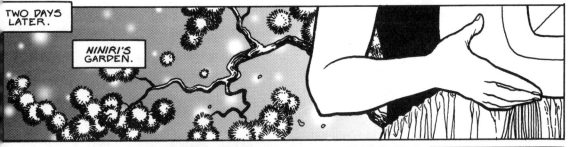

TWO DAYS LATER.

NINIRI'S GARDEN.

DEAR, WOULD YOU LIKE A SWEET?

YOU MAY HAVE AS MANY AS YOU LIKE. THEY'RE ALL SO *DELICIOUS.*

MMM! THIS ONE *ESPECIALLY.* HERE...

WHY DON'T YOU TRY SOME FOR *YOURSELF?*

NO?

≶SIGH≷

PERHAPS LATER.

HOW ABOUT THIS?

LOOK WHAT I'VE BROUGHT YOU.

ANOTHER NICE PRESENT! DO YOU WANT TO *OPEN* IT? *NO?* WELL, MAYBE I SHOULD OPEN IT *FOR* YOU, HM? WOULD YOU *LIKE* THAT?

WELL, *I* THINK SOMEONE SHOULD OPEN IT RIGHT AWAY!

AND DO YOU KNOW WHY THAT IS?

THIS IS WHY! AN ADORABLE SELWIT PUP!

LOOK!

LOOK! LOOK!

ISN'T IT CUTE?

IT'S FOR YOU! IT'S SO *HAPPY* TO MEET YOU, ISN'T IT?

HOW ADORABLE!

HOW...

DEAR...

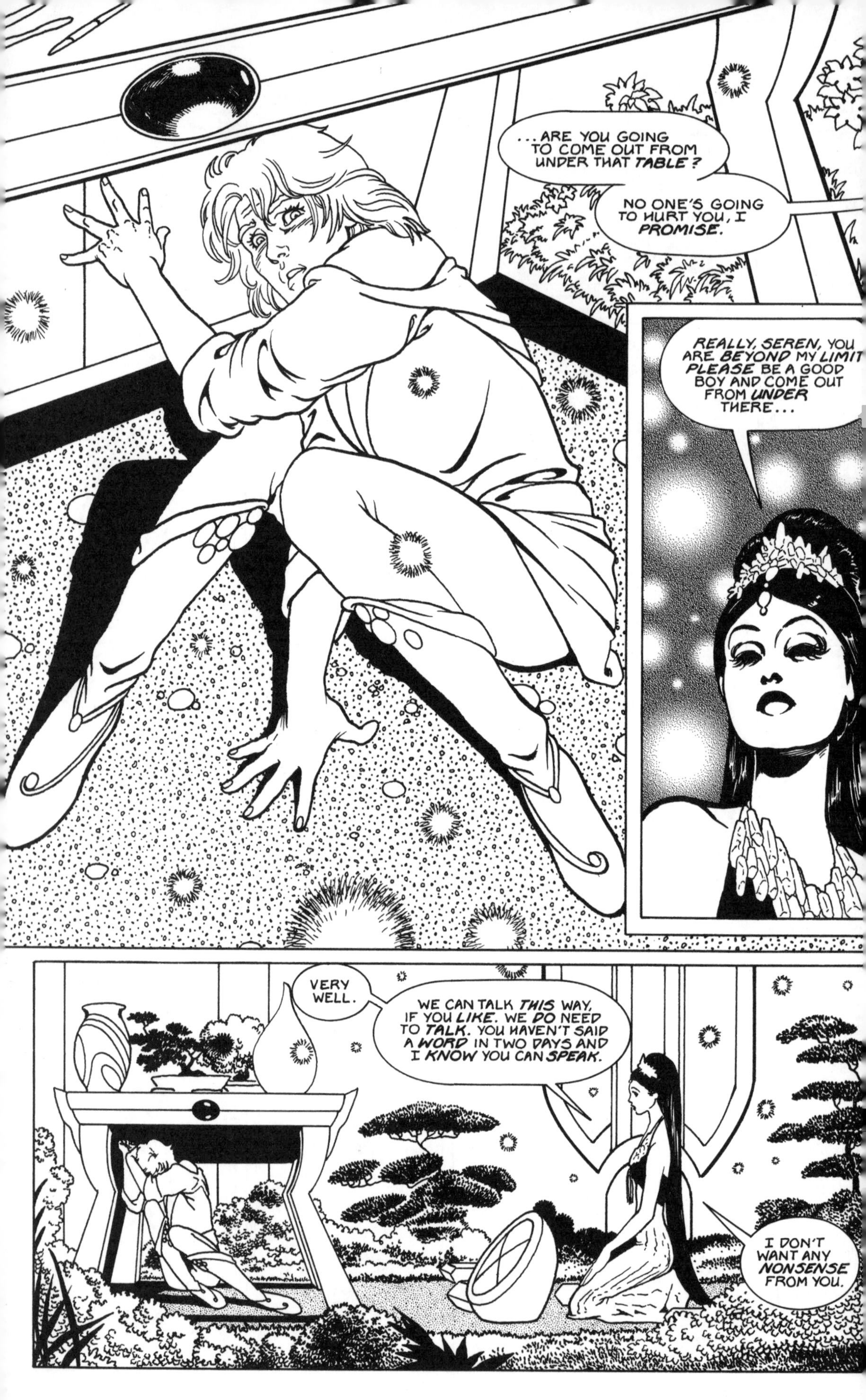
...ARE YOU GOING TO COME OUT FROM UNDER THAT TABLE?
NO ONE'S GOING TO HURT YOU, I PROMISE.
REALLY, SEREN, YOU ARE BEYOND MY LIMIT. PLEASE BE A GOOD BOY AND COME OUT FROM UNDER THERE...
VERY WELL.
WE CAN TALK THIS WAY, IF YOU LIKE. WE DO NEED TO TALK. YOU HAVEN'T SAID A WORD IN TWO DAYS AND I KNOW YOU CAN SPEAK.
I DON'T WANT ANY NONSENSE FROM YOU.

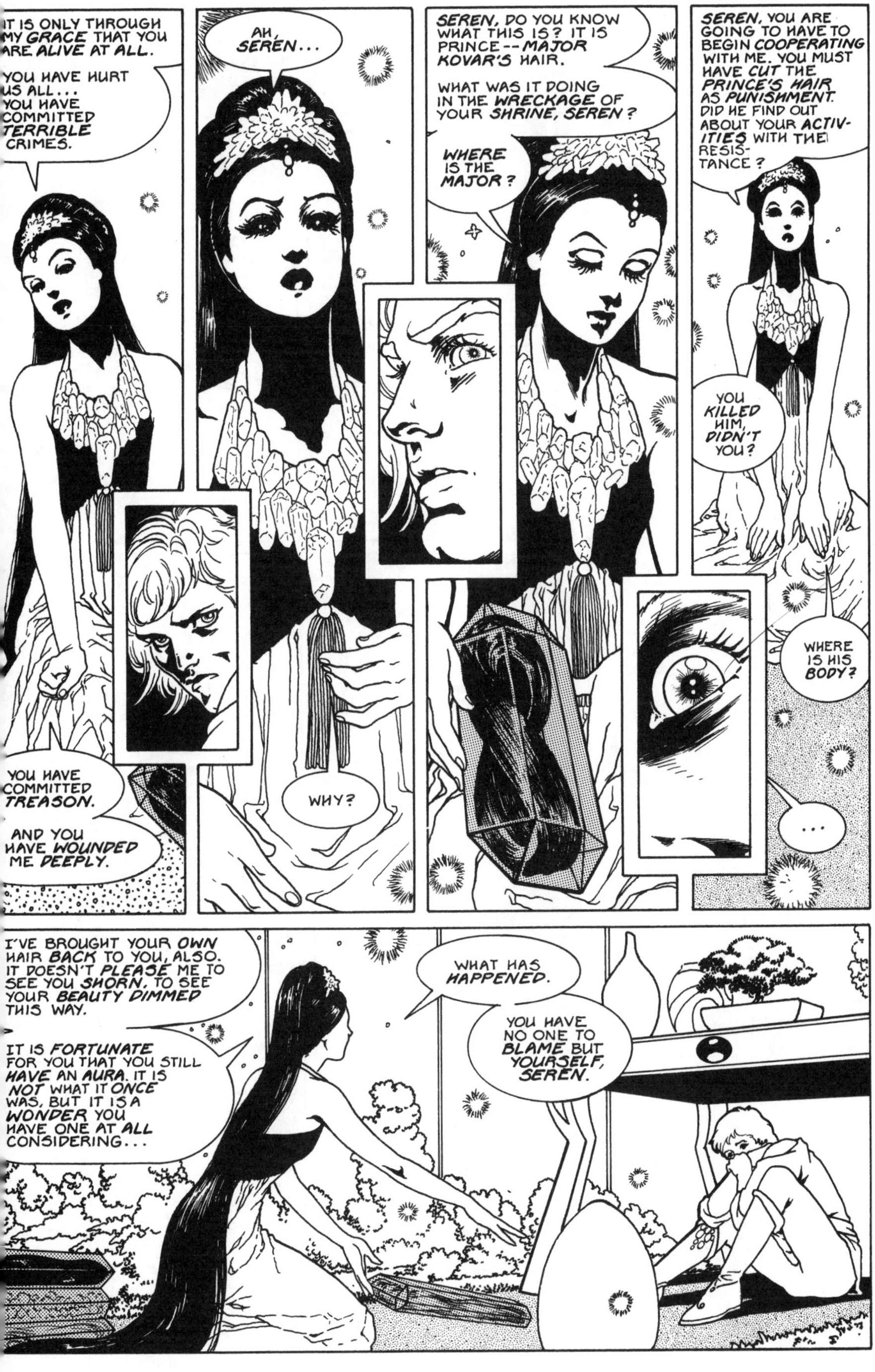
IT IS ONLY THROUGH MY GRACE THAT YOU ARE ALIVE AT ALL.
YOU HAVE HURT US ALL... YOU HAVE COMMITTED TERRIBLE CRIMES.
YOU HAVE COMMITTED TREASON.
AND YOU HAVE WOUNDED ME DEEPLY.
AH, SEREN...
WHY?
SEREN, DO YOU KNOW WHAT THIS IS? IT IS PRINCE--MAJOR KOVAR'S HAIR.
WHAT WAS IT DOING IN THE WRECKAGE OF YOUR SHRINE, SEREN?
WHERE IS THE MAJOR?
SEREN, YOU ARE GOING TO HAVE TO BEGIN COOPERATING WITH ME. YOU MUST HAVE CUT THE PRINCE'S HAIR AS PUNISHMENT. DID HE FIND OUT ABOUT YOUR ACTIVITIES WITH THE RESISTANCE?
YOU KILLED HIM, DIDN'T YOU?
WHERE IS HIS BODY?
...
I'VE BROUGHT YOUR OWN HAIR BACK TO YOU, ALSO. IT DOESN'T PLEASE ME TO SEE YOU SHORN, TO SEE YOUR BEAUTY DIMMED THIS WAY.
IT IS FORTUNATE FOR YOU THAT YOU STILL HAVE AN AURA. IT IS NOT WHAT IT ONCE WAS, BUT IT IS A WONDER YOU HAVE ONE AT ALL CONSIDERING...
WHAT HAS HAPPENED.
YOU HAVE NO ONE TO BLAME BUT YOURSELF, SEREN.

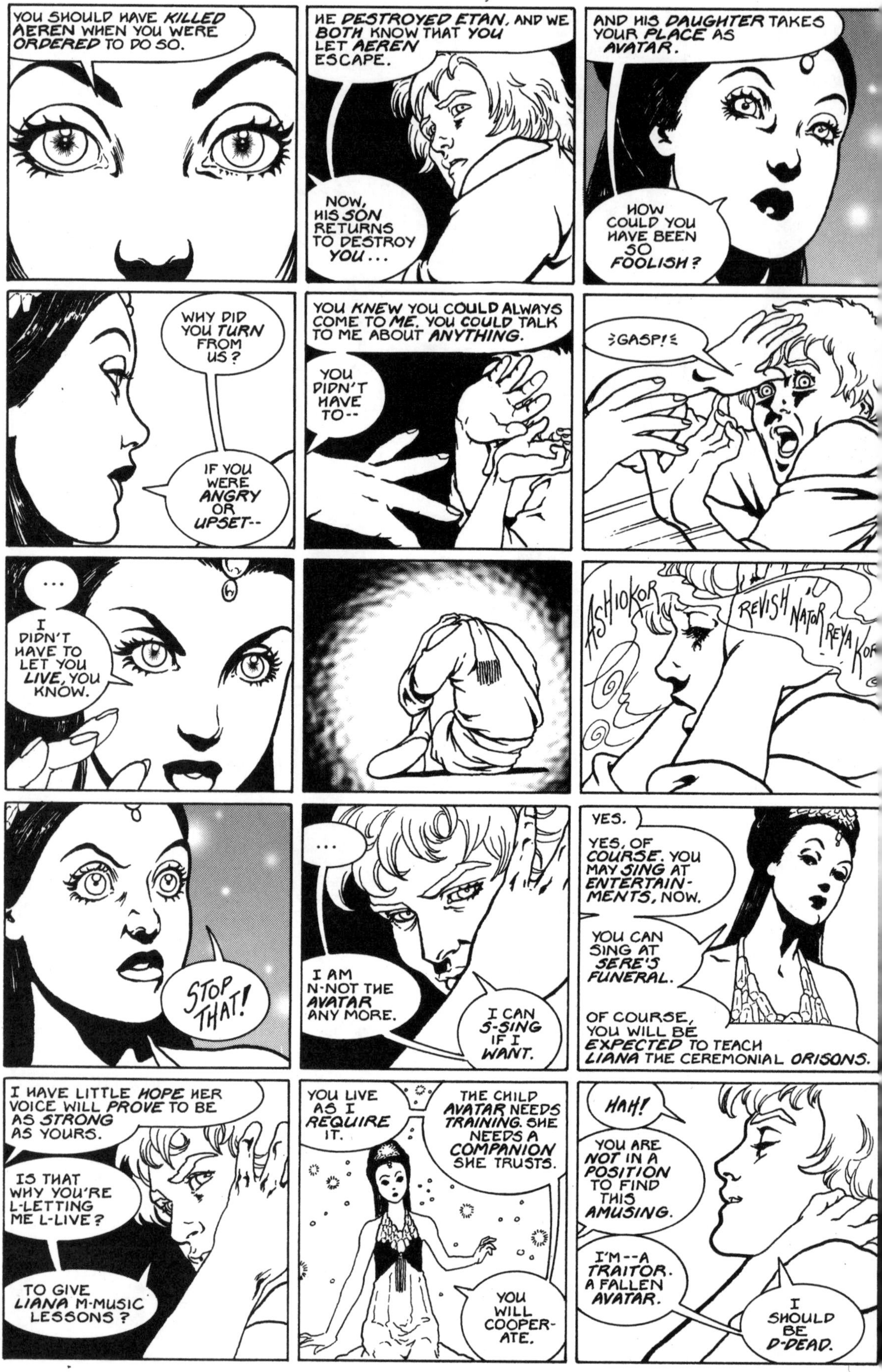
YOU SHOULD HAVE KILLED AEREN WHEN YOU WERE ORDERED TO DO SO.
HE DESTROYED ETAN, AND WE BOTH KNOW THAT YOU LET AEREN ESCAPE.
NOW, HIS SON RETURNS TO DESTROY YOU...
AND HIS DAUGHTER TAKES YOUR PLACE AS AVATAR.
HOW COULD YOU HAVE BEEN SO FOOLISH?
WHY DID YOU TURN FROM US?
IF YOU WERE ANGRY OR UPSET--
YOU KNEW YOU COULD ALWAYS COME TO ME. YOU COULD TALK TO ME ABOUT ANYTHING.
YOU DIDN'T HAVE TO--
GASP!
...
I DIDN'T HAVE TO LET YOU LIVE, YOU KNOW.
ASHIOKOR
REVISH NATOR REYA KOR
STOP THAT!
...
I AM N-NOT THE AVATAR ANY MORE.
I CAN S-SING IF I WANT.
YES.
YES, OF COURSE. YOU MAY SING AT ENTERTAIN-MENTS, NOW.
YOU CAN SING AT SERE'S FUNERAL.
OF COURSE, YOU WILL BE EXPECTED TO TEACH LIANA THE CEREMONIAL ORISONS.
I HAVE LITTLE HOPE HER VOICE WILL PROVE TO BE AS STRONG AS YOURS.
IS THAT WHY YOU'RE L-LETTING ME L-LIVE?
TO GIVE LIANA M-MUSIC LESSONS?
YOU LIVE AS I REQUIRE IT.
THE CHILD AVATAR NEEDS TRAINING. SHE NEEDS A COMPANION SHE TRUSTS.
YOU WILL COOPER-ATE.
HAH!
YOU ARE NOT IN A POSITION TO FIND THIS AMUSING.
I'M--A TRAITOR. A FALLEN AVATAR.
I SHOULD BE D-DEAD.

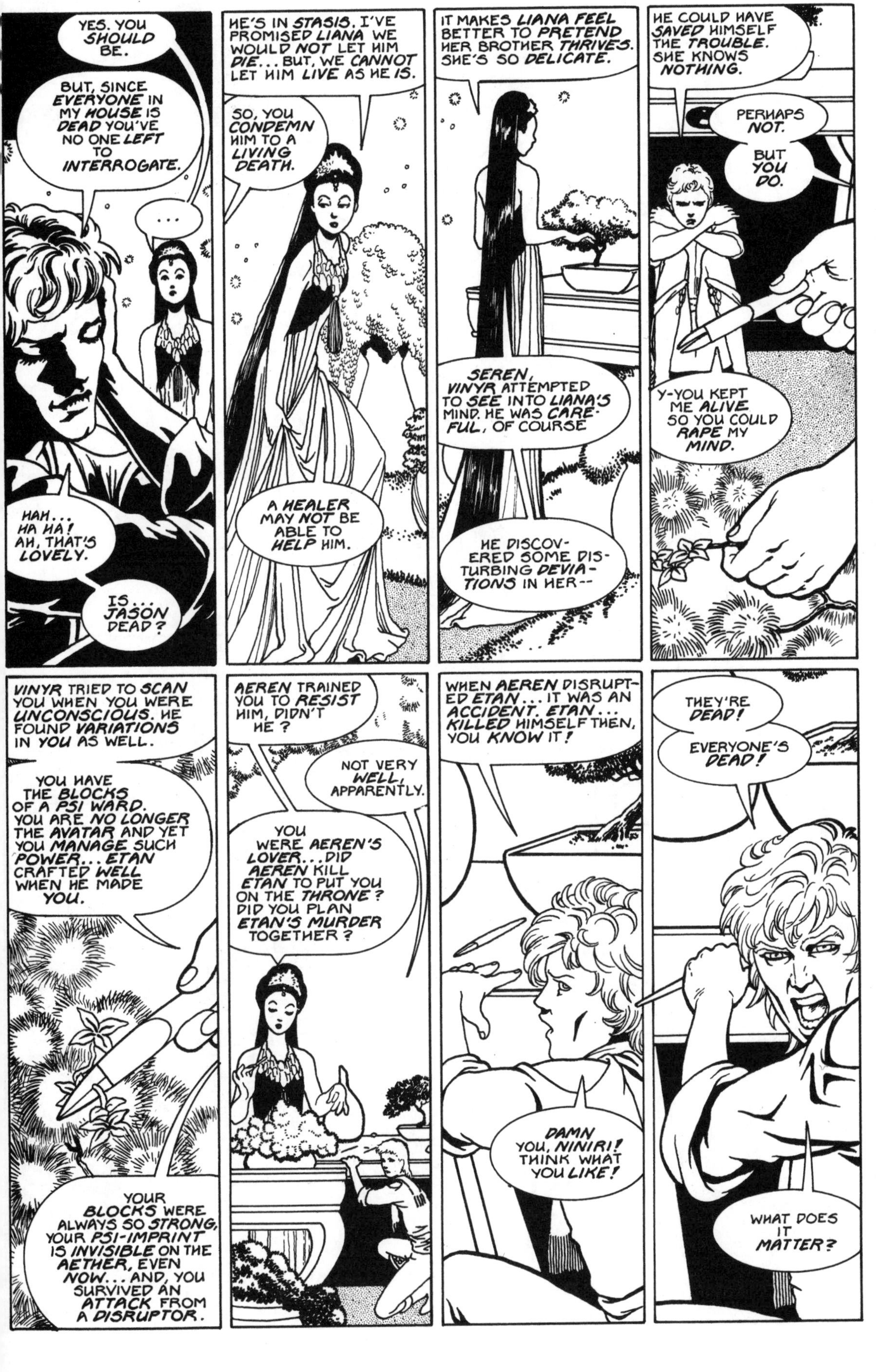
YES. YOU SHOULD BE.
BUT, SINCE EVERYONE IN MY HOUSE IS DEAD YOU'VE NO ONE LEFT TO INTERROGATE.
. . .
HAH... HA HA! AH, THAT'S LOVELY.
IS... JASON DEAD?
HE'S IN STASIS. I'VE PROMISED LIANA WE WOULD NOT LET HIM DIE... BUT, WE CANNOT LET HIM LIVE AS HE IS.
SO, YOU CONDEMN HIM TO A LIVING DEATH.
A HEALER MAY NOT BE ABLE TO HELP HIM.
IT MAKES LIANA FEEL BETTER TO PRETEND HER BROTHER THRIVES. SHE'S SO DELICATE.
SEREN, VINYR ATTEMPTED TO SEE INTO LIANA'S MIND. HE WAS CAREFUL, OF COURSE
HE DISCOVERED SOME DISTURBING DEVIATIONS IN HER--
HE COULD HAVE SAVED HIMSELF THE TROUBLE. SHE KNOWS NOTHING.
PERHAPS NOT.
BUT YOU DO.
Y-YOU KEPT ME ALIVE SO YOU COULD RAPE MY MIND.
VINYR TRIED TO SCAN YOU WHEN YOU WERE UNCONSCIOUS. HE FOUND VARIATIONS IN YOU AS WELL.
YOU HAVE THE BLOCKS OF A PSI WARD. YOU ARE NO LONGER THE AVATAR AND YET YOU MANAGE SUCH POWER... ETAN CRAFTED WELL WHEN HE MADE YOU.
YOUR BLOCKS WERE ALWAYS SO STRONG, YOUR PSI-IMPRINT IS INVISIBLE ON THE AETHER, EVEN NOW... AND, YOU SURVIVED AN ATTACK FROM A DISRUPTOR.
AEREN TRAINED YOU TO RESIST HIM, DIDN'T HE?
NOT VERY WELL, APPARENTLY.
YOU WERE AEREN'S LOVER... DID AEREN KILL ETAN TO PUT YOU ON THE THRONE? DID YOU PLAN ETAN'S MURDER TOGETHER?
WHEN AEREN DISRUPTED ETAN... IT WAS AN ACCIDENT. ETAN... KILLED HIMSELF THEN, YOU KNOW IT!
DAMN YOU, NINIRI! THINK WHAT YOU LIKE!
THEY'RE DEAD!
EVERYONE'S DEAD!
WHAT DOES IT MATTER?

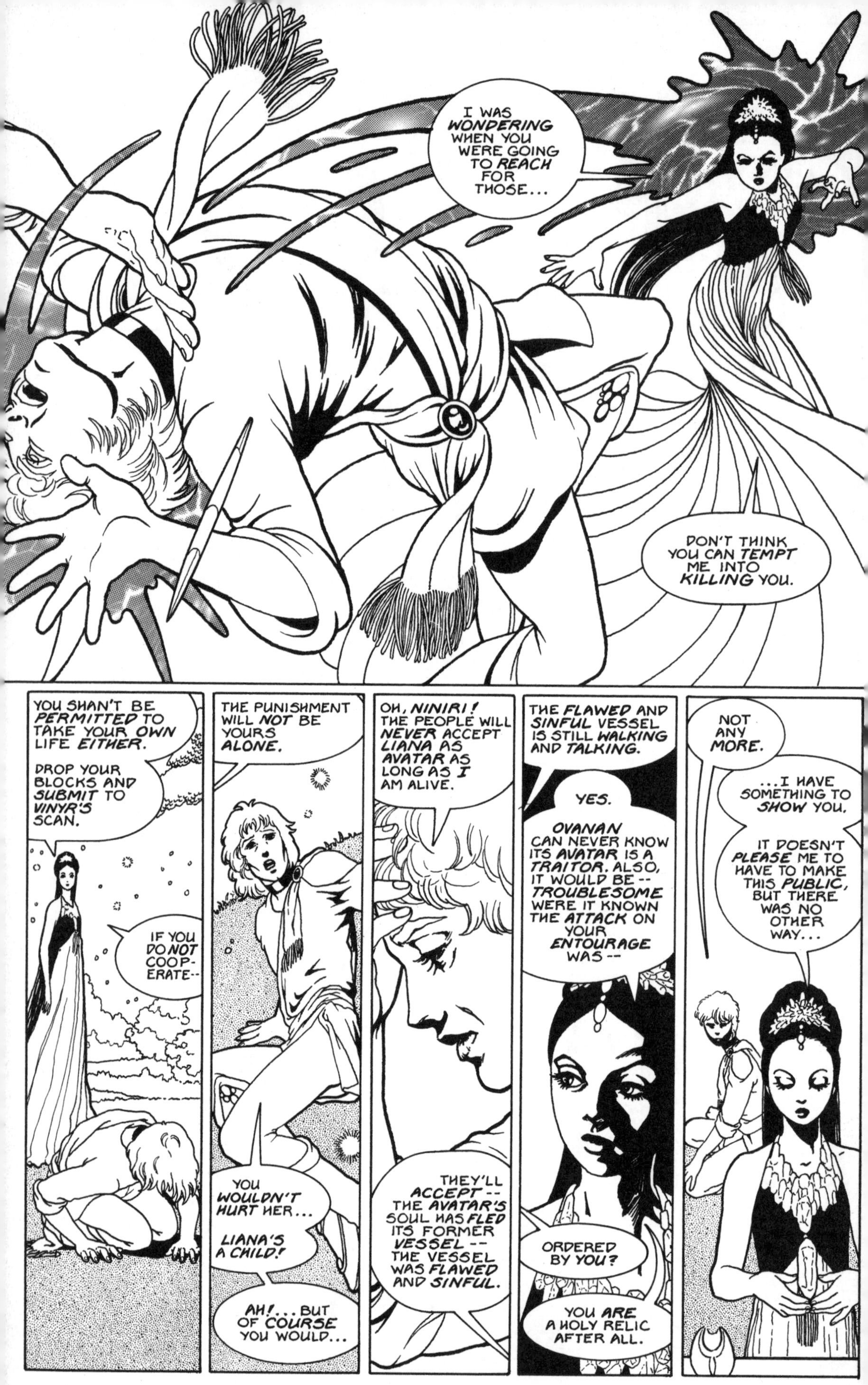
I WAS *WONDERING* WHEN YOU WERE GOING TO *REACH* FOR THOSE...
DON'T THINK YOU CAN *TEMPT* ME INTO *KILLING* YOU.
YOU SHAN'T BE *PERMITTED* TO TAKE YOUR *OWN* LIFE *EITHER*.
DROP YOUR BLOCKS AND *SUBMIT* TO *VINYR'S* SCAN.
IF YOU DO *NOT* COOP-ERATE--
THE PUNISHMENT WILL *NOT* BE YOURS *ALONE*.
YOU *WOULDN'T HURT* HER...
LIANA'S A *CHILD!*
AH!... BUT OF *COURSE* YOU WOULD...
OH, *NINIRI!* THE PEOPLE WILL *NEVER* ACCEPT *LIANA* AS *AVATAR* AS LONG AS *I* AM ALIVE.
THEY'LL *ACCEPT* -- THE *AVATAR'S* SOUL HAS *FLED* ITS FORMER *VESSEL* -- THE VESSEL WAS *FLAWED* AND *SINFUL*.
THE *FLAWED* AND *SINFUL* VESSEL IS STILL *WALKING* AND *TALKING*.
YES.
OVANAN CAN NEVER KNOW ITS *AVATAR* IS A *TRAITOR*. ALSO, IT WOULD BE -- *TROUBLESOME* WERE IT KNOWN THE *ATTACK* ON YOUR *ENTOURAGE* WAS --
ORDERED BY *YOU?*
YOU *ARE* A HOLY RELIC AFTER ALL.
NOT ANY *MORE*.
...I HAVE SOMETHING TO *SHOW* YOU.
IT DOESN'T *PLEASE* ME TO HAVE TO MAKE THIS *PUBLIC*, BUT THERE WAS NO OTHER WAY...

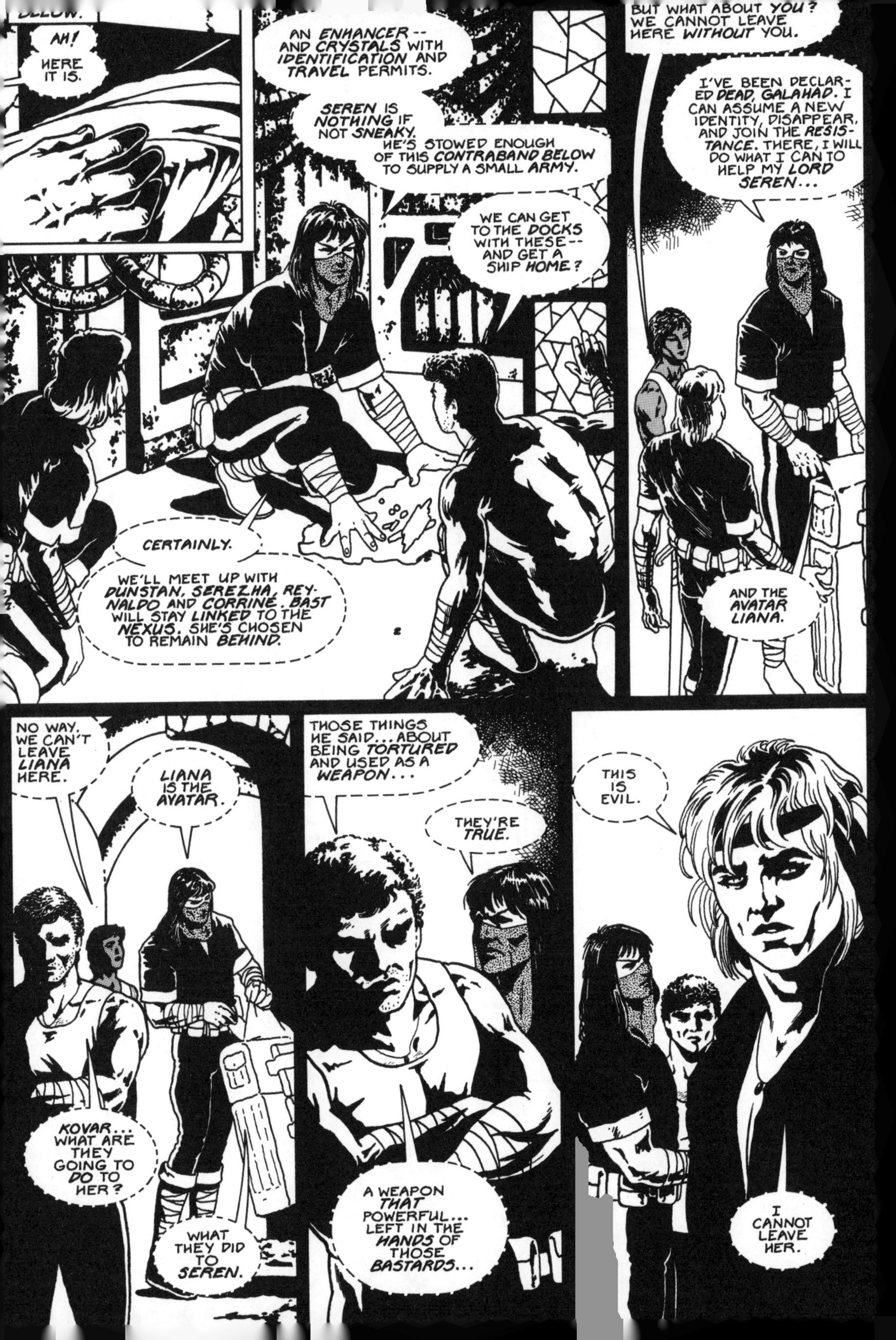
AH!
HERE IT IS.
AN ENHANCER -- AND CRYSTALS WITH IDENTIFICATION AND TRAVEL PERMITS.
SEREN IS NOTHING IF NOT SNEAKY. HE'S STOWED ENOUGH OF THIS CONTRABAND BELOW TO SUPPLY A SMALL ARMY.
WE CAN GET TO THE DOCKS WITH THESE-- AND GET A SHIP HOME?
CERTAINLY.
WE'LL MEET UP WITH DUNSTAN, SEREZHA, REYNALDO AND CORRINE. BAST WILL STAY LINKED TO THE NEXUS. SHE'S CHOSEN TO REMAIN BEHIND.
BUT WHAT ABOUT YOU? WE CANNOT LEAVE HERE WITHOUT YOU.
I'VE BEEN DECLARED DEAD, GALAHAD. I CAN ASSUME A NEW IDENTITY, DISAPPEAR, AND JOIN THE RESISTANCE. THERE, I WILL DO WHAT I CAN TO HELP MY LORD SEREN...
AND THE AVATAR LIANA.
NO WAY. WE CAN'T LEAVE LIANA HERE.
LIANA IS THE AVATAR.
KOVAR... WHAT ARE THEY GOING TO DO TO HER?
WHAT THEY DID TO SEREN.
THOSE THINGS HE SAID... ABOUT BEING TORTURED AND USED AS A WEAPON...
THEY'RE TRUE.
A WEAPON THAT POWERFUL... LEFT IN THE HANDS OF THOSE BASTARDS...
THIS IS EVIL.
I CANNOT LEAVE HER.

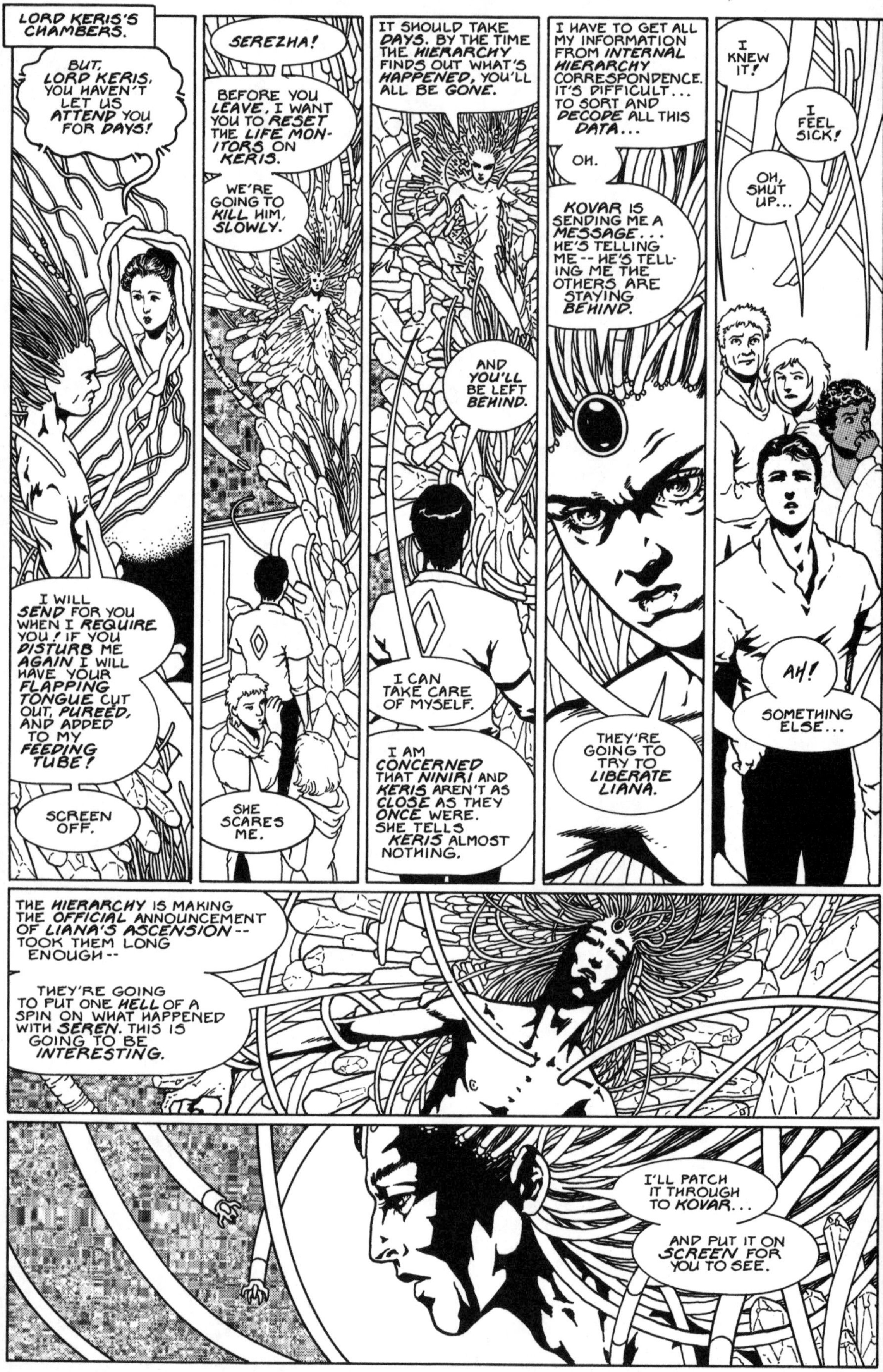
LORD KERIS'S CHAMBERS.
BUT, LORD KERIS, YOU HAVEN'T LET US ATTEND YOU FOR DAYS!
I WILL SEND FOR YOU WHEN I REQUIRE YOU! IF YOU DISTURB ME AGAIN I WILL HAVE YOUR FLAPPING TONGUE CUT OUT, PUREED, AND ADDED TO MY FEEDING TUBE!
SCREEN OFF.
SEREZHA!
BEFORE YOU LEAVE, I WANT YOU TO RESET THE LIFE MONITORS ON KERIS.
WE'RE GOING TO KILL HIM, SLOWLY.
SHE SCARES ME.
IT SHOULD TAKE DAYS. BY THE TIME THE HIERARCHY FINDS OUT WHAT'S HAPPENED, YOU'LL ALL BE GONE.
AND YOU'LL BE LEFT BEHIND.
I CAN TAKE CARE OF MYSELF.
I AM CONCERNED THAT NINIRI AND KERIS AREN'T AS CLOSE AS THEY ONCE WERE. SHE TELLS KERIS ALMOST NOTHING.
I HAVE TO GET ALL MY INFORMATION FROM INTERNAL HIERARCHY CORRESPONDENCE. IT'S DIFFICULT... TO SORT AND DECODE ALL THIS DATA...
OH.
KOVAR IS SENDING ME A MESSAGE... HE'S TELLING ME-- HE'S TELLING ME THE OTHERS ARE STAYING BEHIND.
THEY'RE GOING TO TRY TO LIBERATE LIANA.
I KNEW IT!
I FEEL SICK!
OH, SHUT UP...
AH!
SOMETHING ELSE...
THE HIERARCHY IS MAKING THE OFFICIAL ANNOUNCEMENT OF LIANA'S ASCENSION-- TOOK THEM LONG ENOUGH--
THEY'RE GOING TO PUT ONE HELL OF A SPIN ON WHAT HAPPENED WITH SEREN. THIS IS GOING TO BE INTERESTING.
I'LL PATCH IT THROUGH TO KOVAR...
AND PUT IT ON SCREEN FOR YOU TO SEE.

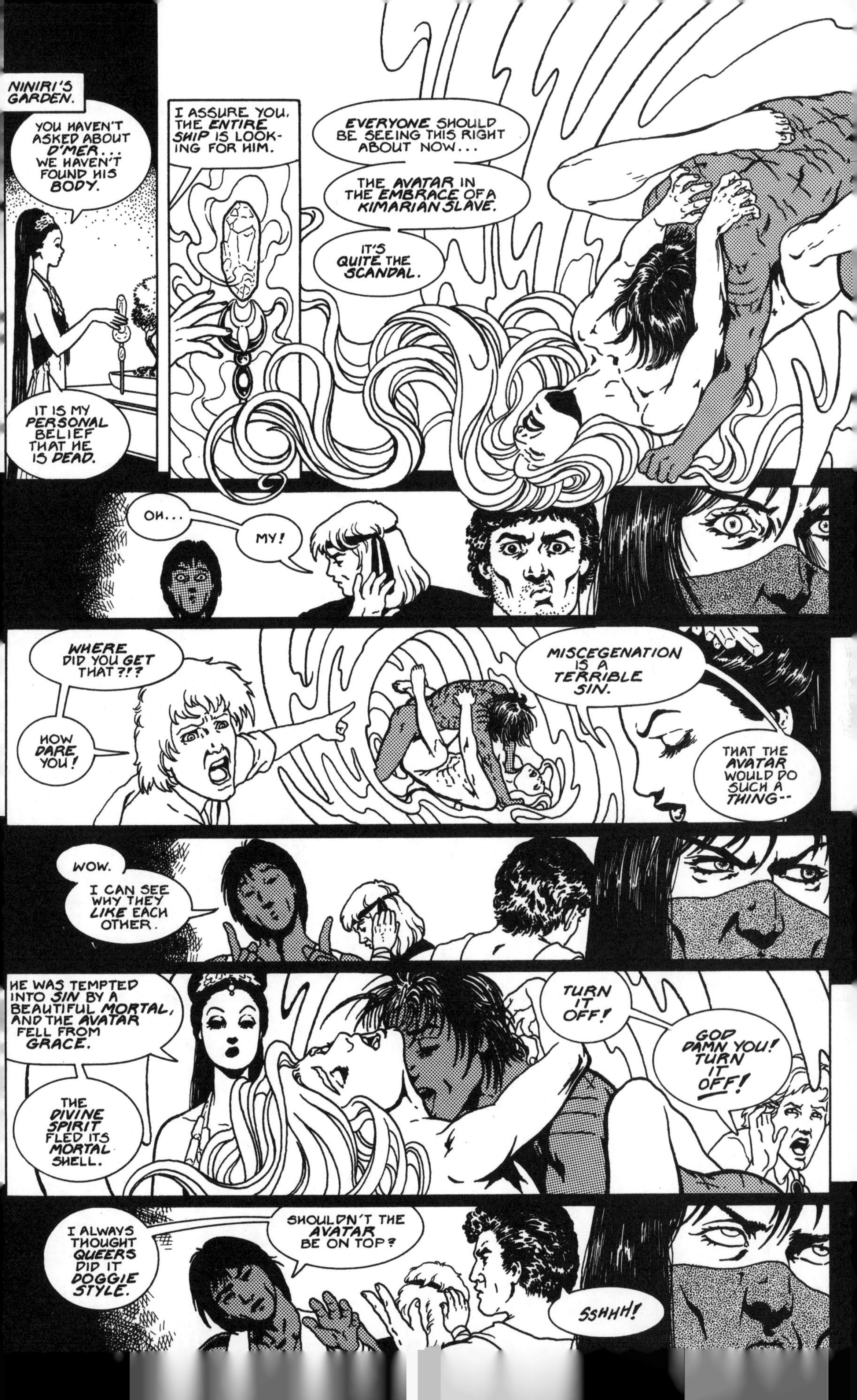
NINIRI'S GARDEN.
YOU HAVEN'T ASKED ABOUT D'MER... WE HAVEN'T FOUND HIS BODY.
IT IS MY PERSONAL BELIEF THAT HE IS DEAD.
I ASSURE YOU, THE ENTIRE SHIP IS LOOKING FOR HIM.
EVERYONE SHOULD BE SEEING THIS RIGHT ABOUT NOW...
THE AVATAR IN THE EMBRACE OF A KIMARIAN SLAVE.
IT'S QUITE THE SCANDAL.
OH...
MY!
WHERE DID YOU GET THAT?!?
HOW DARE YOU!
MISCEGENATION IS A TERRIBLE SIN.
THAT THE AVATAR WOULD DO SUCH A THING--
WOW.
I CAN SEE WHY THEY LIKE EACH OTHER.
HE WAS TEMPTED INTO SIN BY A BEAUTIFUL MORTAL, AND THE AVATAR FELL FROM GRACE.
THE DIVINE SPIRIT FLED ITS MORTAL SHELL.
TURN IT OFF!
GOD DAMN YOU! TURN IT OFF!
I ALWAYS THOUGHT QUEERS DID IT DOGGIE STYLE.
SHOULDN'T THE AVATAR BE ON TOP?
SSHHH!

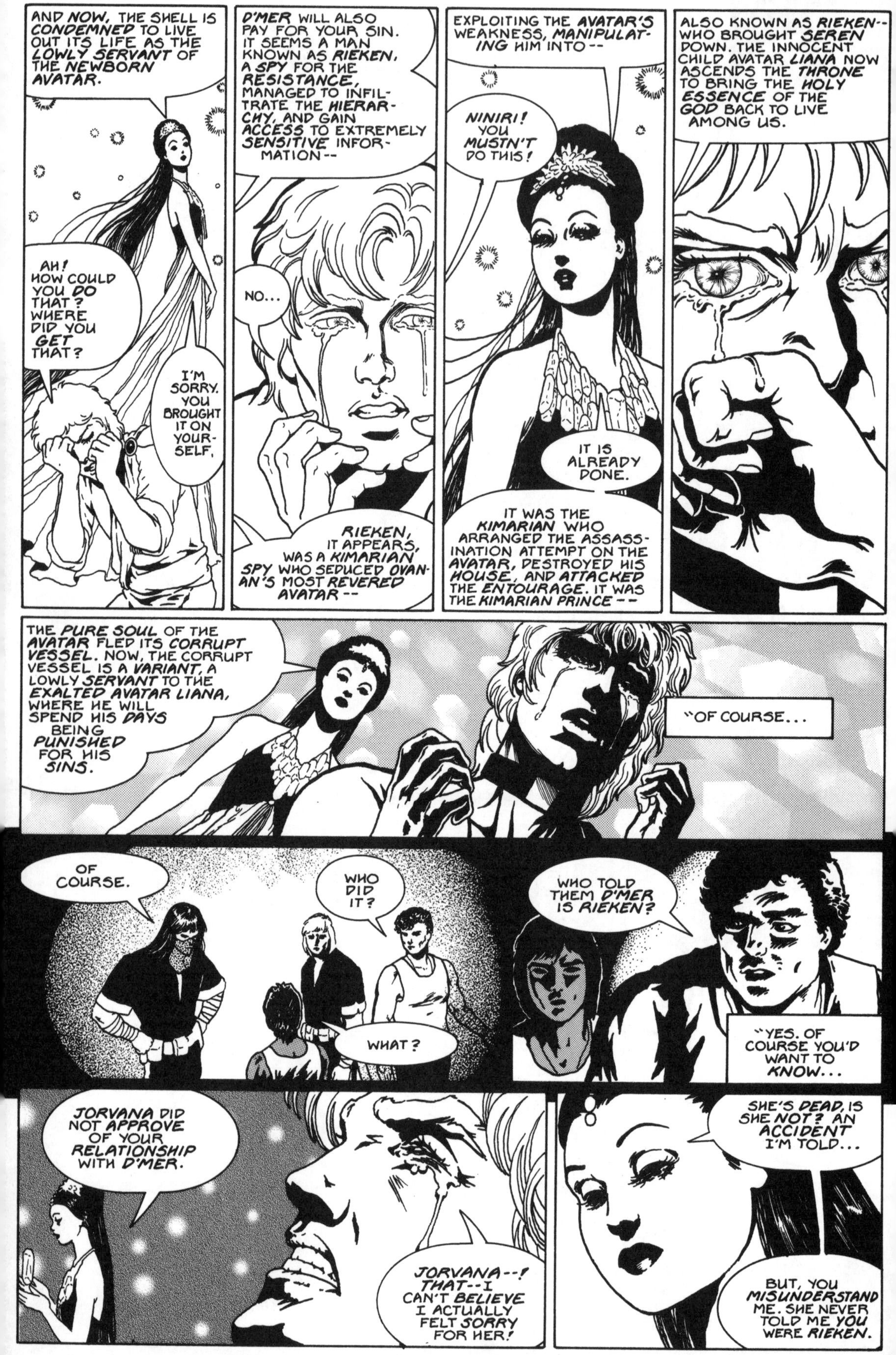
AND NOW, THE SHELL IS CONDEMNED TO LIVE OUT ITS LIFE AS THE LOWLY SERVANT OF THE NEWBORN AVATAR.
AH! HOW COULD YOU DO THAT? WHERE DID YOU GET THAT?
I'M SORRY. YOU BROUGHT IT ON YOURSELF.
D'MER WILL ALSO PAY FOR YOUR SIN. IT SEEMS A MAN KNOWN AS RIEKEN, A SPY FOR THE RESISTANCE, MANAGED TO INFILTRATE THE HIERARCHY, AND GAIN ACCESS TO EXTREMELY SENSITIVE INFORMATION--
NO...
RIEKEN, IT APPEARS, WAS A KIMARIAN SPY WHO SEDUCED OVAN-AN'S MOST REVERED AVATAR--
EXPLOITING THE AVATAR'S WEAKNESS, MANIPULATING HIM INTO--
NINIRI! YOU MUSTN'T DO THIS!
IT IS ALREADY DONE.
IT WAS THE KIMARIAN WHO ARRANGED THE ASSASSINATION ATTEMPT ON THE AVATAR, DESTROYED HIS HOUSE, AND ATTACKED THE ENTOURAGE. IT WAS THE KIMARIAN PRINCE--
ALSO KNOWN AS RIEKEN--WHO BROUGHT SEREN DOWN. THE INNOCENT CHILD AVATAR LIANA NOW ASCENDS THE THRONE TO BRING THE HOLY ESSENCE OF THE GOD BACK TO LIVE AMONG US.
THE PURE SOUL OF THE AVATAR FLED ITS CORRUPT VESSEL. NOW, THE CORRUPT VESSEL IS A VARIANT, A LOWLY SERVANT TO THE EXALTED AVATAR LIANA, WHERE HE WILL SPEND HIS DAYS BEING PUNISHED FOR HIS SINS.
"OF COURSE...
OF COURSE.
WHO DID IT?
WHAT?
WHO TOLD THEM D'MER IS RIEKEN?
"YES. OF COURSE YOU'D WANT TO KNOW...
JORVANA DID NOT APPROVE OF YOUR RELATIONSHIP WITH D'MER.
JORVANA--! THAT--I CAN'T BELIEVE I ACTUALLY FELT SORRY FOR HER!
SHE'S DEAD, IS SHE NOT? AN ACCIDENT I'M TOLD...
BUT, YOU MISUNDERSTAND ME. SHE NEVER TOLD ME YOU WERE RIEKEN.

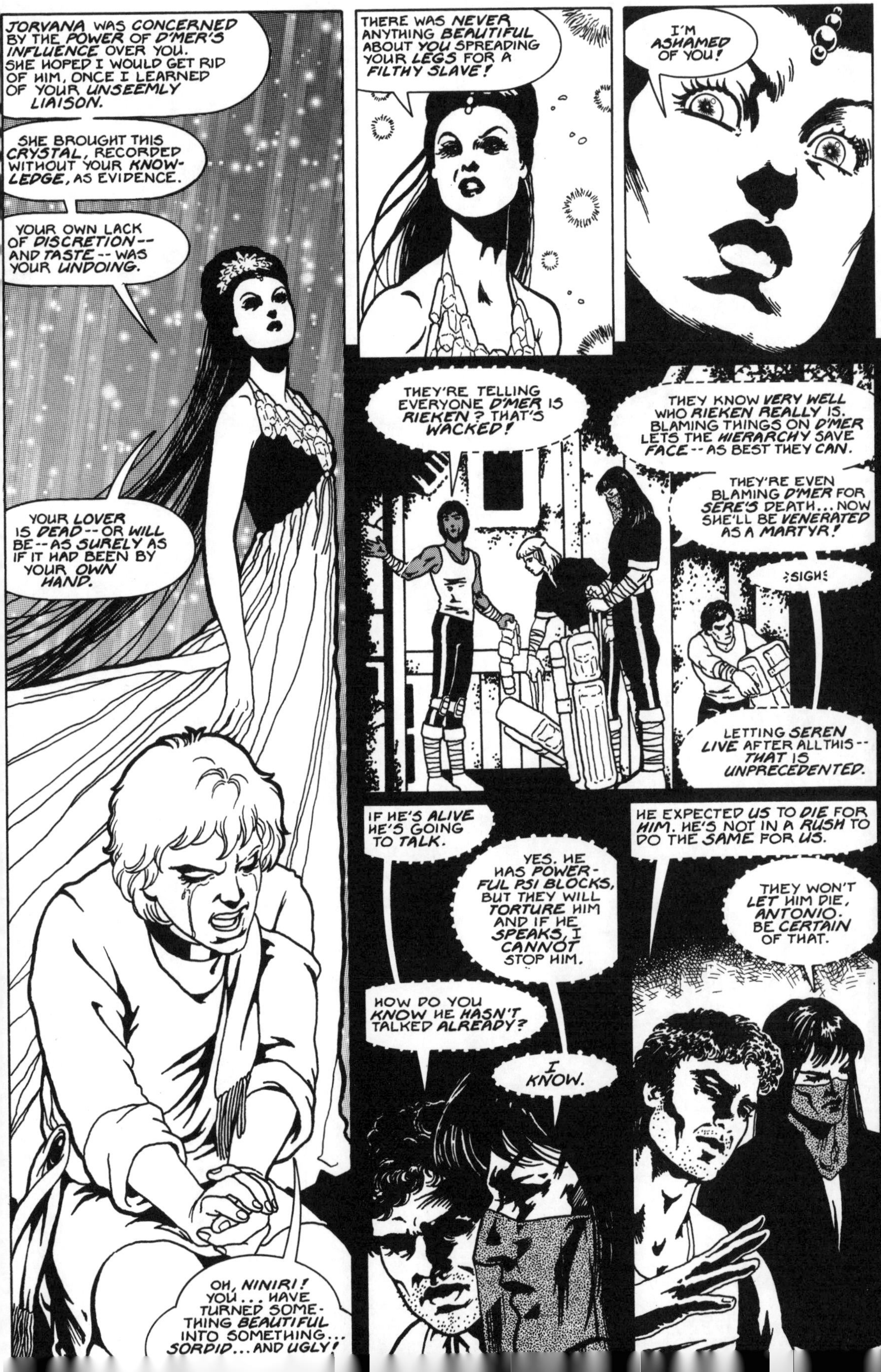
JORVANA WAS CONCERNED BY THE POWER OF D'MER'S INFLUENCE OVER YOU. SHE HOPED I WOULD GET RID OF HIM, ONCE I LEARNED OF YOUR UNSEEMLY LIAISON.
SHE BROUGHT THIS CRYSTAL, RECORDED WITHOUT YOUR KNOWLEDGE, AS EVIDENCE.
YOUR OWN LACK OF DISCRETION -- AND TASTE -- WAS YOUR UNDOING.
YOUR LOVER IS DEAD -- OR WILL BE -- AS SURELY AS IF IT HAD BEEN BY YOUR OWN HAND.
OH, NINIRI! YOU... HAVE TURNED SOMETHING BEAUTIFUL INTO SOMETHING... SORDID... AND UGLY!
THERE WAS NEVER ANYTHING BEAUTIFUL ABOUT YOU SPREADING YOUR LEGS FOR A FILTHY SLAVE!
I'M ASHAMED OF YOU!
THEY'RE TELLING EVERYONE D'MER IS RIEKEN? THAT'S WACKED!
THEY KNOW VERY WELL WHO RIEKEN REALLY IS. BLAMING THINGS ON D'MER LETS THE HIERARCHY SAVE FACE -- AS BEST THEY CAN.
THEY'RE EVEN BLAMING D'MER FOR SERE'S DEATH... NOW SHE'LL BE VENERATED AS A MARTYR!
SIGH
LETTING SEREN LIVE AFTER ALL THIS -- THAT IS UNPRECEDENTED.
IF HE'S ALIVE HE'S GOING TO TALK.
YES. HE HAS POWERFUL PSI BLOCKS, BUT THEY WILL TORTURE HIM AND IF HE SPEAKS, I CANNOT STOP HIM.
HOW DO YOU KNOW HE HASN'T TALKED ALREADY?
I KNOW.
HE EXPECTED US TO DIE FOR HIM. HE'S NOT IN A RUSH TO DO THE SAME FOR US.
THEY WON'T LET HIM DIE, ANTONIO. BE CERTAIN OF THAT.

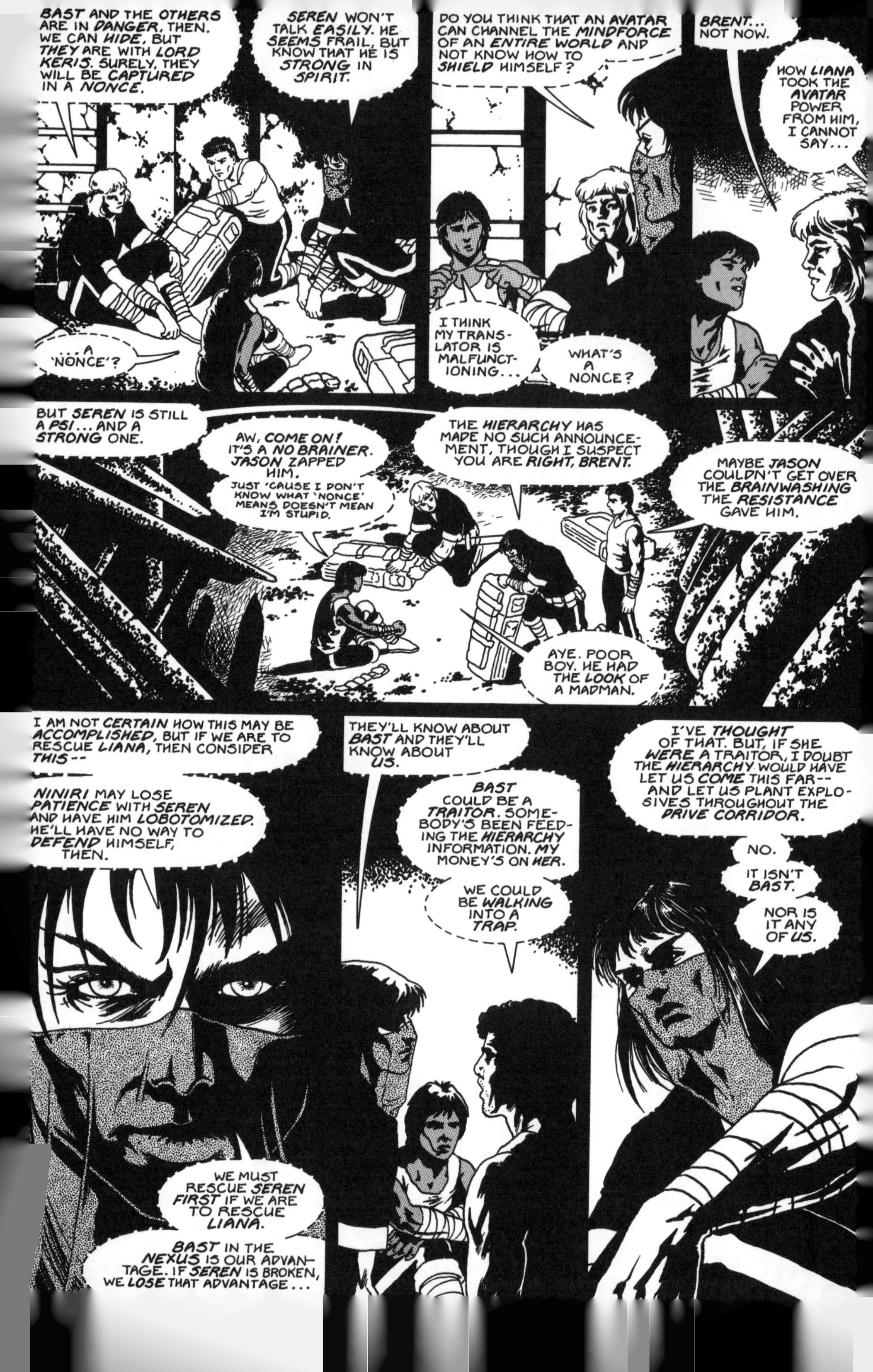
BAST AND THE OTHERS ARE IN DANGER, THEN. WE CAN HIDE, BUT THEY ARE WITH LORD KERIS. SURELY, THEY WILL BE CAPTURED IN A NONCE.
SEREN WON'T TALK EASILY. HE SEEMS FRAIL, BUT KNOW THAT HE IS STRONG IN SPIRIT.
...A 'NONCE'?
DO YOU THINK THAT AN AVATAR CAN CHANNEL THE MINDFORCE OF AN ENTIRE WORLD AND NOT KNOW HOW TO SHIELD HIMSELF?
I THINK MY TRANSLATOR IS MALFUNCTIONING...
WHAT'S A NONCE?
BRENT... NOT NOW.
HOW LIANA TOOK THE AVATAR POWER FROM HIM, I CANNOT SAY...
BUT SEREN IS STILL A PSI... AND A STRONG ONE.
AW, COME ON! IT'S A NO BRAINER. JASON ZAPPED HIM.
JUST 'CAUSE I DON'T KNOW WHAT 'NONCE' MEANS DOESN'T MEAN I'M STUPID.
THE HIERARCHY HAS MADE NO SUCH ANNOUNCEMENT, THOUGH I SUSPECT YOU ARE RIGHT, BRENT.
MAYBE JASON COULDN'T GET OVER THE BRAINWASHING THE RESISTANCE GAVE HIM.
AYE. POOR BOY. HE HAD THE LOOK OF A MADMAN.
I AM NOT CERTAIN HOW THIS MAY BE ACCOMPLISHED, BUT IF WE ARE TO RESCUE LIANA, THEN CONSIDER THIS--
NINIRI MAY LOSE PATIENCE WITH SEREN AND HAVE HIM LOBOTOMIZED. HE'LL HAVE NO WAY TO DEFEND HIMSELF, THEN.
WE MUST RESCUE SEREN FIRST IF WE ARE TO RESCUE LIANA.
BAST IN THE NEXUS IS OUR ADVANTAGE. IF SEREN IS BROKEN, WE LOSE THAT ADVANTAGE...
THEY'LL KNOW ABOUT BAST AND THEY'LL KNOW ABOUT US.
BAST COULD BE A TRAITOR. SOMEBODY'S BEEN FEEDING THE HIERARCHY INFORMATION. MY MONEY'S ON HER.
WE COULD BE WALKING INTO A TRAP.
I'VE THOUGHT OF THAT. BUT, IF SHE WERE A TRAITOR, I DOUBT THE HIERARCHY WOULD HAVE LET US COME THIS FAR-- AND LET US PLANT EXPLOSIVES THROUGHOUT THE DRIVE CORRIDOR.
NO.
IT ISN'T BAST.
NOR IS IT ANY OF US.

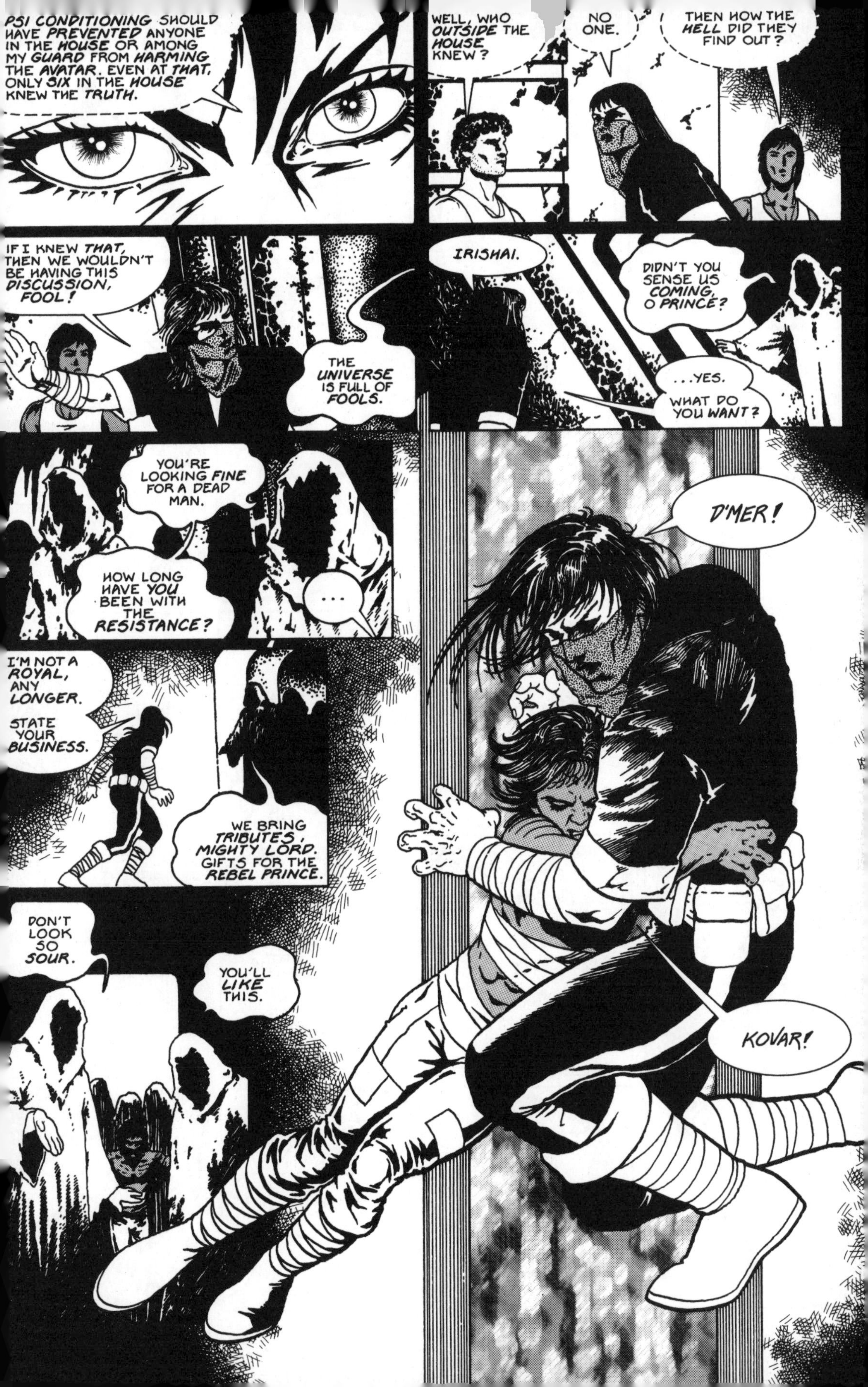
PSI CONDITIONING SHOULD HAVE PREVENTED ANYONE IN THE HOUSE OR AMONG MY GUARD FROM HARMING THE AVATAR. EVEN AT THAT, ONLY SIX IN THE HOUSE KNEW THE TRUTH.
WELL, WHO OUTSIDE THE HOUSE KNEW?
NO ONE.
THEN HOW THE HELL DID THEY FIND OUT?
IF I KNEW THAT, THEN WE WOULDN'T BE HAVING THIS DISCUSSION, FOOL!
THE UNIVERSE IS FULL OF FOOLS.
IRISHAI.
DIDN'T YOU SENSE US COMING, O PRINCE?
...YES.
WHAT DO YOU WANT?
YOU'RE LOOKING FINE FOR A DEAD MAN.
HOW LONG HAVE YOU BEEN WITH THE RESISTANCE?
...
I'M NOT A ROYAL, ANY LONGER.
STATE YOUR BUSINESS.
WE BRING TRIBUTES, MIGHTY LORD. GIFTS FOR THE REBEL PRINCE.
DON'T LOOK SO SOUR.
YOU'LL LIKE THIS.
D'MER!
KOVAR!

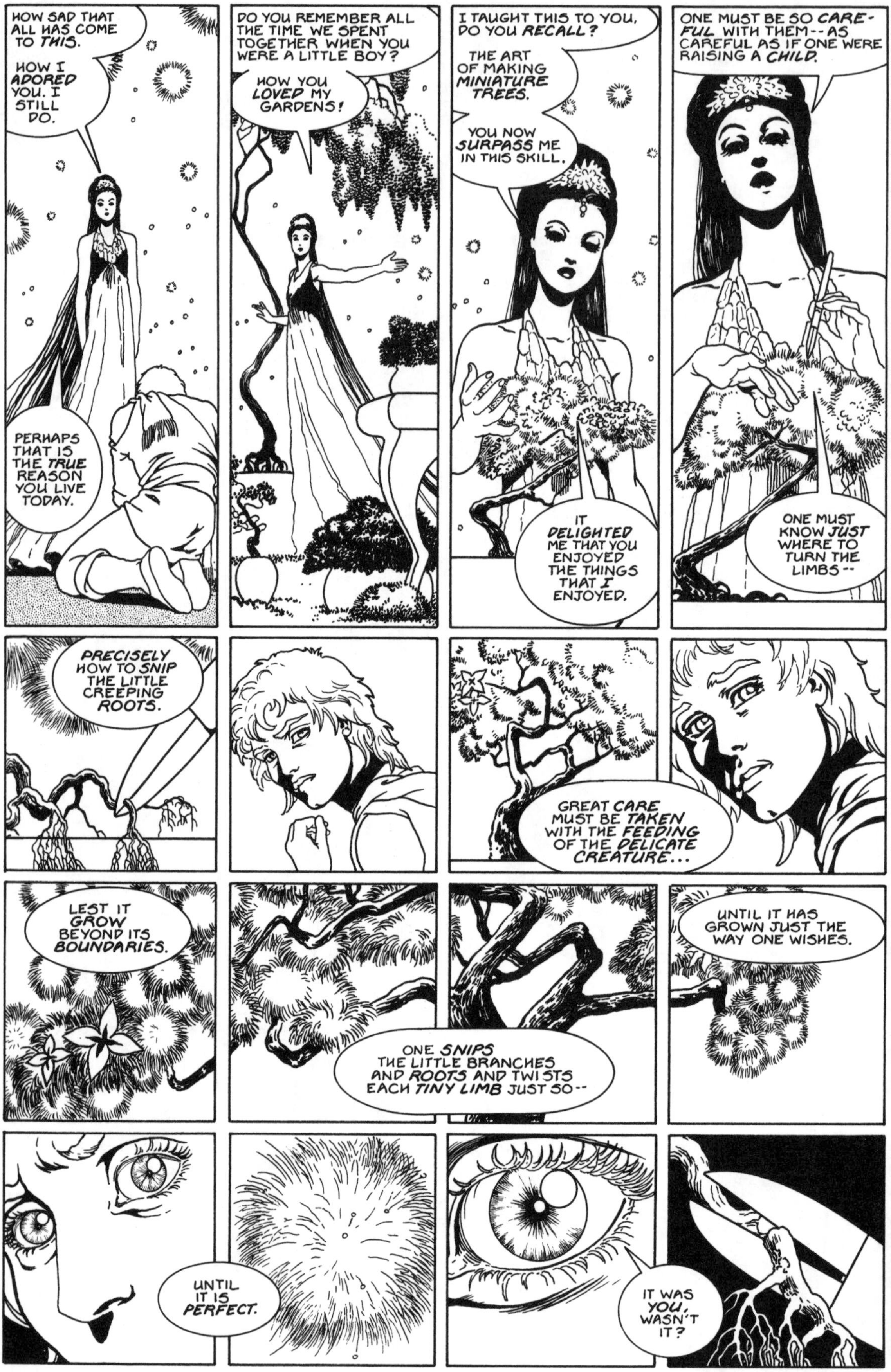
HOW SAD THAT ALL HAS COME TO THIS.
HOW I ADORED YOU. I STILL DO.
PERHAPS THAT IS THE TRUE REASON YOU LIVE TODAY.
DO YOU REMEMBER ALL THE TIME WE SPENT TOGETHER WHEN YOU WERE A LITTLE BOY?
HOW YOU LOVED MY GARDENS!
I TAUGHT THIS TO YOU, DO YOU RECALL?
THE ART OF MAKING MINIATURE TREES.
YOU NOW SURPASS ME IN THIS SKILL.
IT DELIGHTED ME THAT YOU ENJOYED THE THINGS THAT I ENJOYED.
ONE MUST BE SO CAREFUL WITH THEM--AS CAREFUL AS IF ONE WERE RAISING A CHILD.
ONE MUST KNOW JUST WHERE TO TURN THE LIMBS--
PRECISELY HOW TO SNIP THE LITTLE CREEPING ROOTS.
GREAT CARE MUST BE TAKEN WITH THE FEEDING OF THE DELICATE CREATURE...
LEST IT GROW BEYOND ITS BOUNDARIES.
ONE SNIPS THE LITTLE BRANCHES AND ROOTS AND TWISTS EACH TINY LIMB JUST SO--
UNTIL IT HAS GROWN JUST THE WAY ONE WISHES.
UNTIL IT IS PERFECT.
IT WAS YOU, WASN'T IT?

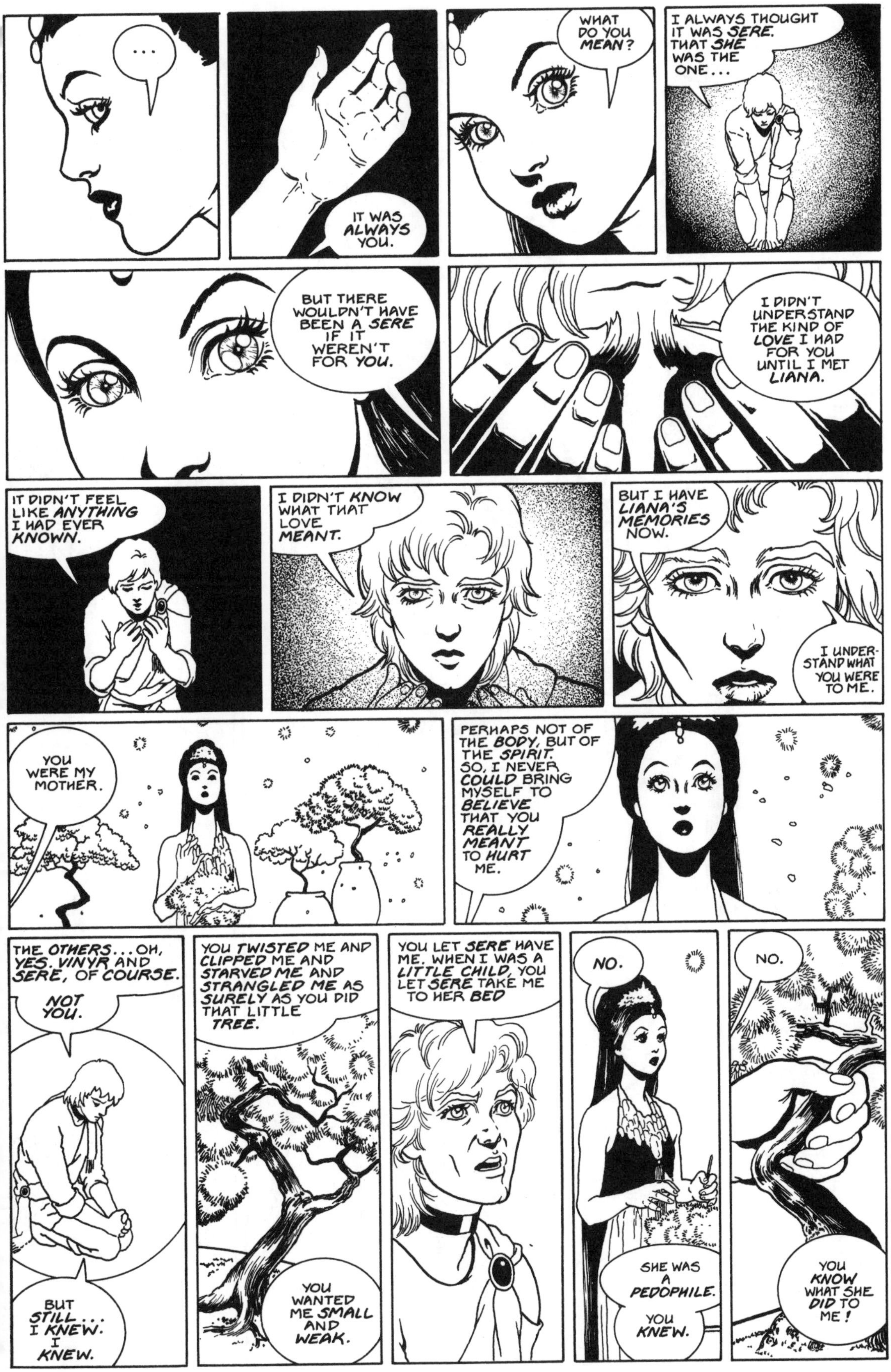
...
IT WAS ALWAYS YOU.
WHAT DO YOU MEAN?
I ALWAYS THOUGHT IT WAS SERE. THAT SHE WAS THE ONE...
BUT THERE WOULDN'T HAVE BEEN A SERE IF IT WEREN'T FOR YOU.
I DIDN'T UNDERSTAND THE KIND OF LOVE I HAD FOR YOU UNTIL I MET LIANA.
IT DIDN'T FEEL LIKE ANYTHING I HAD EVER KNOWN.
I DIDN'T KNOW WHAT THAT LOVE MEANT.
BUT I HAVE LIANA'S MEMORIES NOW.
I UNDER-STAND WHAT YOU WERE TO ME.
YOU WERE MY MOTHER.
PERHAPS NOT OF THE BODY, BUT OF THE SPIRIT. SO, I NEVER COULD BRING MYSELF TO BELIEVE THAT YOU REALLY MEANT TO HURT ME.
THE OTHERS... OH, YES. VINYR AND SERE, OF COURSE.
NOT YOU.
BUT STILL... I KNEW. I KNEW.
YOU TWISTED ME AND CLIPPED ME AND STARVED ME AND STRANGLED ME AS SURELY AS YOU DID THAT LITTLE TREE.
YOU WANTED ME SMALL AND WEAK.
YOU LET SERE HAVE ME. WHEN I WAS A LITTLE CHILD, YOU LET SERE TAKE ME TO HER BED
NO.
SHE WAS A PEDOPHILE.
YOU KNEW.
NO.
YOU KNOW WHAT SHE DID TO ME!

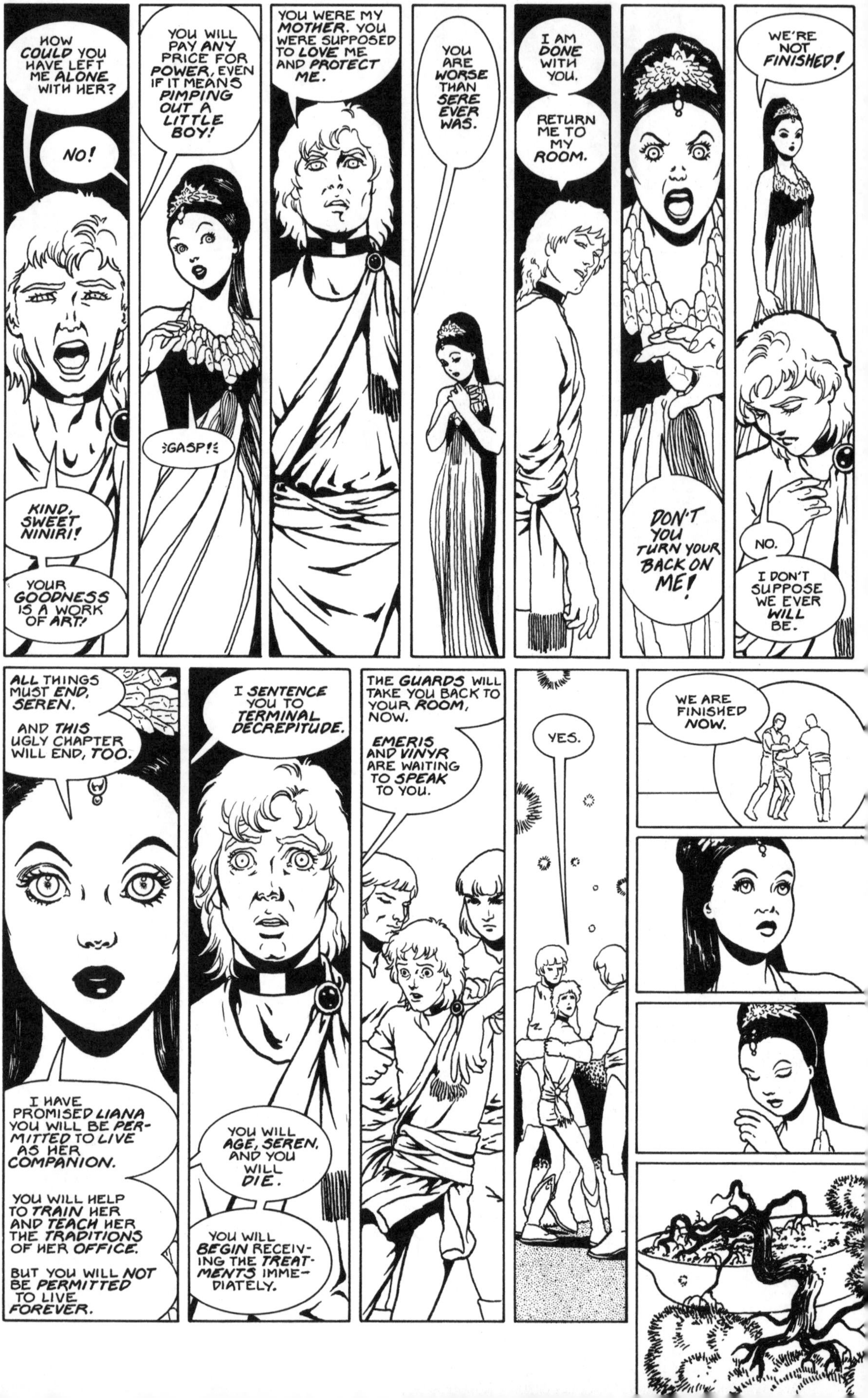
HOW COULD YOU HAVE LEFT ME ALONE WITH HER?
NO!
KIND, SWEET NINIRI!
YOUR GOODNESS IS A WORK OF ART!
YOU WILL PAY ANY PRICE FOR POWER, EVEN IF IT MEANS PIMPING OUT A LITTLE BOY!
GASP!
YOU WERE MY MOTHER. YOU WERE SUPPOSED TO LOVE ME AND PROTECT ME.
YOU ARE WORSE THAN SERE EVER WAS.
I AM DONE WITH YOU.
RETURN ME TO MY ROOM.
DON'T YOU TURN YOUR BACK ON ME!
WE'RE NOT FINISHED!
NO.
I DON'T SUPPOSE WE EVER WILL BE.
ALL THINGS MUST END, SEREN.
AND THIS UGLY CHAPTER WILL END, TOO.
I HAVE PROMISED LIANA YOU WILL BE PERMITTED TO LIVE AS HER COMPANION.
YOU WILL HELP TO TRAIN HER AND TEACH HER THE TRADITIONS OF HER OFFICE.
BUT YOU WILL NOT BE PERMITTED TO LIVE FOREVER.
I SENTENCE YOU TO TERMINAL DECREPITUDE.
YOU WILL AGE, SEREN, AND YOU WILL DIE.
YOU WILL BEGIN RECEIVING THE TREATMENTS IMMEDIATELY.
THE GUARDS WILL TAKE YOU BACK TO YOUR ROOM, NOW.
EMERIS AND VINYR ARE WAITING TO SPEAK TO YOU.
YES.
WE ARE FINISHED NOW.

A Distant Soil™

The story continues in

A DISTANT SOIL:
Coda

**Coming soon from
Image Comics.**

www.adistantsoil.com

Character Spotlight

Bast Abdiyyia

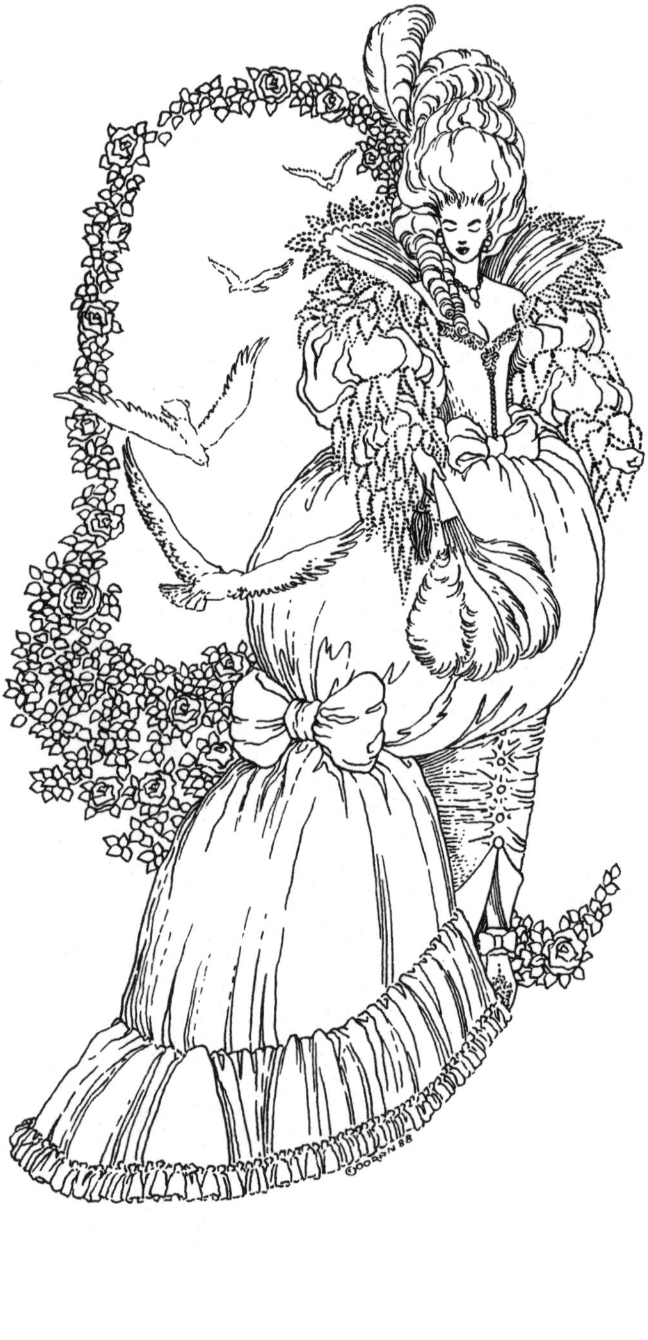

Bast Abdiyyia is a character people either love or hate. I happen to love her, which is why I am reprinting this story.

In the dark ages, when I was a teenaged comic book hopeful, a small press company got a look at my portfolio and decided to publish **A Distant Soil**. This early version of my series was very different from the edition published by Image. Hampered by poor production values and my own uneven drawing skills, heavily edited and rewritten by the editor, I left the project after only nine issues when the company decided they wanted to own my series themselves (and bump me, the creator, out of the picture entirely!)

The acrimonious split was a blessing in disguise. Years later, I was able to completely rewrite and redraw the entire series from page one. As much as I enjoy impressing everyone with how I got my start as a teen comic artist, the work I was doing back then just doesn't compare to what I am doing now.

Except for this story.

First published in color, I have retouched the art for black and white printing. The original color reproduction was so bad, Reynaldo and Brent had green skin and some of my readers thought they were aliens.

At the time, I had just discovered Japanese comics , my favorite being a series called *The Rose of Versailles*, the story of a girl who is raised as a man to be a guard for Marie Antoinette. The joke for those readers in the know, is that the "man" indicated later in the story "R&R", is really a nod to the cross dressing female character from *The Rose of Versailles*.

Whether you're in on the joke or not, it's a story that holds up pretty well, even after all this time! It was the first **A Distant Soil** story that I drew in ink. Previously published stories had been printed entirely from my pencil art, a tedious, laborious technique for doing comics that no one even attempts anymore.

I hope you enjoy this "R&R".

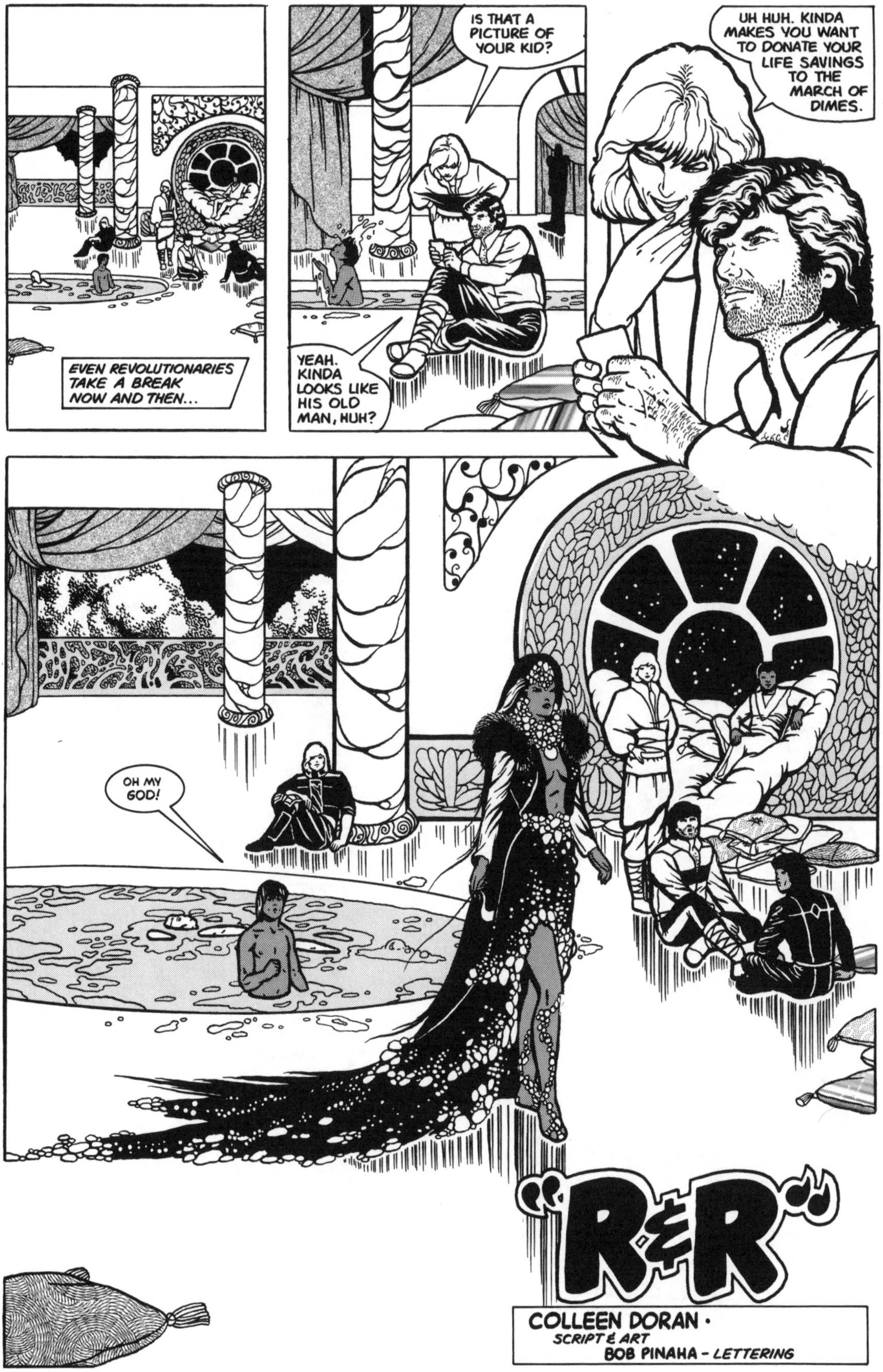
EVEN REVOLUTIONARIES TAKE A BREAK NOW AND THEN...
IS THAT A PICTURE OF YOUR KID?
YEAH. KINDA LOOKS LIKE HIS OLD MAN, HUH?
UH HUH. KINDA MAKES YOU WANT TO DONATE YOUR LIFE SAVINGS TO THE MARCH OF DIMES.
OH MY GOD!
"R&R"
COLLEEN DORAN · SCRIPT & ART
BOB PINAHA - LETTERING

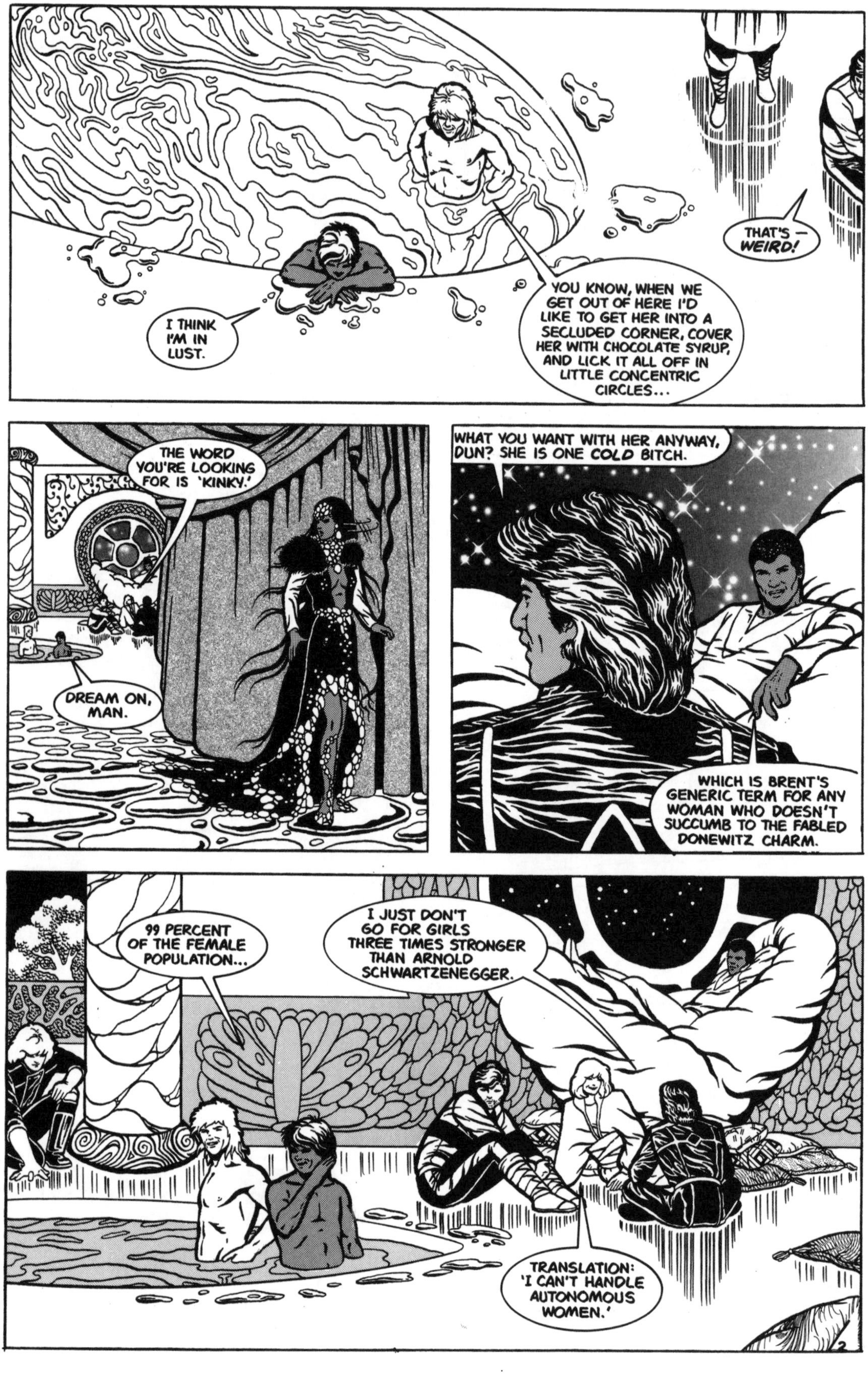

I THINK I'M IN LUST.
YOU KNOW, WHEN WE GET OUT OF HERE I'D LIKE TO GET HER INTO A SECLUDED CORNER, COVER HER WITH CHOCOLATE SYRUP, AND LICK IT ALL OFF IN LITTLE CONCENTRIC CIRCLES...
THAT'S — WEIRD!
THE WORD YOU'RE LOOKING FOR IS 'KINKY.'
DREAM ON, MAN.
WHAT YOU WANT WITH HER ANYWAY, DUN? SHE IS ONE COLD BITCH.
WHICH IS BRENT'S GENERIC TERM FOR ANY WOMAN WHO DOESN'T SUCCUMB TO THE FABLED DONEWITZ CHARM.
99 PERCENT OF THE FEMALE POPULATION...
I JUST DON'T GO FOR GIRLS THREE TIMES STRONGER THAN ARNOLD SCHWARTZENEGGER.
TRANSLATION: 'I CAN'T HANDLE AUTONOMOUS WOMEN.'
2

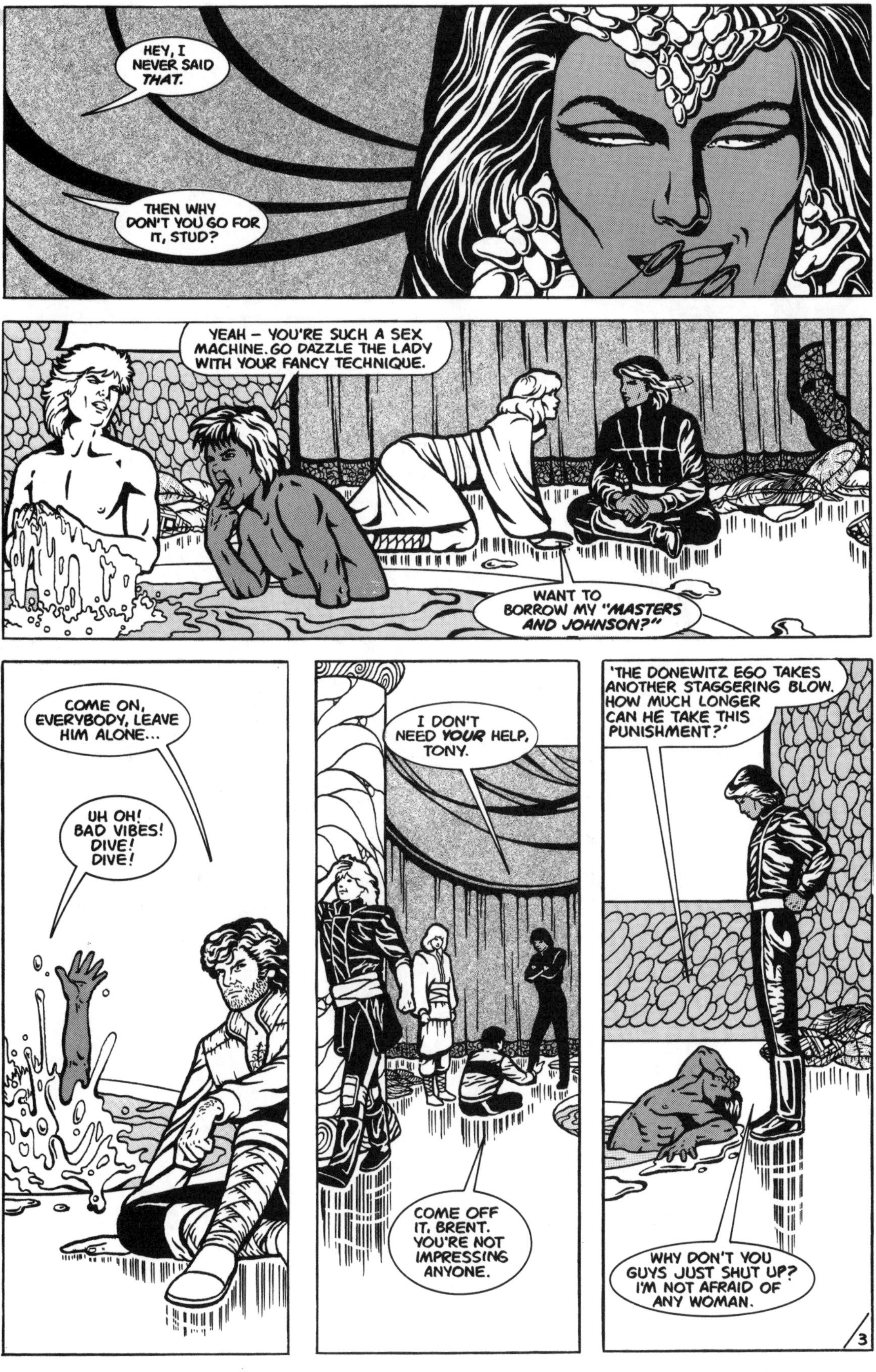
HEY, I NEVER SAID *THAT*.
THEN WHY DON'T YOU GO FOR IT, STUD?
YEAH – YOU'RE SUCH A SEX MACHINE. GO DAZZLE THE LADY WITH YOUR FANCY TECHNIQUE.
WANT TO BORROW MY *"MASTERS AND JOHNSON?"*
COME ON, EVERYBODY, LEAVE HIM ALONE...
UH OH! BAD VIBES! DIVE! DIVE!
I DON'T NEED *YOUR* HELP, TONY.
COME OFF IT, BRENT. YOU'RE NOT IMPRESSING ANYONE.
'THE DONEWITZ EGO TAKES ANOTHER STAGGERING BLOW. HOW MUCH LONGER CAN HE TAKE THIS PUNISHMENT?'
WHY DON'T YOU GUYS JUST SHUT UP? I'M NOT AFRAID OF ANY WOMAN.

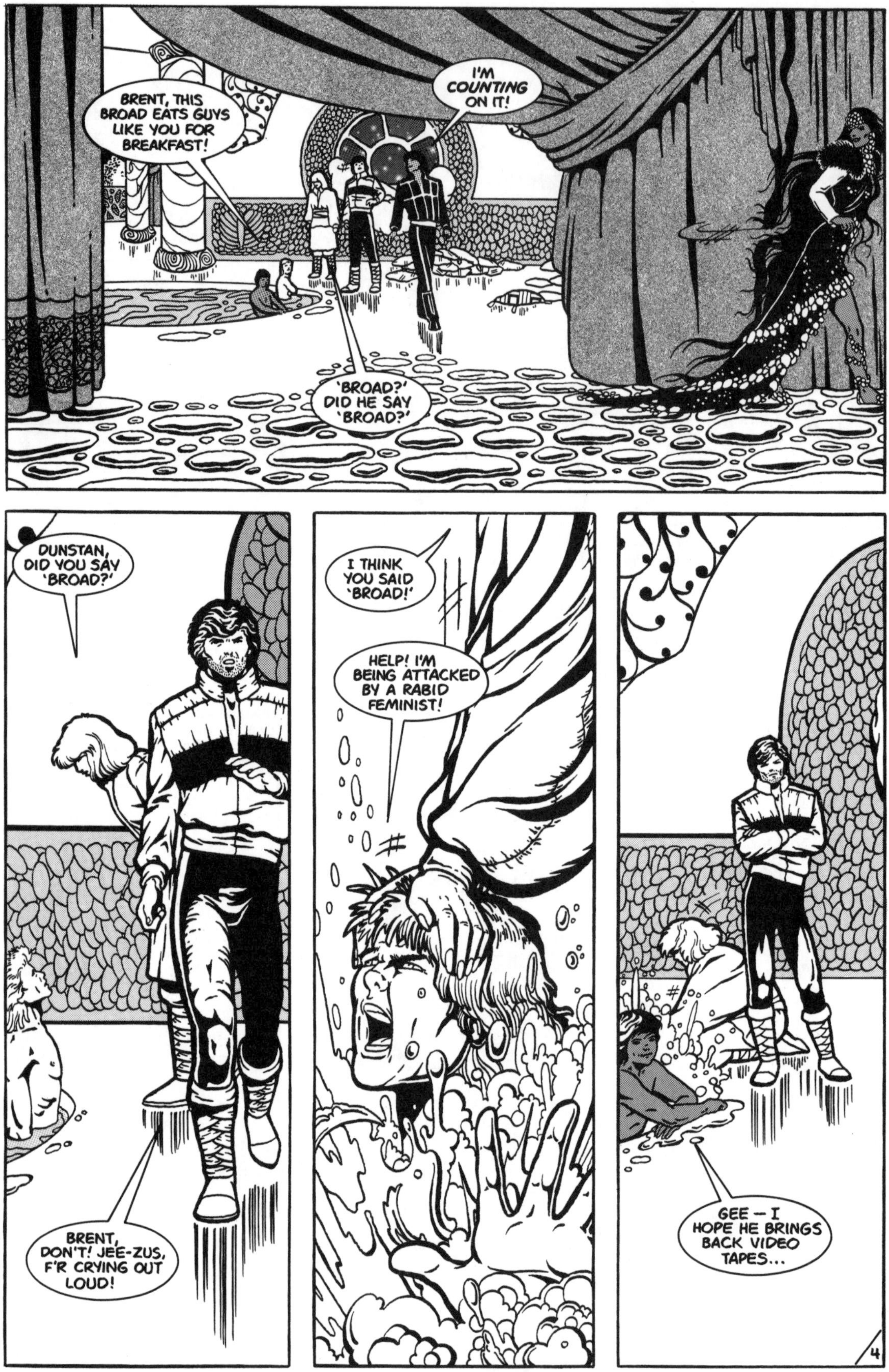
BRENT, THIS BROAD EATS GUYS LIKE YOU FOR BREAKFAST!
I'M COUNTING ON IT!
'BROAD?' DID HE SAY 'BROAD?'
DUNSTAN, DID YOU SAY 'BROAD?'
BRENT, DON'T! JEE-ZUS, F'R CRYING OUT LOUD!
I THINK YOU SAID 'BROAD!'
HELP! I'M BEING ATTACKED BY A RABID FEMINIST!
GEE — I HOPE HE BRINGS BACK VIDEO TAPES...
4

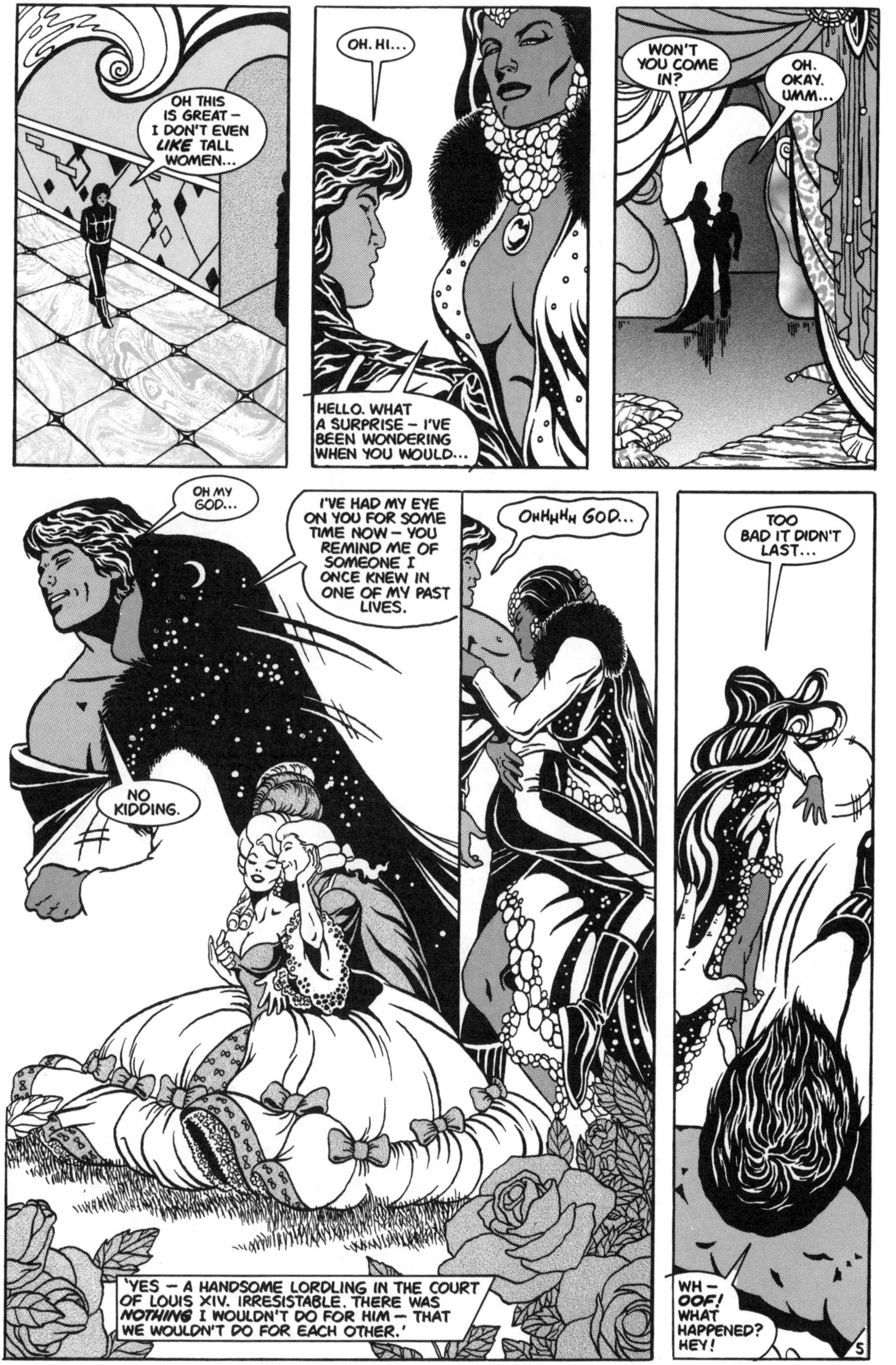
OH THIS IS GREAT — I DON'T EVEN *LIKE* TALL WOMEN...
OH. HI...
HELLO. WHAT A SURPRISE — I'VE BEEN WONDERING WHEN YOU WOULD...
WON'T YOU COME IN?
OH. OKAY. UMM...
OH MY GOD...
I'VE HAD MY EYE ON YOU FOR SOME TIME NOW — YOU REMIND ME OF SOMEONE I ONCE KNEW IN ONE OF MY PAST LIVES.
NO KIDDING.
'YES — A HANDSOME LORDLING IN THE COURT OF LOUIS XIV. IRRESISTABLE. THERE WAS *NOTHING* I WOULDN'T DO FOR HIM — THAT WE WOULDN'T DO FOR EACH OTHER.'
OHHHHH GOD...
TOO BAD IT DIDN'T LAST...
WH — *OOF!* WHAT HAPPENED? HEY!
S

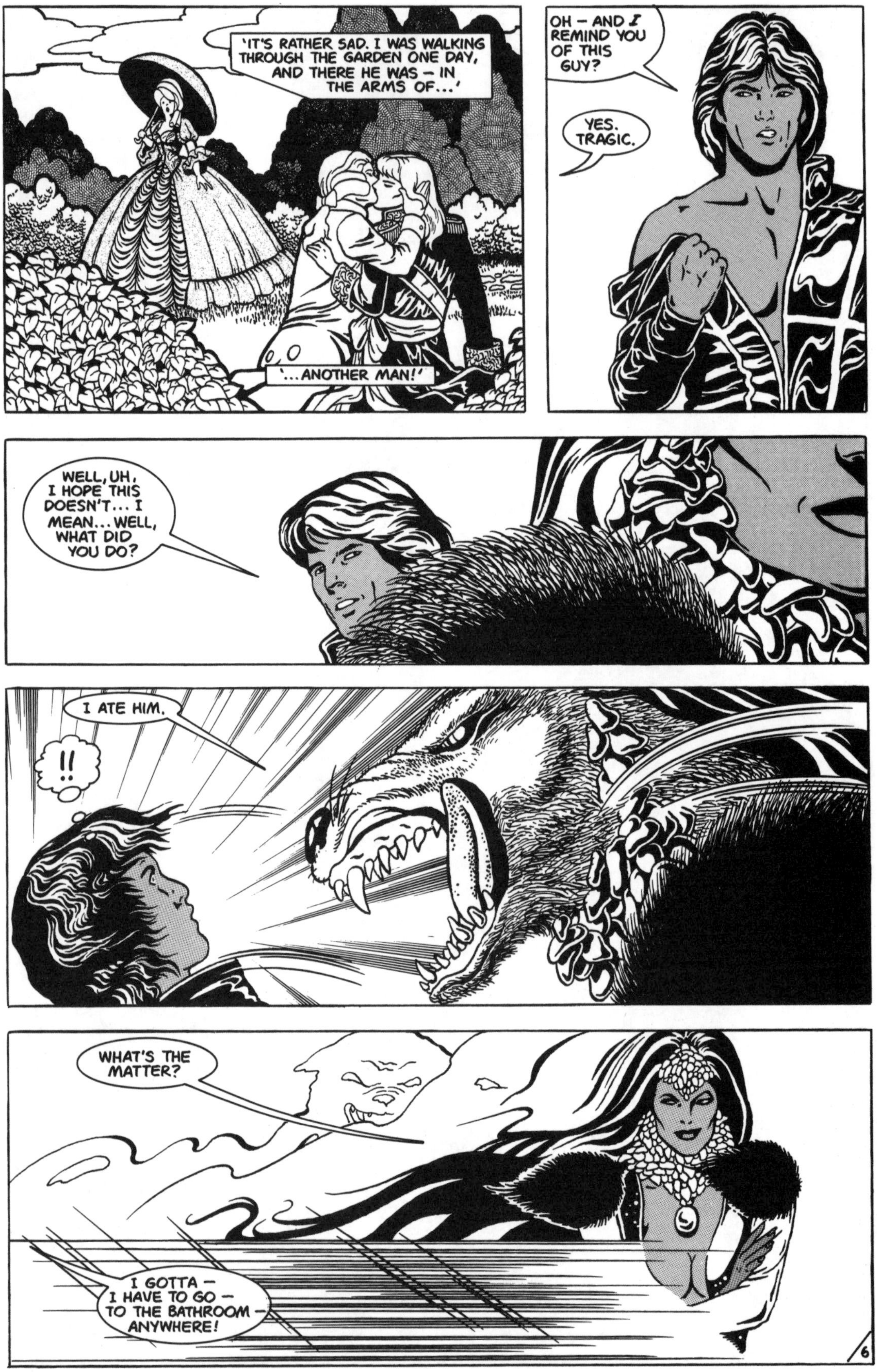
'IT'S RATHER SAD. I WAS WALKING THROUGH THE GARDEN ONE DAY, AND THERE HE WAS – IN THE ARMS OF...'
'...ANOTHER MAN!'
OH – AND I REMIND YOU OF THIS GUY?
YES. TRAGIC.
WELL, UH, I HOPE THIS DOESN'T... I MEAN... WELL, WHAT DID YOU DO?
I ATE HIM.
!!
WHAT'S THE MATTER?
I GOTTA – I HAVE TO GO – TO THE BATHROOM – ANYWHERE!
6

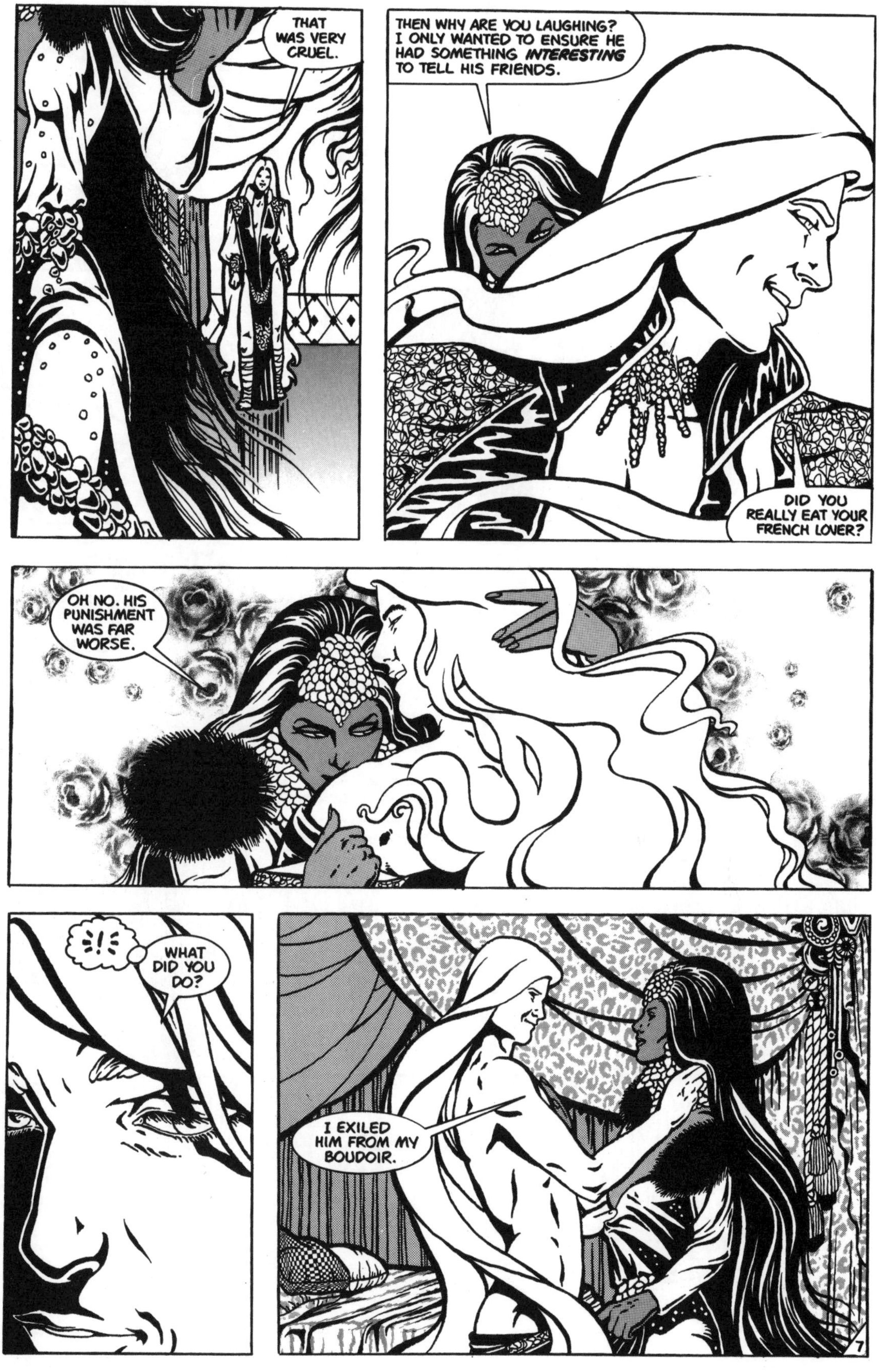
THAT WAS VERY CRUEL.
THEN WHY ARE YOU LAUGHING? I ONLY WANTED TO ENSURE HE HAD SOMETHING *INTERESTING* TO TELL HIS FRIENDS.
DID YOU REALLY EAT YOUR FRENCH LOVER?
OH NO. HIS PUNISHMENT WAS FAR WORSE.
!
WHAT DID YOU DO?
I EXILED HIM FROM MY BOUDOIR.

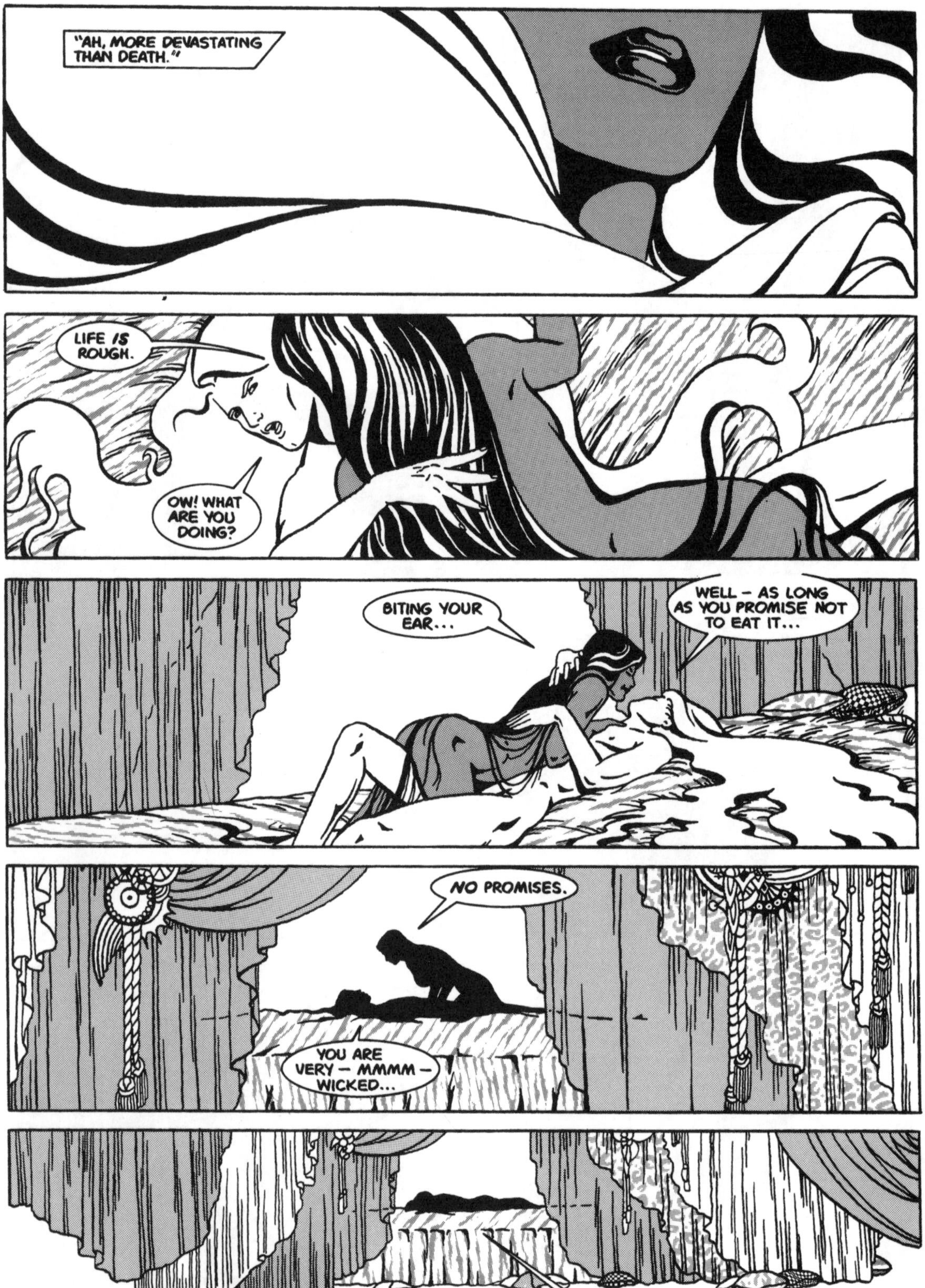

"AH, MORE DEVASTATING THAN DEATH."
LIFE *IS* ROUGH.
OW! WHAT ARE YOU DOING?
BITING YOUR EAR...
WELL - AS LONG AS YOU PROMISE NOT TO EAT IT...
NO PROMISES.
YOU ARE VERY - MMMM - WICKED...
I KNOW...

Afterword

I can't believe it took me three years to get this book out! Two, I thought, two years maximum! But, no! Three years!

Well, two and a half.

I have been a very busy girl.

In addition to all the new work I did on this **A Distant Soil** volume, I also worked as an artist at the Virginia Renaissance Faire, traveled to Europe, studied painting, illustrated a few dozen comics and books, learned to work in the field of animation, and cleaned out my file cabinets which took almost three years by itself and is still an ongoing project.

To all of you out there reading this, my sincere thanks for your patience.

Many, many thanks to my Mummy, my sweetie mummy, who cuts and pastes tone sheets by the hour. She brings me food when I forget to eat. A few weeks ago, she showed up about eight o'clock one night with a plate full of something with homemade chutney on it because she knew I was working and not eating. Mom's are great. "Mother is as close to heaven as I'll ever get", said Lillian Gish.

Thanks to my Dad who worries a lot, and I happen to think that's cute.

Thanks to Jim Valentino, our publisher at Image, and Erik Larsen who brought me into the fold. Thanks especially to Kenny, my designer guy who makes smoochie noises at me over the phone, even when I'm behind schedule. Thanks also to Doug, who never makes smoochies (but that's okay), and thanks to Brent and Traci and everybody at Image because they are all so good to me.

Thanks again to my good pal George Beahm who laughs at me at all the right times. Thanks for all the help and support.

Thanks also to my friends Willow Boudell and Dawn Bromley. Warm regards to Ken Talton.

Much appreciation to my supportive agent and very dear friend Spencer Beck.

Warm thanks to Jeff Smith and Vijaya Iyer, Frank Kelly Freas forever, and Catherine Asaro, Harlan Ellison for the excellent advice (especially the advice that made me money), and to Mary Gray.

Many grateful thanks to all my readers who have been so incredibly supportive and patient.

Colleen Doran
May 2001

Colleen at the Virginia Renaissance Faire.

A Distant Soil™ Items

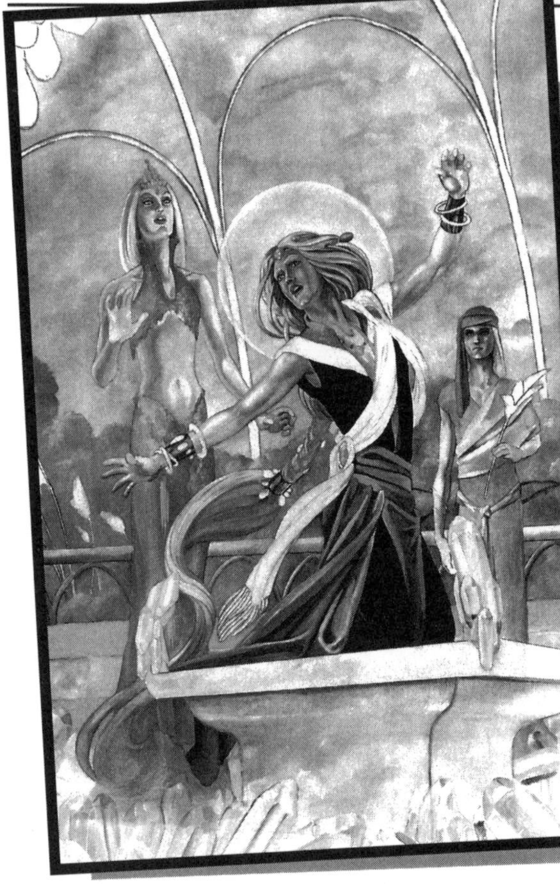

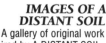

A DISTANT SOIL: THE GATHERING

Volume 1 of the acclaimed graphic novel series collects the first 13 issues of the lead story of the comic book in a big, 240 page, beautifully illustrated trade paperback! With a lovely, gold foil enhanced cover, A DISTANT SOIL: THE GATHERING is available for only $19.95!

A DISTANT SOIL II: THE ASCENDANT

240 page softcover edition for only $18.95!
Also available in a limited edition hardcover, A DISTANT SOIL: THE ASCENDANT, signed and numbered, is only $29.95 and includes a limited edition print and beautiful foil stamped cover.

The hardcover remarqued edition is all that *and* an original full page character drawing for $74.95.

A DISTANT SOIL: The Aria

Volume III in the A DISTANT SOIL saga! The story continues in this all new, beautiful collection! 164 pages of passion and intrigue, politics and betrayal! Available in a signed, numbered hardcover limited edition for $29.95 of only 150 copies. Also available in a remarqued edition of 100 copies, each featuring a hand drawn character portrait of your choice! Only $74.95 (available after July 2001.) Or get the trade paperback edition with handsome, foil enhanced cover for $16.95.

IMAGES OF A DISTANT SOIL

A gallery of original work inspired by A DISTANT SOIL, this 32 page book from Image showcases stellar talents: Charles Vess, Frank Kelly Freas, Dave Sim and Gerhard, Jim Valentino, David Mack, Dave Lapham, Nick Cardy, Curt Swan, Joe Szekeres and others. With full color covers, character biographies and an eight page short story from A DISTANT SOIL! Only $2.95!

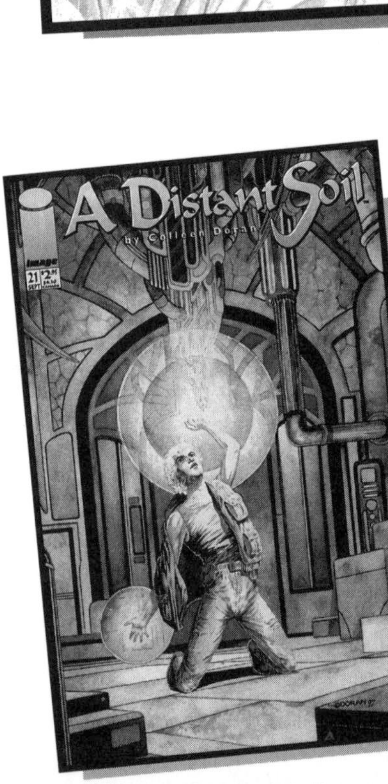

A Distant Soil
image
21

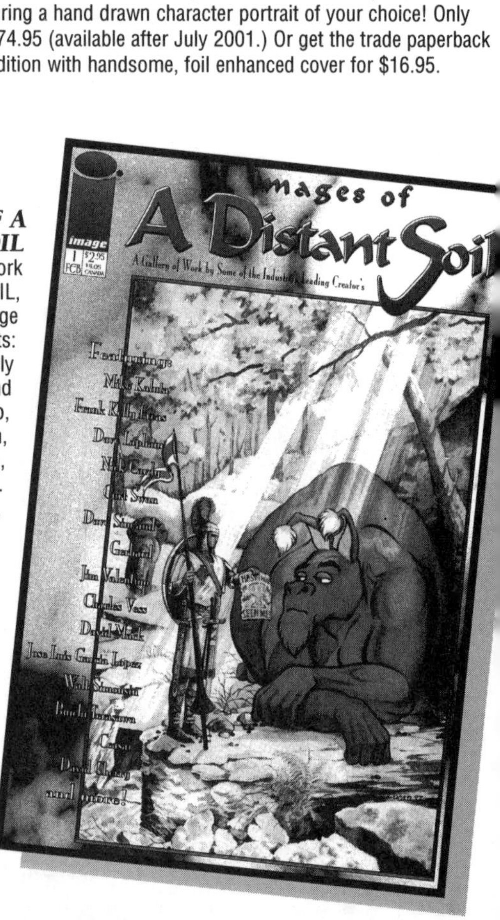

Images of
A Distant Soil
image
1
FCB
$2.95

For more information about A DISTANT SOIL, including never before published art, online interviews with creator Colleen Doran and other great features, visit our website!

www.adistantsoil.com

To find A DISTANT SOIL comics and graphic novels, as well as other work by Colleen Doran and your favorite Image artists, call: 1-888-COMIC-BOOK

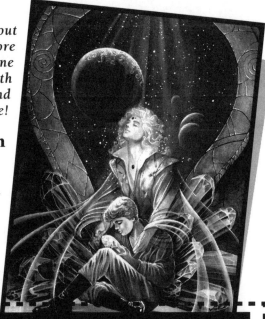

Send to:

Colleen Doran, Colleen Doran Studios
435-2 Oriana Road PMB 610
Newport News • VA 23608 • USA

If you are paying by credit card, please fill this out:

Type of credit card: __________

Card Number: __________

Expiration Date: __________

Your name as imprinted on the card: __________

Your signature: __________

Your Name: __________

Street address: __________

City • State • Zip: __________

ITEM ORDERED	QUANTITY	PRICE EACH	TOTAL

• Important ordering information:
All orders must be in U.S. funds

• Shipping charges:
U.S. orders under $20.00, add $3.00. Over $20.00, add $4.00
Canada, Mexico, overseas: Add $5.00 for order under $20.00.
Add $10.00 for orders over $20.00

• Virginia residents: add 4.5% sales tax

subtotal	
shipping charge	
Total enclosed:	

Biography

Colleen Doran lives in interesting times, but she's not complaining.

Colleen won her first art contest in a Disney sponsored competition at the age of five and has been a professional artist since the age of fifteen.

She is very short and has hair that changes color on a regular basis. Last time we looked at the real color, it was a sort of dishwater blonde.

In addition to spending years working on **A Distant Soil**, an epic that has occupied most of her time and attention since she was twelve, Colleen has illustrated hundreds of other comics, books and magazines.

Her most notable credits include *Anne Rice's The Master of Rampling Gate*, *Clive Barker's Hellraiser*, *Wonder Woman: The Once and Future Story*, *Sandman*, *Amazing Spiderman*, *Captain America*, *Walt Disney's Beauty and the Beast*, *Star Wars Galaxy Magazine* and many others.

She's been profiled in **Comic Book Rebels**, **Women and the Comics**, **Censorship: War of Words** and is the subject of numerous magazine articles and interviews.

Clients include Marvel Comics, DC Comics, Image Comics, The Cahner's Group, Lucasfilm, and The Walt Disney Company. Currently, she continues to illustrate a number of comics projects as well as working in the field of animation.

A Distant Soil has received a number of accolades and honors, the most recent of which being a nomination for the Spectrum Award. It also received the Amy Shultz Award for promoting awareness of child sexual abuse. In 1989 Colleen received a grant from the Delphi Institute to study American pop culture with an international array of cartoonists, and in 1997, she was chosen by Tezuka Productions to be a part of the Japanese/ US comic art seminar in Tokyo, Japan.

Colleen enjoys gardening, hiking and reading. She does not take herself very seriously and doesn't think you should either, but she sincerely hopes you enjoy her work.

Photo credit: George Beahm